C0-AWH-610

The English Church and its Laws
12th-14th centuries

C.R.Cheney

The English Church and its Laws
12th-14th centuries

VARIORUM REPRINTS

London 1982

British Library CIP data   Cheney, Christopher R.
                                 The English church and its laws, 12th-14th centuries.
                                 — (Collected studies series; CS160)
                                 1. Ecclesiastical law — England — History —
                                 Addresses, essays, lectures
                                 I. Title   II. Series
                                 262.9'0942   KD8605

                                 ISBN 0-86078-108-9

Copyright © 1982 by   Variorum Reprints

KD
8785
. C43
1982

Published in Great Britain by   Variorum Reprints
                                  20 Pembridge Mews London W11 3EQ

Printed in Great Britain by   Galliard (Printers) Ltd
                                  Great Yarmouth Norfolk

                                  VARIORUM REPRINT CS160

CONTENTS

This volume contains a total of 348 pages

PREFACE

Thanks in a great measure to F. W. Maitland, it is now an historical commonplace that the *ius commune* of the English Church, from the twelfth century to the Reformation, was not an English growth. It was a *ius commune*, embodied in canonical collections which were applicable — so far as the secular powers permitted — to the whole Latin Church. But each province, each diocese, of the Latin Church enacted laws within certain (or uncertain) limits and committed to writing local customs which touched on ecclesiastical administration and discipline; and these were enforced in the local church courts. Many practical situations which the Corpus Iuris Canonici left on one side were covered in the secular Church by supplementary local law and custom, and in monastic houses by their own customaries, the discipline imposed by visitors, and the decrees of provincial chapters. The title of this volume must be seen in this light. It is this local law-making and law-enforcement which provides the subject of the studies.

The most substantial group (I, VII-X) arose from my concern for over thirty years with the preparation of *Councils & synods with other documents relating to the English Church*, vol.ii, 1205-1313, edited by F. M. Powicke and C. R. Cheney (Oxford, 1964). These were mainly, though not exclusively, investigating the textual transmission of provincial and diocesan laws. The texts published in *Councils & snyods* presuppose these studies and are best read in conjunction with them. No.I ranges rather more widely over the local legislation, a topic of which other aspects appear in essays reprinted in my *Medieval texts and studies* (Oxford, 1973) chapters 6-9. No.XI was prompted by reviewing Austin Lane Poole's contribution to the *Historical essays presented to James Tait* (Manchester, 1933) on the punishment of felonous clerks, dealing with practical questions which arose on one border-line of the two jurisdictions. Despite more recent treatment, particularly of the canonistic and theoretical aspects of the subject, the working of the system in practice may deserve a little more research, as more records of the courts in the later Middle Ages become available. Others among these papers (nos. II, V, VI, XII) go back to an interest of even longer standing in monastic institutions and discipline. Nos. III and IV concern an archbishop of Canterbury whose *acta* I have in recent years prepared for publication in the British Academy's series of English episcopal *acta*. The connection of nos. XIII and XIV with law-making and law-enforcement is tangential but real: I make no excuse for including them in this volume. They deal with men involved in English church government and with the tools which they made and used in the shape of formularies and commonplace books. It is a subject touched on more generally in my *English bishops' chanceries* (Manchester, 1950) and *Notaries public in England in the 13th and 14th centuries* (Oxford, 1972).

I have been sparing in making corrections and additions. Where, to my knowledge, I have been proved wrong in particular interpretations or erred in matters of fact, I have corrected the text or added a note at the end of the article. I have also added references to some later literature, choosing books and articles which give bibliographical guidance. Apart from these corrections and additional notes, the essays are reproduced as they were first printed.

I wish to thank Mrs Eileen Turner and Variorum for including these essays in the series of Collected Studies. Copyright in the papers belongs to the publishers and editors of the books and journals in which they originally appeared, as indicated in the Table of Contents. I am grateful to them all for allowing me freely to have the papers reproduced here.

C. R. CHENEY

Cambridge
November 1981

I

Legislation of the Medieval English Church

PART I

IN 1868 Stubbs, while acknowledging ' the gigantic labour and learning ' of David Wilkins's *Concilia*, declared that ' his work is inadequate, exceedingly defective and incomplete, and (especially in its earlier portions) uncritical '.[1] No one who uses carefully Wilkins's *Concilia* can deny the justice of these strictures. For the earliest period the work of Haddan and Stubbs shows an immense improvement on their predecessor, and their labours have been supplemented by more modern scholars such as Liebermann and Finsterwalder, working on Anglo-Saxon laws and penitentials. But what means has the historian of checking Wilkins in the later periods ? Scholars have occasionally dealt with his texts of particular documents,[2] or pointed to different defects in his general system of editing,[3] but even now the inadequacy of the *Concilia* is not always seen. Modern historians have not always assimilated the criticisms of the Reverend John Johnson, M.A., vicar of Cranbrook, who in 1720 exposed some of the inaccuracies which Wilkins was about to perpetuate, years before the *Concilia* appeared.[4] While much that Wilkins printed has since been published in more accurate and more accessible form, he is still the usual source of reference for the English ecclesiastical laws of the middle ages. This essay is concerned with the parts of the *Concilia* devoted to legatine and metropolitan legislation in England between the twelfth and the fifteenth centuries.[5]

It would be unjust to hold Wilkins responsible for all the

---

[1] *Councils and Ecclesiastical Documents relating to Great Britain and Ireland*, edited, after Spelman and Wilkins, by A. W. Haddan and W. Stubbs, i. (Oxford, 1869), viii. Spelman's *Concilia* (2 vols.) was published in 1639 and 1664 ; Wilkins's *Concilia* (4 vols.) in 1737.

[2] E.g. Hilda Johnstone, ' Archbishop Pecham and the Council of Lambeth of 1281 ', *Essays . . . presented to T. F. Tout* (Manchester, 1925), pp. 171–88.

[3] E.g. H. E. Salter, *Chapters of the Augustinian Canons* (Oxford, 1922), p. 214 ; E. F. Jacob, ' Wilkins's *Concilia* and the fifteenth century ', *Trans. Roy. Hist. Soc.*, fourth series, xv. (1932), 91–131 ; I. J. Churchill, *Canterbury Administration*, i. 367, n. 2.

[4] *A Collection of all the Ecclesiastical Laws . . . of the Church of England*, 2 vols. (London, 1720) ; second edition, [edited by John Baron], 2 vols. (Oxford, 1850–1).

[5] The diocesan constitutions of the same period must be left over for separate discussion. In the conditions of their publication and their textual history they differ from the legatine and provincial canons.

defects of his edition of the canons : in many instances he had good authorities to support him in his errors, and he usually improved upon the editing of Chappuys and Spelman. But the magnitude of his task forced Wilkins to accept a great deal on trust. Like his contemporaries engaged on the conciliar collections abroad, Wilkins proceeded by ' super-position ' rather than by the critical examination of texts already known.[1] A scholar who single-handed edits 3198 folio pages of medieval documents deserves some indulgence. Errors inevitable in 1737 cannot, however, be tolerated two centuries later, and a new edition of the laws of the medieval English Church is urgently needed.

Thanks to Frederick William Maitland it has become a commonplace that the *Corpus Iuris Canonici* and its continental commentators were the law and the authoritative opinion for canonists in medieval England, as in all provinces of the Latin Church. On recognition of this fact depends all understanding of the specifically English law of the medieval Church. For English law there was. It was necessary to extend the knowledge of some sections of the *Corpus*, to reiterate them particularly at certain periods, and to amplify their administrative arrangements. To this end local laws were issued in national, legatine, and provincial synods. The laws glossed by John of Athon and William Lyndwood and later edited by Chappuys and Spelman and Wilkins declared in England the universal law of the Church, and in some respects developed and modified it. While Dr. Z. N. Brooke has demonstrated the papalism of twelfth-century English Church law, Miss Lang quite recently has shown how episcopal administration in the time of Henry III was moulded by the Fourth Lateran decrees.[2] The legal importance of the English canons is sometimes slight, but their precise contents and the occasion of their promulgation always have an historical interest. They indicate the particular needs of the English Church in different periods. They have additional interest in that some parts of them survived in English use after Henry VIII's breach with Rome : the act of 25 Henry VIII cap. 19 declared that such canons, constitutions, ordinances, and synodals provincial, being already made, which were not repugnant to

---

[1] Henri Quentin, *Jean-Dominique Mansi et les grandes collections conciliaires* (Paris, 1900), p. 6 : ' Quiconque voudrait caractériser la méthode commune des collecteurs conciliaires devrait dire qu'ils ont procédé par superposition '. Cf. F. M. Powicke, ' Sir Henry Spelman and the *Concilia*,' *Proc. Brit. Academy*, xvi. (1931), 25–6, 35–6, and E. F. Jacob, ' Wilkins's copy of Sir Henry Spelman's *Concilia* ', *Antiquaries' Journal*, xiii. (1933), 155–8.

[2] Z. N. Brooke, ' The effects of Becket's murder on papal authority in England ' (*Cambridge Hist. Journal*, ii. 1927), and *The English Church and the Papacy* (Cambridge, 1931). Marion Gibbs and Jane Lang, *Bishops and Reform, 1215–1272* (Oxford, 1934), part iii. : ' The reform work of the episcopate on the lines laid down by the Lateran Council of 1215 '.

the laws, statutes, and customs of this realm, should still be used and executed.[1] It is desirable, therefore, that an edition of the laws should have an accurate text, correctly ascribed.

Existing editions do not meet this· need. Some of their pitfalls may be indicated at once by way of warning. Scholars cite from Wilkins canons of Stephen Langton in the council of Oxford which have no demonstrable connexion with this archbishop or this assembly. Canons of St. Edmund are quoted, although there appears to be no reason for supposing that he issued any legislation at all. Passages in the accepted text of the council of Lambeth 1261 are unacceptable ; and canons attributed to Reynolds and Mepham cannot be associated with these archbishops. Through similar defective editing, decrees of English bishops come to be post-dated by 40 or 100 years, or in one instance ante-dated by 150 years. The provincial and legatine canons published by Wilkins, though frequently in need of correction, can seldom be supplemented ; it is otherwise with the collections of diocesan constitutions. In short, the English *Concilia* shares the defects of the great conciliar collections. ' De l'avis de tous ', Dom Quentin wrote in 1900, ' le texte des conciles, une des sources primaires de l'histoire, du droit et de la théologie est, de nos jours encore, plus en retard qu'aucun autre.' [2]

The task of improvement remains for those who are editing a continuation of the *Councils* of Haddan and Stubbs. The following pages will endeavour to explain the inadequacy of the existing editions, and suggest possible ameliorations. First of all, the framing and contents of the English canons will be considered, then the method of their promulgation and preservation. While the immediate object of these discussions is to elucidate the third section, a criticism of the accepted texts, it will be seen that the preliminary questions have a bearing on the efficacy of ecclesiastical government in the later middle ages.

The Framing and Contents of the Canons

Legatine canons were promulgated in England in six councils of the twelfth century (1125, 1127, 1138, 1143, 1151, and 1195) ; the only later ones were those of Otto 1237 and Ottobono 1268.

---

[1] *Stat. Realm*, iii. 460–1 (J. R. Tanner, *Tudor Constit. Documents*, p. 22) ; cf. W. Holdsworth, *Hist. English Law*, i. (third ed.), 592, 594, 596, n. 6.

[2] Quentin, *op. cit.* p. 54. Neither of the valuable revised editions of Hefele's great history of the councils attempts a thorough-going criticism of the texts in the collections. Heinrich Finke in 1891 indicated some of the shortcomings of Hefele-Knöpfler's *Conciliengeschichte*, v. and vi. (Finke, *Konzilienstudien zur Geschichte des XIII Jh.*, Münster, 1891). The uncritical nature of Hefele-Leclercq's *Histoire des Conciles* is sufficiently indicated by the fact that volumes v. and vi. (1912–15) make no use of Finke's studies.

With the exception of York 1195 and probably London 1151, all these councils legislated for both provinces ; likewise did the councils which Anselm held in 1102 and 1108 by primatial authority.[1] For the rest, we are concerned with provincial canons of Canterbury and York. The series apparently begins with Westminster 1175 and London 1200.[2] Those issued in the province of Canterbury from 1222 onwards are mostly printed in the collections of 1504 and 1679, and provided the material for Lyndwood's *Provinciale*. A large majority was issued in meetings of the clergy. It is possible that Archbishop Gray of York issued a general decree by his own authority while visiting his province, and Archbishop Winchelsey apparently did likewise ; but these are instances of a rare practice. We are generally concerned with legislation approved in a national or provincial assembly of clergy.

A few words here seem necessary on the titles by which these assemblies were known. And first to take the most general terms : *Synodus* and *Concilium*. Although by a convenient custom modern writers usually apply ' synod ' to diocesan meetings, reserving ' council ' for assemblies of wider scope, no formal distinction was made in the middle ages. No doubt the wider meaning of synod was more in favour in early times than later, but chroniclers of the twelfth and thirteenth centuries still spoke indifferently of synod and council, and lawyers glossing ancient texts had to recognize the older meaning. Lyndwood agrees that ' commonly is called a synod the council held or assembled by a bishop in his diocese ' ; but also it ' is a general term, signifying a general council which the pope convenes, and a provincial council which an archbishop summons '.[3] For his first statement Lyndwood refers the reader to the canon from whose author one would naturally expect a precise nomenclature of councils : the sixth canon of the Fourth Lateran Council. Innocent III here distinguishes between the *generale concilium* in which he is legislating, the *provinciale concilium* held by a metro-politan, and the *episcopalis synodus* held in each diocese.

These are the terms which will come into general use ; but in 1215 and for some time after, councils of one sort and another were not so clearly labelled. In England *provinciale concilium*

---

[1] For a list of eleventh-century Anglo-Norman councils, see H. Böhmer, *Kirche und Staat in England und in der Normandie*, p. 62, n. 3.

[2] See Part II of this paper.

[3] *Provinciale*, I. iii. 1 *ver.* Synodali (ed. Oxford, 1679, p. 19b) : ' Synodus enim solet dici concilium factum sive congregatum per episcopum in sua diocesi [*Decretales*, v. i. xxv.]. Sed dic, quod Synodus est dictio generalis, significans tam concilium generale, quod convocat papa [*Decretum*, I. xvi. vi.], quam etiam concilium provinciale, quod vocat archiepiscopus [*Decretum*, I. xviii. v.].' Cf. *ibid*. p. 115b. The contrast between diocesan ' synods ' and provincial ' councils ' was not so regularly preserved as Armitage Robinson suggests (*Church Quarterly Review* (1915), lxxxi. 136).

I

is not common until Lambeth 1281.[1] Often, legislators and chroniclers write plain *concilium*. Apart from this, most ambiguity has probably arisen out of the uses of the word *generale*. Hauck has shown [2] that in the eleventh and twelfth centuries the old idea of an ecumenical council was dead, the new idea unborn. A general or universal synod meant something else. According to Leo IX a metropolitan could not hold a universal council without papal consent, and the *Dictatus Papae* declares that ' no synod ought to be called general without the pope's command ' ; in this sense the glossators comment upon the *Decretum*, I. xvii–xviii. It would be natural to suppose that hereafter the word ' general ' was applied only to councils held by the pope or his legate. But in common parlance it was used more widely. German provincial and diocesan councils of the twelfth and thirteenth centuries were usually called ' general synods ',[3] while in England the term ' general ' was applied, not only to nearly all the legatine councils of the period,[4] but to councils undoubtedly held by metropolitan authority. Oxford 1222 is described by two chroniclers and also in a mandate of the dean and chapter of Wells, as a general council.[5] The title is given in a fourteenth-century manuscript to Archbishop Boniface's council of 1258.[6] Wykes describes Reading 1279 as ' a general council

[1] *Reg. Epist. J. Peckham* (Rolls Series), i. 237, etc. ; *Annales Monastici* (Rolls Series), ii. 395 ; iv. 481. Bishop Quivil of Exeter refers (1287) to the ' provincial statutes ' of the legate Ottobono (Wilkins, ii. 160). One chronicler speaks of Westminster 1175 as provincial (see Part II) and one only applies the term to Oxford 1222 (*Walter of Coventry* (Rolls Series), ii. 251). Oxford is so called in synodal statutes of Salisbury (*infra*, p. 213, n. 2). Diceto uses the unusual phrase *concilium regionale* for Westminster 1175 ; and the earliest manuscripts of his history add the marginal note : ' solius papae est concilium generale, Romanae ecclesiae et Constantinopolitanae est concilium universale ' (*Diceto* (Rolls Series), i. 399. Cf. ii. 85). It may be only by the error of a registrar that diocesan canons of Winchester are referred to in the register of Bishop Rigaud (1321) as ' Constituciones Provinciales ' (*Registers of S. de Sandale and R. de Asserio* (Hants. Rec. Soc.), p. 404).

[2] A. Hauck, ' Die Rezeption und Umbildung der allgemeinen Synode im Mittelalter ', *Historische Vierteljahrsschrift*, x. (1907), 465 *seqq.*, especially 467, 472–4.

[3] P. Hinschius, *System des Katholischen Kirchenrechts*, iii. 327, n. 3, 488, 494 ; Hauck, *Kirchengeschichte Deutschlands*, iv. 6, n. 8 ; 7, n. 1. Cf. *ibid.* v. 171, 174, n. 1, and *Hist. Vierteljahrsschr.* x. 467. The king of Aragon in 1304 speaks of the general council held by the archbishop of Tarragona, his suffragans, and others (H. Finke, *Acta Aragonensia*, ii. 844). The archbishop of Dublin in 1348 describes his council as a general council (Wilkins, ii. 746).

[4] *1125*, Winchester Annals (*Ann. Monastici*, ii. 47), *Chron. Angliae Petriburg.* (ed. Giles, p. 82) ; *1127*, Florence of Worcester (Wilkins, i. 410) ; *1138*, *Chron. Angliae Petrib.* (p. 90) ; *1151*, Henry of Huntingdon (Rolls Series, p. 282) ; *1237*, Burton Annals (*Ann. Mon.* i. 253), Waverley Annals (*ibid.* ii. 318), Dunstable Annals (*ibid.* iii. 146), Osney Annals (*ibid.* iv. 84), Gervase of Canterbury's Continuator (Rolls Series, ii. 130) ; *1268*, Osney Annals (*Ann. Mon.* iv. 215), Gervase's Continuator (Rolls Series, ii. 247). Also the national council of *1102*, Eadmer (Wilkins, i. 382).

[5] *Chron. Angliae Petrib.* p. 124 (in a passage derived from the same source Walter of Coventry writes ' provincial council ', ii. 251) ; Matt. Paris, *Chron. Maj.* (Rolls Series), iii. 73 ; *Hist. MSS. Commission, Wells* (1907), i. 75.

[6] Bodleian MS. Ashmole 1146, fo. 50.

in which the constitutions of the general council [*sc.* Lyon II] '
were renewed.[1] Wolsey speaks of Archbishop Warham's intention to hold a ' generail counsail ' with his suffragans in 1518.[2]
We cannot, therefore, on the evidence of title decide the character
of an assembly. When Hoveden describes London 1200 as a
general council,[3] we cannot accept Johnson's gloss : ' That is
National ' ; and the term applied by Bishop Jocelin of Salisbury
to Westminster 1175 does not prove that this assembly was
legatine.[4]

The assemblies in which these canons were promulgated were
variously constituted. In the twelfth century all orders of the clergy
normally attended a legatine council, and the canons were said
to be ' confirmed by all ' [5] or ' by common consent of the bishops '.[6]
The legates of the thirteenth century summoned bishops and
regular prelates to their councils, and all gave their assent. But
the canons were none the less the legate's own, authorized by
the pope's commission to him, not to be altered by metropolitan
authority,[7] and enduring after the termination of the legateship.[8]

The early Church had provided for provincial assemblies to
be summoned by the metropolitan twice a year, but by the
eighth century annual councils became the rule.[9] While this
was confirmed by the Fourth Lateran Council (cap. 6), the later
rule was not perfectly observed any more than the earlier one had
been. Hauck's comment on German provincial councils in the
twelfth and early thirteenth centuries can be applied to England
in that period : ' das Synodalwesen . . . mehr vegetierte als
lebte '.[10] Despite the spasmodic legislation of the thirteenth and
fourteenth centuries, there is no sign of any serious attempt to
bring the bishops together annually for the discussion of ecclesiastical discipline. In 1332 Archbishop Mepham remarked that
a provincial council ought to be held annually, but that he had
been hindered on several occasions from doing his duty in this

[1] *Ann. Monastici*, iv. 281. Cf. Lyndwood's use of the term to designate a provincial council, *infra*, p. 204, n. 4.

[2] Wilkins, iii. 660.   [3] (Rolls Series), iv. 128.

[4] *Sarum Charters* (Rolls Series), 39–40 ; cf. Part II.

[5] Wilkins, i. 408, 414 (1125 and 1138).

[6] *Ibid.* i. 410 (1127). These decrees were confirmed by the king. But the question
of lay attendance and influence in the councils has no place here : cf. Makower,
Constit. Hist. of the Church of England, § 54, notes 16, 25–6 (pp. 357, 359).

[7] Lyndwood, I. ii. 1 *ver.* Observari (p. 11).

[8] Matt. Paris, *Chron. Maj.* iii. 419 (Wilkins, i. 649), undoubtedly referring to
Decretales, I. xxx. x. (Gregory IX).

[9] Hinschius, *Kirchenrecht*, iii. 473 *seqq.* L. Thomassin, *L'ancienne et la nouvelle
discipline de l'église*, II. III. xlv. §§ 3, 9 ; *ibid.* liii. § 9 ; cf. *Decretum*, I. xviii. 2–4,
6–7. The Council of Hertford (672) provided for only one provincial council annually
in England (Haddan and Stubbs, iii. 120).

[10] Cf. Hinschius, *loc. cit.* especially p. 491 ; Thomassin, II. III. liii. § 3 ; *ibid.* lvii.
§§ 4, 7.

matter.[1] A contemporary canonist, John of Athon, referred to the same rule : he suggested as the explanation of its neglect that a council brings no monetary profit, but only expense.[2] In the province of York, to judge by surviving records, councils were less frequent than in the southern province. The same irregularity prevailed abroad. While the period 1230–1310 was particularly fruitful in law-giving in Germany, Hauck only indicates about forty provincial councils in this space of eighty years.[3] M. Lacger observes that ' conciliar activity was particularly intense in the province of Bourges in the thirteenth century ' ; but he can only enumerate twenty-two councils between 1213 and 1315.[4] This irregularity explains and justifies the unavailing attempt of the fifteenth-century reformers to maintain a less ambitious rule. The councils of Pisa (1409) and of Basel (1433) ordered triennial provincial councils, and provided for their session if the metropolitan neglected to summon them.

The subject of English provincial assemblies has received a great deal of attention. Much learning has been devoted to the discussion of their composition and the source of their authority. But the discussion has always been more concerned with the fiscal and political activities of the councils than with their legislative work, and sometimes history has been obscured in a cloud of polemic.

This study is only concerned with provincial councils as legislative bodies. From the Lateran decree [5] one would suppose that their object was purely to maintain ecclesiastical discipline. The talk is all ' de corrigendis excessibus, et moribus reformandis '. The measures to be taken are twofold. First, ' the canonical rules and chiefly those which are ordained in this general council ' shall be read over again, so that the bishops may enforce their observance. Secondly, the metropolitan and suffragans, having received reports on the condition of the province, shall make

---

[1] Wilkins, ii. 561 (*Reg. Rad. de Salopia* (Somerset Rec. Soc.), i. 103–5) ; cf. *ibid.* 680 (Stratford, 1341). About the same time (1322) the legatine canons of Valladolid (Palencia) complained that provincial councils were not celebrated regularly, and demanded that in future they should be summoned once every two years (Hefele-Leclercq, *Hist. des Conciles*, VI. 793–4). Chichele, in a mandate of 1417, referred to the ancient salutary rule that metropolitans should annually hold councils with their suffragans (Churchill, *Canterbury Administration*, ii. 165).

[2] (Whereas the complementary duty of visitation had at least the compensation of procuration fees.) John of Athon on Ottobono, Praefatio *ver.* Provincialium (supplement to Lyndwood, ed. Oxford 1679, i. 79*b*). Cf. Gibbs and Lang, *op. cit.* pp. 143–8.

[3] *Kirchengeschichte Deutschlands*, v. 133–44 ; iv. 20 n 1. In Scotland some thirty meetings are recorded in three centuries (D. Patrick, *Statutes of the Scottish Church* (Scot. Hist. Soc.), p. xliii).

[4] Not all were provincial councils (*Revue d'hist. ecclés.* xxvi. (1930), 294, 284).

[5] IV. Lat. Conc. cap. 6 (*Decretales*, v. i. xxv.).

ordinances in the council and enforce them, ' publishing them in
the episcopal synods to be held annually in each diocese '. This
order was apparently followed by Langton at Oxford 1222, and
was certainly observed in the province of Rouen somewhat later.[1]
The proceedings began with a recital of the Lateran decree, and
finally the council issued new legislation of its own.

Whatever the composition of the provincial council, whether
it be called ' council ' or ' convocation ',[2] there can be little doubt
as to the usual authority for its legislative acts. The presiding
archbishop promulgated canons, on the advice and with the
assent of his suffragan bishops. The Lateran Council mentioned
no others in the provincial council. No other authority was
needed. For one purpose or another, representatives of the
clergy might be called upon to attend the council or convocation ;
their petitions or advice might even exercise a considerable effect
on the nature of the laws promulgated ; but this did not alter
the fact that the legislation needed only to be authorized by the
bishops. The metropolitan's authority was held to be streng-
thened by that of his co-bishops. In 1281 the suffragans of
Canterbury protested that the archbishop ought only to make
constitutions in a provincial council,[3] and Lyndwood said that
he should not carry through arduous business without his suffragans.[4] So, in the canons of councils commonly recur such phrases
as ' sacro approbante concilio statuimus ', ' auctoritate presentis
concilii statuimus '.[5]

The assembly of bishops was the core of the council. Athon
makes this clear in his gloss on London 1237 : ' To a provincial
council, where matters are to be ordained which concern the
state of the province, the bishops are to be cited ; and other
subjects are to be invited, not forced, to attend '.[6] Lyndwood
speaks to the same effect : ' To a provincial council, bishops are
to be summoned, and not others of necessity. . . . But if others
come they are to be admitted. . . . And others shall be summoned
whose affairs are being dealt with, or because their advice is

---

[1] Dunstable Annals (*Ann. Mon.* iii. 76), *Chron. Angliae Petrib.* pp. 124–5 ; Walter
of Coventry, ii. 251. Cf. *Regestrum Visitationum Odonis Rigaldi*, pp. 286, 356, 387, 481.

[2] Cf. Churchill, *op. cit.* ii. 168–70, and the valuable essay of J. Armitage Robinson,
' Convocation of Canterbury : its early history ' (*Church Quarterly Review*, lxxxi.
(1915), 81–137).

[3] Quoted, Churchill, i. 361. Pecham replied that he would not act *contra iuris
formam*.

[4] *Provinciale*, ii. iii. 5 *ver.* Fratrum nostrorum (p. 104). Cf. Anselm's statement,
infra, p. 208.

[5] Cf. for Germany, Hauck, *Kirchengesch.* v. 149, n. 3.

[6] Proemium *ver.* Et consensu (Lyndwood supplement, i. 5*a*) : ' Ad consilium
. . . provinciale, ubi statuenda sunt aliqua, quae tangunt statum provinciae episcopi sunt citandi ; et ceteri subditi invitandi, non cogendi [*Decretum*, i. xviii. 4 ;
ii. i. vii. 4] '.

needed.'[1] In connexion with this should be read Lyndwood's
remarks : ' the authority of a provincial council . . . binds all
in the province ' (i.e. the suffragans' subjects), and ' archbishops
and bishops . . . can make constitutions '.[2]

There is sufficient evidence that English practice from the
thirteenth to the fifteenth century harmonized with these legal
opinions. The canons of Lambeth 1261 were issued in the name
of the archbishop of Canterbury and his suffragans, with their
seals attached.[3] At the council of Lambeth 1281 Pecham made
constitutions as if by his own authority, although, going beyond
the requirements of the canon law, he had summoned the ' inferior
prelates ', and punished absentees.[4] Mepham employed the
formula ' by authority of the present council and with the consent
of our suffragan brethren ', and Stratford and Islip used similar
terms ; but their councils none the less contained clergy besides
the bishops.[5] During the fourteenth and fifteenth centuries the
inferior prelates and proctors of the clergy were being called
to provincial councils, and from late in the fourteenth century
provincial constitutions sometimes mention the consent of ' all
the clergy '.[6] The change is comparable to the change taking
place in the councils of the state. The old idea of a council of

---

[1] *Provinciale*, III. ix. 3 *ver.* Provinciali concilio (p. 154a) : ' Verum est quod ad
provinciale concilium vocandi sunt episcopi, et non alii de necessitate. . . . Si tamen
alii veniant, admittendi sunt quod dic ut *extra* [III. x. x.]. Vocabuntur etiam alii
de quorum factis agitur, vel quia ipsorum consilium est necessarium.' In fact the
decretal (of Innocent III) states more than Lyndwood suggests : ' ut capitula ipsa
[cathedralium] ad huiusmodi concilia *debeant invitari*, et eorum nuncii ad tractatum
admitti, maxime super illis quae ipsa capitula contingere dignoscuntur '.

[2] *Ibid.* I. iii. 1 *ver.* Contradictione ; I. xiv. *ver.* Iuramento (pp. 21a, 70b).

[3] Brit. Mus. Cotton Ch. xvi. 29 *ad fin.* Pecham's ordinance for the university of
Oxford, issued at Reading 1279, bore the bishops' seals (Wilkins, ii. 39). The provincial canons of Rheims were in this period usually ratified by the seals of the bishops
(Th. Gousset, *Actes de la province ecclés. de Reims*, ii. 368 (1233), 385 (1239), 409 (1270),
480 (1304)).

[4] Wilkins, ii. 63 : ' universos nostrae provinciae praelatos inferiores, quos conciliorum tractibus interesse iubent sancti canones, vocandos decrevimus '. *Ann.
Monastici*, iii. 288 : ' absentes graviter sunt puniti '. Cf. process against the de-
faulters, and their submission, 1282 (*Reg. Epp. J. Peckham*, iii. 1069). In 1216 the
abbots of the province of Salzburg refused to appear in the council and were therefore
excommunicated (Hauck, *Kirchengesch.* v. 150, n. 3). The provincial council of
Bourges 1267 fixed penalties for non-attendance on all classes of the clergy who
might be summoned to a council (*Revue d'hist. ecclés.* xxvi. 289) ; likewise the legatine
council of Buda 1279 (R. Hube, *Antiq. Constitutiones . . . Gneznensis* (St. Petersburg,
1856), pp. 85-6). Cf. Hinschius, iii. 497, n. 2.

[5] Wilkins, ii. 552 (1328), 675 (1342) ; iii. 13 (1351/2). To the council of 1341, ' abbates,
priores, clerus, et capitula vocati non fuerant praecise sed causative, videlicet si sua
crederent interesse ' (Murimuth, *Contin. Chronicarum*, p. 122 ; cf. Wilkins, ii. 680). Cf.
Stratford's letter (1347) summoning to a council, besides the suffragans, ' singula
capitula conventus et collegia per unum clerusque cuiuslibet diocesis per duos pro-
curatores ydoneos, si sua crediderint interesse et causas vel negocia habuerint in
huiusmodi concilio provinciali tractanda '. *Reg. J. Trillek* (Canterbury and York
Soc.), pp. 306-7.

[6] Wilkins, iii. 234 (1398), and Churchill, i. 369, n. 2 (1415, 1416).

I

bishops is giving way before the notion of a representative assembly, just as it is superseded in the Church Universal by the new conception of a general council. But the acceptance of this principle probably never affected the authority of the legislation; the consent of the representatives in the provincial council was formal.[1]

The law of the Church was applied in much the same way abroad. While a full survey has no place here, a few examples of continental practice may be mentioned. Proctors of the cathedral chapters attended provincial councils of Rouen and Rheims in the thirteenth century : but at Rouen the bishops alone authorized the actions of the councils, and at Rheims they alone sealed the canons to which the capitular proctors had given consent.[2] To the thirteenth-century German councils came the inferior prelates, and proctors of the cathedral chapters appeared late in the century. From this period onwards German provincial canons are usually said to be by authority of the bishops and other prelates.[3]

The nature of the legislation issued by these councils differs from century to century rather than according to the nature of the assembly, national, legatine, or provincial. Of the twelfth-century canons Dr. Brooke observes : ' The Councils did not attempt, did not even make a beginning towards, the creation of a code of Church law. A Council was an effective way of calling attention to the abuses within the Church, of getting general assent to the remedying of them, and, above all, of putting on the participants the onus of doing their share in enforcing the laws—the old laws—against these abuses.' [4] The relation of the local to the universal law is set forth by Gratian : provincial councils, he says, are not able to make new law, but they may enjoin the observance of laws already made.[5]

The twelfth-century canons are mostly confined to the repetition of passages from papal law-books, often word for word. Later local legislation completes and glosses, rather than repeats, the law of the *Corpus Iuris*. Thus, for example, in England, Oxford 1222 adds to the Lateran decree on vicarages a fixed minimum salary for vicars, and makes special rules for the

---

[1] For further details, see W. Wake, *The State of the Church* (1703), pp. 95–118, especially pp. 113–15. Arundel's canons of 1408 appeared with the authority of the bishops and other prelates at the petition of the lower clergy (Wilkins, iii. 315).

[2] *Reg. . . . Odonis Rigaldi*, pp. 123, 125 ; Gousset, *Reims, loc. cit. supra*, p. 201, n. 3.

[3] Hauck, *Kirchengesch.* v. 149–50. In the province of Salzburg the archbishop and suffragans alone confirm canons.

[4] Z. N. Brooke, *The English Church and the Papacy*, p. 101.

[5] *Decretum*, I. xviii: ' Episcoporum igitur concilia [*sc.* provincialia] . . . sunt invalida ad diffiniendum et constituendum, non autem ad corrigendum. Sunt enim necessaria episcoporum concilia ad exortationem et correctionem, que etsi non habent vim constituendi, habent tamen auctoritatem imponendi et indicendi, quod alias statutum est, et generaliter seu specialiter observari preceptum.' Cf. Hinschius, iii. 330–1, 492.

differentiation of Jews and Christians. In later times the legislators are chiefly concerned to deal with the questions of clerical
privilege and heresy with measures suited to their particular
provinces. The character of these regulations made it necessary
to establish the inferiority of the local law to the common law of
the Church. This principle is recognized in an interesting way
in the provincial canons of Rouen. On at least four occasions
in the thirteenth century the archbishop prefaced his canons
with a limiting clause : the legislation is not to introduce new
law : it is only to be binding in so far as it embodies ' those
things which are found in the law, the statutes of Gregory IX,
and bishops' synodal decrees '.[1] Here we see the council's anxiety
to prevent disputes over the meaning of the canons, which might
arise from interpretations of them in a sense contrary to the
common law.

Lyndwood enunciates the same principle and expounds it
according to the great glossators.

> Archbishops and bishops (he says)[2] . . . can make constitutions
> to declare or recall the common law, and where there is no penalty in the
> law can fix penalties, and can add to an old penalty. They can also
> add to papal constitutions and supplement them and for the correction
> of manners can make precepts, prohibitions, and penal statutes, so long
> as they do not subvert the common law. . . . They can also make
> statutes on those matters which belong to their jurisdiction, so long as
> they do not oppugn general laws.

Elsewhere Lyndwood observes that a penal constitution cannot
annul or restrict the law made by a superior authority, and that
an archbishop cannot annul legatine constitutions for this reason,
though he may supplement them by the addition of a penalty.[3]

[1] *Reg. . . . Odonis Rigaldi*, pp. 287, 357, 387, 482 : ' Placet sancto concilio quod
ea que secuntur inferius firmiter observentur, ita quod reverendi patres, O. dei gracia,
Rothomagensis archiepiscopus, et eius suffraganei, et eorum subditi, ad eorum ob-
servacionem, tanquam de novo statuta fuerint, nullatenus obligentur ; scilicet quantum
ad ea que in iure sive in statutis Gregorii pape IX, sive in synodalibus episcopalibus
inveniuntur expressa '. Archbishop Anselm obtained papal confirmation of the
acts of his council 1102 (Wilkins, i. 382). Archbishop Hildebert of Tours had the
acts of his provincial council of Nantes 1123 confirmed by Honorius II (Migne, *Patr.
Lat.* clxxi. 253–4). Archbishop Boniface sought (in vain) for confirmation of the
canons of Lambeth 1261 (Wilkins, i. 759). But there is no sign that this was a usual
practice or considered necessary.

[2] *Provinciale*, I. xiv. *ver.* Iuramento (p. 70*b*) : ' Possunt . . . archiepiscopi et
episcopi constitutiones facere iuris communis declaratorias et revocatorias, et ubi
poena deficit in iure, possunt poenas apponere, et veterem poenam augere. Possunt
etiam constitutionibus papalibus addere, et eas supplere, et ad correctionem morum
statuta facere praeceptoria, prohibitoria, et poenalia, dum tamen ius commune non
subvertant ; secundum Hostien. qui hoc notat in *d.c. ut singulae* [de off. Archipr.]
et idem *Jo.* in *no. post eum*. Possunt etiam in his, quae ad ipsorum iurisdictionem
pertinent, statuta facere, dum tamen legibus generalibus non obsistant ; prout notatur
per Jo. An. in *no. extra. de off. le. c. ulti. in prin.*'.

[3] *Ibid.* III. v. 2 *ver.* Innodatus ; III. ix. 3 *ver.* Adiiciendo (pp. 137*b*, 154*a*).

So, when Archbishop Pecham ordered the observance of a decree of the legate Ottobono, his was a precept ' potius executivum . . . quam auctoritativum ', for Ottobono's decree was already binding and had the greater authority.[1]

Another limitation to the validity of provincial canons is stated by Lyndwood. Custom might be invoked against them in certain circumstances. If a provincial constitutio had never been accepted by the subjects of the bishops and never applied, and if the breaking of it caused no scandal, then it might lapse : ' contrary custom excuses neglect '. But where the infringement caused scandal, the excuse of contrary custom could not avail.[2]

The Fourth Lateran Council provided a means of preparing the legislation of provincial councils, that is, for deciding what portions of the general law of the Church called for special emphasis or elaboration at the moment. The bishops in council were to appoint fit persons (' idoneas personas, providas videlicet et honestas ') for each diocese, who should in the course of the year carefully investigate what stood in need of reform ' simpliciter, et de plano, absque ulla iurisdictione '. They were to bring their reports to the metropolitan and his suffragans in the next council, to facilitate their work. The reports would provide the material for new constitutions.

It may be confessed straightway that there seems to be no direct evidence of this order being regularly obeyed in any part of Europe. Only in certain diocesan canons, notably those of Bishop Richard le Poore of Salisbury (1217–22), provision was made for the appointment of two or three fit persons in each deanery, to report on the locality at the bishop's command.[3] This canon is plainly modelled on chapter vi of the Lateran Council. Lyndwood knew of it under an ascription (probably false) to Archbishop Edmund, in texts which read ' at the archbishop's command '. Naturally, Lyndwood saw in it the order of the Lateran decree, and commented that it seems to go somewhat farther, requiring inquisitors in each deanery. The men, he observed, are not officials with jurisdiction, but only appointed to make a report ; the result of their report is simply action in the provincial council, not prosecution by the archbishop ; the archbishop may therefore appoint them in the dioceses of his suffragans.[4] But Lyndwood's treatment is academic : one cannot

---

[1] *Provinciale*, I. ii. 1 *ver*. Observari (p. 11a). Cf. Maitland, *Canon Law*, pp. 24–6.

[2] *Ibid*. III. i. 1 *ver*. Cappis clausis (p. 118b). Cf. Athon, Otho xiii. *ver*. Et cappis clausis (p. 37a).

[3] Ch. 44. *Sarum Charters* (Rolls Series), p. 144. The canons attributed to Bishop Giles (1257–62) refer to the same institution as a custom of the diocese : ' duo debent esse inquisitores docti et discreti ' (Wilkins, i. 714). Cf. Gibbs and Lang, *Bishops and Reform*, pp. 144, 147.

[4] *Provinciale*, v. i. 1 *ver*. Duo vel tres (p. 277b) : ' Haec constitutio aliquid adiicere videtur ultra id quod legitur [*Decretales*, v. i. 25] quod loquitur de personis . . . per

infer that the rule was maintained in England, and apparently
no English records witness to it. For the most part, continental
records give the same negative result. Inquisitors appear in the
diocesan synod,[1] but not in the provincial council. There is
one interesting exception. A sign of these reporters, as valuable
as it is unusual, appears in the register of Archbishop Rigaud of
Rouen.[2] At his provincial council 1251/2 :

with the advice of the suffragan bishops were elected as inquisitors good
men and true who should inquire in their dioceses about the things which
appertain to the reform of manners and the correction of excesses, and
report whatever they should find worthy of reformation and correction
to the next provincial council, according to the form of the general
council.

The names of two inquisitors for each diocese follow. Nothing
more is heard of them until the council of 1257. When the
inquisitors last appointed were asked for their reports, ' they
were all negligent except the inquisitor [*sic*] of the diocese of
Rouen. Then we appointed others. . . . ' Two years later the
inquisitors in the council excused themselves for not holding
inquiry because some had deceased and the survivors did not
like inquiring without their colleagues. At the next council
few of the inquisitors appeared, and they vouchsafed no information. With that, the archbishop, by common consent,
ordered that the duty of inquiry should devolve on the archdeacons.

So, in the only instance [3] where one finds the Lateran decree
enforced, it failed to work effectively. Absence of other evidence
does not permit us to say with certainty that inquisitors were
unknown elsewhere : we could not hope for reference to them
in most of the conciliar documents which survive ; it is only
highly probable that some trace would remain if the inquisitors
regularly were appointed and did their work.

But we ought not to assume too readily that the principle
behind the Lateran decree was ignored. Archbishop Rigaud
finally decided that each archdeacon should bring a report to the
provincial council : and in England there are traces of a somewhat similar practice. Either the suffragans or the representatives
who eventually came always to accompany them took the place

---

singulas diœceses ad talia in concilio generali referenda assignandis ' (*ibid. ver.*
Mandatum archiepiscopi, *ver* Aliorum clericorum). Elsewhere, he calls this kind of
inquiry ' inquisitio generalissima ' (*ibid.* I. ii. 2 *ver.* Inquirant (p. 17*b*)).

[1] Especially where heresy was rife. E.g. Narbonne (1227), Mansi, *Ampl. Collectio,*
xxiii. 24 ; Salzburg (1418), Mansi, xxviii. 981–2.

[2] *Reg. . . . Odonis Rigaldi,* 125, 286, 356, 387.

[3] One fifteenth-century council (Sens 1461) mentions the institution. Two *testes
synodales* for each diocese were appointed in the provincial council (Mansi, xxxii. 431).

I

of formally appointed inquisitors. They were sometimes if not always requested to bring local grievances to the notice of the assembly. Thus the legate Ottobono writes (1268) to an English bishop to call a synod of deans, archdeacons, abbots, priors, and others of his diocese, to resolve on *reformanda* so that when the time comes to meet the writer the latter may better be able to ordain what is necessary to correct abuses.[1]   Archbishop Mepham, summoning bishops to his council in 1328, orders them to deliberate beforehand with their clergy ' de gravaminibus et defectibus dicti concilii studio reformandis '.[2] Similarly Archbishop Stratford, in his summons to a provincial council in 1347, says ' we desire you [to discuss] with the religious and clergy of your diocese the depravities and excesses needing reform, so that on the said day at the said place there may be obtained a fuller and more mature report upon them, whence what is fitting can more conveniently be ordained '. Bishop Trillek, for one, held such an assembly and reported to the archbishop that he had not troubled to write anything down, because the religious and clergy aforesaid had reported to him nothing worthy of reform at the council.[3]

These records all point in one direction. They suggest that legatine and provincial canons were alike founded on the particular demands and deficiencies of the people concerned. In this respect they resemble closely the injunctions issued by prelates after a visitation. They are not for the most part systematic codes of law. An inquiry discovers certain faults and these give rise to legislation. The legislation will adopt well-known phrases and reiterate generally accepted canons, but it will reflect the special needs of the province in which it is uttered. This may be illustrated from the preamble to Archbishop Thoresby's canons for the diocese of York. On matters for which earlier laws sufficiently provide there is no need to promulgate new ones. Since the archbishop finds good laws on certain topics, issued by his predecessors Greenfield and Zouche, ' *ex abundanti* we renew the same ordinances and constitutions '. He recites them in full and passes on to legislation of his own. This of course resembles closely the method of medieval visitors, who

---

[1] *Ante*, xv. (1900), 119–20.

[2] Wilkins, ii. 548–9. The bishop of Exeter (absent from the council) sent to the archbishop the names of those he had consulted, and their *gravamina*. Cf. [Edmund Gibson], *Synodus Anglicana* (1702), pp. 147–69.

[3] *Reg. Joh. Trillek* (Canterbury and York Soc.), pp. 307–8, 310. Thomassin gives a continental example (*L'ancienne et la nouvelle discipline*, II. III. lvii. § 7) : Gregory XI ordered (1374) the suffragans of Narbonne to hold diocesan synods before the provincial council to decide in them upon proposals to make in the council. The same practice of ordering preliminary diocesan assemblies might be adopted when the council had to discuss secular affairs (e.g. 1297 and 1309, *Reg. Rob. Winchelsey* (Cant. and York Soc.), p. 199 ; Wilkins, ii. 313).

often incorporated a selection of previous injunctions in their own.[1]

Sometimes one can do more than draw a parallel with the visitation process. Legislation might grow out of a visitation,[2] or a synod might be the outcome of a visitation and the occasion of using whatever information had been gained during the inquiry. An early instance of the latter procedure is afforded by the diocesan statutes of Meath (? 1216) : the bishop orders archpriests to send the *acta visitationis* and reports on the condition of churches to the diocesan synod, where the amending of abuses can be discussed.[3]

The evidence is sparse, but convincing. Legatine and provincial laws were designed to supplement the common law of the Church, sometimes simply to renew it. Always the choice of material was governed by two considerations : the immediate needs of the locality and the compatibility of the local with the universal law. The purpose and authority of local canons are summed up in the archbishop of Canterbury's preamble to Westminster 1175, as it is given by the *Gesta Henrici II :* [4]

In the Church of God, according to the ancient custom of the fathers, councils are gathered together so that those who occupy the higher office of pastors may by common counsel order the lives of their subjects according to the established rules of conduct and restrain with more considered censure the enormities that are always rife. We, therefore, adhering to the rules of the orthodox fathers rather than establishing anything fresh, have thought fit to promulgate in your midst certain canons which we order to be firmly and inviolably observed by all of our province (*universis provincialibus nostris*). For we account them transgressors of the holy canons who shall presume to contravene the statutes of this sacred synod.

[1] Wilkins, iii. 69. A special request from the clergy might lead to a re-statement of an earlier provincial canon : thus in 1421 Sudbury's constitution ' Capellani stipendiarii ' was renewed (Wilkins, iii. 402). For the renewal of visitation injunctions see, e.g. *Reg. Epp. J. Peckham* (Rolls Series), i. 82, 223 ; iii. 845.

[2] E.g. *Reg. Walter Gray* (Surtees Soc.), p. 217 ; *Reg. Epp. J. Peckham* (Rolls Series), ii. 737 ; iii. 794, 797 ; *Reg. H. Hethe* (Cant. and York Soc.), pp. 354–5. Dr. Frere suggests that Grosseteste's constitutions were injunctions after visitation ; at least he is justified in observing that they agree ' not merely in contents and general plan but in detail and wording with (*a*) the Articles of 1233 and (*b*) the instructions given by Grosseteste to his Archdeacons in 1236 '. Frere, *Visitation Articles and Injunctions, Introduction* (Alcuin Club coll. xiv.), p. 98 ; cf. p. 104.

[3] Wilkins, i. 547. It was after a tour of England which included the visitation of several monasteries that Cardinal John of Ferentino held a council at Reading in October 1206, in which, it is said, ' he confirmed the church law throughout the whole kingdom ' (*ante*, xlvi (1931), 444). Cf the archbishop of Tours in his provincial council of Saumur (1253), c. 1 : ' Nos sanctorum canonum et praedecessorum nostrorum volentes servare statuta, et ea quae visitando provinciam Turonensem correctione novimus indigere, corrigere cupientes, vocatis venerabilibus fratribus Turonensis provinciae episcopis, etc. . . .' (quoted, Thomassin, I. I. xlvi. § 4).

[4] *Gesta Henrici II.* (Rolls Series), i. 84–5 (Wilkins, i. 476).

The Method of Publishing Canons

A precious indication of the method of publishing canons in the early twelfth century comes from the letters of Archbishop Anselm. After the national council of London 1102 the archbishop wrote as follows to William the archdeacon : [1]

Sententias capitulorum concilii expositas nolo vobis aut alicui ad praesens mittere, quia quando in ipso concilio expositae sunt, non potuerunt ad plenum et perfecte recitari, propterea quia subito sine praemeditatione, ac competenti tractatione, sicut oportuerat, sunt prolatae. Unde quaedam videntur addenda, et forsitan quaedam mutanda, quod non nisi communi consensu coepiscoporum nostrorum volo facere. Volo ergo eas dictare, et prius eisdem episcopis ostendere, cum primo convenerimus, quam per ecclesias Angliae dictatae et expositae mittantur. Nomina tamen rerum, de quibus ibi locuti sumus, vobis mittimus, ut secundum quod recordari poteritis nos de illis decrevisse, faciatis.

Not only does this letter emphasize the authority of the assembled bishops : it also tells us that the canons were drafted hastily for a perfunctory recital in the council, and that with the advice of the bishops a new recension was later to be made,[2] of which copies would be circulated among the churches. Very little later evidence is forthcoming on the drafting of canons. It is conceivable that in the canons printed by Wilkins *s.a.* 1173 we have a first recension of Westminster 1175, though the discrepancies are very wide. When Otto held his legatine council in 1237 the bishops asked for and obtained opportunity to see the statutes which the legate proposed to issue : they met together a day before the council to discuss the statutes, but apparently made no alterations in them.[3] The provincial canons of Lambeth 1261 were based on the provisions made by all the clergy three years earlier. Those of London 1341 underwent revision. The possibility remains that other canons first appeared, in the council at which they were promulgated, not in their final form.

The canons were usually recited publicly in the council. At Westminster 1175, Archbishop Richard made Benedict, his chancellor, read the canons to the assembly.[4] At Oxford 1222, Langton's canons were read together with those of the Fourth

---

[1] Wilkins, i. 383 (Migne, *Patr. Lat.* clix. 94–5, reading *sciatis* for *faciatis*).

[2] Perhaps this was the purpose of the council which Anselm announced to the archbishop of York for Christmas 1103 (*Hist. Church of York* (Rolls Series), iii. 25–6). But Anselm left England for three years after Easter 1103, and his own words, as well as William of Malmesbury's (*Gesta Pontificum* (Rolls Series), pp. 117–18), suggest that the canons of 1102 as we have them are only the first draft.

[3] Matt. Paris, *Chron. Maj.* iii. 418 (Wilkins, i. 648); cf. Finke, *Konzilienstudien,* p. 70, n. 1.

[4] ' In communi de scripto legi fecit Benedicto eius cancellario solempniter legente statuta concilii sui sub hac forma. . . .' Gervase of Canterbury (Rolls Series), i. 251–2.

Lateran Council.[1] The legate Otto, at London 1237, 'had the statutes read aloud and distinctly and ordered them firmly to be observed '.[2] Boniface's canons were publicly recited on the last day of the council at Lambeth 1261 ; [3] so also Ottobono's and John Pecham's, in 1268, 1279, and 1281.[4] One is encouraged to believe that this was a regular practice in England by the fact that it was usual abroad.[5]

A formal reading at their first promulgation apparently sufficed to make these constitutions binding on the auditors. To secure general observance it was usual in the thirteenth century and after to demand that the bishops should publish the canons within their own jurisdiction. Thus archbishops are to publish legatine canons in their provincial councils and bishops to publish provincial canons in their diocesan synods. The latter was indeed a rule already incorporated in the *Decretum* (I. xviii. xvii.) from the council of Toledo 693, and it was re-peated in the Fourth Lateran decree (cap. 6). Much later Lynd-wood observed that six months is the normal period allowed to lapse before publication by the bishops, but that the metropolitan may demand that they publish his constitutions within that period.[6]

Although a single publication was all that the law required,[7] recitation of the canons at regular intervals was sometimes de-manded. There was no general rule, and the urgency of certain topics—causes of excommunication, concubinary priests, or matters of monastic discipline—produced regulations for the repetition of select chapters. While the canons of Oxford 1222 were to be recited in bishops' synods ' as it should seem expedient ', the excommunication clause was to be recited therein every year, and four times a year in the parish churches.[8] Ottobono ordered the archbishops and bishops to have his statutes read diligently word by word in their synods every year. Pecham renewed this

---

[1] *Supra*, p. 200, n. 1.   [2] Matt. Paris, *Chron. Maj.* iii. 420 (Wilkins, i. 649).

[3] Spelman, *Concilia*, ii. 315.

[4] Wykes, *Ann. Mon.* iv. 215; cf. *Chron. Petroburgense*, p. 19 ; Wilkins, ii. 51. Cf. Part II of this study.

[5] E.g. Gousset, *Actes . . . Reims*, ii. 357, 474, 520 ; *Reg. . . . Odonis Rigaldi*, 287, 357, 387, 482, 586 ; further references in Hinschius, iii. 501, n. 5.

[6] *Provinciale*, I. ii. 2 *ver.* Ut ius exigit (p. 18*b*). In 1342 Stratford ordered the suffragans to publish his constitutions and bring them to the notice of the public. In 1408/9 Arundel ordered them to publish his statutes canonically in their synods and chapters.

[7] Athon, Ottobono xxxvi. *ver.* Annis singulis (p. 141*a*) : ' de iure sufficeret notitia post publicationem unicam, una cum fluxu duorum mensium a tempore publicationis huiusmodi, ad arctandum quemcumque subditum '. Cf. Wilkins, ii. 711. The two-month limit was enforced by Archbishop Thoresby of York 1367 (*ibid.* iii. 72).

[8] Wilkins, i. 593. Visitation articles of the fourteenth century inquire about parish priests : ' an publicent inter parochianos suos excommunicaciones latas in constitucionibus Oxon' ? ' (Exeter Coll. MS. 31, fo. 243). For discretion allowed to priests in the reciting of sentences, cf. Greenfield at York (Wilkins, ii. 415).

order and further demanded that the legate's canon *de concubinariis* (cap. 8) should be read in the quarterly rural chapters.[1]
Pecham, and after him Thoresby of York, issued in his council
a kind of catechism which parish priests might use for the regular
instruction of their flocks.[2] Frequent repetition of sentences
of excommunication was also demanded by Pecham, and the
whole of the canons of Reading 1279 was to be read ' twice a year,
viz. in the two general chapters of each archdeaconry '.[3] In
his provincial council 1309, Winchelsey ordered that in all
cathedral churches should be read quarterly the sentences of
excommunication, and statutes (probably those concerning
clerical privilege) of Langton, Otto, and Ottobono : the inferior
clergy were to recite them once a year.[4] The monastic orders
made their own regulations for reading canons that concerned them. Among the articles of monastic visitation preserved by the Burton annalist is the inquiry : ' whether the
statutes of the Council of Oxford, in so far as they concern religious . . . are read several times a year in chapter ? '[5] The
Benedictine General Chapter of York in September 1273 demanded
that the statutes of the legate Ottobono should be read in every
(conventual) chapter after the reading from the Rule ; and the
English Augustinians in 1325 and 1340 ordered the reading of
canons of Oxford and Ottobono.[6]

The question now arises : how did the prelates obtain their
copies of the canons of a council ? The question is important
for any estimate of the value of existing texts. Were they
official productions of the legate's or archbishop's chancery,
delivered in the council ? Or were they dispatched to the various dioceses after the council was over ? Or was it incumbent
upon all diocesans to make their own clerks take copies from an
authentic original ?

It is probably impossible to answer these questions with
certainty, but the scanty evidence suggests that custom changed.
From the passage in St. Anselm's letter already quoted we might
infer that the archbishop was responsible for sending out copies
of the canons after the council was over. But this is not certain.
The next piece of evidence, likewise inconclusive, comes from

---

[1] Wilkins, ii. 15, 51, 36.

[2] *The Lay Folks' Catechism* (Early Engl. Text Soc. O.S. 118). Cf. the tract appended to Quivil's diocesan constitutions for Exeter.

[3] Wilkins, ii. 35, 56, 36. The excommunication clause of Reading is found in
two thirteenth-century MSS. appended to earlier diocesan canons (Wilkins, i. 601 ;
Brit. Mus. MS. Reg. 7 A, ix. fo. 90ᵛ), also following a fourteenth-century text of the
Legenda (Bodleian MS. Hatton 109, fo. 62ᵛ).

[4] *Reg. Simonis de Gandavo* (Cant. and York Soc.), i. 378 (Wilkins, ii. 402).

[5] *Annales Monastici*, i. 485.

[6] *Chapters of Engl. Black Monks* (Camden Soc.), i. 250 ; *Chapters of Aug. Canons*
(Cant. and York Soc.), pp. 14, 19.

Lambeth 1261. The canons were then issued in the form of letters patent, with the seals appended of all the bishops at the council.[1] The formality of this utterance suggests at least the possibility that the clerks attending the council may have prepared on the spot sufficient copies to be sent sealed to all dioceses. More than two centuries ago William Wake pointed out the fact that the canons of Reading 1279 were very quickly copied into Godfrey Giffard's register : ' We may venture to conclude (he says) that the copy entred this same year, and that written within six weeks after the Council was ended, into the register of the bishop of Worcester was taken from that which he brought with him to publish, or cause to be published, in that diocese.' In fact, this record only proves that the bishop obtained a copy expeditiously : we are still left in doubt as to how precisely he obtained it.[2]

Fuller information for the province of Canterbury begins in the middle of the next century. How Mepham's canons were published we cannot say, in the absence of his register, but the evidence from the pontificates of Stratford and Islip points to a new departure in Islip's time, here as in other branches of administration. Six months after his provincial council of October 1342 Archbishop Stratford transmitted the canons provided in the council directly to the bishop of Wells and presumably to the other suffragans, desiring that the bishops should bring them to the notice of all whom they concerned.[3] But with Islip the dean of the province comes between the archbishop and the rest of his suffragans. Even as early as the twelfth century the bishop of London, as dean, had summoned his colleagues to a provincial council ; [4] now he takes an important part in the publishing of canons. Islip's various constitutions, each concerned with a separate subject, were not all promulgated in councils ; but they usually were issued in the form of letters directed to the bishop of London, whose duty it was to pass them on to the other suffragans of the province. Consequently, his constitution on stipendiary priests (1350) appears in Trillek's

[1] Brit. Mus. Cotton Ch. xvi. 29. Cf. Rouen 1267 (Pommeraye, *S. Rotomag. Ecclesiae Concilia*, p. 258), and Compiègne 1270 (Gousset, *Actes . . . Reims*, ii. 409-10).

[2] Wake, *State of the Church*, p. 220. Cf. Council of Benevento 1331 : the suffragans and parish priests are to obtain within a month a copy of the provincial constitutions ' scriptam manu notariorum curiae nostrae, aut alicuius alius, cui duxerimus committendum ' (Mansi, *Ampl. Coll.* xxv. 974–5).

[3] *Reg. Rad. de Salopia* (Somerset Rec. Soc.), ii. 463. On another reading of the evidence the canons were issued only two months after a council in March 1342/3 (cf. Part II of this study). Archbishop Thoresby of York only issued his provincial canons after the council was over. The canons were agreed in the chapter-house at York, but sealed and dated at Thorpe ' quoad consignationem ', 29 September 1367 (Wilkins, iii. 70, 72). Cf. Morton's procedure 1486/7 (*ibid.* iii. 620).

[4] Migne, *Patr. Lat.* cxc. 933 (Gilbert Foliot, bishop of London, to the bishop of Salisbury).

I

Hereford register with the covering letter of the bishop of London.[1] This is henceforth the usual method of publication in the province of Canterbury. It is fully displayed in the canons of Archbishop Arundel 1408/9. They were issued in letters close to the bishop of London ; he was told to send copies under his seal and letters to the other suffragans, and all were to publish them canonically in their synods and chapters.[2] So also on 23 October 1414 Chichele dispatched the decree of a provincial council to the bishop of London, who sent a copy of it on 6 November to the bishop of Chichester.[3]

The evidence shows the archbishop and the dean of the province concerned to supply all the suffragans with copies of canons. Nothing suggests that the inferior prelates were directly supplied with official copies of provincial canons.[4] It was for

---

[1] *Reg. Joh. Trillek*, pp. 157 *seqq.* (cf. Churchill, *op. cit.* i. 359, n. 2). This was not conciliar legislation, and for such mandates as this the archbishop sometimes wrote directly to each suffragan (Churchill, i. 359, n. 1) ; but the bishop of London was again the intermediary when a new edition was issued ' de fratrum nostrorum consilio et assensu ' 9 November 1362 (*Reg. S. de Sudbiria, London* (Cant. and York Soc.), p. 193). Cf. the statutes on festivals of Islip (*ibid.* p. 188) and Chichele (*Reg. R. Mascall, Hereford* (Cant. and York Soc.), pp. 89, 122). This method is concealed by some texts. Compare the original form of the constitution on festivals sent by Islip to the bishop of London (Oxford ed. 1679, p. 57) with the versions composed from copies received by the bishop of Salisbury (Wilkins, ii. 560 ; All Souls Coll. MS. 42, fo. 278ᵛ ; Camb. Univ. Lib. MS. Add. 3575, fo. 328ᵛ ; Hereford Cath. MS. P. 7. vii. fo. 149 ; Holkham MS. 226, p. 80), the bishop of Lichfield (Brasenose Coll. MS. 14), and the official of the archdeacon of Oxford (Bodl. MS. Wood empt. 23, fo. 173, All Souls Coll. MS. 42, fo. 174).

[2] Oxford edition, 1679, p. 68.

[3] *Reg. R. Rede* (Sussex Rec. Soc.), i. 160. Brit. Mus. Cotton Charter xv. 12 is the original sealed letters patent of the bishop of London to the dean of St. Paul's (1 April 1398) reciting Archbishop Roger's conciliar canon on festivals (8 March 1397/8). The practice of the monastic general chapters is interesting in this connexion. The English Benedictine Chapter 1426 ordered the proctor of each house to draft a copy of the statutes before leaving the general chapter, and to have it sealed and endorsed by the president (*Chapters of Eng. Black Monks*, ii. 177–8). Augustinian houses were told in 1325 only to accept copies of capitular statutes if they were authenticated with the presidents' seals ; but Mr. Salter is unable to say whether 150 or 160 copies were drawn up and sealed in the chapter, or whether each set of visitors exhibited a sealed copy in each house and allowed it to be copied (*Chapters of Aug. Canons*, pp. xvii, 14). In the Cistercian Order, after 1212, each abbot took with him from the general chapter a copy of the ' definitiones generales ' (*Statuta . . . Ord. Cist.*, ed. J. M. Canivez, i. 390). For further information on the preservation of Benedictine chapter acts and the extant copies of their statutes see W. A. Pantin, ' Chapters of the English Black Monks ' (*Trans. Royal Hist. Soc.*, fourth series, x. (1927)), pp. 196 *seqq.*

[4] The provincial council of Rouen 1335 ordered that each bishop should receive a copy of the canons. Then it ordered bishops to see that the parish clergy had the provincial and diocesan constitutions copied, and expounded them to the people in the vernacular (Pommeraye, *Concilia*, pp. 297–8) ; cf. provincial canons of Dublin 1351 (Wilkins, iii. 18). The legate Ottobono ordered (1268) that copies of his canons should be had by bishops, cathedral chapters, and monastic superiors (Wilkins, ii. 15). In Germany the legate Conrad had ordered (1225) archbishops, bishops, archdeacons and deans to publish his constitutions, and ordered abbots and other prelates of churches and monasteries to have them copied (Mansi, xxiii. 8). The same order occurs in the provincial canons of Salzburg 1386 (Mansi, xxvi. 723).

the bishops and for the monastic orders to take measures necessary for the further diffusion of the canons. They had to be possessed by those who had to read them regularly. Consequently, the obligation is expressed in diocesan statutes. The bishop of Meath ordered his archpriests to see that copies were made of provincial statutes, to be recited and expounded in the rural chapters.[1] One recension of Poore's constitutions for the diocese of Salisbury makes a similar order to the archdeacons in respect of the council of Oxford ; [2] and in order to ensure a knowledge of the excommunication sentences of 1222 both Grosseteste of Lincoln and Insula of Durham incorporate them verbatim in their own constitutions.[3] By inference from continental practice and from the method of diffusing diocesan constitutions we may suppose that the clergy either paid a fee to the bishop's clerks for copies of the canons or borrowed exemplars which they themselves copied.[4]

Before we turn to the existing texts upon which a new edition of the canons must be based, some further evidence may be indicated regarding the possessors of the canons in the middle ages. Two fairly well-defined periods appear. From what has gone before, we should anticipate that the twelfth-century canons were not very widely diffused : for the legislators made no demand for their recital and we do not know of any distribution of official copies. But in the thirteenth century and afterwards it was clearly obligatory on every diocesan to have by him a copy of legatine and provincial canons, and the regular prelates and lower clergy were obliged to possess some sections of the law ; these obligations are reflected in the contents of medieval catalogues and extant texts.

Canons earlier than the Fourth Lateran Council are not common in medieval catalogues,[5] and they are not quoted in the later middle ages. The existing manuscripts mostly date from the twelfth century. The canons are found inscribed in books which belonged to cathedral or episcopal libraries ; they were not considerable enough to warrant a volume to themselves and so

---

[1] Wilkins, i. 547.

[2] Worcester Cath. MS. Q. 67, fo. 144ᵛ (marginal addition).

[3] Grosseteste implies that it was not usual for parish churches to have the provincial canons : ' Et quia in multis ecclesiis, ut credimus, non est scriptum Oxoniense concilium, principium ipsius . . . duximus hic adiungendum ' (*Epp. R. Grosseteste* (Rolls Series), p. 162). Miss Lang infers the contrary (Gibbs and Lang, *op. cit.* p. 114).

[4] In 1303 the bishop of Worcester sent to the dean of Bristol an ordinance of Archbishop Winchelsey concerning the deanery : he ordered the dean, if requested by the mayor and corporation, to make them a copy of this mandate under his seal (*Reg. Ginsborough* (Worc. Hist. Soc.), pp. 7-8). Canons of Salzburg 1418 : persons requiring copies of the canons pay for them (Mansi, xxviii. 979).

[5] Ch. Ch., Canterbury : ' Concilia Lanfranci ' (James, *Ancient Libraries of Canterbury and Dover*, p. 31, no. 137) ; Dover : ' Statuta Ricardi archiepiscopi ' (*ibid.* p. 466, no. 211).

I

LEGISLATION OF THE

they were often inserted in a continental law-book, of which they formed a natural supplement. Brief canons of Archbishop Richard are preserved in a collection of Alexander III's decretals, immediately following the decrees of the council of Tours.[1] Some of these canons have also survived in copies made at the time by careful chroniclers. Thus we are entirely dependent on one manuscript of Henry of Huntingdon for the canons of 1151, on the *Gesta Henrici II* and Hoveden for the complete series of 1175 and on Hoveden for those of 1195. Their relationship with the archbishop's chancery and the great monastic houses gave some of these writers the opportunity to see and copy the laws. It would seem that the canons were meant to be preserved, but never widely diffused, and after the Fourth Lateran Council they were not much regarded.[2]

The second period begins with the provincial canons of Oxford 1222. From now onwards the canons of councils were frequently copied and widely diffused, and the effective by-laws of the English Church came to be only those laws which canonists dated after the Fourth Lateran Council. The *Summa Summarum*, a fourteenth-century compilation, draws upon the provincial canons of Oxford 1222, Reading 1279, Lambeth 1261 and 1281, and the legatine canons of Otto and Ottobono. Similarly, John of Athon, who comments on Otto and Ottobono, does not look back to the twelfth-century constitutions. Lyndwood, composing his *Provinciale* about 1430, omits those twelfth-century canons which were issued by metropolitan authority. Of some fifty surviving collections in which scribes of the fourteenth century and after brought together canons provincial and legatine, only two preserve any twelfth-century canons besides those of 1175.[3] And this corresponds with Lyndwood's list of the ' constitutiones quas habemus in regno Angliae ',[4] in which he gives both provincial and legatine canons from 1222 to 1415. These canons occur frequently in medieval catalogues of cathedral and monastic libraries,[5] and about one quarter of the extant collections can be

---

[1] Brit. Mus. Cotton MS. Claudius A. iv. fo. 191ᵛ (Wilkins, i. 474).

[2] Cf. Z N. Brooke, *The English Church and the Papacy*, pp. 101 *seqq.*

[3] The fifteen texts of the 1175 canons are all defective and ascribed to the year 1065 ; cf. Part II of this study.

[4] *Provinciale*, v. xv. 2 *ver.* Minima (p. 319). Here as elsewhere he shows a striking disregard of the northern province. He apparently worked on collections of canons as we have them to-day, and in ascribing the canons of 1175 to Langton's successor Richard Wethershed substituted for the error of his texts a fresh one of his own making.

[5] E.g. Ch. Ch., Canterbury : *c.* 1300 (James, *Ancient Libraries*, nos. 294, 584, 654, 732, 733, 1501, 1605, 1627, 1637, 1823) ; St. Aug., Canterbury : fifteenth century (*ibid.* nos. 1550, 1552, 1834, 1835) ; Dover : 1389 (*ibid.* nos. 220, 222, 244, 262, 267, 277, 278, 279, 285, 290, 370, 408) ; Durham : 1395 (*Vet. Cat. Eccles. Dunelm.* p. 47), 1421 (*ibid.* p. 124) ; Peterborough : *c.* 1400 (*Serapeum*, 1851, pp. 156, 185 ; *ibid.* 1852, pp. 3, 18, 36).

certainly associated with particular cathedrals or monasteries. Only rarely were the canons copied into chapter muniments,[1] and they do not often figure in episcopal registers, until the time when they were issued by the dean of the province and were enregistered along with other correspondence concerning the province.[2]

Before the bulk of legislation produced collected editions in the fourteenth century, the canons might be preserved by those responsible for their publication with papal decrees and law-books,[3] or on separate small *rotuli*,[4] or in the original charter form of the original.[5] Following the orders to recite the canons regularly in chapter, monasteries equipped their libraries with collections of excerpts bearing on the monastic life. Select canons were sometimes incorporated with the kalendar, obituary, and other material used in daily chapter. St. Augustine's, Canterbury, for instance, possessed in the fifteenth century, ' collecciones Roberti de Clare in quibus continentur decretales et constituciones legatorum super ordinem monachorum ', and, in another volume, a selection of Mepham's constitutions.[6] The statutes of Ottobono for religious were preserved with the provincial chapter statutes and the local chronicle at St. Mary's Abbey, York,[7] and Norwich cathedral priory had a copy for refectory reading.[8] A Durham priory manuscript (B. iv. 41) and the Launceston priory register (Tanner MS. 196) each contains statutes from the legatine and provincial councils concerning regulars. On the other hand, the inferior members of the secular clergy had no use for the canonical prescriptions on monasticism : one of these persons, in the diocese of London in the thirteenth century, copied parts of Oxford 1222 into his theological and legal miscellany, omitting the monastic chapters.[9] The clause *de concubinariis* of Ottobono was diffused more widely than the whole series of legatine canons

[1] E.g. Salisbury Cathedral muniments, Liber Evidentiarum C ; Bodleian MS. Ashmole 1146 (Chichester).

[2] *Reg. Godfrey Giffard Worcester*, fo. 89ᵛ. Cf. *Reg. J. Trillek*, p. 157. M. Lacger has found provincial statutes of Bourges 1267 in a register of the bishopric of Rodez. Others came from the archives of the archbishopric of Albi (*Rev. d'hist. ecclés.* xxvi. 285, n. 6, 286, n. 4, cf. 292).

[3] E.g. Caius Coll. Cambridge MS. 44 contains Oxford 1222 with the second and fourth *Compilationes*.

[4] E.g. Ch. Ch., Canterbury, Chartae antiquae O. 138 (Oxford 1222); L. 138ᵃ (Lambeth 1261).

[5] E.g. Brit. Mus. Cotton Charter xvi. 29 (Lambeth 1261).

[6] James, *Ancient Libraries*, pp. 376, 406 (nos. 1550, 1834).

[7] MS. Bodley 39, fo. 42ᵛ. Cf. the order of the Benedictine Chapter of 1343 (*Chapters*, ii. 40).

[8] 1308. H. W. Saunders, *Introduction to the . . . Rolls . . . Norwich*, p. 143.

[9] MS. in the possession of the Rt. Rev. the Bishop of Lewes, fo. 5ʳ. A fifteenth-century collection of extracts (' constituciones provinciales que ad usum faciunt cotidianum ') is found in Caius Coll. MS. 235, with a text of the *Articuli Cleri* and formulas for episcopal visitation and the dedication of a church.

because Pecham had ordered this one clause to be read in all rural chapters.[1] From the inventories made at visitations for the chapter of St. Paul's Cathedral, London (1297), it appears that the parish churches were expected to possess, besides the (diocesan) synodal statutes, the *articuli consiliorum* (probably sentences of excommunication), *Capitula Octoboni* (perhaps a selection from Lambeth 1268), and the statutes of Pecham.[2]

The canons from 1222 onwards did not owe their diffusion simply to the ordinances for their copying and recitation. If those ordinances were frequently neglected, another pressing demand produced more copies, and more comprehensive copies. For the councils were now concerned less to repeat papal decrees than to add fresh by-laws. The ecclesiastical lawyer had constant recourse to them : in them he found the local arrangements for clerical discipline and statements of clerical privilege against lay power. The canons of Canterbury had an extended effect in the fifteenth century, when the provincial council of York (1462) accepted such previous legislation of the southern province as was not repugnant to York canons.[3] Canons were therefore copied for the practitioner in the courts christian as well as for those who had the cure of souls.

There was no official attempt (so far as we know) to furnish the lawyer with an authentic edition of the canons. On the continent a collection of earlier canons, revised, sifted, and arranged by subject, was undertaken by various metropolitans of the fourteenth and fifteenth centuries, and the collections so arranged had the same stamp of authenticity as the books of

---

[1] *Supra*, p. 210. Copies in MS. All Souls Coll. Oxon. 63; Univ. Library Cambridge MS. Addit. 3468 (an Ely book, cf. Bodleian, MS. Rawl. B. 278); *Vetus liber archidiac. Eliensis*, p. 7.

[2] *Visitations of Churches belonging to St. Paul's* (Camden Soc. N.S. 55), pp. 2–62 *passim*. Of 16 churches 7 lack ' statuta synodalia ', 8 lack ' articuli conciliorum ', 11 lack ' Capitula Octoboni ' and 12 lack Pecham's Statutes. Articles for parochial visitation (Brit. Mus. MS. Harl. 52 fo. 26) demand that in each church there be ' statuta synodalia et articuli conciliorum et capitula Ottoboni et statuta J. de Pecham archiepiscopi '.

[3] Wilkins, iii. 580, 663. Already there had been some borrowing. Canons of York, 1258–9, demand the observance of Oxford 1222 (Brit. Mus. MS. Lansdowne 397, fos. 245, 252ᵛ), and Durham canons repeat the Oxford sentences 1274–83 (Wilkins, ii. 28); Greenfield in 1311 refers to Lambeth 1261 (*ibid.* ii. 415). Northern manuscripts contain canons of the southern province (e.g. Brit. Mus. MS. Cotton, Vitell. A. II ; Durham Cath. MS. B. iv. 41). The copying of canons in another province was not uncommon : thus Westminster 1175 was used at Rouen 1190 (Seckel, in *Deutsche Ztschr. für Kirchenrecht*, 3 Folge, ix. 1899, 176, n. 45), and London 1200 cites Rouen c. 23 (Wilkins, i. 507). The Mainz collection of 1310 had currency in Magdeburg, Salzburg, and Prague (Hauck, *Kirchengesch.* v. 145). Cf. the copying of Southern Chapter statutes by the Benedictine Chapter of York. In 1499 the collegiate church of Bishop Auckland (dioc. of Durham) received with other books for its library : ' Constituciones secundum usum Cantuariensis provincie cum glosa Willelmi Sherwode [? *read* Lyndwode] in pergameno ' and ' Liber Belial' et Constituciones Cant' in pergameno ' (*Register of R. Fox, Durham* (Surtees Soc. 1932), pp. 95–6).

decretals issued by the popes.[1] But in England these examples were only followed by York in the sixteenth century, when Wolsey issued a meagre collection of his predecessors' canons arranged systematically.[2] In the province of Canterbury the task was left to private individuals. Badius Ascensius, dedicating the first printed edition to William Warham in 1504, expressed the wish that the archbishop would take in hand the publishing of a collection. But the wish was never gratified. The collections of the provincial constitutions that were made do not agree in contents : when Lyndwood came to arrange the material after the manner of the *Corpus Iuris* and comment upon it, there were many variants from which he had to choose. Some forty existing manuscripts and more than a dozen printed editions of his *Provinciale* [3] witness to its great utility and influence ; but it was no more an official compilation than Gratian's *Decretum* had been.

EXTANT TEXTS AND THEIR EDITING

Some general reflections on the state of the texts will clear the way for a chronological survey of the canons. The province of Canterbury provides most of the material and most of the problems. From what has gone before, it will be evident that while our knowledge of the twelfth-century councils depends on relatively few and early texts, for the councils after 1215 a large number of less authentic copies survive. Contemporary official enregistrations begin to be common in the second half of the fourteenth century, and then the less trustworthy copies can be easily discarded : but for the councils between 1222 and 1342 we must rely on the manuscript collections such as Lyndwood used and on isolated texts of dubious authority. The questions of textual accuracy and correct ascription are most difficult

---

[1] Archbishop Peter of Mainz made a systematic collection in 1310, because the canons of his predecessors were ' in diversis chartulis seu libellis dispersas ', whence doubt about their authenticity arose (Mansi, xxv. 299). Prague followed Mainz in form and largely in substance in 1346 and 1355 (*ibid.* xxvi. 75, 382), also Magdeburg in 1370 (*ibid.* xxvi. 567). In Poland a provincial council of Gnesen (1357) reissued and recited preceding canons and caused copies to be made (R. Hube, *Antiquissimae Constitutiones . . . Gneznensis* (St. Petersburg, 1856), p. 207). In 1420 Archbishop Nicholas of Gnesen, echoing Peter of Mainz in his preamble, published a collection of canons in five books ' sub certis et consuetis titulis ', invalidating for the future all other previous constitutions (*Statuta sinodalia et provincialia etc.* n.p. or d. (? Cracow, 1512), fo. 52ᵛ ; (*Statuta provincie Gnesnensis antiqua revisa diligenter et emendata* n.p. or d. (? Cracow, 1513), fo. [5]).

[2] Wilkins, iii. 662 *seqq.* There is, however, an indication that before this time the archbishops of York had a collected edition, albeit incomplete, of provincial canons. In 1466 Archbishop Neville recited canons of a provincial council (1440–52), found in the register of Archbishop Kemp, their author : ' non tamen in libro statutorum provincialium inter alia inscriptas et incorporatas ' (Wilkins, iii. 604).

[3] The (first) Oxford edition of 1483 is the only one of five editions of the *Provinciale* printed before 1500 to contain Lyndwood's gloss.

to answer in this middle period, from Langton to Stratford. It may be said that the legislation of the English Church in this period exceeds in bulk and importance all that was produced in other periods of the middle ages.

The existence of the collections has an important bearing on the textual history of the canons. It means that for the period after 1222 there are more varieties than for the earlier canons. It may have meant, moreover, that the original copies ran a greater risk of quick destruction than before. It certainly has meant that editors, seeking a complete series of the canons, have tended to choose the latest and fullest collection they could find, and disregard the early isolated texts. The editions of 1504 and 1679 [1] represent approximately a family of fifteenth-century manuscript collections, copying most of their worst errors and introducing others. Spelman and Wilkins also drew on the collections for many of the canons. While it is true that Wilkins was not content to print from one manuscript, his choice of additional texts seems sometimes to be quite arbitrary. Relying on his predecessors' and friends' transcripts, he frequently ignores valuable texts which lay at hand in manuscripts he purports to employ. Nor can we always tell what Wilkins means when he writes ' collatum cum codice . . . '. Sometimes he has made the merest superficial comparison and left his chief text unaltered ; sometimes he gives a more or less full collation ; but occasionally at least he conflates two texts without any warning in the apparatus. The result is an edition which includes as part of the original many notes and additions of later medieval copyists, to say nothing of those Latin titles and paraphrases of the text which the reader cannot always recognize as Wilkins's own.

The task of the modern editor is in some places lightened by the survival of authentic texts hitherto neglected. But it is usually hard to establish their authority. For each set of canons belonging to the period 1222–1342 there are on an average some fifty texts available. Their provenance is usually doubtful, and even those which bear the recommendation of cathedral muniments often differ among themselves. Most of these numerous manuscripts are obviously far removed from the original. In none does the scribe say whence he takes his copy. Seldom do two texts agree. There are peculiar transpositions, or variant phrases, or passages added or omitted. All the traditional ingenuity of the genealogist is required to relate these texts

---

[1] *Constitutiones legitime seu legatine regionis anglicane : cum subtilissima inter-pretatione domini Johannis de Athon : triplicique tabella. Necnon et constitutiones provinciales ab archiepiscopis Cantuariensibus edite : et summa accuratione recognite : annotate et Parisiis coimpresse* (edited by J. Chappuys, printed by W. Hoepli, Paris, 1504, Short-title Cat. 17108). A similar text of the provincial canons forms the second supplement to the edition of Lyndwood's *Provinciale* printed at Oxford, 1679.

by hypothetical links one with another ; and there is constant danger of imputing paternity when the relationship is really more remote.

These many varieties enforce an unwelcome truth. They are due in part to careless copying, in part to deliberate disregard of the copyist's original. Some of the earliest texts are written very poorly, titles are garbled, passages left out by haplography. Although Gervase of Canterbury must have had access to an authentic text of the contemporary council of Westminster 1175, he omits one chapter of the canons, and the omission occurs again in the only later manuscripts which give an approximately correct text.[1] Two of the earliest manuscripts of Oxford 1222 make nonsense by combining the first half of chapter xxxv (in Wilkins's sequence) with the second half of chapter xxxiv ; [2] and Wilkins's own text differs from nearly all the manuscripts in reading 'maneria' for 'misericordia' in chapter xlix. Such slips are not infrequent. The greater pitfall, however, results from the copyist's habit of improving on his original. Small phrases were embellished : ' deus ' became ' deus omnipotens ', ' excommunicamus ' became ' excommunicamus et excommunicatos nunciamus '. Frequently the copyist altered the order of the canons, whether with the desire for a particular sequence, or because he had omitted something and later rectified the mistake. The multitude of variants in word-order, seldom significant in themselves, likewise testifies to the fact that the scribe was not concerned to give a scrupulously accurate verbal copy. Nor was he always much concerned with the history of the canons : some of the extant manuscripts assign Oxford 1222 to the years 1200, 1216, 1221, 1232. The lack of any historical purpose appears also in the lengthy additions made from later legislation.[3] Two sets of canons were conflated,[4] and the continental *Concilia* print in Oxford 1222 a clause on festivals not otherwise known.[5]

Chapter headings and divisions deserve mention here. In nearly all cases the earliest manuscripts of canons make only the broadest divisions into paragraphs and give no chapter titles. Having regard to all the evidence, we may infer that as originally issued the paragraphs were probably neither numbered nor separately entitled. These aids to easy reference were doubtless

[1] Gervase of Canterbury (Rolls Series), i. 251 ; Bodleian MS. Rawl. C. 428, fo. 111ᵛ ; Lambeth MS. 171 fo. 9. Chapters 7 and 8 both end ' anathema sit innodatus '. The latter chapter is omitted. There seems no reason to doubt its authenticity.

[2] Caius Coll. MS. 44 ; Brit. Mus. MS. Reg. 11 B. V.

[3] A MS. of Axbridge Corporation and Cambridge Univ. Lib. MS. Addit. 3575 each incorporates in Oxford 1222 two chapters from Lambeth 1261.

[4] Cf. Lambeth 1261, discussed in Part II.

[5] Also printed in *Lincoln Cathedral Statutes*, ed. H. Bradshaw and C. Wordsworth, iii. 539–41. Bodleian MS. Digby 58 interpolates chapters of the so-called ' Legenda ' of Oxford in the text of Lambeth 1281.

added very soon, but they cannot be regarded as authoritative, and can seldom even contribute to a classification of the texts.[1]

While any medieval documents of which many texts survive exhibit some of the same features, there are peculiar difficulties in dealing with this class of legislative material. The legislative text was modified more freely than most texts, literary, scientific, or dogmatic, because the modifications would not be noticed. This is not to deny that minute verbal changes in the later recension of a document may be of the utmost significance ; [2] but there are seldom signs of official revision and re-publication which might be taken to account for most of the variants in the canons here under consideration. Copyists were seldom sufficiently intelligent to emend, but were only too prone to simplify. The colourless style of the canons was perhaps improved by copyists' experiments in transposition and expansion, and if the scribe grafted a canon of another growth, it might easily pass unnoticed : for the subject-matter, like the style, of some laws remained the same from century to century. Errors of ascription passed uncorrected and were exaggerated with fantastic results. Men accepted the authority of canons ordained (it was said) by Archbishop Richard in 1065 and others ascribed to Archbishop Stephen in 1200 ; all that lawyers cared for was the law : the impossibility of these dates raised no objection ; and when the error has passed muster for 600 years or so we may despair of rectifying it.

When the ascription of a canon is doubtful, we can only hope to gain certainty with the help of outside evidence. The doubtful canon may appear in other legislation of earlier or later date. While papal legislation is not likely to be modelled on local canons,[3] there is practically no limit to the amount of borrowing among the latter. But a connexion is more often suggested by similarity than by identity. Here the argument from verbal parallels must be used with extreme caution ; the same formulas, often founded on biblical and patristic phrases, may recur independently in several sets of canons. On the other hand, legislators seldom quoted exactly the canons they took for their guide or authority, and frequently departed far from their original.[4] Even when a connexion can be proved it is not neces-

---

[1] This is of course paralleled in secular legislation, and the editor of Bracton's *De Legibus* arrives at the same conclusion regarding the book- and chapter-divisions of that work.

[2] See Mr. Pantin's remarks on the Benedictine chapter statutes (*Chapters*, I. xiii).

[3] Though a universal law might occasionally be moulded on a local law, e.g. 4 Lat. Conc. c. 51.

[4] Hauck's argument that the early Mainz canons precede the Third and Fourth Lateran Councils because they express the same ideas in different words, seems quite inconclusive ; Hauck makes the early date appear probable for entirely different reasons (' Die angeblichen Mainzer Statuten von 1261 . . .' in *Theologische Studien Th. Zahn dargebracht*, p. 83).

sarily direct : two sets of canons, one dubious, one certain, may both have drawn upon an unknown original. A solution of the problem depends always on the existence of some external evidence—quotation from or reference to the canons—and this is often lacking. The problem of dating a canon may lead us sometimes to question its authenticity, and for settling this question the character of the surviving manuscripts is important. One must remember the habits of copyists compiling useful but unofficial reference-books, adding notes and references to the canons they copied, illustrating a provincial law with a constitution from their diocese.

Turning to the state of the texts, one is reminded of the problems which confront Professor Woodbine in his study of forty-six manuscripts of Bracton's *De Legibus*. He too points to the evidence for many missing manuscripts ; but in the case of Bracton's book most of the copies were made within a century of the original, whereas the thirteenth-century canons were being copied for two hundred years and more. Like the copyists of Bracton, those who compiled the collections of English canons seldom followed one copy right through the series. One cannot assume, therefore, having collated two texts of Oxford 1222 and found them alike, that the accompanying texts of Lambeth 1281 must belong to the same family. Only in a few cases have more than one scribe been employed on the body of a collection, but there is often evidence that scribes had several different exemplars. This is indicated by such phrases as ' Quere istam constitutionem sub meliore forma posterius ', ' Hec constitutio sequens est constitutio Johannis Pecham secundum aliquos libros ', ' Westmonasterii vel Lambethe, anno domini 1270 aliter 1272 '.[1] Further confusion is introduced into the family history by the rubricators, who naturally do not always follow the first scribe's exemplar, but use another copy or their own imagination in composing suitable titles and chapter headings.

The editor of these constitutions has to face the task of classifying these many texts ; and modern canons of criticism prescribe a course of action for him. He should arrange his texts in families, and establish the relation of these groups to one another and to their archetype or original. Then, if the archetype or original does not emerge in any one manuscript, he should compose his edition from the readings of those texts which are nearest to the archetype.

For the preliminary process of classification Dom Henri Quentin offers a method which has been applied with highly interesting results to the Vulgate texts of the Old Testament.[2]

---

[1] *Constitutiones legitime* . . . (Paris, 1504), fos. 152r, 141v, 138r.

[2] See H. Quentin, *Mémoire sur l'établissement du texte de la Vulgate*, iere partie, *Octateuque* (Collectanea Biblica Latina, vi), (Rome, 1922) ; and by the same writer, *Essais de critique textuelle* (Paris, 1926).

It involves the complete collation of a portion of the work ; an examination of the exceptional variants, and of the agreements of pairs in all ' variantes à témoins multiples ' ; and finally a classification of these latter variants by groups of three, in search of instances in which two of the trio are found never to be in agreement against the third.[1] Assuming the production of a conflate text on these lines to be ideally desirable when no authentic original survives, we have yet to decide whether circumstances permit its production. At the risk of some repetition, the following facts must be taken into account.

In the literary works to which Dom Quentin applies his method, there is no great likelihood that many copies were made from the original. It is, therefore, reasonable to hope that the original or the archetype of the existing texts may be reached through the construction of a genealogical tree of one, two, or three branches. Dom Quentin does indeed in each case achieve this fairly simple arrangement. And in these instances the distinction between original and archetype, upon which he insists, is undoubtedly of great importance for a right approach to textual criticism. But the conciliar legislation does not conform nicely to this arrangement. Here original and archetype are probably one.[2] The canons were transcribed in numerous copies immediately upon publication, and we have to deal with descendants of perhaps as many copies as there were bishoprics and great religious houses throughout the province.

The variant readings are extremely numerous : as has been noted, copyists cared very little for the precise wording of the original. But these variants do not provide the right data for classification. In these texts, written within a century or two of the original, having a restricted vocabulary, expressing fairly familiar concepts in commonplace terms, there was seldom any occasion for scribes to go far astray. A long list of unique variants does not assist the inquiry, the exceptional variants are numerous enough to be useful, but the ' variants à témoins multiples ' are for the most part unsuitable for classification. An overwhelming majority is of the sort described by Professor

---

[1] Where A and B are never found in agreement against C (expressed by the equation AB > C = O), C is intermediate between A and B and the relationship of the texts is represented by one of the following figures :

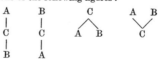

[2] Dom Quentin postulates an archetype differing from the original when an obviously false reading is found in all texts ; but in the conciliar material the original may be responsible for the error (cf. the mis-dating of the regnal year in the canons of Lambeth 1261, see Part II of this study).

Woodbine as ' non-determinative ',[1] and Dom Quentin's principle must be upheld : ' dans le choix des variantes à retenir pour classer les manuscrits, il ne faut garder que les particularités sans intérêt pour les copistes '.[2] None of the canons is of great length—not longer than the first seven or eight chapters of Genesis—and very few of the common variants can be utilized. The material to work upon is therefore meagre.

Further, it may be noted that Dom Quentin relies on each copyist introducing the average number of variants.[3] But in the conciliar texts, at least, this is certainly not suggested by the statistics of unique variants.

Coming to apply this method of classification to the actual texts, we find the natural consequence of these facts. The sixty texts of Oxford 1222 may be chosen for the experiment. The construction of a concordance and the selection of exceptional variants reveal some close relationships. But when we proceed further to a classification by groups of three, the zero equation necessary for a positive result $(AB > C = O)$ does not appear. Or rather let us say that, while we cannot attempt all the 34,220 groups of three contained in sixty texts, we do not obtain the zero equation in the groups which appear most likely to yield that result, except in cases where other data have already given the same information. This after all is precisely what might be expected. We have seen reason to suppose that many of the families are only related with each other through the original ; and most of the variants are ones which may recur at any point in the pedigree, through careless alteration, or occasionally through ' correction ' by the copyist's reference to another text.

The comparative exactness of Dom Quentin's method (and even he only claims ' certitude non absolue mais morale ' (*Essais,* p. 89)) does not carry the inquiry very far. We are confronted with many families and no ascertainable connexion between them. Does our material offer any other data upon which to base a classification ?

There seems to be no infallible method to bring to light the original, no cast-iron rule to replace that on which Dom Quentin relies. But our texts of certain of the canons contain at least one valuable clue to classification besides that of verbal variants. The arrangement of chapters in a set of canons differs in the various texts, and by classifying the *form* of the texts we arrive at a grouping which at once agrees with the grouping by verbal variants and adds further particulars. By a cautious comparison of these families we may arrive at their inter-relationship. The

---

[1] See Bracton, *De Legibus et Consuetudinibus Angliae,* ed. G. E. Woodbine, i. 98 *seqq.*

[2] *Essais de critique,* p. 65. But here Dom Quentin's strictly objective method demands an estimate of the objectivity of the copyist, and it can hardly be contended that all copyists were alike in their desire and ability to correct their original.

[3] *Op. cit.* pp. 88–9.

I

224 LEGISLATION OF THE MEDIEVAL CHURCH

principle propounded by an eighteenth-century critic is adopted :
of several readings that is the best which best explains the origin
of all the others,[1] and the results can be checked by the application
of the verbal tests discussed above. There can be no question of
scientific accuracy in the method, but some results can be claimed
to be highly probable.[2]

Once a pedigree has been composed, the editor is ready to
embark on the preparation of a text. Dom Quentin has been
fortunate in resolving the genealogy of the Vulgate texts into three
branches only, all derived from a single lost archetype. From the
heads of these three traditions he reconstructs the archetype,
accepting the authority of two against the third in cases of discrepancy. This method cannot be applied to the councils. The
genealogy of form does not place any extant manuscript in direct
relationship with any other : it only relates the two families to
which the manuscripts respectively belong.[3] To reconstruct the
lost parent-text all the manuscripts must be considered, for all
may derive from the first parent through lost generations.
Furthermore, when the classification is by form there is no
guarantee of the purity of one line against another : a line in
which the form has changed ten times may preserve a better text
than a tenth copy in the form of the original. Finally, in con-
structing a conflate text we are faced with the question which so
often worried medieval electoral bodies : is the choice of *maior
vel sanior pars* of any use as a rule of conduct ?

Our conclusion is opposed to the construction of a conflate
version. The texts can perhaps be classified, but not with certain
accuracy. On the other hand, we are not bound down to any
one text, as Friedberg was in editing the *Corpus Iuris Canonici ;*
for no ascertainable text alone has, or ever had, the force of
law. It seems best to select a manuscript which belongs to an
early generation in the family-tree, to print it with only such
alterations as are required to make sense where the scribe wrote
nonsense, and to give select collations from other families. In
details the method must naturally vary according to the state
of the texts. The edition will not present the reader with the
original nor yet the archetype ; it will not pretend to do more
than provide the reading of one manuscript out of many, a manuscript (nevertheless) which has the merit of belonging to an early
generation. The apparatus will only notice variants which
modify the meaning of the canon.

[1] J.-J. Griesbach, cited by Quentin, *op. cit.* p. 31.
[2] For the application of this method see the discussion of Oxford 1222 in Part II
of this study.
[3] Cf. Dom Quentin (*op. cit.* p. 103) : ' Mes généalogies s'appliquent non aux manuscrits eux-mêmes, mais aux types de transmission du texte qu'ils représentent '.

Legislation of the Medieval English Church [1]

PART II

EARLY TWELFTH-CENTURY CANONS

THE texts of the canons before Archbishop Richard of Canterbury (1174–84) will not be considered in detail here. The canons do not appear in any of the late collections, with the exception of the Bodleian MS. Rawl. C. 428 and MS. Lambeth 171, manuscripts closely related throughout, and probably both written at Worcester in the fourteenth century. They contain the canons of 1075, 1076, 1108, 1125, 1127. Wilkins apparently errs in assigning to the year 1153 (i. 425) a constitution of William, archbishop of York. The text whence Wilkins took the constitution (MS. Cotton, Vitell. A. ii. fo. 115) bears no date ; on the other hand it forms part of the canons issued by William Greenfield in 1306, and very probably originated then.[2] The whole character of the constitution conforms best with the later date.[3]

CANONS OF ARCHBISHOP RICHARD

The council which Richard of Dover held at Westminster in May 1175 has been often regarded as a national and legatine council. There is, however, nothing in the account of the council or its canons which proves this, and one finds indications to the contrary.

Some colour is given to the view that Westminster 1175 was intended to be a national synod by the words of Ralph

---

[1] See *supra*, pp. 193–224.

[2] Wilkins, ii. 285, following Spelman, *Concilia*, ii. 438, from the burnt MS. Cotton, Vitell. D. v. ; also in Brit. Mus. MSS. Lansdowne 397, fo. 245 ; Cotton, Vitell. A. ii. fo. 94 (formerly fo. 110).

[3] The Irish canons of Cashel 1172, printed by Wilkins (i. 472) from Hoveden and Giraldus Cambrensis, occur in a fifteenth-century register from Waterford cathedral (Brit. Mus. MS. Harl. 3765, fo. 32ᵛ). Regarding the legatine council at Mellifont 1152 noted by Wilkins (i. 425) it should be observed that synodal decrees of a bishop of Meath (Wilkins, i. 547) cite an ordinance by the legate at the Council of Kells 1152 (cf. J. F. Kenney, *Sources for the Early History of Ireland*, i. 768–9).

de Diceto, who lived at the time and wrote not many years after
the event. He says :

> Habitum est concilium regionale Lundoniis . . . praesidente Ricardo
> Cantuariensi archiepiscopo et apostolicae sedis legato. Roger Eboracensis
> archiepiscopus concilio non interfuit, nec qui eius absentiam allegarent
> transmisit, cum iuxta priscam consuetudinem ad vocationem Cantuariensis
> ecclesiae, vel interesse debuerit, vel iustam absentiae causam per nuntios
> et per epistolam probabiliter allegare.[1]

Clearly de Diceto was aware that those earlier councils which were
not legatine had been primatial and national : [2] he does not
use the term ' provincial council ', and he reverts to the archbishop of York's obligation to attend apropos of London 1200.
In some circles in the southern province this tradition of primatial
councils may well have survived, but it is difficult to believe that
it had any practical significance at all. The list of those present
at Westminster 1175 [3] shows that the attendance was limited
to prelates of the province of Canterbury. The fact that the
clerks of the archbishop of York appeared in order to protest
does not imply that the council was national : the king and
his son were present as well, but that did not transform the
ecclesiastical assembly into a royal council.

As regards the idea that the council was legatine, the evidence
is equally unsatisfying. De Diceto's evidence militates against
the possibility. The chroniclers besides de Diceto who refer to
Westminster 1175 state the archbishop's legatine and primatial
dignities, but speak of his holding the council with his suffragans.[4]
Further, we may note that while Richard might claim primatial
authority to hold a national synod, he could not hold a legatine
national synod, for his commission applied only to his own
province.[5]

Thus contemporary evidence that the council was legatine
is entirely lacking, while de Diceto's words do not suffice to prove
it primatial. On the other hand, the words of the council give
positive evidence. Richard's preamble refers to the salutary
custom of holding councils in a way which at least best applies
to the custom of holding provincial councils by metropolitan
authority ; and he enjoined the observance of the canons ' universis provincialibus nostris '.[6] We do not, therefore, have to
rely on the doubtful testimony of William of Newburgh, who

---

[1] R. de Diceto (Rolls Series), i. 399 ; *ibid.* ii. 169. Cf. Matt. Paris, *Hist. Anglorum*
(Rolls Series), i. 392.

[2] Cf. Wilkins, i. 325, 327, 369.   [3] *Gesta Henrici II*, i. 84.

[4] *Ibid. loc. cit.* ; Gervase, i. 251.

[5] ' Dominus papa eidem provinciae suae legationem indulsit ' (*Gesta Henrici II*,
i. 70) ; noted by H. Tillmann, *Die päpstlichen Legaten* (p. 34), who treats Westminster
1175 as a ' Legatenkonzil ' (*ibid.* p. 36, n. 123).

[6] Quoted *supra*, p. 207.

I

calls this ' provinciale concilium ' ; [1] all the other evidence points the same way.

The canons of Westminster 1175 are preserved by two contemporary chroniclers, ' Benedict Abbas ' and Gervase of Canterbury.[2] The former gives eighteen canons, each with a title professedly stating the source. This was the version used by Spelman, whom Wilkins followed in his edition. Gervase omits not only all chapter headings but also (presumably by haplography) the eighth chapter of Benedict's text. While it is strange that no other texts of the canons earlier than the fourteenth century are known, there can be no doubt that their attribution is correct.[3] The later manuscripts all agree in the strange title : ' concilium celebratum apud Westmon. tempore Ricardi archiepiscopi, a.d. mlxv° '.[4] The only fourteenth-century texts, two practically identical Worcester manuscripts, follow the chroniclers' text in general, and like Gervase omit chapter 8. They add fresh descriptive chapter headings.[5] The fifteenth-century texts, thirteen in number, depart farther from the original. Each omits cc. 3, 8, 10, 11, 13[2], 14, 15, 17. Representatives of this class are to be seen in the apparatus of Wilkins's edition and in the text of the *Constitutiones*, 1504 (fo. 142[v]). Although these texts may possibly contain some reading of the original which is otherwise lost, they undoubtedly represent a corrupt tradition developed very late.

The Oxford edition of 1679 prints (p. 10) twelve canons ascribed to Richard Wethershed *c.* 1230. They consist of the selection of 1175 found in the texts described above, with the exception of chapter 18, for which is substituted the chapter on doctors found in Bishop Poore's constitutions (ch. 94) and in ' Edmund ' (ch. 34).[6] No known manuscript attributes any of these canons to Wethershed ; but Lyndwood undoubtedly treated certain chapters of the series as though they came from

---

[1] *Chron. Stephen, Henry II and Rich. I* (Rolls Series), ii. 203. Miss Churchill notes this as the first use of the term in England (*Cant. Administration*, i. 361).

[2] They were copied from the *Gesta Henrici* by Hoveden and thence abridged by Walter of Coventry.

[3] Ch. 13[1] is cited very soon after the council in a letter from Bishop Jocelin of Salisbury (*Sarum Charters*, pp. 39–40), and the Annals of Tewkesbury refer to ch. 14 in connexion with the council (*Ann. Mon.* i. 51). Five canonistic collections make use of the canons during the next few years (see E. Seckel, *Ztschr. f. Kirchenrecht*, 3 Folge, ix. (1899), p. 186). Johnson's arguments against this date (*Collection*, ii. *s.a.* 1229) are not valid.

[4] Bodleian MS. Rawl. C. 428, fo. 111[v], &c. Lambeth MS. 538, fo. 147[v], describes the council as at Westminster 1066.

[5] MS. Rawl. C. 428, fo. 111[v]; Lambeth MS. 171, fo. 9. Classification by groups of three establishes that they derive from the Gervase rather than the Benedict tradition, and stand intermediate between the texts of the chroniclers and the late abbreviated versions.

[6] The Oxford edition of ' Edmund ' makes the opposite substitution of ch. 18 of 1175 for ch. 34.

I

this archbishop. The Oxford editor, accepting Lyndwood's ascription (which seems to be quite unjustified), attached it to the whole
series dated 1065 in the edition of 1504, and interpolated the final
chapter on doctors, still in accordance with Lyndwood's ascription.
    Wilkins (i. 474) printed another set of short canons of Arch-
bishop Richard *s.a.* 1173. They are known only in one manuscript
(Cotton, Claud. A. iv. fo. 191ᵛ), a twelfth-century collection of
decretals of Alexander III which includes the canons of Tours
(1163) and gives ' Concilium Ric' Cant' archiepiscopi ' as ch. 24
of the collection. Haddan and Stubbs remark that the editor's
dating is impossible, since Richard was not consecrated until
1174. They suggest that ' these canons . . . look much more
like an abridged copy (with a few additions) of the canons of
. . . 1175 '.[1] But the comparison is not close : sixteen out of
the thirty-seven canons have no parallel in those of 1175, and
two more introduce another element.[2] Their ascription remains
in doubt. It may be that we have here a new recension of the
canons of 1175, issued in a later provincial council by the same
archbishop.

CANONS OF ARCHBISHOP HUBERT

    Wilkins printed from Hoveden the canons issued by Arch-
bishop Hubert at York 1195 and at London 1200.[3] The attendance at the council of York was apparently limited to clergy of
the diocese, but the wording of chapter 16 (' ad archiepiscopum
vel episcopum ') suggests that the canons were intended for at
least the province of York. Hubert held this council by virtue
of a legatine commission which embraced all England, granted
in 1195.[4] No other text but that preserved by certain manuscripts of Hoveden is known.
    London 1200 was almost certainly a provincial council. Again,
as in 1175, de Diceto remarks that the archbishop of York was
supposed to attend ' ad vocationes Cantuariensis ',[5] but this is
not sufficient to prove that the council was held by primatial
authority or that its decrees were meant to extend beyond the
province of Canterbury. That Hubert's legateship expired with
Celestine III admits of little doubt. Whatever the relationship
may be between the legatine commissions to twelfth-century
archbishops of Canterbury and the status of *legatus natus* enjoyed by archbishops of the fourteenth century,[6] the position of

---

[1] *Councils,* i. 382 n.

[2] Ch. 27 : vicarii *perpetui* ; ch. 35 : ex dispensatione *inter principes.*

[3] Wilkins, i. 501 *seqq.,* 505 *seqq.* (Hoveden (Rolls Series), iii. 294 *seqq.,* iv. 128 *seqq.*).

[4] Hoveden, iii. 290–3 ; Diceto, ii. 125 ; *Epistolae Cantuar.* (Rolls Series), p. 370.

[5] Diceto, ii. 169.

[6] Churchill, *Canterbury Administration,* i. 153 *seqq.* Cf. Stubbs, *Const. Hist.* iii.²
308 ; Makower, *Const. Hist.* pp. 287–8 (§ 34, n. 15).

Hubert is apparently clear. In Celestine's lifetime, after 1195, Hubert is regularly called legate ; after Celestine's death he is called archbishop.[1] There is no sign that Innocent III renewed his commission. The pope addresses him in 1198 and 1199 simply as archbishop, and Hubert styles himself ' archbishop ' or ' archbishop and primate of all England '. [2] If this were not sufficient proof, we should still have the definite words of Thomas of Marlborough, who was bound to be interested in the legal powers involved in the legateship : ' legatione autem finita post annum ', and ' postquam legatus insignia legationis deposuit '.[3] It is therefore clear that Hubert cannot have issued his canons of 1200 by legatine authority, however complete was their reliance upon papal legislation.[4]

Besides the Hoveden copy, the London canons occur in an extremely carelessly written manuscript of the thirteenth century (Brit. Mus. Reg. 7 C. vii. fo. 53ᵛ), which belonged to the Austin priory of St. Bartholomew's, Smithfield. Here they are dated in the second year of King John, thus after 18 May 1200. But the Smithfield manuscript raises difficulties. Besides transposing chapters 10–13 and 14 of Hoveden's text, it adds five new chapters, of which the fourth repeats parts of chapter 10. The third and fifth of these additions contain phrases in the form of a bishop's command (' per episcopatum nostrum '). It seems possible that here we have to do with a clumsy conflation of two recensions, of which one at least had been revised for diocesan use.

CANONS OF ARCHBISHOP STEPHEN LANGTON

The Council of Oxford 1222.—One of the earliest assemblies held in the province of Canterbury by metropolitan authority, this was the first provincial council to legislate in England after the Fourth Lateran Council. The fundamental importance of Innocent III's decrees for the later administration of the Church is reflected in Langton's canons. It would be going too far to state that England received the papal legislation *via* Oxford, for individual bishops had reiterated some of the decrees between 1216 and 1222 ; [5] nevertheless the council of Oxford was regarded

---

[1] Professor Stenton has, however, drawn attention (*ante*, xlvii. 486) to a charter of Hubert employing the legatine style in the first year of King John.

[2] *Epist. Cantuar.* 391, 393, 443, 394 ; Diceto, ii. 164.

[3] *Chronicon abbatiae de Evesham* (Rolls Series), pp. 106, 246. Marlborough, in speaking of the special tutelage of the archbishop over the abbey of Evesham, uses the word *legatus* (pp. 258, 259, 183), but clearly with the special sense ; cf. p. 107 : ' suo speciali legato quamvis iam non generali '.

[4] Dr. Brooke, who treats them as legatine canons, points out their copying of the Lateran decrees and their reiterated recognition of the authority of Rome (*English Church and the Papacy*, p. 104).

[5] See Gibbs and Lang, *op. cit.* pp. 105–30.

I

by later canonists as the starting-point of English provincial legislation. It is continually referred to until the end of the middle ages.[1] In view of these facts, it is particularly desirable that an authentic text of the canons should be found. At present, three different versions are in print and are quoted indifferently. The version most often cited is that given by Wilkins, but an examination of the manuscripts tends to discredit his choice. The task of improvement is not an easy one, however, and the conclusion is not so certain as could be wished. We know very little about the council itself. Maitland, in a most attractive essay, told what is known of one sad episode. A deacon was burnt, burnt because he had turned Jew for love of a Jewess ; and that fired the imagination of several chroniclers. On the other activities of the council they give less detail. Perhaps it is just as well ; at least there are no fabulous embellishments to hide what happened. We simply learn that the Lateran decrees were recited and some other canons promulgated.

The extant manuscripts of these canons, as might be expected, are numerous, but no one text bears the obvious stamp of authenticity. Of sixty texts only seven date from the thirteenth century, and probably none of them comes within thirty years of the council. Many more manuscripts must have existed in the thirteenth century, and the earliest of the survivals may stand at the end of a long line of copies. In addition, several diocesans incorporated sections of Oxford 1222 in their own constitutions, not long after the council. We are thus provided with many additional texts of the excommunication clause from the constitutions of Bishop Grosseteste, which had a wide circulation. Four types of variation must be considered in a survey of the texts : (i) the sequence of the fifty canons varies in many ways ; (ii) several additions to Wilkins's text appear in some manuscripts ; (iii) the chapter headings vary ; (iv) the text varies in detail. It is not possible to essay an arrangement which comprehends all four classifications at once. Reasons have already been given for preferring a classification of forms to any other. An arrangement of the canons according to sequence can be checked by application of verbal tests.

Only one of the extant texts follows exactly the sequence of Wilkins's chief authority, Brit. Mus. MS. Cotton, Otho A. xvi.[2]

---

[1] Cf. the fifteenth-century copyist's note in MS. Cotton, Vitell. A. ii. fo. 48 : ' et fuerunt prime provinciales constituciones in regno Angl' ut patet in constituc' Joh. Pecham '. As late as 1444 the Benedictine General Chapter adopts the rule of the Council of Oxford respecting abbot's chaplains (Pantin, *Chapters*, ii. 193).

[2] Thus in Thomas Smith's catalogue (1696), p. 68 ; but the manuscript disappeared in the Cottonian fire, 1731, and Wilkins followed Spelman in quoting it always as Otho A. xv. (also missing).

and all but two [1] differ from the Cotton manuscript in the arrangement of chapters 42 to 50. Leaving earlier transpositions out of account for the moment,[2] we find that forty-eight of the texts are susceptible to arrangement under one of three heads : [3]

Group I : in which the order of the last chapters is 42, 50, 43–9, conclusion.

Group II : in which the order is 42–4, 50, 45–9, conclusion.

Group III : in which the order is 42, parts of 45 transposed, 43–4, first sentence of 45, 50, 46–9, conclusion.

It is interesting to observe that in this classification the entire contents of both Groups II and III are found in nearly all texts, including that printed by Wilkins,[4] whereas the various manuscripts of Group I contain several additions to the accepted text. One is tempted to take the highest common factor as represented in Groups II and III and treat all the other material in Group I as extraneous ; especially since the history of legal texts is generally one of interpolation, addition rather than subtraction. But there are cogent reasons for preferring Group I.

[1] Brit. Mus. MS. Arundel 438 and Balliol Coll. MS. 301 (approximately). For convenience of reference, the number of chapters in Wilkins's text are used. Chapter 50 is taken to end at ' carnes comedere ', and the following part, beginning ' Ut autem omnia ', will be referred to as the conclusion.

[2] Twenty-three of the forty eight grouped texts transpose parts before c. 42 : these provide ten varieties.

[3] Five complete texts do not come into this arrangement (Otho A. xvi. ; Arundel 438, fo. 69 ; Balliol 301, fo. 183 ; Camb. Univ. Libr. MS. Dd. ix. 38, fo. 44ᵛ ; Pembroke Coll. Camb. MS. 131, fo. 73), and a sixth has not been examined (Trinity Coll. Dublin MS. 526, p. 65). The remaining six are too imperfect to permit classification (Caius Coll. Camb. MS. 349, fo. 126ᵛ ; Brit. Mus. MS. Reg. 9 B. ii. fo. 23 ; Lambeth MS. 778, fo. 1 ; New Coll. MS. 107, fo. 123ᵛ ; Bodleian MS. Tanner 196, fo. 149 ; Durham Cath. MS. B. iv. 41, fo. 30). Tanner 196 is, however, sufficiently complete to show descent from Group I.

Group I(a) : Bodleian MSS. Rawl. C. 100, fo. 105 ; Rawl. C. 100, fo. 114 ; Rawl. C. 428, fo. 102 ; Hatton 109 (formerly 24), fo. 46 ; Bodley 794, fo. 158 ; All Souls Coll. MS. 42, fo. 212 ; Exeter Coll. MS. 31, fo. 218 ; Brit. Mus. MS. Cotton, Vitell. A. ii. fo. 48 ; Lambeth MS. 171, fo. 10 ; Ch. Ch. Canterbury, Chartae antiquae O. 138 ; Hereford Cath. MS. P. 7. vii. fo. 123ᵛ ; C.C.C. Cambridge MS. 271, fo. 73.

Group I(b) : Bodleian MSS. Selden supra 43, fo. 38 ; Wood empt. 23, fo. 105 ; C.C.C. Oxon MS. 72, fo. 25 ; Camb. Univ. Libr. MS. Ii. ii. 7, fo. 164 ; Caius Coll. MSS. 38, fo. 99, 44, fo. 153 ; Trin. Coll. Camb. MS. 1245, fo. 113 ; Brit. Mus. MSS. Reg. 5 E. xii. fo. 65, Reg. 9 B. ii. fo. 14, Reg. 11 B. v. fo. 186 ; Cotton, Vespas. E. iii. fo. 103 ; Harl. 52, fo. 64, Harl. 3705, fo. 1.

Group II : Balliol Coll. MS. 158, fo. 136 ; Exeter Coll. MS. 41, fo. 173 ; Brasenose Coll. MS. 14, fo. 158 (formerly fo. 156); Camb. Univ. Libr. MSS. Gg. vi. 21 (= Wilkins's ' Eliensis 235 '), Ii. iii. 14, fo. 218, Addit. 3575, fo. 263 ; Peterhouse MS. 84, fo. 140 ; C.C.C. Camb. MS. 84, fo. 169 ; St. John's Coll. Camb. MS. 88, fo. 92ᵛ ; Brit. Mus. MSS. Harl. 335, fo. 38, Harl. 2349, fo. 11 ; Lambeth MS. 538 (formerly 17), fo. 55ᵛ ; Axbridge Corporation MS. fo. 1 ; Holkham MS. 226, fo. 1 ; Labbe and Cossart, *Concilia* (1730), xiii. 1065 ; Lyndwood, index to *Provinciale* (ed. Oxford, *c.* 1483).

Group III : Bodleian MS. Ashmole 1146, fo. 63 ; Magdalen Coll. MS. 185, fo. 15ᵛ ; Caius Coll. MS. 487, fo. 136 ; Ch. Ch. Canterbury MS. E. 9 ; Salisbury Cath. Liber Evid. C. p. 383 ; *Constitutiones* (ed. Paris, 1504), fo. 121 (ed. Oxford, 1679), p. 1.

[4] Exceptions : Harl. 335 and Holkham 226 make the small addition to ch. 42 found in Group I. Camb. Univ. Libr. Addit. 3575 and Axbridge both interpolate the same chapter from the canons of Lambeth 1261.

Not only do twenty-five of these forty-eight texts fall into
Group I ; this group also contains sixteen out of the twenty-two
of these texts which can with probability be dated before *c.* 1400,
and all but one of those which can be dated probably before
c. 1350. In general, the argument for authenticity which is
based upon the date of surviving copies is worthless, but here
the field of comparison is broad, and the preponderance of one
type in the earlier period is so marked that we are justified in
taking Group I as the nearest descendants of the original. The
very diversity of the early texts within this group suggests that
in their common sequence, 42–50–43, they preserve the authentic
order. The material of the canons, otherwise of little help,
tends to confirm this choice. The subject-matter of chapter 50
follows most naturally after chapter 42.[1]

Within Group I there are many varieties of sequence, but one
main subdivision. In Group I (*a*) cc. 41–50 (which concern the
regular clergy) follow immediately on cc. 31–5 (which also concern
regulars). In Group I (*b*), all or part of the irrelevant cc. 36–40
stands in between the two monastic sections. It may further
be observed that all of Group III place the monastic material
together, while in all of Group II cc. 36–40 stand in between the
two monastic sections. The unclassed texts, Otho A. xvi. and
Arundel 438, agree with Groups I (*b*) and II in this respect. Here
again there seems to be a choice between distinct lines of descent.
The more logical sequence is undoubtedly that which places
cc. 41–50 immediately after cc. 31–5. But that is no reason
for preferring it. On the contrary, any copyist might wish to
bring the monastic material together, whereas no two copyists
would be likely to agree in inserting cc. 36–40 between cc. 35
and 41. An examination of ecclesiastical legislation of this
period will often show a rough arrangement according to subject,
but seldom any classification strictly carried out : canons were
often isolated out of their natural context.[2] It therefore
seems best to explain the sequence of Groups I (*a*) and III as
the result of copyists' attempts to produce an arrangement
according to subject-matter. We thus arrive at Group I (*b*)
as the tradition nearest to the original. This set includes ten
varieties of sequence in thirteen manuscripts. When they are
viewed in connexion with the other groups there can be little
doubt as to the original order. Four early manuscripts of
Group I (*b*) (families **a** and **d**) [3] agree in reading 1–42, 50, 43–9,
conclusion. No single variation of this order appears in more

---

[1] Ch. 50 reads : ' statutum istud, vel illud de indumentis [*sc.* ch. 42] . . . '. None
of the printed texts presents the canons in this sequence, and the text chosen for
Spelman's *Concilia* and adopted by Wilkins falls into none of the three usual categories
given above.   [2] Cf. Pantin, *Chapters,* i. 61.
   [3] Brit. Mus. MSS. Reg. 9 B. ii. fo. 14, Reg. 11 B. v., Harl. 52 ; Caius Coll. MS. 44.

than two of the other texts. The same sequence in cc. 1–42 is vouched for by the other groups : transpositions are numerous but always peculiar. They cannot be correlated without reference to the order 1–42. As regards sequence, therefore, **ad** probably come nearest to the original.

Additions to and omissions from the accepted text can be fitted without violence into the grouping by sequence. The omissions are negligible. The additions which have to be considered are four :

(i) A chapter appears between cc. 9 and 10 of Wilkins's text : ' Item volumus ut in ecclesiis religiosorum et in prebendatis secundum formam generalis concilii vicarii ordinentur '.[1]

(ii) There is an addition to ch. 42 after ' Monachus infra annum xviii non recipiatur nisi evidens utilitas vel necessitas aliud inducat ' : ' Idem in canonicis regularibus observetur '.[2]

(iii) A new chapter is inserted after ch. 48 : ' *Ne inclusi aliquo loco constituantur sine licencia episcopi* '.[3]

(iv) An addition is made to ch. 50 after ' nec elemosinarius possit contra hoc dispensare ' : ' Quoniam si quid fuerit mittendum, per eum qui preest licite mittatur '.

With two exceptions in two differing manuscripts, no texts of Groups II and III contain any of these additions. Addition (i) appears in several manuscripts of Group I whose sequence suggests authenticity,[4] and in MS. Ashmole 1146 (Group III). Addition (ii) does not appear in Group I (*b*), but mainly in Group I (*a*). Its character is such that it might be added by any copyist. While in this chapter Langton was modifying a Benedictine regulation of 1219,[5] there seems to be no corresponding rule made by the English Augustinian canons, either before or after 1222.[6] Addition (iii) occurs only in four closely related texts of Group I (*a*), of which at least two come from Worcester cathedral priory. Lyndwood treated it as the second part of a canon ascribed to Edmund, but in none of the manuscripts of ' Edmund ' does it appear. At present its origin is unknown.[7] The other peculiarities of these texts make them suspect, and this

---

[1] Bodleian MS. Rawl. C. 100, fo. 105 ; Ashmole 1146 ; Camb. Univ. Libr. MS. Ii. ii. 7 ; Caius Coll. MSS. 38, 44 ; Brit. Mus. MSS. Reg. 11 B. v., Harl. 52.

[2] Hereford Cath. P. 7. vii. ; Holkham 226 ; Harl. 335 ; C.C.C. Oxon 72 ; Rawl. C. 100, fo. 114 ; Cotton, Vitell. A. ii. ; Wood empt. 23. The last four MSS. read *regulariter* for *regularibus*.

[3] Rawl. C. 428 ; Lambeth 171 ; Exeter Coll. 31 ; Bodley 794. The chapter is found printed in Lyndwood, pp. 214–15 (beginning : Ad haec districtius . . .).

[4] It does not appear in the **a** family (Reg. 9 B. ii. fo. 14).

[5] ' Infra xx annum monachi non recipiantur nisi commendabilis utilitas vel necessitas aliud induxerit ' (Pantin, *Chapters*, i. 10).

[6] The *Statuta primaria* of the Premonstratensian Order forbid the admission as canon of anyone ' qui decimum octavum suae aetatis annum non exegerit ' (dist. I, cap. xv. ; J. Le Paige, *Bibliotheca Praem. Ord.* p. 794*b*).

[7] Unless it is to be attributed with other canons to Mepham, cf. *infra*, p. 414.

I

chapter must be treated as an interpolation unrecorded until
the fourteenth century.   Addition (iv) is the only one which is
found in a large number of texts ; it is common to nearly all the
texts in the sequence of Group I,[1] including families **a** and **d**.
While no exact parallel has been found in other legislation, the
passage which it follows is taken, in part verbatim, from the
Benedictine chapter acts of 1219, and perhaps the same meaning
should be attached to this addition as to the note in the chapter
statute : ' presidentem vero ab hac necessitate exceperunt '.[2]
No explanation can be offered of the omission of the passage
from the parent texts of Groups II and III.

There seems to be no reason to distrust the conclusion to which
we are led by considering the sequence of the canons.   The
acceptance of the **ad** section means the rejection of two additions
(ii and iii) and the possible rejection of another (i).   It is proposed
to make a manuscript of the **d** family (Caius Coll. 44) the basis of
a new edition.   It may be thought rash to select a text containing a passage which is found only in seven out of nearly
sixty manuscripts.   True, there is no obvious reason why the
canon should not have been promulgated at Oxford 1222.   It was
in accord with the Fourth Lateran Council,[3] it had not been
pronounced in England before, and it is not found in later canons.
Some such antecedent ordinance is implied by the following
canons of the council.   On the other hand, this canon is not quoted
by later legislators, and if it be authentic it is necessary to suppose that it was inexplicably omitted from the original of all the
surviving texts save seven.   Its survival in a fourteenth-century
text of Group III, from the archives of Chichester, adds to the
likelihood of authenticity ; for this manuscript represents a
tradition independent of **ad** and, with a closely related thirteenth
century copy in the archives of Salisbury Cathedral, provides
a text remarkable for its general purity.   Yet it remains possible
that the passage was interpolated, and **a** may thus be preferable
to **d**.   On this point it would be unwise to dogmatize until unknown early manuscripts come to light.   Meanwhile the **d** form
may be accepted, with reservations as to addition (i).

One cannot too strongly emphasize that the choice of a
d text does not imply a belief that this text is necessarily purer
than another.   All that is claimed is that here is a manuscript
which resembles the original fairly closely in general form and
contents.   A similar text or a much purer one might be found in

---

[1] Not in Hereford Cath. P. 7. vii.

[2] Pantin, *Chapters*, i. 10. Cf. *Customaries St. Aug. Cant.* &c. (H. Bradshaw Soc.),
i. 172 ; ii. 116, 256 ; and *Customs of Aug. Canons*, ed. J. W. Clark, p. 160.

[3] Ch. 32, which mentions prebendal but not monastic churches. Cf. Poore's
constitutions, ch. 108, and Archbishop Hubert's London canons, ch. 14 (Wilkins,
i. 508).

a far distant family, and no manuscript in any particular line of descent can be expected to have the monopoly of ' good ' readings. The Caius College MS. 44 certainly contains many obvious and peculiar blunders. It is, however, encouraging to note that where the manuscripts are divided more or less evenly between two readings, the manuscript of our choice usually embodies the preferable reading.[1]

The so-called ' Legenda ' of Oxford.—In certain texts of Oxford 1222 is found a series of canons mainly on the sacraments. Wilkins printed them from MS. Hatton 109 (then Hatton 24), where they appear separately, and treated them as an appendix to Oxford 1222. Not all the manuscripts agree with Wilkins's text, some are linked to the preceding canons of Oxford in other ways, some bear totally different titles. Anyone who examines the thirty-two texts which contain this material in one form or another will admit the complexity of the problem they present. Ten distinct varieties can be traced. The ascriptions range from Langton at Oxford 1222 or 1230 to Reynolds at Oxford 1322 or Mepham at Lambeth. The problem becomes more confusing when one observes that parts of these canons appear verbatim in the provinces of Rouen, Rheims, and Mainz.[2] No attempt is made here to solve all the problems which the *Legenda* and cognate documents raise : their relationship with Oxford 1222 is all that is in question at the moment. On this point a definite answer is possible.

The *Legenda* has been misunderstood because of its juxtaposition to the canons of Oxford in the printed editions. When the manuscripts are studied it is seen to be nothing other than a miscellaneous set of canons suitable to be read in a synod. Two thirteenth-century texts contain practically all that is in Wilkins's text of the *Legenda* with a good deal besides. The Caius College MS. 349 [3] is a miscellaneous collection originally in several volumes, of works useful for a parish priest or prelate. They include the tract ' *Qui bene presunt* ' and the fourth book of the *Sentences*. The fourth section begins (fo. 124) with a poem on penance. Then on fo. 126ᵛ comes ' Consilium Oxonie '. The text is extremely incomplete,[4] but it is terminated by the usual conclusion and followed without interruption by the greater part of the *Legenda*, beginning : ' Baptismus cum reverentia '.[5] Then comes, still without break, cc. 14–16 of the

---

[1] E.g. ch. 1 : abducant, obducant ; ch. 9 : scripta, presumpta ; ch. 31 : volumus, nolumus ; ch. 36 : legis, predicacionis. In each case Caius MS. 44 adopts the second reading.

[2] Cf. Mansi, xxii. 731, 1181 ; xxiii. 30.

[3] M. R. James's catalogue ; New no. 542 ; T. James, no. 266 ; Bernard, no. 769.

[4] Omissions : cc. 1–4, 14–16, 18–25, 27, 28¹, 29–35, 41–50.

[5] Only ch. 10 is omitted, and this appeared above, being identical with Oxford 1222, ch. 28³.

Fourth Lateran Council and ch. 20 of Oxford 1222 with a modified ending. MS. Bodley 843 contains three books.[1] The second contains Peter Comestor's *Allegoriae*, followed by a sermon and, in another early thirteenth-century hand, the passage which concerns us (fo. 122). It bears no title. Beginning with ' Baptismus cum omni reverentia ' it proceeds through the *Legenda* as the Caius text does. Like the latter it continues with cc. 14–16 of the Fourth Lateran, but then diverges into a series of decrees on monastic life, taken in part from Oxford 1222. It concludes with Langton's decree against concubinary priests recorded by Wendover *s.a.* 1225.

These sets of canons are most instructive. Each contains much material from the authentic canons of Oxford, but not the same material. There are other differences besides, but the *Legenda* section is the same in both. Only the Caius MS. suggests by its title that these are canons of Oxford, and here the authentic canons have the normal conclusion, thus marking off the *Legenda* from what has gone before. Other features tell against the ascription to Oxford. Comparing these canons (as given in the Hatton MS.) with the undoubted canons of Oxford, Miss Lang calls attention to ' various clauses of similar import differently expressed ', and to the excommunication clauses which ' not only differ to some extent in import but also in the number of times they are to be pronounced in the year '.[2] Moreover, in their present form at least, they are expressed as diocesan pronouncements : matters demanding a diocesan bishop's attention are reserved ' ad nos vel gerentes vices nostras '.

After these observations on the early manuscripts the later texts fall into their proper place. In the fourteenth-century Hatton MS. the *Legenda* does not follow immediately the canons of Oxford : its title is ' Statuta de legenda in synodo edita in consilio Oxon' per dominum Stephanum quondam Cant' Archiepiscopum a.d. m cc° xxii° '. This is immediately followed by the *incipit* of the Oxford sentences of excommunication and by the *incipit* of Oxford ch. 5.[3] Surely this was but a way of indicating that first among the statutes to be read in a synod were these chapters of Oxford 1222 ? What follows after was *Legenda* also, but it did not emanate from the council. We must

---

[1] *Summary Cat. Western MSS.* no. 2576. Described as ' written in France (?) ' : the first book (late twelfth century) consists mainly of works of St. Ambrose, and the third (early thirteenth century) is the *Enchiridion Ecclesiasticum* of John, bishop of Avranches.

[2] *Bishops and Reform*, p. 116.

[3] Wilkins makes a misleading abbreviation of the title : ' Statuta legenda in concilio Oxoniensi edita . . . '. The Hatton text concludes (fo. 62ᵛ) : ' Expliciunt statuta legenda in synodo ut supra continentur in consilio Oxon' '. Two fifteenth-century MSS. give the same *incipits :* Camb. Univ. Libr. Ii. iii. 14, fo. 221ᵛ, and Balliol Coll. 158.

at once return to Caius College MS. 349. It begins with the
Oxford sentences and continues with ch. 5. Obviously the
intervening chapters were not for recital in a diocese, for they
are injunctions addressed to bishops. The same principle explains the selection of chapters which follows : it omits generally
those concerning the lower prelates and the regular clergy. We
may conjecture that this selection was designed for recital in
an archdeacon's synod or chapter. It should be observed that
while the Hatton MS. begins with the indication of a form
resembling Caius 349, so also its final chapter-title ' De vita et
honestate clericorum ' (which does not correspond to the following quotation from Oxford cc. 8 and 9), suggests that cc. 14–16
of the Fourth Lateran were meant to follow, as in both our early
texts.

This same arrangement is found in other groups of manuscripts. In a late fourteenth-century collection of constitutions
(Pembroke Coll. Camb. MS. 131, fo. 87) the *Legenda* occurs with
the title ' Concilium apud Oxon' secundum celebratum ibidem
a.d. m° ccc° vicesim.'. Its preamble will be found also in
Grosseteste's diocesan constitutions.[1] Here, as in Caius 349,
Oxford, ch. 5, follows the sentences of excommunication. Immediately afterwards comes the first chapter of the *Legenda*
under the title ' De baptismo '. The Pembroke College MS.
is unfortunately defective at the end of the *Legenda*, but two
more manuscripts which have the same introductory matter continue with cc. 14–16 of the Fourth Lateran and other material.[2]

Nothing would be gained by giving an analysis of the other
forms in which the *Legenda* is found. Many more varieties
could hardly make more certain our conclusion, which is this.
Parts of Oxford 1222 were ordered to be recited regularly in
synods. Other canons were to be read also. The cc. 14–16 of
the Fourth Lateran were specially suitable : Archbishop Rigaud
of Rouen regularly had them read in councils.[3]   And in addition there was a group of canons giving instruction on the
administration of the sacraments. These drew on material
common to several countries, found in fragments in many diocesan canons of the thirteenth century. But we cannot say
that they were ever issued as the canons of a council.[4] They
formed the core of a fluctuating mass of canons, disciplinary

[1] *Epist. R. Grosseteste* (Rolls Series), pp. 162–4, beginning : ' Et quia in multis
ecclesiis ut credimus non est scriptum Oxoniense concilium '.

[2] Caius Coll. MS. 38, fo. 111 (fourteenth century) ; Harl. 3705, fo. 70ᵛ (fifteenth
century). Ch. 16 of the Fourth Lateran also appears in the midst of the *Legenda* in
the group Rawl. C. 428 (fo. 107ᵛ), &c.

[3] E.g. *Regestrum . . . Odonis Rigaldi*, pp. 286, 387, 481.

[4] Cf. MS. Bodley 843, fo. 125ᵛ : ' a tempore huius sancte synodi '. On the other
hand, neither this MS. nor Wilkins's text in any place makes an order ' auctoritate
presentis concilii '.

and homiletic.[1] We have called them *Legenda*, but they were
only a portion of the material suitable to be recited in the synod,
they might be altered to taste, and they were only one of several
such miscellaneous collections.[2]

The whole connexion of the *Legenda* with Oxford 1222 seems
to arise from the ignorance of copyists. As in the case of a
famous book, *De imitatione Christi*, the title of the first section
has been read as the title of the whole work.[3] The general
title *Statuta legenda in synodo* which appears in some texts, drops
out ; the sub-title comes to be repeated on each page ; and
fresh generations of copyists, faced with two sets of Oxford canons,
label the canons of 1222 ' Oxon I ' and the *Legenda* ' Oxon II '.[4]
It is easier to destroy the connexion of the *Legenda* with Oxford
1222 than to discover its origin. Continental parallels have
been noted, Archbishop Hubert's canons contain similar passages,
likewise the earliest English diocesan constitutions. For the
present we must leave the problem unsolved, saying with Mansi : [5]
' Undenam tanta affinitas, uter ex alio acceperit, dicant docti '.

So-called canons of Stephen Langton.—Spelman printed (ii.133)
s.a. 1206 three canons purporting to be provincial constitutions
published by Langton at Lambeth. These were reprinted with the
same title by Wilkins (i. 530–1), *s.a.* 1209. Mansi (xxii. 752) gave
them the date 1204. They concern the payment of mortuaries,
the holding of scot-ales, and the celebration of the Mass. No
less than seventeen texts record these canons, and most ascribe
them to Langton.[6] Ten more contain only the second part of

---

[1] The first six (each headed ' ex synodali statuto ') are interspersed with the
canons of Lambeth 1281 in Bodleian MS. Digby 58, fo. 97.

[2] Others are ' Constituciones cuiusdam episcopi ', printed by Wilkins (i. 656)
from Cotton MS. Vespas. E. iii. fo. 138 (now fo. 148) ; New Coll. MS. 222, fo. 1 ; and
probably ' Edmund ' (see *infra*, p. 401). Cf. the references in the midst of a fifteenth-
century collection of canons (Camb. Univ. Library MS. Gg. 21, fo. 61^v : ' Nota
constituciones recitandas in sinodo, scilicet Othonis c. *de archidiaconis* et Oxon'
c. *Ut archidiaconi*, et c. *presbiteriorum* [*sic*]. Jo. Stratford' c. *statuimus* et c. *avida* (?)
et c. *humana* et Othonis *ad baptismum* et constitucio *licet ad profugandum* et in constitucionibus Redyng' c. iiii et Pecham c. iii et Ottoboni c. *ingredientibus.*'

[3] Rubricators of these collections constantly carry the same title over several
distinct and incongruous documents ; hence cataloguers who depend on the guidance
of running titles omit much in their descriptions.

[4] E.g. Trin. Coll. Camb. MS. 1245 (' Constituciones iste celebrate etiam Oxon'
a.d. m°—'). MS. Harl. 3705, fo. 70^v, gives the heading ' Constituciones Oxon' 11°,
quidam dicunt quod sunt Stephani Langthon edite in manerio suo de Lambeth a.d.
12—'. Magdalen Coll. MS. 185, fo. 14, attributes the *Legenda* to Stephen at Oxford
1230 ; Pemb. Coll. Camb. MS. 131, fo. 87, dates it Oxon' 1320 ; Caius Coll. MS.
38, fo. 111, dates it Oxon' 1322. In the group represented by Lambeth MS. 171
it was easy for the *Legenda* to become merged with the authentic Oxford canons,
since the concluding paragraph of Oxford was omitted. In the Dover priory catalogue
of 1389 the *Legenda* is termed ' Constituciones prime Stephani archiepiscopi ' (M. R.
James, *Ancient Libraries*, p. 472, no. 277).

[5] Mansi, xxii. 1181.

[6] Camb. Univ. Libr. MS. Ii. iii. 14, p. 386, and Balliol 158, fo. 164^v, said : ' Winchelsey at Merton ' ; the latter was altered in the fifteenth century to ' Langton at
Lambeth '. Camb. Univ. Libr. MS. Addit. 3575, fo. 290, attributes the canons to Islip.

the chapter on mortuaries, sometimes associated in these texts with Langton, sometimes with Winchelsey. It stands as a constitution of Winchelsey *s.a.* 1305 in Spelman (ii. 433) and Wilkins (ii. 279). Lyndwood introduced a new ascription, not vouched for by any known manuscript. He quoted the whole of the first canon [1] and attributed it to Archbishop Simon Langham. Following him, Johnson ascribed all three canons to Langham *s.a.* 1367.

In spite of the number and variety of texts it is not difficult to reject them one and all. There are no manuscripts earlier than the late fourteenth century ; all their ascriptions are false.[2] We need scarcely trouble to dwell upon the processes of corruption, since we can establish the origin of the canons beyond doubt.

The first chapter purports to explain ' the statute of our predecessor R. concerning mortuaries ' ; it says that, although the reason for the payment was not inserted in the original statute, it was in fact understood to be compensation for the withholding of tithe.[3] This first chapter is found in the diocesan canons of Bishop Giles of Salisbury, 1257–62.[4] Two recent predecessors of Bishop Giles might be designated by the initial R. No legislation on mortuaries occurs in the well-known canons of Bishop Richard Poore, but we find the canon for which we are looking in unpublished canons of Bishop Robert Bingham 1238–46.[5] The discovery of the original canon as well as its revised form puts the provenance of the latter beyond doubt. The second chapter appears also among the canons of Bishop Giles, and we may reasonably suppose that it originated with him.[6]   The

---

[1] *Provinciale*, I. iii. 1 (p. 19, cf. p. 22).

[2] Finke pointed out the impossibility of the dates 1204, 1206, 1209 (*Konzilienstudien*, p. 41). Leclercq's edition of Hefele places the supposed council at Lambeth in 1213 (*Histoire des Conciles*, v. ii. 1232). It may be noted that the terms of the first and second canons imply diocesan, not metropolitan, authority.

[3] The reference to ' our predecessor R.' led Lyndwood to suppose that the original statute was that attributed in some texts to R. Winchelsey and renewed, therefore, not by S. Langton but by S. Langham (*Provinciale*, I. iii. 1 *ver*. Interpretatione (p. 22*b*)). In fact, however, the ' Winchelsey ' texts, like all the others, give the reason for payment, missing from the original statute.

[4] Wilkins, i. 718.

[5] MS. Harl. 52, fo. 124ᵛ. This fourteenth-century text, the only known copy, is described as ' Constitutiones domini Roberti episcopi Sar'.' The canons can be attributed to Bingham by virtue of the present quotation and also by a thirteenth-century footnote to the Salisbury Liber Evid. C. p. 367, which gives the *incipit* of Bingham's canons.

[6] The later texts do, however, contain an extra clause, which practically repeats the first clause. It may represent a lost later recension of the Salisbury canons. No explanation can be offered of the fact that two diocesan canons of the thirteenth century, York 1258–9 and Winchester 1246–61 (Brit. Mus. MS. Lansdowne 397, fo. 248ᵛ, and Salisbury Liber Evid. C. fo. 402), in condemning scot-ales, speak of the excommunication of those attending these gatherings declared in the Council of Oxford. When Grosseteste denounces scot-ales he does not mention Oxford (*Epist. R. Grosseteste*, p. 73).

third chapter is taken directly from Robert Bingham (fo. 123). These canons have therefore no connexion with Langton, Winchelsey, or Langham. Having been extracted from a collection of Salisbury canons,[1] their origin was forgotten, they became attached to these great names and acquired authority throughout the province of Canterbury.

The editions of 1504 (fo. 150) and 1679 (p. 10) and Wilkins (i. 597) print another document as a canon of Stephen Langton. This occurs in some fourteen texts, none earlier than the late fourteenth century. Most of them bear the title : ' Constitutio domini Stephani archiepiscopi super plures casus in quibus simplex sacerdos non potest absolvere nisi in articulo mortis sed mittere debet ad superiorem '. Against the ascription to Stephen Langton may be urged the following points : the document is not cast in the form of a provincial constitution ; no manuscript mentions Langton's surname [2] or comes within a century of his lifetime ; no reference to it occurs in the legislation of the next two centuries. Its actual origin remains unknown.

Canon of Canterbury province, 1225.—Roger of Wendover preserves a decree of the archbishop of Canterbury and his suffragans which, he says, was published in the year 1225.[3] Nothing suggests that this was issued in a provincial council, unless it be the co-operation of archbishop and suffragans. The clergy did indeed come together in this year, but with the king and magnates at a secular council, to discuss secular business. But for the St. Albans' chronicler the decree would be unknown ; for its origin is not stated when it ends the extended series of *Legenda* in MS. Bodley 843, fo. 125ᵛ. It is surprising that a provincial constitution should come so near to utter disappearance. We do not know how widely it was circulated ; since it added little to the regulations of Oxford 1222, as an isolated text it would tend to be neglected.

So-called Canons of Archbishop Edmund

For the past 500 years St. Edmund has been taken for the author of a series of forty-one canons. Lyndwood included many of them in the *Provinciale*,[4] and they are found in all the printed editions of *Concilia*. Lyndwood was not prepared

---

[1] This sort of thing was frequently done. Two more of Bishop Giles's canons appear isolated, without title, in a thirteenth-century gradual (Bodleian MS. Rawl. liturg. d. 3, fo. 111ᵛ).

[2] Camb. Univ. Libr. MS. Gg. vi. 21, fo. 61, adds ' Langeton ' to the title, in the margin.

[3] *Flores Historiarum* (Rolls Series), ii. 287 ; Wilkins, i. 607.

[4] Lyndwood ascribes cc. 16–18 of ' Edmund ' to Archbishop Sudbury (*Provinciale*, v. xvi. 14–16 (pp. 342–3)), and is copied by the Oxford editor (p. 59).

to suggest the occasion of their issue, and later editors have been content to date them *c.* 1236, without assigning them to any particular ecclesiastical council. No other evidence exists that the archbishop ever held a synod of his diocese or province. While the editors assume that the canons were provincial, it has long been observed that their terms imply only diocesan authority.[1] Miss Lang has recently pointed out the original source of all these canons : ' the first thirty-eight were word for word repetitions of clauses in the Salisbury constitutions [of Richard Poore 1217–22] without any sort of variation. The thirty-ninth and forty-first clauses are repetitions of clauses in the " Legenda " and the only original contribution is the last part of the fortieth clause concerning tithes.' [2]

Poore's constitutions were a remarkably comprehensive collection, and besides drawing on material which was the common source of many other diocesan canons, they were directly used by later prelates. Even so, it is somewhat surprising to find a selection of them appropriated by the archbishop of Canterbury, without alteration and with negligible additions. One is impelled to inquire into the authority for the ascription to Edmund.

Seventeen texts of the canons have been noted. Several correspond closely to Wilkins's text, but three at least stop short at ch. 38 ; that is to say, they contain nothing but the selection from Poore.[3] The other texts divide cc. 39–41 from the Poore series by the note : ' In aliquibus libris iste constituciones sunt posite inter constituciones provinciales Oxon' ideo istas ad illas constituciones factas adde, de confirmacione, de decimis, de bonis '.[4] All these texts entitle the canons ' constituciones provinciales sancti Edmundi Cant. archiepiscopi ', but give no further clue to their origin. Lyndwood gives no more information.[5] No manuscript is earlier than the latter part of the fourteenth century ; nor in all the thirteenth and fourteenth centuries does any reference to these canons appear. One is surely justified in rejecting the ascription to Edmund. The evidence admittedly is mainly negative, but in all respects it corresponds with the

[1] Johnson, *Collection*, *s.a.* 1236, notes to cc. 5, 17, 31 ; Hefele-Leclercq, v. ii. 1547.

[2] *Bishops and Reform*, pp. 118–19. The last part of ch. 40 consists of references to authorities later than St. Edmund's time.

[3] All Souls Coll. MS. 42, fo. 232ᵛ ; Trin. Coll. Camb. MS. 1245, fo. 119 ; Hereford Cath. MS. P. 7. vii. fo. 133. Lyndwood includes a selection of cc. 1–38 only. Cc. 39–41 occur elsewhere in the Hereford MS. (fo. 159ᵛ) headed ' Langetone '. In MS. Harl. 335, fo. 38, they follow the conclusion of Oxford 1222 without any break.

[4] Exeter Coll. MS. 41, fo. 201, &c.

[5] While in twelve cases he adopts his usual formula ' Constitutio quae est Edmundi ', he occasionally uses phrases which indicate dubiety : ' Dicitur fuisse Edmundi ' (*Provinciale*, p. 71), ' Attribuitur Edmundo archiepiscopo ' (pp. 26, 160, 204), ' Intitulatur Edmundo in quibusdam libris ' (p. 28).

evidence against the so-called canons of Westminster 1065 and Langton at Lambeth ; and these can be proved on other grounds to be spurious.[1] In each case a late compiler has made extracts from existing material and provided a new title. In this instance we see two stages of development, in which extracts were first made from Poore, and parts of the *Legenda* later added.

CANONS OF ARCHBISHOP BONIFACE

Councils of the years 1258–61.—The texts of the canons issued in these years bear a variety of titles, and greatly differ among themselves in contents. In order to have a clear impression of their relationship, we shall summarize the circumstances of their issue.

On 19 April 1258, after a royal council at which the prelates had refused assent to an aid,[2] Archbishop Boniface of Canterbury summoned bishops, deans of cathedral and other churches, abbots, priors, and archdeacons with proxies, to a council at Merton on 6 June.[3] This assembly elaborated articles for the protection of the Church's privileges against encroachments by the lay power ; the articles were based upon *gravamina* drawn up by Grosseteste some years earlier,[4] and those who now drafted them reserved the right to make further alteration.

It is open to doubt whether this was a national or a provincial assembly of the Church, and whether the articles were issued at Merton or at Westminster. The Burton Annals ascribe the proceedings to a meeting of ' Archbishop Boniface, his suffragans and the prelates of the realm with the clergy ' at Merton.[5] Other texts .of the articles give more details, to some extent contradictory. Wilkins observed that an All Souls' manuscript dates the articles 8 June 1258 at Westminster ' in solenni conventione praelatorum et cleri Anglicanae ecclesiae '.[6] The time and place dates can be reconciled with the Burton Annals by the supposition that the articles were issued on the third day of the council and that the assembly had moved from Merton to Westminster, a not unusual proceeding. All texts agree in addressing the articles in the name of Boniface and his suffragans, and several of them

---

[1] It is significant that the MSS. containing the ' Edmund ' canons (with the exception of MS. Rawl. C. 100) are precisely those which contain the abridged version of ' Westminster 1065 ', and furthermore all contain the so-called canons of Langton.

[2] Matt. Paris, *Chron. Maj.* v. 676, 680 ; Treharne, *Baronial Plan of Reform*, i. 65.

[3] *Ann. Mon.* i. 411 *seqq.* (Wilkins, i. 736).

[4] *Ann. Mon.* i. 425 *seqq.* Cf. the documents of 1257, *ibid.* i. 401 *seqq.* ; Matt. Paris, vi. 353 *seqq.* (Wilkins, i. 724 *seqq.*).   [5] *Ann. Mon.* i. 412 (Wilkins, i. 736).

[6] Wilkins, i. 736 n., 740 n. ; All Souls MS. 42, fo. 222ᵛ. Manuscripts agreeing approximately with this text are Harl. 2349, fo. 54 ; Harl. 3705, fo. 24 ; Lambeth 778, fo. 13 ; Bodleian, Ashmole 1146, fo. 50 ; Caius Coll. 487, fo. 155 ; Ch. Ch. Canterbury MS. E. 9, fo. 37ᵛ.

actually entitle the council a provincial council. On the other hand, the wording of the articles suggests that they were intended to apply to the whole English Church. In view of this, and of the words of the Burton annalist, one may suppose that the council was intended to be national, that the archbishop of York was prevented by death and his suffragans by other reasons from attending, and that prelates and clergy of both provinces answered the summons. This would reconcile an address in the name of Boniface and his suffragans with other details which suggest a national council.[1] The agreement on these articles in June 1258 did not mean that they at once became accepted law in either province. They were merely a draft, as yet not framed in the peremptory language of the canons. At this revolutionary moment in the history of the State, the prelates may well have waited to see what turn events would take at the parliament at Oxford. For a parliament of magnates and clergy was timed to meet three days after the articles were issued, on 11 June at Oxford. And among the provisions of this parliament, the agenda for the new council of twenty-four included the amending of the state of the Church.[2] It was perhaps as a result of this that a national ecclesiastical meeting came together at Oxford in the summer of 1258.[3] A committee of four bishops presented the articles of Merton or Westminster for the consideration of the assembly; but some were absent and some were doubtful, and so the business was left unfinished.[4]

The articles remained without revision or ratification for three years. In May 1261 they were transformed into formal legislation. On May 8 the prelates of both provinces had met at London to hear the papal legate's demand for an aid. Their answers were postponed to two councils, at which the clergy of Canterbury and York met the legate, at London and Beverley on the 16 and 23 May respectively.[5] Both these councils ordained certain new statutes concerning the state of the English Church, which they ordered to be observed along with others formerly provided at Oxford. This is the story of the *Flores.* No other evidence supports this statement as regards the provincial council at

---

[1] In the dating clause of All Souls MS. 42 (Wilkins, i. 740 n.) the witnesses include the archbishop and his suffragans; other MSS. containing this clause read ' archiepiscopi ' for ' archiepiscopus '. But Sewall de Bovill had died 10 May 1258, and it was September before Godfrey Ludham was consecrated at Viterbo.

[2] Stubbs, *Select Charters* (9th ed.), p. 381.

[3] Its composition is uncertain. Matthew Paris says ' the prelates of all England were summoned generally ', v. 707 (Wilkins, i. 740).

[4] This depends entirely upon Paris. He does not identify the statutes with the earlier Articles, but the statutes which he gives in the *Liber Additamentorum* are in fact the Articles (Brit. Mus. MS. Cotton, Nero D. i. fo. 134, Wats's edition (1684), i. 1123 ; cf. collation in *Ann. Mon.* i. 412 *seqq.*).

[5] *Flores Histor.* (Rolls Series), ii. 465, 468 (Wilkins, i. 755 n., 755–6).

Beverley, and the reference of the *Flores* to what had been provided at Oxford obscures the relationship of the articles with the
canons of 1261. From the canons themselves we can tell approximately what came of the council of the southern province.
Before the day appointed to meet the legate at London (16 May),
the southern prelates had held an independent provincial council
at Lambeth, which ended on 13 May. On that day were promulgated a series of provincial canons based mainly upon the
articles of 1258, which had been shelved at Oxford in the same
year. According to the continuator of Gervase of Canterbury
(who tells us the names of the suffragans present), the statutes
of the legate Otto (1237) were also recited in the council. Then
the king's clerks came and appealed against the canons, as did
also the Lord Edward with Peter of Savoy, ' and so the council
dissolved without result '.[1]

Considering the plain-spoken reproof of the secular power
which is to be found in every chapter of these canons, the king's
opposition was not surprising. The archbishop appealed to the
pope for confirmation of the canons ; the king protested to the
pope against them ; [2] and on 30 January 1263 Urban IV informed the king that at the latter's request he was not confirming
Boniface's canons, although he could see nothing objectionable
in them.[3] This rebuff has permitted later partisan writers such
as Prynne to treat the canons of Lambeth 1261 as void. But
medieval canonists, at least, regarded them as of equal authority
with other provincial legislation. Pecham affirmed that the pope
had eventually confirmed them,[4] Greenfield of York quoted them,
Stratford renewed several of their chapters, and Lyndwood included the whole series in his *Provinciale*. Lyndwood observed
that most of Boniface's canons are penal and concern ecclesiastical
privilege and its violation ; ' but since these constitutions are
but little observed, I will (he says) be brief in the glossing of them :
I intend however to show in what respects they harmonize with
the common law and where they can be based upon common law '.[5]

At first sight, the varying texts of the articles and canons
present some difficulties. We can fortunately be fairly sure of
the original form of each document and thence see the development of conflate versions. About a dozen manuscripts of the
1258 articles remain. Of these the texts in the Burton Annals [6]

¹ Gervase (Rolls Series), ii. 212–13. He assigns these canons to the first meeting,
on 8 May 1261.
² Appointment of proctors by the king, 27 May 1261, printed by Prynne from the
patent rolls (*Records*, ii. 990, cf. 26 November 1261 ; *ibid.* iii. 21).
³ *Foedera* (Record Comm.), i. 424 (Wilkins, i. 759).
⁴ C. of Reading, 1279 : MS. Harl. 52, fo. 80 ; MS. Bodley 794, fo. 182.
⁵ *Provinciale*, II. ii. 1 *ver.* Contingit (p. 92a). Johnson misunderstands this (*Collection, s.a.* 1261, note to ch. 5).
⁶ From which Wilkins printed, i. 736 *seqq*.

and the *Liber Additamentorum* must claim precedence, for they are the only ones probably written before the council of 1261. All the other texts contain more or less additions and alterations derived from the new recension of 1261.

For Lambeth 1261 we have a choice of about fifty manuscripts, of which some have not been fully examined. But one manuscript is singularly valuable. Cotton Charter xvi. 29 gives the canons in the form of a charter. The hand is contemporary, the form suggests an original official copy sealed with the seals of the archbishop and his suffragans.[1] We probably have here the original or a copy made from the original for delivery to a bishop. This text differs materially from Wilkins's.[2] A full dating clause gives the occasion as 13 May 1261 at Lambeth, and contains the names of three of the bishops who ratified the canons with their seals.[3] Ten manuscripts agree very closely indeed with the Cotton charter,[4] while eight more show only minor variations. A comparison of this form of Lambeth 1261 with the articles of 1258 shows that most of the material was used again, often in the same words. It had to be reframed as definite legislation, and being concerned with the province substitutes ' provincia Cant.' for ' regnum ' or ' ecclesia anglicana '. Six entirely new chapters were inserted at the end. Since one of this group of texts was printed by Spelman there is no need to notice further the many modifications of the articles, and it is no part of our present task to comment upon the historical significance of the revision.[5]

The connexion of the two documents led later copyists, who were oblivious to the historical circumstances, to attempt to embody in one text all the constitutions of Archbishop Boniface.

[1] According to the terms of the dating clause. The document has been so seriously damaged by fire that it is impossible to be sure that seals were originally attached.

[2] Wilkins, i. 746 *seqq.* This purports to be made from four texts. The first two of these (Otho A. xvi. and Vitell. A. ii. fo. 65ᵛ) provided Wilkins with the correct version, but he prefers, without note or comment, the testimony of two inferior texts and in his conflation selects the latter's impossible and misleading dating clause. Spelman had printed correctly from the first text. J. Armitage Robinson noted the divergence and followed Spelman (*Church Quarterly Rev.* lxxxi. 92, n. 1).

[3] The bishops of London, Worcester, and Salisbury are perhaps specified by name because they were the three bishops in the Council of twenty-four. The dating clause wrongly states the regnal year as ' anno regis Henrici tercii quadragesimo quarto ', and it is important to notice that the error is common to the other manuscripts which preserve this form of the text. The correct regnal year is only found in one MS. (Bodley 794, fo. 139 : in the title ; dating clause omitted).

[4] Brit. Mus. MSS. Cotton, Otho A. xvi., Cotton, Vitell. A. ii. fo. 65ᵛ, Harl. 52, fo. 69. Arundel 438, fo. 87ᵛ ; Bodleian MSS. Ashmole 1146, fo. 55, Rawl. C. 100, fo. 127 ; Univ. Coll. Oxon. MS. 148, fo. 207 ; Ch. Ch. Canterbury, Chartae antiquae L. 138ᵃ ; Salisbury Cath. Liber Evid. C, p. 290 ; *ibid.* p. 391.

[5] As a rough indication : the following passages from the Articles, appearing in Wilkins's text of 1261, have to be omitted. Cc. 4 (from ' Et si reddantur '), 9 (to ' quo apparuit impetrata '), 14, 16, 17, 18, 19 (last sentence).

These conflate versions appear late in the fourteenth century, and find their way into numerous later collections. Occasionally the articles would be taken as the basic text and only a few additions be grafted from the canons ; [1] but conflate texts in which Lambeth 1261 predominates had the wider circulation. One form was used by Lyndwood, another chosen by Wilkins. Several forms have been distinguished and classified, but their value for preparing an edition of the canons is negligible.

Constitution of Archbishop Boniface on tithe.—A decree on the payment of tithes is ascribed to Boniface in most of those manuscripts in which it appears as an isolated canon. Wilkins printed it without this ascription from a copy which follows immediately upon a decree of Archbishop Gray of York.[2] The identical decree occurs twice again in the *Concilia :* it is the last of Giles of Salisbury's diocesan canons (1257–62), and the first of the provincial canons ascribed to Winchelsey at Merton (1305).[3] The date of the Salisbury manuscripts shows that the canon was at least current in the thirteenth century. Unfortunately, no contemporary text ascribes it to Boniface. But the ascriptions of the later manuscripts are instructive. Some speak of a constitution of the bishops of all England, published at Merton ; [4] others of a general statute at London by Archbishop Boniface and his suffragans.[5] These doubtful alternatives are those which confront us with regard to the articles of 1258. One may perhaps legitimately conjecture that this decree on tithes was issued in the same assembly. On the other hand, the appropriation of a provincial canon by the bishop of Salisbury without reference to the metropolitan authority, is hard to understand. An examination of the canons on this subject attributed to Winchelsey supports the theory of diocesan origin. Unless some contemporary reference comes to light, we cannot say whether Boniface ever reissued the canon first published by the bishop of Salisbury.

[1] E.g. Bodleian MS. Seld. sup. 43, fo. 50ᵛ.

[2] Wilkins, i. 698–9, from MS. Cotton, Vitell. D. v. (fo. 9ᵛ of the remnant). The title is ' Constituciones synodales de decimis feni, agnorum . . . '. The MS. is of the fifteenth century.

[3] Wilkins, i. 719–20 ; ii. 278. Cf. Lyndwood's note : ' Haec est constitutio Roberti Winchelsey Cant' archiepiscopi secundum aliquos libros, secundum alios est Bonifacii, vel alias est constitutio communis episcoporum congregatorum apud Merton in communi concilio, prout vidi in uno libro valde antiquo ' (*Provinciale*, I. xvi. 5 *ver.* Quoniam (p. 191*b*)).

[4] E.g. Lyndwood, *ut sup. ;* MS. Ashmole 1146, fo. 79 ; MS. Hatton 109, fo. 55 ; New Coll. MS. 92, fo. 177ᵛ ; MSS. Harl. 106, fo. 11, and Harl. 2349, fo. 63, read ' bishops of all England ' ; Brasenose Coll. MS. 14, fo. 176ᵛ, reads ' Boniface at Merton '.

[5] E.g. MS. Reg. 9 B. ii. fo. 146ʳ ; Exeter Coll. MS. 31, fo. 226 ; MS. Rawl. C. 428, fo. 118ᵛ ; MS. Wood empt. 23, fo. 157ᵛ ; C.C.C. Oxon MS. 72, fo. 48ʳ ; Lambeth MS. 171, fo. 21. MS. Trin. Coll. Camb. 1440, fo. 54, describes it as ' concilium de Lamethe editum a Bonefacio archiepiscopo Cantuar' '. It appears as a provincial constitution of Boniface in the fourteenth-century *Summa Summarum*, MS. Bodley 293, fos. 123ᵛ–124.

Manuscripts of the provincial constitutions ascribed to Pecham were described by C. Trice Martin in 1885. While his list was inevitably incomplete, it remains a valuable guide to some of the main varieties of texts.[1]

Canons of Reading, 1279.—There are at least forty-three extant manuscripts of these canons, of which Martin noted twenty-five. Nothing would be gained by enumerating them here, or by detailing their many divergencies from Wilkins's text. This will certainly have to be modified at many points, but the variations seldom affect the general sense of the canons. In one important respect, however, the printed editions need alteration. As the canons now stand they have the appearance of independent legislation comparable to that of Pecham's predecessors. It was as new legislation that they interested medieval canonists, and they came to be looked at in this light. But it was only at the expense of omitting from copies all traces of the original form of publication. The result is as incomplete as one actor's lines taken out of a play and presented without the cues. Pecham's own canons were only one player's part. Several manuscripts emphasize this by their title : the constitutions of Archbishop Pecham with his additions and declarations on certain chapters in the constitutions of Oxford, Lambeth, Otto and Ottobono, and Lyon [II].[2]

The whole *acta* have fortunately been preserved in a few manuscripts [3] and have left traces in many more. These texts make it clear that the business of the council of Reading was to reiterate large portions of the conciliar legislation of the thirteenth century, with comparatively few additions. In this the council resembled that held by Pecham two years later at Lambeth ; here also the earlier canons were recited, but here Pecham's additions formed a compact body of new law.[4] The proceedings opened by the archbishop's statement of his intention to recite the canons of Ottobono ('quod utilitatem aliorum [*sc.* Stephani

---

[1] *Reg. Epist. J. Peckham* (Rolls Series), III. cxxiii–cxliv. Pecham's activity in the councils of Reading and Lambeth has more recently been the subject of investigation by Professor Hilda Johnstone (*Essays presented to T. F. Tout* (1925), pp. 171–88).

[2] E.g. Brit. Mus. MS. Reg. 9 B. ii. fo. 21 ; Bodleian MSS. Ashmole 1146, fo. 63, Wood empt. 23, fo. 127ᵛ.

[3] Brit. Mus. MS. Harl. 52, fo. 79 ; Bodleian MSS. Ashmole 1146, fo. 63, Bodley 794, fo. 178, Wood empt. 23, fo. 127ᵛ ; Exeter Coll. MS. 31, fo. 226ᵛ ; Trin. Coll. Camb. MS. 1245, fo. 124ᵛ. Other manuscripts not yet examined may also preserve this form. Johnson had shrewdly guessed its existence (*Collection, s.a.* 1279, ch. 3).

[4] Cf. Winchelsey's council of 1309 in which he ordered the publication of the statutes and ordinances of Otto and Ottobono and Stephen together with sentences of excommunication (Wilkins, ii. 402, *Reg. Simonis de Gandavo* (Cant. and York Soc.), pp. 378–80). A collection of this material 'sub compendio', arising out of Winchelsey's order, is contained in the Cambridge Univ. Libr. MS. Dd. VII. 14, fos. 7 *seqq.*

et Octonis] pro maiori parte in se videtur includere '),[1] with certain
other matter of his own making ; then the canons of Boniface
in defence of ecclesiastical privilege, with more additions ; thirdly,
Magna Carta and the excommunication of its violators ; fourthly,
sentences of excommunication extracted from four councils. After
this the recital of Ottobono's canons began.[2] When Ottobono's
chapter on baptism had been read, the archbishop made ' declaracio super eodem capitulo ' (MS. Bodley 794, fo. 178ᵛ). This
is ch. 4 of Wilkins's text, and it cannot be understood except as
a pendant to Ottobono's canon. When the ' declaracio ' had been
read, the recitation of the legatine canons was resumed until,
at ch. 8, Pecham halted again to add an extra penalty to Ottobono's
' de concubinariis ' : this is Wilkins's ch. 5. And so the recital
continued. The cc. 1 and 2 of Wilkins were ' adiecciones ' and
' declaraciones ' which could only be understood if the other laws
had just been read.[3] Finally, the sentences of excommunication
' taken from the four councils ' (Wilkins, ch. 3), followed upon
the recital of Lambeth 1261.[4]

While some manuscripts give the preamble and all the references to the canons which were read, others [5] have preserved
the original order of Pecham's ' adiecciones ' : cc. 4, 5, 1, 2, 3.
All these texts in the preferable form reverse the order of the
second and third excommunication clauses, thus agreeing with
both the council of Oxford in which they originated and the
council of Lambeth (1281) which repeated them.

Undated canons of Pecham (Wilkins, ii. 48–9).—The first three
chapters given by Wilkins are preserved together in a text of
the mid-fourteenth century (MS. Harl. 52, fo. 81ᵛ), and in others.
They may well have been issued in a provincial council by Pecham,
but the manuscripts give no clue to their date. There is no justi-

---

[1] MS. Bodley 794, fo. 178.

[2] Some texts begin with the *incipit* of Ottobono's statutes : Camb. Univ Libr. MS.
Ii. ii. 7, p. 421 ; Balliol Coll. MS. 301, fo. 189ᵛ ; Brit. Mus. MS. Reg. 9 B. ii. fo. 21.

[3] Note, e.g. the words ' presens legati constitucio Octoboni ' in ch. 1. Bodley
794, fo. 180, gives in full the constitution of Pope Gregory X, *Licet canon*, and Wood
empt. 23, fo. 130, gives *Nemo deinceps*.

[4] Cf. MS. Harl. 52, as described by Martin, *Reg. Ep. J. Peckham*, iii. cxxv. Bodl.
794 misplaces some of the material and adds cross-references. It also adds the note
that Pecham at Reading excommunicated pluralists (fo. 182, also in Harl. 52. Cf.
ch. 1 and Johnson's note thereon).

[5] Besides all the MSS. in page 407, note 3 *supra :* Worcester Reg. God. Giffard, fo.
89ᵛ ; Public Record Office, Exch. T.R. Dipl. Doct. 1576 (printed by H. Cole, *Original
Documents*, p. 362), Exch. T.R. Bks. 274, fo. 295 ; Brit. Mus. MSS. Reg. 10 C. 1,
fo. 15, Harl. 3705, fo. 31, Addit. 6158, fo. 132 ; MS. Bodley 794, fo. 144 ; Balliol Coll.
301, fo. 189ᵛ ; Camb. Univ. Libr. MS. Ii. ii. 28, fo. 2 ; Lambeth MS. 778, fo. 18ᵛ.
Peterhouse MS. 84, fo. 147ᵛ, is in the order of Wilkins's text, but at ch. iv. is the note :
' De pueris baptizandis, et ista constitucio et cetera sequequens [*sic*] addunt ad constituciones Octoboni et in quibusdam libris scribuntur in principio istarum constitu-
cionum de Redyng, et hoc videtur melius propter clausulam positam in constitucione
proxima que incipit Que autem a nobis, &c.'.

fication for dating them 1280 as Wilkins does, or for appending them to Reading 1279 as in the Oxford edition.[1] The two parts of ch. 4 need separate consideration, for they are usually found isolated from the rest and from each other. The second part, beginning ' Ceterum advertentes ', safeguards the trees growing in cemeteries, and its ascription rests on slender evidence.[2] The first part (' Ad doctrinam ') states the obligations of parishioners in the maintenance of church buildings and furniture.[3] The many divergencies between the manuscripts of this canon can be mostly explained as careless copying ; but the titles also vary. While the fourteenth-century manuscripts ascribe the canon to Pecham, five of the fifteenth century make Winchelsey the author.[4] We may probably accept the canon as Pecham's, but we have no evidence that it was associated with others or issued in a provincial council.[5] The ascription to Winchelsey will be understood by reference to other canons on this subject appearing under his name.

So-called Canons of Archbishop Winchelsey

On the authority of several fifteenth-century manuscripts Wilkins printed (ii. 278–83) a group of canons ascribed to Winchelsey. They agree for the most part, but not entirely, with those given in the Oxford edition of 1679. Both editions ascribe many of the canons to a provincial council held at Merton in 1305. The manuscript evidence is copious and confusing. While some late texts present the whole series as one set of canons, they are more often found isolated.[6] It will therefore be best to examine the authenticity of each in turn.

Canons on tithe.—The first section (Wilkins, ii. 278) is neither more nor less than the canon ascribed in many manuscripts to

---

[1] To Martin's list of texts (pp. cxxxix *seqq.*) should be added : C.C.C. Camb. MS. 84, fo. 187 ; Peterhouse MS. 84, fo. 154ᵛ ; Trin. Coll. Camb. 1245, fo. 136ᵛ ; Hereford Cathedral MS. P. 7. vii. fos. 123, 142ᵛ ; *Constitutiones* (Paris, 1504), fo. 141ᵛ. Cf. *infra*, n. 3.

[2] It is found in Lambeth MS. 778, fo. 27 ; MS. Harl. 3705, fo. 41ᵛ ; and Magdalen Coll. Oxon MS. 185, fo. 11.

[3] Brit. Mus. MSS. Cotton, Vitell. A. ii. fo. 53ᵛ, Cotton, Cleop. D. III, fo. 190 (formerly fo. 191) ; Bodleian MSS. Ashmole 1146, fo. 78ᵛ, Wood empt. 23, fo. 153ᵛ ; All Souls Coll. MS. 42, fo. 254 ; Exeter Coll. MS. 31, fo. 237ᵛ ; Hereford Cathedral MS. P. 7. vii. fo. 143. Cf. the canon of Archbishop Walter Gray of York (Wilkins, i. 698) : the best edition is W. Farrer's, *Cockersand Chartulary* (Chetham Soc.), I. i. 50–3 ; an additional text is in Wilkins, iii. 676.

[4] Winchelsey at Merton ' 1360 ' : Bodl. MS. Seld. sup. 43, fo. 72ᵛ. Winchelsey on his provincial visitation : Brit. Mus. MS. Cotton, Cleop. D. III, fo. 190 ; Exeter Coll. MS. 31, fo. 237ᵛ. Robert on his metropolitan visitation of Worcester diocese : All Souls Coll. MS. 42, fo. 248 ; Hereford Cath. MS. P. 7. vii. fo. 143.

[5] One fourteenth-century MS. (Harl. 2349, fo. 114ᵛ) ascribes the canon to Pecham on his provincial visitation.

[6] The ascription to Merton is not supported by outside evidence. Apparently there is no other mention of any ecclesiastical meeting at Merton in 1305.

Archbishop Boniface, found also in the canons of Bishop Giles
of Salisbury (*supra*, p. 406). The second section (ii. 279) may be
divided into three parts, ending (*a*) ' particulariter decimentur ',
(*b*) ' duximus relinquendum ', and (*c*) ' precipimus observari '.
II (*a*) is found with a slightly different opening in the Salisbury
canons of Robert Bingham ; [1] it appears again in the Winchester
canons of John Gerveys, 1262–7, and the Exeter canons of Peter
Quivil, 1287.[2] II (*a*) and ii (*b*) occur together in York canons
1258–9, and in Durham canons 1274–83.[3] Section ii (*c*) is not
known elsewhere. Comparing it with ii (*a*) one realizes that
the two sections overlap so much that they could scarcely have
been issued together. Many manuscripts of Winchelsey only
include sections (*a*) and (*b*),[4] and like the earlier diocesan texts
reverse the order of the last two sentences.[5]

Two more canons on tithe (not in Wilkins) are attributed to
Winchelsey in some texts.[6] One of these (' Sancta ecclesia
constituit ') was used by Lyndwood as a canon of Winchelsey,[7]
but its form suggests a circular letter from a bishop or archdeacon
to his parish clergy rather than a provincial canon. The second
canon (' Quoniam in signum ') is likewise clearly a diocesan
enactment (' nostre diocesis locis ') : it is found complete in the
York canons of 1258–9,[8] and part of the Exeter chapter on tithe
appears to be modelled upon it.[9]

The tithe canons are thus proved to be earlier than Winchelsey
and are suspect as a collection. The twenty-four manuscripts
which ascribe the whole or part of them to Winchelsey date only
from the fifteenth century, and other ascriptions, to Otto, Pope
Innocent IV, and Ottobono, are found in fourteenth-century
texts of section ii (*a* and *b*).[10] It is tempting to explain their
frequent appearance in the diocesan canons of both provinces
by a legatine origin ; but no other evidence points to any general

[1] MS. Harl. 52, fos. 124ᵛ–5.

[2] *Reg. Joh. Pontissara* (Cant. and York Soc.), i. 231 (Wilkins, ii. 297) ; Wilkins,
ii. 159.

[3] Brit. Mus. MS. Lansdowne 397, fo. 252 ; Wilkins, ii. 29.

[4] Cf. Oxford edition, 1679, p. 35.

[5] Thus ending : ' valeat impedire '. The penultimate sentence in this order is
omitted entirely from the Oxford edition.

[6] E.g. Seld. sup. 43, fo. 73ᵛ.

[7] *Provinciale*, III. xvi. 7 (p. 199*b*). Cf. *Constitutiones* (Oxford 1679), p. 36. Copies
in All Souls Coll. MS. 42, fo. 255ᵛ ; Camb. Univ. Libr. MSS. Gg. VI. 21, Addit. 3575,
fo. 341ᵛ ; Pembr. Coll. Camb. MS. 131, fo. 56 ; Brit. Mus. MS. Harl. 335, fo. 82 ;
Lambeth MS. 538, fo. 194ᵛ.   Spelman attributed the canon to Mepham 1332.

[8] Lansdowne 397, fos. 251ᵛ–252.

[9] Found without title following Winchelsey, Hereford Cath. MS. P. 7. vii. fo. 128.

[10] Reg. 9 B. ii. fo. 146ᵛ, and Harl. 2349, fo. 113, agree with the Salisbury form : the
former MS. ascribes the canon to Innocent IV, the latter has no heading. Ashmole 1146,
fo. 42ᵛ, and Harl. 2349, fo. 22ᵛ, agree with the York form and ascribe it to Ottobono.
Ch. Ch. Canterbury MS. B. 10, fo. 4ᵛ, attributes the Salisbury form of II(*a*) to the
legate Otto. Brit. Mus. MS. Harl. 2349, fo. 113, and Ch. Ch. Cant. MS. E. 9, fo. 59,
give the same section without ascription.

legislation by the legate Otto beyond the canons of London 1237. We have to consider whether the Salisbury canon of Bingham could be the origin of canons of Winchester, Exeter, and York (and thence Durham) ; and whether the circulation of the York and Durham canons suffices to explain their presence in the Canterbury collections. If we deny the Salisbury canons this influence, we must postulate a common original before the death of Bingham (1246). If we deny that the York canons could have been copied unofficially into so many Canterbury collections, then we must suppose that Winchelsey renewed them. The problem cannot be considered apart from that of the so-called canon of Boniface on tithe, also attributed to Winchelsey, and it may be helpful to remember the history of some other diocesan canons. The collections which include these ' Winchelsey ' canons contain other material with equally suspicious titles. The formation of the manuscripts, their ambiguous titles, and rubrics added afterwards, combined with the easy circulation of a canon from one diocese or province to another, permit us to reject this unhistorical ascription. Without more definite evidence we may conjecture that the Salisbury canons were sufficiently well known to be borrowed at York as well as in the southern province, and that in the fifteenth century the earnest collector of legislation on tithe brought together all the diocesan pronouncements he could find, under the name of one archbishop.[1]

Canon on mortuaries (Wilkins, ii. 279).—This canon, found in many late texts along with ' Winchelsey ' on tithe, has already been shown to originate in a diocesan canon of Salisbury (*supra*, p. 399). The arguments against its renewal by Winchelsey are those which apply to the canons on tithe.

Canons on parishioners' obligations (Wilkins, ii. 280).—Following ' Winchelsey ' on tithe and mortuaries, under the same ascription to a council at Merton, is found a canon (' Ut sciant parochiani ') which closely resembles the canon of Pecham on the obligations of parishioners.[2] At the end, however, is an appendix of extra obligations for providing books and vestments. In several copies the note is added : ' Quere istam constitucionem sub meliore forma inferius '. The canon does appear in a revised form, in which the material of the appendix is distributed in suitable places in the body of the canon. Lyndwood ascribes this revised form to Winchelsey,[3] and this agrees with three

---

[1] A study of the personnel of the English episcopate shows the possibility of frequent transmission (cf. Gibbs and Lang, *op. cit.* appendixes, and Patrick, *Statutes of the Scottish Church*, pp. lii *seqq.*). On the passage of capitular statutes and customs from one cathedral to another, cf. Bradshaw and Wordsworth, *Statutes of Lincoln Cathedral*, esp. i. 33 *seqq.*, 61 *seqq.*, 166 ; iii. 268 *seqq.*

[2] Also isolated texts in Balliol Coll. MS. 158, fo. 164ᵛ ; Camb. Univ. Libr. MSS. Ee. v. 13, fo. 10, Ii. iii. 14, p. 387.

[3] *Provinciale*, iii. xxvii. 2 (p. 251a).

I

manuscripts,[1] but most of the manuscripts have other ascriptions. Some give the alternative ' Roberti de Wynchelsey et secundum quosdam Simonis Islep ' ; [2] some name Archbishops Robert and Walter [Reynolds] ; [3] two name Archbishop Walter alone ; [4] and others say ' Roberti et Walteri et secundum quosdam Simonis Islep '.[5]

The evidence shows that several decrees were issued on this subject during the late thirteenth and early fourteenth centuries. To establish the original times and forms is probably beyond the historian's powers. The subject-matter partly explains this. In each case the body of the canon is nothing but a list of articles to be provided and cared for in the churches. This list was all that mattered. No sanctity attached to the wording of the list, and the preamble might be paraphrased or simply omitted ; [6] the order in which the articles were mentioned would freely be altered. The titles are significant, too : for the canon issued or modified in a visitation would probably assume variant forms more easily than one promulgated in a provincial council. It might be issued by its author's successor, and thereafter go by his name.[7] One can therefore only postulate different canons where the divergencies touch the actual obligations.[8]

In this state of uncertainty conjecture is perhaps permissible. It appears from an analysis of form and contents that Winchelsey first issued a canon which in all essentials agreed with the canon ' Ad doctrinam '. It did, however, present the material in a somewhat different form, and this fact supports the ascription of ' Ad doctrinam ' to Pecham. It is suggested that this new form

---

[1] Camb. Univ. Libr. MS. Dd. ix. 38, fo. 57 ; Caius Coll. MS. 38, fo. 118ᵛ ; Pembr. Coll. Camb. MS. 131, fo. 86 : ' Constitucio generalis iuxta decretum dicti domini Roberti in visitacione sua a.d. 1305. Inprimis statuit et decrevit . . .'

[2] All Souls Coll. MS. 42, fo. 275ᵛ ; Balliol Coll. MS. 158, fo. 184 ; Exeter Coll. MS. 41, fo. 202ᵛ ; Camb. Univ. Libr. MS. Gg. vi. 21, n. 13.

[3] Camb. Univ. Libr. MS. Mm. iv. 41, fo. 7 ; C.C.C. Camb. MS. 189, fo. 31ᵛ ; Brit. Mus. MSS. Cotton, Faustina A. viii. fo. 41ᵛ, Harl. 335, fo. 15, Reg. 9 E. ii. fo. 1 ; Brasenose Coll. MS. 14, fo. 152ᵛ (formerly fos. 147ᵛ, 150ᵛ) ; St. John's Coll. Camb. MS. 88, fo. 55. The last three say ' in eorum visitacione metrop.'. These three also agree with the texts ascribed to Reynolds and with an untitled text (*Vetus Liber Archidiaconi Eliensis*, p. 150) in commencing with the words ' Inter cetera provisum et ordinatum est '. Hereford Cath. MS. P. 7. vii. fo. 149ᵛ, ascribes the canon to Archbishops Winchelsey and William.

[4] MS. Bodley 794, fo. 187 ; Camb. Univ. Libr. MS. Addit. 3468, fo. 84ᵛ. The latter says : ' in sua visitacione metropolitana '.

[5] C.C.C. Camb. MS. 84, fo. 29ᵛ ; Peterhouse MS. 84, fo. 163ᵛ ; Holkham MS. 226, p. 72 ; *Constitutiones* (Paris 1504) fo. 146ᵛ.

[6] Thus ' Imprimis statuit et decrevit . . . ' (*supra* n. 1). Cf. Bodl. MS. Wood empt. 23, fo. 153ᵛ : ' ipsis innotescat quod . . .'.

[7] This perhaps explains the ascription of the canon ' Ad doctrinam ' to Winchelsey (*supra*, p. 409, n. 4).

[8] And here one must allow for careless copyists : e.g. *Vetus Liber Archid. Eli.* p. 150, and Brasenose Coll. MS. 14, fo. 152ᵛ, and MS. Reg. 9 E. ii. fo. 1, all omit the passage between ' reparacionem (navis) ' and ' (reparacionem) librorum '.

may be seen in a faulty text of the early fourteenth century.[1] It contains the same material as Pecham's canon, but the preamble and the order are those of the canon ascribed in some manuscripts to Robert and Walter. After he had thus repeated his predecessor's rules, Winchelsey apparently renewed his visitation decree, slightly modified, as a circular letter (' tenore presentium innotescimus . . . '). This is preserved in the so-called canons of Merton, as printed by Wilkins (ii. 280) omitting the appendix included in this version. With Archbishop Reynolds, more burdens were laid upon parishioners. A new decree was framed which owed much to Winchelsey's earlier visitation form ; but for those persons who already possessed Winchelsey's text it was convenient to insert the additions by way of an appendix (' Item compellendi sunt parochiani . . . '). This composite text and the revised form issued by Reynolds are those found in Wilkins's *Concilia* (ii. 280). As regards the ascription to Islip, no fourteenth-century text mentions his name, and his register has no record of the canon. This hypothesis may claim to account for the principal varieties of the manuscripts. Further evidence is needed before we can pronounce definitely on the authors of these canons and the circumstances of their publication.

Canon on stipendiary priests (Wilkins, ii. 280 *seqq.*).—None of the twenty-two texts of this canon which have been noted is earlier than the fifteenth century ; in details the selection of a text may therefore be expected to raise difficulties. The renewal of the canon by Courtenay in 1391 is of value, but only gives a paraphrase of Winchelsey's words.[2] All the known texts agree in ascribing the canon to Winchelsey, but only half of them give any clue to the time of its publication : these agree in dating it 1305.[3] Seven of these eleven texts state that the constitution was ' facta in visitacione '. Courtenay on the other hand declared that his predecessor's canon was ordained ' in concilio provinciali '.

Canon on fornicators (Wilkins, ii. 283).—This canon, while reminiscent of earlier diocesan canons of Winchester,[4] differs in deferring the penalty of marriage until a third offence. It is found with other canons ascribed to Winchelsey in fifteenth-century manuscripts, seldom with a clear ascription and never with a date. But like some of the tithe canons, it was issued before Winchelsey's time in the diocesan canons of York, 1258–9.

---

[1] After 1331. Bodl. Kent rolls 6ᵈ, a roll of legal records, &c., from Tonbridge Priory : ' Hec est decretum domini Roberti nuper Cant' archiepiscopi in sua visitacione provinciali '.

[2] Wilkins, iii. 213, from Courtenay's register, &c.

[3] Excepting Lambeth MS. 538, fo. 174ᵛ, which is dated 1306.

[4] 1246–61, Salisbury Cath. Liber Evid. C, fo. 400ᵛ ; 1261–7, *Reg. Joh. de Pontissara*, i. 224. Cf. Brit. Mus. MS. Lansdowne 397, fo. 247.

I

So–called Canons of Archbishops Reynolds and Mepham

Of the various sets of canons printed in the *Concilia* collections under the names of Reynolds and Mepham, only the well-authenticated canons of the council of London 1328/9 stand up to criticism. First of all may be dismissed the canons ascribed by Spelman to Archbishop Reynolds (ii. 488 *seqq.*). These are Stratford's canons printed by Wilkins (ii. 675 *seqq.*) from the same manuscript.[1] They must be considered in connexion with the other canons of Stratford.

Both Spelman (ii. 500) and Wilkins (ii. 560–1) attribute to Mepham 1332 a canon which from the dating clause clearly belongs to Islip 1362.[2] In addition Spelman gives two canons which we have found elsewhere ascribed to Winchelsey.[3] The first is undoubtedly Winchelsey's, the second is probably not a provincial constitution (*supra*, p. 410). In any case there is no good manuscript authority for Spelman's ascription.

Among the manuscripts containing all or part of the so-called *Legenda*, no less than thirteen fifteenth-century texts contain the same selection and agree in the title : ' Constituciones provinciales domini Stephani Mepham Cant' archiepiscopi edite apud Lambeth '.[4] It is by no means impossible that Mepham should have issued as his own a number of canons which, as we have seen, had already been in circulation for a century. It is, however, likely that in reissuing these canons a prelate would make some alterations and additions. The only new element here is the chapter ' Ne inclusi ', which is also found in one late text of the *Legenda* ascribed to ' Oxon ii° ',[5] and in certain fourteenth-century texts of Oxford 1222.[6] On the other hand, ch. 8 of Mepham's canons of 1328 resembles ch. 5 of these canons. Finally, the third, sixth, and ninth of these canons are in the form of diocesan laws, like the corresponding portions of the *Legenda*.

All these considerations cast doubt on the ascription to Mepham. The situation is complicated by their pretended association with Reynolds. Lyndwood selected from a text of the *Legenda* (possibly such a one as Trin. Coll. Camb. MS. 1245), cc. 2 to 8. He says that he had seen them ascribed to Mepham,[7] but he ascribed them to Reynolds because, he says, ' iuxta quotationem communem ' they are dated 1322 and entitled

<hr/>

[1] Brit. Mus. MS. Cotton, Vitell. A. ii. fo. 92ᵛ (now fo. 83ᵛ).

[2] Spelman printed (ii. 611) a more correct text with the right date, from Islip's register. This also appears in the Oxford edition of 1679 (p. 57) but not in Wilkins.

[3] ' Presbiteri necnon . . .' (Wilkins, ii. 280) ; ' Sancta ecclesia . . .' (Oxford ed. 1679, p. 36).

[4] *Legenda*, cc. 3², 4–7, 9–11, ' Ne inclusi ', 13². Printed in *Constitutiones* (Paris, 1504), fo. 145ᵛ, and Spelman, ii. 497. Spelman's text (MS. Cotton, Otho A. xvi.) and most others omit ch. 10. Note the borrowing of Langton's Christian name.

[5] Trin. Coll. Camb. MS. 1245, fo. 116ᵛ.   [6] *Supra*, p. 393.

[7] The ' Mepham ' selection does not include cc. 2, 3¹, and 8 of the *Legenda*.

' C. Oxon. 2 ' ; since Reynolds was archbishop then, he must have been their author.[1]   On the basis of Lyndwood's text the Oxford editor of 1679 composed his ' provincial constitutions of Archbishop Walter Raynold published in the Second Council of Oxford, 1322 ', and Wilkins printed from this source.[2]   But no manuscript authority vouches for this.   It is apparently nothing but a selection from a normal series of the *Legenda* with the ascription to Oxford 1222 corrupted to 1322.

In conclusion, there seems no more reason for ascribing these canons to Reynolds or Mepham than there was reason for ascribing them to Langton.   They were in common circulation during the thirteenth and fourteenth centuries, and copyists who did not know their origin were constrained to attach them to a familiar name. Finally, a few of them received a special sort of sanction when they were taken by Lyndwood for commentary in the *Provinciale*.

CANONS OF ARCHBISHOP STRATFORD

Three sets of Stratford's canons were published by Wilkins.[3] In the first series there are nine canons, of which eight agree very closely with portions of the second set.   Such alterations as there are suggest that a revision was carried out for the council of October 1342, and that this first set was an earlier version, related to the later one as the articles of 1258 were related to the canons of 1261.   Some phrases are softened : ' apparitorum turba pestifera ' becomes ' apparitorum onerosa multitudine ' ;   one chapter, ' de bigamia ', is not included in the later series.   The title given to the first set in the only known text is : ' Constituciones edite et nondum publicate et a quibus fuit appellatum '.[4]   This agrees with our information about the provincial council held in October 1341.   Wilkins gives the summons to a council on 19 October 1341,[5] and the king's letter to the prelates warning them before the council to do nothing contrary to the royal dignity.[6]   From Murimuth we learn that at this council the publication of canons ' pro libertatis ecclesiasticae conservatione et morum reformatione '

---

[1] *Provinciale*, I. iv. 4 *ver*. Cum quanta (p. 32*b*).

[2] Oxford ed. pp. 39–40 ; Wilkins, ii. 512 *seqq*.

[3] Wilkins, ii. 675 *seqq*., 696 *seqq*., 702 *seqq*.

[4] MS. Cotton, Vitell. A. ii. fo. 83ᵛ (formerly fo. 92ᵛ) (fifteenth century).   A later fifteenth-century hand added, ' Iste sunt constituciones domini Walteri Reynold, archiepiscopi edite a.d.m° ccc sed deficit hic prima constitucio eiusdem super ornamentis que incipit : Inter cetera ' (cf. *supra*, p. 412, n. 3), whence Spelman's attribution of the canon to Reynolds (ii. 488).   The reference to Mepham precludes this. Immediately preceding this series fo. 82ᵛ formerly fo. 91ᵛ) is ch. 12 of the second series, without title (cf. Wilkins, ii. 679).

[5] Wilkins, ii. 680, from the Ely register.   Also in Grandison of Exeter's register (ed. F. C. Hingeston-Randolph, ii. 968 *seqq*.) and Winchester Cathedral chartulary (ed. A. W. Goodman, p. 222).

[6] Wilkins, ii. 681, from Wells register.   Also in *Cal. Close Rolls, 1341–43*, p. 335.

I

was postponed to another council.[1]   Furthermore this agrees
with the terms of the summons to a council in 1342.

In September 1342 Stratford sent out his summons for a
provincial council to meet at London ' on the Monday after the
Translation of Saint Edward the king, that is the 2 id. October '
[14 October].[2]   But before this, convocation had been summoned
at the king's demand for 9 October,[3] and the second set of canons,
a revision of the first, is usually dated in the manuscripts
10 October 1342.[4]

Series iii is described in Wilkins as being issued in a provincial
council ' on the Wednesday after the feast of Saint Edward king
and martyr ' 1342 [19 March 1342/3].[5]   But there is apparently
no other record of a council on this day and not all the manuscripts
agree upon the dating.   Several texts give the feast of ' Saint
Edward ' or of ' Saint Edward the king ' : [6] it is at least possible
that there has been a confusion of the saints and their feasts,
and that we ought to read ' the Wednesday after the translation
of Saint Edward the king '.   This gives a date two days after
that for which Stratford summoned his council : 16 October
1342.[7]   On this hypothesis the second and third sets of canons
belong to the same council.   It was not, however, until the following May that Archbishop Stratford sent the canons in their
final form to his suffragans.[8]   These final canons we believe to
be the third series only, published with all the details of origin,
names of witnessing bishops, a preamble and a demand for future
observance.   This view is supported by the discovery of a text
which combines the second and third series.[9]   Here, among the

[1] Murimuth, *Contin. Chronicarum* (Rolls Series), p. 122.

[2] Wilkins, ii. 710, from Lincoln register.   Also in *Reg. Rad. de Salopia* (Somerset
Rec. Soc.), ii. 454.

[3] Wilkins, ii. 696 n., from Lincoln register.   Also *Foedera*, II. ii. 1209.

[4] Some texts say ' secundum aliquos libros ' : Holkham MS. 226, fo. 51 ; cf. Brit.
Mus. MS. Harl. 335, fo. 77 ; Peterhouse MS. 84, fo. 156 ; Hereford Cath. MS. P. 7.
vii. fo. 151.   Lyndwood gave no date and stated that he found no certain reference to
the council in registers or chronicles (*Provinciale*, III. vi. 4 *ver.* Concilio (p. 140*a*) ;
cf. II. ii. 4 *ver.* Concilii (p. 98*b*)).   Trin. Coll. Camb. MS. 1245, fo. 140ᵛ, names John
Mepham, London, 10 October 1313 ; apart from the confusion of names, the date is
an easy misreading of mcccxlii.   Lambeth MS. 538, fo. 135, reads 10 Oct. 1344.
Brasenose Coll. MS. 14, fo. 183, gives the year only : 1344.   The name *Extravagantes*
given to the canons in the Oxford edition 1679 apparently has no medieval authority.

[5] Some texts add ' aliter 1343 ' [i.e. 24 March 1343/4] ; others without the full
dating clause read ' 1343 '.   These canons are twice dated 1343 by Lyndwood, but
he dates them 1342 in his list of provincial canons (*Provinciale*, I. ii. 2 *ver.* Editae
(p. 17*b*), I. ii. 3 *ver.* Constitutiones (p. 18*a*), v. xv. 2 *ver.* Minime (p. 319*b*)).

[6] Bodl. MS. Seld. sup 43, fo. 75 ; Lambeth MS. 538, fo. 176ᵛ.

[7] Bodl. MS. Rawl. C. 100, fo. 132, reads 25 Oct. 1342, and gives the list of bishops
present as it occurs in other texts of the third series.

[8] *Reg. Rad. de Salopia*, ii. 463.   This delay may explain the dating 1343, in several
texts of the third series.

[9] MS. Harl. 52, fo. 93.   Without title, immediately preceding the usual text of
the third series with title dated 1343 (fo. 103).   Some of the textual peculiarities are

canons of the second series, preserved in their normal order, are scattered the sixteen chapters of the third series in an unusual sequence, omitting the publication clause and showing some other peculiarities. The chapter ' de bigamia ' from series i. is also included. It seems possible that in October 1342 the council had all this material before it for consideration, and that those chapters which form the third series, dealing partly with the limits of lay jurisdiction, were reserved for recasting and issued six months later. The publication of the second series remains doubtful. We cannot say whether it was accepted straightway and published in the council, or whether it was copied as the residue after the third series had been published. Though rarer than the third series, it is preserved in more than a dozen texts, and Lyndwood accepted its authority.

In Part I of this study evidence was brought together to explain the usual fate of the laws, and the usual process of their corruption, whether in text or title. The following survey of particular texts has only been concerned with those legatine and provincial canons from the twelfth to the fourteenth century which call for the most drastic revising in a new edition. Some of the conclusions expressed should be regarded rather as hypotheses, tentative and wanting correction. They will at least serve a purpose by stating the problems.[1] While each set of canons presents its peculiar difficulties to the editor, in the matter of ascription the evidence of all has to be correlated. The cardinal defects of Wilkins's treatment of the laws are his ignorance of the general state of the texts, and his faulty reproduction of them. Modern editors can not ignore what Wilkins ignored ; nor can they correct as Wilkins sometimes corrected.

found in MS. Seld. sup. 43, fo. 75, and MS. Bodley 794, fo. 149 (imperfect), is apparently the beginning of a similar text. The text of the third series which follows is called ' Constituciones Nove ' (fo. 150). From a late fourteenth-century index to the chartulary of St. Swithun's at Winchester, it appears that this volume formerly contained a conflate text, of which the rubrics correspond to those of the Harleian manuscript (*Chartulary of Winchester Cathedral*, ed. A. W. Goodman, pp. 247–8).

[1] Strikingly similar problems concerning the secular laws and their publication, the defects of the unofficial collections and their acceptance by past editors, are discussed by H. G. Richardson and G. O. Sayles in ' The early statutes ', *Law Quarterly Review*, L (April and October 1934), and separately (London : Stevens, 1934).

I

ADDITIONAL NOTES

This paper formed prologomena to Councils & synods, with other documents relating to the English Church , vol.ii (pts 1 & 2) 1205-1313, ed. F.M. Powicke and C.R. Cheney (Oxford 1964), and has relevance to vol.i (pts 1 & 2) of that work,871-1204, ed. D. Whitelock, M. Brett, and C.N.L. Brooke (Oxford 1981). Further volumes on the later Middle Ages are in preparation. The topic is also the subject of studies VII-X below and of two papers, 'Textual problems of the English provincial canons' and 'William Lyndwood's Provinciale', in C.R.Cheney, Medieval texts and studies (Oxford 1973). The indices of Councils & synods i and ii give more complete guides to the manuscripts.

Pp.385-8:   For the C. of Westminster 1175 see Councils & synods,i.965-93.

P.388 line 5: The text in BL ms. Cotton Claud. A iv is fully discussed and more plausibly explained by M.G. Cheney,'The Council of Westminster,1175',Studies in Church History,11 (1975) 61-8 and Roger,Bishop of Worcester (Oxford 1980) 219- 21. It is re-edited in Councils & synods,i.978-81.

Pp.388-9:   ' Council of London ' is better described as 'Council of Westminster':see Councils & synods,i.1055-8.

P.389 n.1:   This charter is spurious:see English episcopal acta, iii, ed. C.R. Cheney (British Academy, forthcoming)no.593.

Pp.395-8:   These texts were reviewed in the light of new evidence in study VII below; ms. Bodley 843 fos.122r-125v is there shown to contain statutes of an unidentified English diocese, 1222x 1225 (printed in Councils & synods,ii.139.)

P.404 para.2: See J.W.Gray,'Archbp Pecham and the decrees of Boniface', Studies in Church History, 2 (1965) 215-9. For the texts in question see Councils & synods, ii.662,685-6,834,845-8.

P.415 para.3: See also Brenda Bolton, 'The Council of London of 1342', Studies in Church History, 7 (1971) 146-60.

P.415 para.3: The C. of Lyon II (Sext 1.12.1) deprived bigamous clerks of their privilege and after this clerks were sometimes found by a lay jury to be bigamous and were, if convicted of felony, hanged without reference to the ordinary (cf. below,study XI 216-7,227 n.1). Although archbp Stratford condemned the practice in his first council (Wilkins, Concilia,ii.677 c.5),the chapter was dropped in his later legislation. The clergy,however,won their claim for reference to the ordinary to prove bigamy ('as in times past in cases of bastardy') in Stat.18 Edw.III st.3 c.2 (cf.Gabel, Benefit, pp.87-90).

II

A Monastic Letter of Fraternity to Eleanor of Aquitaine

THE document given below from a late thirteenth-century copy
is apparently unknown in any other form and has been hitherto
unnoticed. It indicates a connexion between Queen Eleanor and
Reading Abbey, throws light upon the liturgical practices at
Reading in the twelfth century, and provides an unusually early
example of a monastic letter of fraternity addressed to an individual. The letter must be dated by the abbacy of Roger,
1158–65,[1] of whom little is known. By it Eleanor receives the
assurance that at her death all shall be done for her as is
customarily done for a monk of Reading after his decease. The
queen died at a great age in 1204 and was buried like her second
husband within the abbey of Fontevrault. Here, and in other
churches besides Reading, the queen was remembered in prayer
by virtue of special agreements. Apart from those churches
which had promised prayers for the royal family in return for
a confirmation of privileges,[2] others had promised Eleanor to
maintain her anniversary. About 1168 the promise was made
by the canons of St. Hilaire of Poitiers and incorporated in a
charter from the queen,[3] and a twelfth-century note in a book of
St. Swithun's, Winchester, may well apply to Eleanor : ' regine
Anglie concessimus plenariam societatem '.[4] Eleanor's name
appears also in the obituary-kalendars of Canterbury and Rouen
cathedrals,[5] and of the abbey of Lire.[6] The list of churches which
commemorated the queen could probably be extended, but it is
doubtful whether any other document records these commemora-
tions so explicitly as does the letter from Reading.

The prayers of a religious community were often solicited by
secular clergy and layfolk in the early middle ages, and the

---

[1] Cf. *ante*, xxxvii. 400–1.

[2] E.g. 1154–66, St. Katherine's Priory, Lincoln (*Registrum Antiquissimum Lincoln.*,
ed. C. W. Foster, i. 121) ; 1155, the Hospitallers in England (*Recueil des actes d'Henri II*,
ed. L. Delisle, i. 98) ; 1156–9, the leprosary of La Flèche (*ibid.* i. 212) ; 1190, the
Templars in England (*Records of the Templars in England*, ed. B. A. Lees, pp. 139–41).

[3] *Recueil des actes d'Henri II*, i. 425–6.   [4] Brit. Mus. MS. Addit. 29436, fo. 45ʳ.

[5] J. Dart, *Cathedral Church of Canterbury*, app. p. xxxv ; *Recueil des historiens de la
France*, xxiii. 363.

[6] *Ibid.* xxiii. 471.

Durham *Liber vitae* is a splendid English memorial to the practice. The persons inscribed in this book participated in a general commemoration of the departed, and sometimes received the benefit of prayers while they were still alive. Almost any monastic cartulary containing documents of or before the twelfth century records grants to the house for which the benefactor was made ' particeps omnium beneficiorum que fiunt vel fient in ecclesia '. In the same period it became usual to celebrate by definite services the death of each regular inmate of a monastery, and this benefit was extended to monks of other houses by reciprocal confraternities. It was originally less common for other persons to obtain from a church the honour of a special obituary service and a special perpetual anniversary ; [1] but in course of time the system of fixed celebrations for individual monks, both in their own and in associated houses, was extended to those seculars, clerical and lay, who by their favour or donations merited the regard of the community. Gradually the names of distinguished layfolk appear alongside of those of abbots and monks in the obituary-kalendar.[2]

It seems likely that until the thirteenth century, at least, the secular who was admitted to fraternity by a monastery seldom received at his decease, and at subsequent anniversaries, all those honours paid to a professed monk. Even when the grant goes beyond the general statement of ' participation in all benefits ' to a promise of services ' as for a professed brother ', there is sometimes no mention of an anniversary. Frequently both obsequies and anniversaries are celebrated according to terms peculiar to the agreement.[3] Reading's grant to Eleanor would, therefore, seem to be exceptionally early and exceptionally extensive. Moreover, while such grants as this most often record, as the consideration, a substantial gift by the would-be confrater,[4] the Reading grant is represented merely as a response to the queen's request.

[1] Molinier, *Les obituaires français au moyen âge*, pp. 40–1.

[2] The examples given by the Rev. Prebendary Clark-Maxwell (' Some Further Letters of Fraternity ', *Archaeologia*, lxxix. 180–1) are of the fourteenth and fifteenth centuries ; likewise the long series printed in *Durham Obituary Rolls* (Surtees Soc.), pp. 106–20.

[3] Molinier, *Obituaires français*, p. 116. Cf. Clark-Maxwell, ' Some Letters of Confraternity ', *Archaeologia*, lxxv. 27, 30–1. This is also true of confraternities among monasteries. In sixty agreements in a list made at St. Mary's Abbey, York, about the end of the twelfth century, only the monks of four houses enjoy commemoration ' sicut de nostris ', together with nine individual prelates and monks of other houses (Brit. Mus. MS. Addit. 38816, fos. 37ʳ–39ʳ).

[4] The Bernardine customs of Cluny do indeed say that ' there are many faithful, as well poor as rich, who, after being brought into our Chapter, receive our fraternity ' (quoted, Clark-Maxwell, ' Some Letters ', p. 30), but this is not incompatible with the view that the admission of confraters, like that of oblate children and monks *ad succurrendum*, was usually accompanied by a gift.

Since our knowledge of early fraternity is mainly gained incidentally from charters, the form of this document is of interest.
The late Rev. Prebendary Clark-Maxwell only discovered one
English letter of fraternity earlier than the year 1200, and that
one, from Newhouse (O. Praem.), is at least twenty years later
than the Reading example.[1] A still earlier letter of fraternity
is worth noticing. It lacks the full details of the Reading document, and mentions the usual benefaction as a reason for the
grant. Stephen, count of Brittany, endowed the abbey of St.
Mary's, York, and a late twelfth-century copy preserves the grant
of fraternity which he received at some time between 1093 and
1112. Unlike the other twelfth-century letters it is in the form
of letters patent :

Stephanus sancte Marie Eboraci abbas primus omnibus sancte matris
ecclesie filiis orationes et salutem. Sciat fraternitas vestra quia ego communi consilio fratrum meorum hanc convenientiam pepigi comiti Stephano
pro soca Clistone quam ipse in elemosina ecclesie nostre dedit ; videlicet,
duos monachos in eadem ecclesia perpetualiter tenere, missam quoque
unam pro eo ipso vel vivente vel mortuo cantare, et anniversarium suum
unoquoque anno celebrare. Quam convenientiam omnibus successoribus
meis sicuti proficuum predicte elemosine habere voluerint, inviolabiliter
tenendam trado, et quantum mee potestati committitur firmiter precipio
quod si quis hanc sanctionem violare presumpserit, inobedientie reus sit.[2]

It has been remarked that the Reading letter gives fuller details
than most records of fraternity. This is the more interesting
since the abbey offered to Queen Eleanor the normal benefits of
a deceased monk. Reading was founded from Cluny, and may
have adopted the written customs of Cluny for the conduct of
its daily life,[3] but no customary of the English house is known to
exist. Nor does a confraternity-list of the abbey inform us of
the custom at the obsequies of its own monks.[4] The letter to

---

[1] Printed in ' Some Further Letters ', p. 187, from the original, Brit. Mus. Charters,
Harl. 43, B. 14. The earliest document in Clark-Maxwell's list is a grant by the abbots
of Cîteaux and Clairvaux of participation in the benefits and prayers of the Order,
1183–4 (' Some Letters ', p. 27). Moreover, only one grant from an English Cluniac
house is known : Lenton Priory, 1237 (*ibid.* p. 33 ; ' Some Further Letters ', pp. 179,
183).

[2] Brit. Mus. MS. Addit. 38816, fo. 34ᵛ, headed : ' De anniversario Stephani comitis
Brithannie '. The copy adds : ' Undecimo kal. Maii. Obit Stephanus comes Brithannie
et Hadewyse uxor eius. In conventu vinum tantum per abbatem de Kirkeby Stephan.'
The abbey ordinal gives the day of Count Stephen's anniversary as xi kal. Maii (*Chronicle
of St. Mary's Abbey, York* (Surtees Soc.), p. 112). Evidently it was celebrated by a
pittance not mentioned in the agreement. Where this MS. reads *Clistone, Cliftone* is
presumably intended. On the grant of Clifton to St. Mary's, York, see *Early Yorks.
Charters, IV,* ed. C. T. Clay, pp. 3–4, 131–2 ; for other grants by Count Stephen in
return for prayers see *ibid.* pp. 4, 9.

[3] A copy of *consuetudines cluniacenses* was in the abbey's library (*ante,* iii. 122).

[4] Brit. Mus. MS. Cotton Vespas. E. v, fos. 37 (formerly fo. 21) *seq.*, a thirteenth-
century list. Twenty-eight English and French monasteries are named, with varying

Eleanor comprises, as it were, a brief chapter of the missing customary. In general, the regulations correspond to those described elaborately in other English monastic records, but there are a few differences. Whereas for a monk of Reading there was a daily celebration of mass for a year and the daily allowance of his prebend to the almoner, elsewhere a shorter period of commemoration was probably the rule.[1] The Durham monks celebrated masses for thirty days for each of their brethren.[2] Some twelfth-century agreements for reciprocal intercession among monasteries arranged for the same period of thirty days, *tricenale* or *tricennarium*.[3] It was no new practice then : ' Tricenale quod instituit benedictus Gregorius ', says the York ordinal ; and the thirteenth-century customaries show the term of thirty days still commonly in use.[4] In the thirteenth century, at least, Reading celebrated for monks of Lewes ' tricenarium quem cantant vi sacerdotes unus post alterum, singuli quinque missas '.[5]

In the matter of almsgiving, the arrangement at Reading is unusual. One group of English abbeys in the twelfth century arranged by their bond of confraternity to provide a monk's prebend for thirty days ; [6] Reading likewise provided ' procurationem tricenariam ' at the death of the abbot of St. Wandrille ; [7] and St. Swithun's, Winchester, promised ' per xxx dies corredium unius monachi ' for Abbot Simon of Reading.[8] The Canterbury customary differs from the practice at Reading in allotting a sum

celebrations. The other side of the contract with St. Swithun's, Winchester, is found in Brit. Mus. MS. Addit. 29436, fo. 44ᵛ (quoted by Birch, *New Minster and Hyde Abbey*, p. 49 n.). While Savigny does not appear in the Reading list, the latter abbey subscribed to the mortuary roll of Abbot Vitalis, 1122–3 (Delisle, *Rouleaux mortuaires*, p. 343 ; *Rouleau mort. du bienheureux Vital*, pl. xlix).

[1] E.g. ' Constitutiones Lanfranci ', *Concilia*, ed. Wilkins, i. 358 *seqq.* ; *Customaries of St. Aug. Canterbury*, &c., ed. E. M. Thompson, i. 349 *seqq.*, 368 *seqq.* ; Customary and ordinal of York, *Chron. St. Mary's, York*, pp. 102 *seq.*, 121.

[2] *Liber vitae* (Surtees Soc., ed. A. H. Thompson), i. xix.

[3] Thus between Peterborough and Ramsey : ' a singulis sacerdotibus tricenale integrum persolvetur ' (Madox, *Formulare Anglicanum*, p. 82 ; cf. *ibid.* p. 301). Rather later, Bury and Westminster arrange to celebrate a *tricennarium* for every monk (Widmore, *Hist. of Westm. Abbey*, p. 233). The monks of St. Mary's, York, celebrated thirty masses for monks of Cerne, and arranged with Ramsey Abbey (before 1114) that ' abbates vero utriusque loci trigintale ex integro [habeant] ut mos est ' (Brit. Mus. MS. Addit. 38816, fos. 37ʳ, 37ᵛ) ; cf. *ibid.* (fo. 39ʳ) : ' Pro magistro Dionisio et Roberto monachis sancti Edmundi unusquisque sacerdos unam missam, ceteri vero psalmos qui ad eos pertinent. Insuper recipientur in primo tricennario quod fiet in ecclesia post auditum obitum eorum . . . Statutum est quod in tribus tricennariis que fiunt per annum pro familiaribus accipiet elemosinarius victum ad xii pauperes.'

[4] *Chron. St. Mary's, York*, pp. 13, 103, 121 (cf. S. Greg. Dialog. iv. 55) ; *Customaries of St. Aug. Canterbury*, &c., i. 351, 368.

[5] Brit. Mus. MS. Cotton Vesp. E. v, fo. 37ʳ.

[6] Dugdale-Caley, *Monasticon*, ii. 19 (Malmesbury, Evesham, Whitby, York). Cf. the practice at York, *supra*, n. 4. At Ramsey and Worcester the monks' prebends were paid for thirty days, the prelates' for a year (Clark-Maxwell, ' Some Letters ', p. 20).

[7] MS. Cotton Vesp. E. v, fo. 37ᵛ.　　　　　　[8] MS. Addit. 29436, fo. 46ʳ.

of money to the poor on the burial day, the thirtieth day, and anniversaries.[1]

It does not appear that the diet of the monks of Reading was improved on the occasion of obits in the twelfth century. The pittances with which burials, trentals, and anniversaries came to be celebrated in monasteries were more usual in the later middle ages.

About forty years had passed before the monks of Reading were called upon to use their intercessions and distribute their alms on Eleanor's behalf, according to the terms of this grant. The abbot from whom it emanated had long since died ; the abbey's cartularies contain no copy of the letter.[2] A kalendar, written probably in the second quarter of the thirteenth century, for the use of the almoner of Reading, is disquietening. Among the few non-monastic obits, King Henry II and King John appear, but Queen Eleanor's name is missing.[3]

Salisbury, Muniments of the Dean and Chapter,[4] Liber Evidentiarum C., no. 290 (p. 213, formerly fo. 95)

a. Dei gracia regine Angl' ducisse Normannie et Aquitanie et comitisse Andeg' Rogerus fratrum [5] Radingensium servus et humilis eorundem fratrum conventus in eternum regnare cum illo cuius regnum est omnium seculorum. Gaudemus et deo gracias agimus de religiosa cordis vestri devocione, regina venerabilis, quod inter opes et delicias regias nequaquam nobis anime vestre dominatur oblivio et inter tot et tanta regni temporalis negocia eterne pocius salutis et delectacionis geritis sollicitudinem. Inde est quod et nostre humilitati preces porrigere dignata est regia vestra sublimitas ut quod pro uno professorum [p. 214] nostrorum post obitum suum in domo nostra fieri solet, hoc vobis in fine concederemus. Non carebit [6] humilitas fructu suo ; satisfacimus ut iustum est beneplacito vestro ; et hoc ipsum quod sit sicut imperastis vobis significamus. Cum tamen omnium bonorum beneficiorum ecclesie nostre specialiter et inter primos tam in vita quam post transitum vestrum [7] de seculo vobis iure debetur [8] participacio, pro monacho nostro apud nos abeunte agitur in primis vigilia,[9] cum consuetis psalmis cantibus et lectionibus, deinde missa solempnis in conventu ; singuli sacerdotum tres missas privatim ei solvunt [10] et qui sacerdotes non sunt ter quinquaginta psalmos. Ipsa die pascuntur in hospicio pro anima defuncti xiii pauperes et ad communis elemosine augmentum dantur [11] centum panes. Ab ipsa die per totum

---

[1] *Cust. St. Aug. Canterbury, &c.,* i. 351.

[2] I am obliged to Professor Stenton for this information.

[3] MS. Cotton Vesp. E. v, fos. 11ᵛ *seqq.* Unfortunately no obits are entered after February in the kalendar of the Reading MS., Brit. Mus. Harl. 978, fos. 15ᵛ *seqq.*

[4] I am obliged to the dean and chapter of Salisbury for their kindness in facilitating my use of this manuscript and in permitting the publication of this document.

[5] MS. fratri.   [6] MS. cabit.   [7] MS. nostrum.   [8] MS. debatur.

[9] For a full description, see *Cust. St. Aug. Canterbury,* &c., i. 347 *seqq.,* 353 ; *Chron. St. Mary's, York,* pp. 102, 106.

[10] MS. solunt.   [11] MS. dotum.

annum unaquaque die sabati eligitur unus sacerdos et nominatur in capitulo qui cotidie in ipsa ebdomada missam pro eo celebret, et per totum annum exit de refectorio cotidie procuracio unius monachi que datur pro eo alicui maxime indigenti ad hoc electo. Completo anno rursus in capitulo sicut prima die absolvitur anima defuncti et anniversarium eius fit in conventu, scilicet, vigilia et missa solempnis, unusquisque sacerdotum unam pro eo missam celebrat, reliquorum [1] singuli quinquaginta psalmos. Nomen defuncti et dies anniversarius ex libro capituli annuatim in conventu recitatur et statim post capitulum cantantur pro eo et pro aliis fratribus et amicis nostris defunctis septem psalmi quos sancti patres ad hoc instituerunt,[2] et ipsa die singulis annis datur pro eo ad elemosinam procuracio unius monachi. Hec ergo omnia quemadmodum rogastis, o domina, concedimus et statuimus ex parte dei et nostra ut pro vobis agantur plenarie in ecclesia nostra cum vos dominus de presenti eduxerit. Concedimus quoque insuper et anniversarium [3] vestrum solempniter pro vobis in conventu perpetuo celebrandum. Conservent [4] vos et semper valere faciant [5] rex regum castaque misericordie mater angelorum regina virgo Maria, amen.

ADDITIONAL NOTE

P.492 line 15: Monasteries very often lost or suppressed the record of their obligations to observe anniversaries. The matter was fully discussed by August Molinier (above,p.489 n.1),133-50, and more diffusely by G.G.Coulton, Five centuries of religion, iii (Cambridge,1936),65-86,620-5. In this particular case, colour for discontinuance may be seen in the absence from the above letter of any suggestion that the queen had given a quid pro quo.

---

[1] MS. riliquorum.

[2] The seven penitential psalms: cf. ' Psalmi defunctorum ' (*Cust. St. Aug. Canterbury*, &c., i. 370 ; Molinier, *Obituaires français*, p. 118).

[3] MS. anniversirium.   [4] MS. Conserva et.   [5] MS. faciat.

III

Hubert Walter and Bologna

The early life of Hubert Walter, archbishop of Canterbury from 1193 to 1205, remains obscure despite the efforts of modern historians to recover the details. We do not know, within a decade, when he was born: two books written a few years ago respectively offered as probable dates c.1140-45 or earlier and c.1150-60.[1] We know from Hubert's own words that he was 'nurtured' or 'educated' in the household of his uncle, Ranulf Glanvill, but at what age or during which years we cannot tell. The uncertainty about Glanvill's early career makes matters worse.[2] The obscurity would lift to some extent if it could be proved that Hubert Walter added to the training in English law which he must have received in Glanvill's household and as Glanvill's colleague on the bench a background of academic study at Bologna. This was suggested by Mr. H. G. Richardson in his introduction to *The Memoranda Roll of 1 John*.[3] He supported this suggestion with one Bolognese record and one story told by Giraldus Cambrensis. Mr. Richardson's high authority naturally led others to accept the idea that Hubert Walter had formal training in the learned law, so that his Bolognese education was stated as a fact by Professor G. O. Sayles in *The Medieval Foundations of England*, by the late Dr. A. L. Poole, *From Domesday Book to Magna Carta*, by Professor Frank Barlow, *The Feudal Kingdom of England*. Dr. F. J. West, in *The Justiciarship in England*, mentioned the idea of a Bolognese training without actually subscribing to it. In 1956 I questioned the relevance of Mr. Richardson's 'evidence' in a footnote to my Ford Lectures, and repeated my objection more fully in *Hubert Walter* (18-19). Professor Charles Young, likewise, in his study of *Hubert Walter* (7 note 9), agreed in dismissing the Richardsonian argument. Meanwhile, Messrs. Richardson and Sayles reiterated Mr. Richardson's earlier view in *Law and Legislation from Æthelberht to Magna Carta* (Edinburgh 1966) 74, and in a footnote courteously chided me for seeming to contradict the evidence. I feel obliged to make a

---

[1] C. R. Cheney, *Hubert Walter* (Leaders of Religion Series; London 1967) 17; C. R. Young, *Hubert Walter, Lord of Canterbury and Lord of England* Durham N.C. 1968) 5. While preferring a date c.1155, Prof. Young allows that 'an earlier date of birth, although not likely, is by no means impossible'.

[2] See the interesting speculations of J. C. Russell, in 'Ranulf de Glanville', *Speculum* 45 (1970) 69-79.

[3] *The Memoranda Roll for the Michaelmas Term of the First Year of the Reign of King John, 1199-1200* . . . (Pipe Roll Soc. new series 21; 1943) lxii.

more reasoned justification of my long-standing doubts, the more so because the problem of Hubert Walter's legal education seems to remain an open question.[4]

Before looking at the facts of the case, it may be well to ask what we are looking for. Do those who speak of Hubert Walter as a student of Bologna mean simply that he passed a year or two there in elementary studies or claim that he had a prolonged and substantial training in the learned law and emerged equipped to appear as proctor or advocate in an ecclesiastical court? Since it has been inferred that 'Hubert appeared professionally before Alexander III' a full course in law seems to be what is in question.

The facts which have been adduced are two: (1) an entry in the Obituary of the Austin canons of San Salvatore and S. Maria de Reno at Bologna,[5] and (2) a story told by Giraldus in the *Gemma ecclesiastica* about an archbishop who appeared before Pope Alexander III 'in magna multorum et magnorum audientia'.[6] Let us examine these in turn, and first the entry in the Obituary. This record has long been recognized to be of very great interest to historians of Bolognese legal studies, since it contains the names of students extending over a long period, from about 1140 to about 1300. Among the names some are evidently English. And among these, under 12 July in the calendar, is the entry: 'a. d. 1205 obiit venerabilis frater Cantuariensis archiepiscopus Humbertus.'

In 1893 A. Allaria, writing about English scholars at Bologna,[7] identified nineteen names in the Obituary as of Englishmen, including Cardinal Boso and Archbishop Hubert. Six others of the nineteen were designated *magistri*. Four of the nineteen gave gifts 'pro opere Sancti Thome'. Now we know that a newer and grander altar had been built in San Salvatore in honour of St. Thomas of Canterbury as a result of scholars' subscriptions by the end of the twelfth century, though it still wanted consecration in June 1202.[8] It is tempting to assume that all of Allaria's nineteen Englishmen were scholars. But the Obituary, like all documents of the kind, is not confined to one class or profession.[9] There are to be found in it canons of S. Maria de Reno and their relatives, a monk of Vallombrosa, a master mason, various women. The Emperor Frederick I appears as *patronus*. One *Robertus anglicus* († 1254) is described as *frater noster*. One person (not English) is described as *scholaris*, and there are a good many *magistri*. The total number of names is very large: on a rough estimate there must be between 800 and 1000. The common denominator in the miscellaneous group is the *quid pro quo*. Benefactors were commem-

---

[4] Rudolf Hiestand, in *Histor. Zeitschrift* 212 (1970) 661.

[5] J. C. Trombelli, *Memorie istoriche concernenti le due Canoniche di S. Maria de Reno e di S. Salvatore insieme unite* (Bologna 1752) 343. The obituary (317-: 55) is excerpted in M. Sarti and M. Fattorini, *De claris archigymnasii Bononiensis professoribus* (2nd ed. Bologna 1888-96) 2.285-8, but this entry is omitted.

[6] Giraldus Cambrensis, *Opera*, ed. J. S. Brewer et al. (Rolls Series 1861-91) 2.345.

[7] A. Allaria, in *Dublin Review* 112 (1893) 66-83.

[8] Trombelli 398; Allaria 83; *Letters of Pope Innocent III concerning England and Wales*, ed. C. R. and Mary G. Cheney (Oxford 1967) no. 422 (pp. 68, 230-31).

[9] Cf. Trombelli 319.

orated in return for some gift, which is often recorded. No consideration appears against the names of some canons or of the *fratres*. The *fratres* had entered into confraternity with one or other of the establishments and had doubtless compounded at the time of entry for their commemoration after death. Archbishop Hubert was one of the *fratres*. This offers no presumption that he figures here because he was a scholar.

True, many English scholars went to Bologna, and it is reasonable to assume that some of Allaria's nineteen Englishmen were scholars. But Bologna lay on a main road to Rome. It was an important mercantile centre. An altar of St. Thomas might well attract the visits and offerings of well-to-do Englishmen who halted there for different reasons. If we associate the English element in the Obituary with the altar of St. Thomas, we may point to Archbishop Hubert's devotion to the cult, as evidenced at Acre, c.1191-93 and in his later proposal for a chapel in Lambeth in honour of the martyr. It may also be worth noting that the archbishop was a *confrater* of the English house of Austin canons at Merton.

We have no record that Hubert Walter visited Bologna apart from the evidence of this Obituary, but it is possible to suggest a time. In Spring 1193, when he was bishop of Salisbury, returning from the Third Crusade, he travelled from Rome to find his captive king in Germany, and may have passed that way. He certainly was not in Italy later than this, and he is unlikely to have spent any length of time there in the ten years before the Crusade, when he is intermittently recorded in England. But, we may ask, was a personal visit needed to secure a place in a confraternity? Surely not. May not this entry simply mean that Archbishop Hubert made some gift or bequest to the church which earned him the title and privilege of *frater*? Or had some one of his English friends made an offering on his behalf? We know that Simon de Camera, bishop of Chichester, in 1207 bequeathed a hundred marks for the soul of his former master, the archbishop.[10] To sum up, the appearance of Hubert Walter's name in this list is compatible with a hypothesis that he was once a student at Bologna, but by itself it is not evidence.

A story of Giraldus Cambrensis in the *Gemma ecclesiastica* tells of an illiterate archbishop who displayed his ignorance of Latin in the presence of Pope Alexander III.[11] Since the whole object of this chapter of the *Gemma* is to show the deficiencies of prelates, this story cannot conceivably relate to Archbishop Hubert, who at the time of Alexander III's death in 1181 did not hold any ecclesiastical dignity, still less the archbishopric. The term 'miserabilem antistitem', which Giraldus uses, could not fit him. Nor can Giraldus be blamed for suggesting that his arch-enemy was the subject of this particular anecdote. The whole chapter consists of a dozen *exempla* about various exalted persons, regulars as well as secular clergy. This is the ninth story. The sixth story is 'de archiepiscopo' and nos. 7 and 8 'de archiepiscopo eodem'; and since stories 7 and 8 are laid at Archbishop Hubert's door in the *De invectionibus* (1.5),[12]

---

[10] *Rotuli litterarum clausarum*, ed. T. D. Hardy (Record Commission 1833-34) 1.92 and Cheney, *Hubert Walter* 177.

[11] Giraldus Cambrensis, *Opera* 2.345.

[12] Ibid. 3.29-30.

84

all three must be directed against him. No. 9, with which we are concerned, is also an 'exemplum de archiepiscopo', but this time not 'de archiepiscopo *eodem*'; and it is followed by *exempla* about a bishop, a prior, an abbot, and a bishop who is recognizably William Longchamp. There is no reason to suppose that the subject of no. 9 was the same as the subject of the three preceding stories. Nor did Pollock and Maitland or Kuttner and Rathbone, when they referred to this chapter of the *Gemma* for tales about Hubert's illiteracy, countenance this particular identification or infer that 'Hubert appeared professionally before Alexander III'.[13]

In the absence of genuine evidence for Hubert Walter's sojourn as a student at Bologna, we can only fall back upon conjecture and probability. So little is known of his early years that a Bolognese period is not absolutely excluded. But no contemporary who wrote about Hubert ever breathed a word about it. He never received the title of *magister*. His links with the king's court in the 1180's, his poor reputation as a scholar, give no support. We need tangible evidence before entertaining the idea.

Corpus Christi College,
Cambridge.

---

[13] See F. Pollock and F. W. Maitland, *History of English Law* (2nd ed. Cambridge 1898) 1.133 and S. Kuttner and Eleanor Rathbone in *Traditio* 7.323, invoked by Richardson and Sayles, *Law and Legislation* 74 n. 2.

IV

Levies on the English clergy for the poor and for the king, 1203

A t the turn of the twelfth-thirteenth centuries taxation in England, apart from scutage, was exceptional.[1] It was only tentatively applied in different ways to various classes of people, with procedures which are never clearly recorded and results which are mostly unknown. The policy was, it seems, hesitant and the action unpopular; so that, even though the tax on income and movables of 1207 (on which we are better informed) was amazingly profitable, King John's government never attempted anything like it again. One of the most difficult problems confronting the civil government was how to tap the wealth of the Church. And here the modern historian is short of evidence on what the Crown attempted and what it achieved.

The attempt in the year 1203 to get money from the clergy is of all occasions the most obscure, and historians have generally shied away from the question. The government decided to tax the land-owning classes by a fractional levy of one seventh; whether it was a levy on revenue or movables remains doubtful.[2] The land-owners presumably included the bishops, cathedral churches, and religious houses. But was the tax more far-reaching? The records of chancery and exchequer do not help, beyond showing that religious houses did indeed pay *auxilia* and *dona*.[3] The chroniclers are mostly silent. The seventh is, however, mentioned in related notices by writers of Bury St Edmunds and St Albans. As elsewhere in their work, they reflect a common source, but the picturesque account of Roger Wendover of St Albans is not wholly matched by the Bury annalist. The latter simply says: 'Money was collected throughout England for an aid to the king (*in regis auxilium*), a seventh part of all revenues (*reddituum*) of laymen and conventual monasteries.'[4] Wendover, with rhetorical colouring, tells

1. See G. L. Harriss, *King, Parliament and Public Finance to 1369* (Oxford, 1975), ch. I: 'The origins of national taxation.' I am grateful to Professor J. C. Holt for helpful comments on a draft of the above note, and must particularly thank Mr M. G. Snape for help with the Durham manuscript. Sir Richard Southern kindly assured me that the letter from Archbishop Hubert does not occur in collections of Peter of Blois's correspondence and that in his view the style does not suggest that Peter composed it.

2. S. K. Mitchell, *Studies in taxation under John and Henry III* (Yale Univ. Press, 1914), pp. 61–3, and *Taxation in medieval England* (Yale, 1951), p. 133; S. Painter, *The reign of King John* (Johns Hopkins Press, 1949), pp. 130–1; J. C. Holt, *The Northerners* (Oxford, 1961), p. 147.

3. *Pipe Roll 5 John* (Pipe Roll Soc. n.s. 16), *passim* for 'dona'. The Dorset membrane (p. 160) lists 'auxilia' of abbots and priors in the county.

4. *Ungedr. anglo-norm. Geschichtsquellen*, ed. F. Liebermann (Strassburg, 1879), p. 142; Taxster in *Flor. Wigorn. chronicon*, ed. B. Thorpe (Eng. Hist. Soc. 1848–9), ii. 165.

us more, not all of it correct. King John, he says, returned from France on 6 December and, accusing his earls and barons of deserting him in Normandy, took from them 'a seventh of their movables (*mobilium*), nor did he in this robbery refrain from laying hands on conventual and parochial churches. He had Archbishop Hubert of Canterbury to act for him in the matter of the church property, Geoffrey fitz-Peter in the matter of lay property; and these two spared no one in carrying out their orders.'[1] If Wendover is right, the tax was levied on movables and the parochial clergy were mulcted as well as the monks; but it would be rash to accept his story without corroboration. Uncertain as we are, it is at least worth noting a tax which the king imposed at about the same time in the Channel Islands. Letters patent of 13 August 1203 to the bailiff of Jersey and Guernsey ordered that bishops, abbots, abbesses, and clergy, knights, vavassors and others, who had revenue and tenements in the islands should give, for defence of the islands, a fifth of their revenues (*reddituum*) for a year or of their fees or alms.[2] In England, four years later, the clergy were again asked for a tax, and made heavy weather about consent to the levy of a 'thirteenth'. In 1207 bishops eventually saved their faces, if not their pockets, by paying substantial *dona* in order to be quit 'of the aid provided in the council at Oxford'. What was done about the rectors of parishes is unknown.[3] Likewise in 1203; we do not find any concrete evidence for the extraction of money from the parochial clergy.

Two other records do, however, relate to levies on the clergy in 1203. They confirm that on this as on previous occasions Hubert Walter was the royal agent to extract from the Church a contribution to the country's needs at a crucial juncture in foreign affairs. They also show another side of his activity, otherwise totally unrecorded and of exceptional interest.

Our first source is a letter from Bishop Herbert Poore of Salisbury to Archbishop Hubert, found among the miscellaneous archives of the archbishopric which silted up in the muniments of the prior and convent of Canterbury after Hubert's death.[4] Although published by R. L. Poole in 1901, it has been neglected by most of the historians of the period.[5] In it the bishop answers a letter, or letters (*litteris* is

1. Wendover, *Flores. hist.* (ed. H. O. Coxe) (Eng. Hist. Soc. 1841–4), iii. 173.
2. *Rotuli litt. patentium*, ed. T. D. Hardy (Record Comm. 1835), p. 33*b*.
3. See *Councils and Synods* (ed. F. M. Powicke and C. R. Cheney) (Oxford, 1964), II. i. 5–9.
4. Canterbury D. and C. Muniments, Ch. Ch. letters, vol. 2, no. 225, printed in *Hist. MSS Comm. Reports on various collections*, i. (1901), 233–4. The protocol, not printed by Poole, reads: 'Venerabili patri in Christo H. dei gratia Cantuariensi archiepiscopo totius Anglie primati H. divina permissione Sar' episcopus salutem et tam devotam quam debitam in omnibus reverenciam.' On p. 234, line 16, for *nostre* read *vestre*.
5. It is summarized by C. R. Young, *Hubert Walter, lord of Canterbury and lord of England* (Durham, N. Carolina, 1968), pp. 92–93, who does not discuss its significance, and is briefly mentioned by C. R. Cheney, *From Becket to Langton* (Manchester, 1956), p. 145, n. 3.

ambiguous), on several topics. In the first place, it seems, the archbishop has asked the bishop of Salisbury to admonish the clergy of his diocese, both resident and non-resident, to give poor-relief according to precise instructions ('secundum certam formam in eisdem litteris prescriptam'). He has also ordered the bishop to convene the said clergy and induce them to grant an aid (*auxilium*) to the king. The bishop replies that he has received some assurances on almsgiving, but has hesitated over the second matter (the king's aid) because he cannot secure the presence in rural chapters of even a tenth part of those clergy who have charge of the churches in his diocese. Those present comprise annual vicars together with relatively few parsons and perpetual vicars. They refuse to give him a definite answer without the greater and better part ('maiori et saniori parte') of those absent. Will the archbishop therefore advise by letter what he decides should be done to induce or compel the absentees? So far, without this advice, the bishop has been unable to take action against so many, who are too far distant to be assembled in so short a time; but in this, as in other matters, he will be prompt in compliance as is proper (*secundum deum*) when he hears what the archbishop proposes.[1]

The second source, which is printed below, has apparently passed unnoticed. It only survives, to my knowledge, in a formulary and legal miscellany written soon after 1300 and given to Durham cathedral priory by brother William of Gisburne.[2] It purports to be a letter from H. (Hubert Walter) archbishop of Canterbury to G. (Geoffrey Muschamp) bishop of Coventry. If the initials are correct the outside limits of dating are 21 June 1198 × 13 July 1205. The writer affects a *style ampoulé* which is rare in the chancery-products of the archbishops of Canterbury in this age, and for elegance it does not compare with letters of John of Salisbury or Peter of Blois, who had written in the archbishops' service. A homiletic preamble occupies more than half the space. It draws morals from the alternation of adversity and prosperity, famine and plenty, and then announces that famine and other ills have increased of late because works of mercy are neglected. The archbishop is therefore providing 'with the advice of his brethren' that each bishop in his diocese shall exhort clergy and laity to help the poor and engage more than usually in fasts and prayers and other good works. Specifically the prelates have provided that resident clergy are to be urged and, if need be, compelled to help the poor in their parishes lest they die of starvation. Non-resident clergy are to be treated likewise, and made to give a quarter of their revenue

1. The rest of Bishop Herbert's letter is taken up with replies to the archbishop's complaints about his part in the election of the abbess of Wilton and about opprobrious words attributed to Mr Roger of Winsham.

2. The manuscript includes among other things the Summa of Richard de Pophis, letters of Peter de Vineis, etc. Archbishop Hubert's letter is immediately followed by the letter of Pope Gregory X to the Emperor Michael Palaeologus from the Council of Lyon, 28 July 1274 (Potthast 20869).

in alms. By a rather abrupt and clumsy transition ('Propterea . . .') the mandate orders – 'sicut alias statutum est' – special prayers to be said daily in the mass, and processions to be held every Friday for the Holy Land, for the king who is unjustly beset by enemies, for the peace of the Church and the realm, for good weather and good crops. Thus may God's anger be averted and peace and plenty ensue.

Can this be regarded as a genuine mandate of Archbishop Hubert? The company it keeps in the only known copy is not reassuring. On the other hand, it was not unusual for genuine letters of political or ecclesiastical interest to be incorporated in formularies and letter-books along with documents of much later date, both genuine and spurious. The *Liber epistolaris* of Richard de Bury furnishes examples.[1] In favour of taking this text seriously we may say that it is hard to see what purpose would have been served by inventing it at a later date. Even granted that the motives of forgers and writers of fiction are inscrutable, comparison with the letter of Bishop Herbert Poore described above is a very strong argument for confidently assigning this letter to the same period. One is forced to conclude that this is a mandate sent out – or the draft of a mandate intended to be sent out – by Archbishop Hubert to the suffragans of his province and probably to the province of York.

Something of the sort, if not precisely in this form, drew the bishop of Salisbury's response, and it throws light on the circumstances which he took for granted. We learn from this letter why the archbishop made his appeal to the beneficed clergy to help the poor. This, incidentally, confirms the date which we assign to Bishop Herbert's letter because of its reference to an aid for the king. 1203 is the year. In 1203 it is recorded by several chroniclers that there was famine in the land. The Cistercian annals of Margam, in south Wales, say that this produced a dreadful mortality among the poor. The Waverley annals say the same and add that shortages of food drove the monks of Waverley to dispersal in other monasteries. Ralph of Coggeshall speaks of severe floods in many parts of England in April. This was not just an exclusively Cistercian rumour. The Tewkesbury annals speak of serious famine, with corn at an exorbitant price.[2] At Michaelmas the exchequer took account of the trouble, for the sheriff

---

1. Ed. N. Denholm-Young (Roxburghe Club, 1950). Another similar miscellany from Durham is described by C. R. Cheney, in 'Law and letters in fourteenth-century Durham: a study of C.C.C.ms. 450', *Bull. John Rylands Univ. Libr.* lv (1972), 60–85.

2. *Annales monastici* (Rolls series), i. 26, 57; ii. 255, *Chron. R. Coggeshall* (Rolls series), p. 142. This was not, it seems, a year of general dearth on the Continent, though shortages of wine led to a rise in prices at Reims. F. Curschmann, *Hungernöte im Mittelalter* (Leipziger Studien, vi, 1900), p. 161. Figures drawn from a rather small sample of prices for grain and stock in England in these years agree with the non-quantitative evidence cited above: see D. L. Farmer, 'Some price fluctuations in Angevin England', *Econ. Hist. Rev.* (2nd series), ix (1956–7), 34–43. 'During the first decade of the thirteenth century,' says Mr Farmer, 'prices rose to levels which were rarely to be exceeded until the great famine of 1314–16' (p. 39).

of Gloucester accounted for feeding 100 poor people at Gloucester, and 200 at Bristol, by order of the king's writ, from 20 April to 1 August. Over the same period similar sums were paid to the poor as royal alms in Devon and Cornwall.[1] This royal benefaction was renewed and extended to other regions in May–August 1204,[2] but never in the later years of the reign. The exceptional shortage in 1203 had brought severe after-effects in the following spring and summer. But if we ask what were the results of the bishops' admonitions, revealed in these two letters, we come up against a wall of silence.

That the letter to the bishop of Coventry and the letter from the bishop of Salisbury are connected seems undeniable, but it is disconcerting to find no trace in the former of a demand for a clerical *auxilium*. The mandate for prayers and processions does indeed refer to the attacks made upon the king by his enemies. This chimes in with the conditions of the year 1203, when the assault of Philip Augustus on the Angevin power approached a crisis. But the letter proposes no material help from the clergy: nothing beyond pious practices. Assuming that it survives in the form in which it was dispatched to the dioceses, it must surely have been accompanied or followed by some explicit instruction to the bishops, however delicately worded, to levy an aid from the parochial clergy. One cannot date these letters with any exactness. Archbishop Hubert was in England throughout 1203, but the known occasions when he met his suffragans are few and the possible times many. The records of distributions to the poor, on the pipe rolls, shows that food-shortage had made itself felt, at least in the west country, by the middle of April 1203.

One final comment on this obscure episode: the juxtaposed demands on the clergy, for almsgiving and for taxpaying, which in a modern context seem to be totally distinct, did not appear in that light at the beginning of the thirteenth century. Both arose from the moral obligation binding the clergy to come to the pecuniary aid of the unfortunate; the canon law took account of this duty to perform a work of mercy. A letter of Pope Gelasius I, constantly quoted by canonists down to Gratian (*Decretum*, C. 12 q. 2 c. 27), required the assignment of a quarter of clerical income to poor-relief, and Archbishop Hubert's letter appears to refer to that canon. As regards taxpaying, the demands of lay governments had recently led to legislation on the subject of taxation in the Third Lateran Council (1179). It was mainly concerned to denounce extortion from the clergy, but it declared that they should contribute to the pecuniary needs of lay princes and magistrates if bishops decided that the needs of the community as a whole justified a voluntary gift (c. 19: *Extra*, 3.49.7). As Gabriel Le Bras pointed out, in his first published work, the

1. *Pipe Roll 5 John*, pp. 58–59, 71, 80.
2. *Pipe Roll 6 John* (Pipe Roll Soc. n.s. 18), pp. 80, 94, 106, 121, 146, 187, 248.

council drew no distinction between the claims made on the clergy's charity by destitute individuals and those made by an unfortunate lay government.[1]

Cambridge

Durham, Cathedral Library MS C. iv. 24, fo. 101ʳ. s. xiii/xiv:

H dei gratia Cantuariensis archiepiscopus venerabili in Christo fratri G. Coventrensi etc. Dominus ac redemptor noster Iesus Christus qui nos omnes salvos fieri cupit, multis modis ad benefaciendum nos allicit et ad ea que salutis sunt incitat et invitat. Nunc enim prospera largiendo mulcet ut attrahat, nunc eadem subtrahendo et per adversa flagellando minatur ut convertat. Interdum namque beata prestat cum pace tempora, secundat vota, conservat sanitates corporum, et frugum ac fructuum fructuosa pietate tribuit habundantiam, ut sic miser homo creatorem et redemptorem suum saltem per beneficia recognoscens se coram eo in gratiarum actiones devotus incurvet et per bona opera placere studeat a quo habet ut in tanta prosperitate et habundantia letus vivat. Interdum vero quia hiis inpinguatus miser homo recalcitrat, et ex prosperitate nimia infatuatus et elatus deum deserit et servit operibus tenebrarum ut ei vexatio tribuat intellectum,[2] in eum pius dominus indignationis sue flagella convertit ut qui in prosperitate nesciebat bene agere, saltem per tribulationem et angustiam discat ad dominum proclamare, sicut scriptum est*ᵃ*:[3] et clamaverunt ad dominum cum tribularentur et dominus necessitatibus eorum liberavit eos. Sicut autem ne longe petamus exempla circa nos actum cernimus dum tam preterita quam presentia tempora contemplamur. Vidimus enim, vidistis et vos, olim tempora respectu modernorum plurimum beata, quando ex divini muneris gratia et arridebat terris fertilitas et pace populus letabatur, quando in habundantia dabat terra germen suum, et pomis arbores replebantur*ᵇ*,[4] quando non capiebant pre multitudine granum horrea et vino torcularia redundabant,[5] in quibus divine largitatis muneribus, quia servare nescivimus mensuram et modum, immo de multitudine divitiarum nostrarum incaute gloriantes[6] errare cepimus et peccare, in usum vitiorum stulte que ad exercitium virtutum acceperamus, invenerunt nos mala quorum non est numerus. Sicut enim iam sentire possimus et videre, data est terris peccatis nostris exigentibus pro fertilitate sterilitas, pro habundantia panis et vini fames valida, bella pro pace, pro longitudine vite magna mortalitas et dierum nostrorum abbreviatio. Set cur multiplicata sunt tot mala in terra nisi pro peccatis et negligentiis nostris, cur in sterilitatem est conversa fertilitas nisi quia nos in operibus caritatis steriles sumus dum proximos nostros fame videmus interire nec eis cum possimus subvenimus, cur nunc singulis annis frugibus et fructibus fraudamur nisi quia diebus istis plusquam prius fraus et dolus inundaverunt super terram, cur bella

1. *L'immunité réelle* (Thèse de doctorat, 1920), p. 63. See also Harriss, *op. cit.* p. 63 on the contemporary view of taxes being justified on the plea of necessity, or emergency, and J. W. Baldwin, *Masters, Princes, and Merchants* (Princeton, 1970), i. 237, ii. 172, on the right of prelates to compel their clergy to give alms to the poor in times of scarcity.

2. *Cf.* Isa. 28:19. 3. *Cf.* Ps. 106:13.
4. *Cf.* Lev. 26:4. 5. *Cf.* Prov. 3:10.
6. *Cf.* Ps. 48:7.

seviunt et unde nunc tanta mortalitas nisi quia in pace deo non servivimus nec intelleximus ut debuimus nos per eum vivere et valere. Verum si sapimus saltem per hec flagella ad dominum convertemur, et qui per iniquitates nostras eum offendimus de cetero per caritatis opera quibus potissime placatur et per nostre vite emendationem eum^c studebimus complacere. Sic enim Ninivite, cum eis denuntiatum per prophetam quod eorum civitas infra quadraginta dies subverteretur,[1] induerunt se cilicio et spergentes cinerem super capita sus in ieiunio et fletu divinam a se indignationem averterunt. Querit enim salutem nostram pius dominus, et quia nos diligit ideo^d verberat et castigat.[2] Castigat enim pater filium quem diligit. Quapropter non simus hiis similes de quibus dictum est: percussi eos et non doluerunt,[3] set revertamur ad dominum et custodiamus vias eius, subveniamusque pro posse proximis nostris fame pereuntibus ne nobis quod absit mors eorum imputetur. Scriptum est enim: pasce fame morientem. Quisquis enim pascendo hominem servare poteris^e, si non paveris occidisti. Sic autem facientibus miserebitur pius dominus dabitque nobis pacem pro bellis, pro dolore gaudium, pro inopia copiam, et animas inanes satiabit dominus bonis.[4] Verum quia nobis qui dominici gregis curam suscepimus non sufficet solum bene velle nisi et subditos ad bene agendum verbo et exemplo studeamus invitare, de consilio fratrum nostrorum providimus ut singuli per diocesim suam tam clericos quam laicos ad subveniendum pauperibus et ad ieiuniis et orationibus aliisque bonis operibus plus solito insistendum diligentius exhortentur. Et ut clericorum exemplo alii efficacius ad pietatis officia incitentur, de eorumdem fratrum nostrorum consilio et assensu est provisum ut clerici apud beneficia sua residentes ad subveniendum pro posse suo pauperibus parochianis suis et egenis ne fame pereant diligenter moneantur, et ubi salubrem admonitionem recipere noluerunt salubriter compellantur. Hii vero qui non resident ad quartam^f partem reddituum pauperibus viduis et egenis pupillis et orphanis misericorditer^g prestandam attentius similiter moneantur, et opportune et importune ad hoc modis omnibus reducantur, arguendo, obsecrando, increpando et si necesse fuerit discrete compellantur.[5] Murmurare autem vel egre ferre non debent si Christo ad eorum hostia mendicanti quartam refundant, qui eis totum dedit, set nec de rigore constitutionis huius conqueri nec sub sarcina ista quasi gravi suspirare debent, cum antiquis canonibus nullo canone quoad hunc [fo. 101v] articulum abrogatis cautum^h fuerit ut quarta pars obventionum ecclesiarum annuatim^j pauperibus distribueretur. Que est igitur invidia si quod singulis annis pauperibus dari statutum fuit vel semel hoc tempore necessitatis tribuatur. Propterea pro terra Ierosolomitana, pro rege qui ab inimicis suis iniuste impugnatur ut nostis, pro pace ecclesie et regni, pro serenitate aeris et terre fertilitate fiant sicud alias statutum est singulis diebus speciales^k orationes in missa, necnon in qualibet ebdomoda sexta feria tam a viris religiosis quam aliis ecclesiasticis viris fiant processiones, nudis pedibus, cum orationibus, disciplinis, ieiuniis, aliis operibus deo gratis, ut sic placatus

1. *Cf.* Jonah 3:4. 2. *Cf.* Heb. 2.6.
3. *Cf.* Jer. 5:3. 4. *Cf.* Ps. 106:9.
5. A quarter was required from unlicensed absentees by diocesan statutes of Worcester, 1240 (*Councils & Synods*, ii. 314, *c.* 70, *cf.* Salisbury, 1257–68, *ibid.* ii. 564, *c.* 38). The legate Ottobuono generalized the rule and provided an incentive for archdeacons to enforce it in the Council of Lambeth, 1268 (*ibid.* ii. 758, *c.* 9).

altissimus indignationem suam avertat a nobis, nobisque simul et regi ac regno pacem tribuat et frugum ac fructuum habundantiam. Quapropter cum quod ad honorem dei et pauperum subventionem necnon ad utilitatem puplicam de communi ut diximus fratrum nostrorum consilio provisum est velimus ut iustum est generaliter observari, fraternitati vestre mandamus, monemus et in peccatorum remissionem iniungimus quatinus hanc nostram et fratrum nostrorum provisionem salubrem per diocesim vestram[1] firmiter ab omnibus observari faciatis, provisuri attentius ut sic quatenus ad vos pertinet hoc opus dei exequi studeatis quod inde merito debeatis tam apud deum quam apud homines commendari. Valete.

a	est *repeated* MS	*g*	misciditer MS
b	replebebantur MS	*h*	tantum MS
c	cum MS	*j*	annuatim MS
d	ide MS	*k*	spūales MS
e	poterius MS	*l*	nostram MS
f	quartem MS		

V

The Papal Legate and English Monasteries in 1206

PAPAL legates in thirteenth-century England received rough treatment from the pens of English chroniclers. Not in Matthew Paris
alone, but in the majority of monastic writers, we find harsh words
about the proud foreigners who came to drain England of her
wealth. We know well enough that this does not fairly represent
the truth, that in fact papal legates were notable instruments of
reform in the English church as well as tax-gatherers ; but the
evidence of their activities is not always very clear. Even the
work of the celebrated Otto and Ottobono for the reform of
English monasteries is not well known. The appearance of a set
of legatine injunctions consequent upon the visitation of St.
Mary's Abbey, York, may be thought to justify the collection of
all available evidence about their author and his work in England.
In the sum it is scanty. The visitation took place in the year 1206
and the legate was master John of Ferentino, cardinal deacon
of S. Maria in via lata.[1]

---

[1] He was elevated to the cardinalate in 1205 and died in 1216 (Eubel, *Hierarchia
catholica* (1898), i. 4). He is called indifferently Ferentinus, Florentinus, de Ferentino.
He is not to be identified (as in *Annales Monastici* (Rolls Series), iii. 28–9 notes) with the
abbot of St. Giovanni de Casamari, legate in England in 1203, who was not a cardinal.
The records of the cardinal's mission are mostly summarized in H. Tillmann, *Die*

The legate arrived in England (May 1206[1]) at a time of stress, when Hubert Walter was only a few months dead and the dispute of factions in the Canterbury election was at its height. Innocent III had on 30 March quashed the proceedings of all parties, postponing the hearing of the case until 1 October.[2] King John replied to this on 26 May. Within ten days he sailed for France, to hold together the little that remained of his vanishing continental dominions. He only returned to England in December.

Apart from references connecting the legate John with particular monasteries, to be mentioned in due course, we have to rely mainly upon the account of his mission given by Roger of Wendover. Wendover says that John Ferentinus came into England in 1206 :

traversing the country he accumulated a great sum of money and at length held a council at Reading on the morrow of the feast of St. Luke the evangelist.[3] This done and his baggage bestowed with great care and diligently guarded, the hasty traveller betook himself to the sea and bade England farewell.[4]

To this statement the *Historia Minor* of Matthew Paris adds the reason why the legate held a council : ' ne nihil fecisse in spiritualibus videretur '.[5] The *Brut y Tywysogion* says that here the legate ' confirmed the church law throughout the whole kingdom '.[6] But unfortunately the details of the business seem to be utterly unrecorded.

The object of the legate's visit to England is not clear, unless we take Wendover's view that Cardinal John came to collect money. That this was part of his business is certainly probable ;[7] but at all events he was concerned with other matters as well. The first reference to his legateship is in the register of Inno-

---

päpstlichen Legaten in England bis zur Beendigung der Legation Gualas (1218) (Bonn, 1926), 92–3.

[1] Winchester annals (*Annales Monastici*, ii. 79) ; ' post Pascha ' [2 April] in the Worcester annals (*Ann. Mon.* iv. 394).

[2] Potthast, *Regesta pontificum*, nos. 2732–5.

[3] [19 October] : thus the Worcester and the St. Edmund's annals (*Ann. Mon.* iv. 394 and Liebermann, *Ungedruckte a.-n. Gesch.-quellen*, p. 145). The Tewkesbury, Dunstable and St. Albans chronicles say ' die S. Lucae ' (*Ann. Mon.* i. 58, iii. 29 ; Liebermann, *op. cit.*, 168).

[4] Roger of Wendover, *Flores* (Rolls Series), ii. 14 (cf. Matthew Paris, *Chronica Majora* (Rolls Series), ii. 495). Ciacconi says without giving his authority that the legate stayed in England for two years (*Vita pontificum*, etc. ed. Oldoini (Rome, 1677), ii. 24), but the cardinal subscribed a papal letter on 28 June 1207 (Potthast, p. 466). Moreover the Winchester-Waverley annals say that he stayed in England ' circueundo ecclesias Anglicanas a Pascha usque ad festum Sancti Martini (11 November) ' (Liebermann, *op. cit.*, 184).

[5] *Historia Anglorum* (Rolls Series), ii. 107 (cf. *Flores Hist.*, Rolls Series, ii. 132).

[6] Rolls edition, p. 261.

[7] Cf. Waverley Annals, *s.a.* 1205 (*Ann. Mon.* ii. 257), and the king's prohibition of a clerical meeting ' super Romescotto solvendo ' in May 1207 (wrongly dated in *Foedera* (1816), i. 94 and Wilkins, *Concilia*, i. 514; cf. *Rot. Lit. Pat.* (1835), p. 72 a, and Hardy's Itinerary of King John, and Tillmann, *op. cit.*, p. 93, note 117).

cent III ; as early as 1 February 120⅚ the pope ordered him to restrain King John from molesting the dean of Salisbury, and other clergy and laymen ; and Ciacconi declares (probably on no better authority) that this was the object of his mission.[1] Another letter of the pope addressed to the legate on 25 March 1206 ordered the latter to give leave to the prior and convent of Glastonbury to elect an abbot.[2] At this time the see of Bath was vacant and the Glastonbury monks fought (in the end successfully) against the union of the bishopric and their abbey. A month later (23 April) letters testimonial in favour of Jocelin of Wells, bishop-elect, were sent by the English bishops and King John to the cardinal legate, as well as to the pope himself.[3] The cardinal had not yet arrived in England, if we may trust the dating of a papal letter to which he subscribed at the Lateran, dated 4 May 1206.[4]

These details cannot be said to illuminate the legate's work very much. A few other references, however, of some importance, show him to have been concerned with the state of English monasteries.

On 10 June 1206 the pope commissioned him to inquire into the condition of the priory of St. Petroc at Bodmin (Cornwall), with a view to granting the convent's request that it should be converted into an abbey.[5] The legate apparently did not agree with the convent's view of the matter, and St. Petroc's remained a priory to the end of its days. No further reference to the cardinal's legateship occurs in the papal registers. Turning to English records we find that the legate, during his sojourn in England, inspected some charters of St. Augustine's, Canterbury,[6] and visited Eve-sham Abbey, Ramsey Abbey,[7] and St. Mary's, York. Dr. Helene Tillmann suggests the possibility that Cardinal John was the legate who rejected the complaints of the monks of St. Albans against their abbot ; it cannot have been Guala, as stated in the *Gesta Abbatum* (Rolls edition, i. 252), but it may have been Nicholas of Tusculum.[8] From the Dunstable annals we learn that John of

---

[1] Potthast, no. 2676 ; Ciacconi, *loc. cit.* Wendover describes the king's exactions in the preceding year (ii. 10).

[2] Potthast, no. 2727.

[3] Only the king's letter is dated. A sub-contemporary rubric describes the cardinal John as ' tunc venienti legato in Angliam '. The letters are printed from exemplifications of 1242 in *Archaeologia*, LII. ii. 106–7. ' Joscelino Bathon. electo ' is witness to a charter of King John on 20 April 1206 (*Hist. MSS. Comm. Report, Rutland Collection*, iv. 55). He was consecrated at Reading on 28 May by the bishop of London (Paris, *Chron. Maj.* ii. 495 ; *Ann. Mon.* ii. 257, iv. 394).

[4] Hontheim, *Hist. Trevirensis diplom.* (1750), i. 646 (Potthast, no. 2767 and p. 466).

[5] *Reg. Innocent. III* (Migne's *Patr. Lat.* 215), lib. ix, n. 80 (Potthast, no. 2803). The priory had been received under papal protection in 1203 (Potthast, no. 1962).

[6] *Hist. MSS. Comm., Rept. V*, appendix, p. 442 b.

[7] The abbey expended forty shillings on his entertainment (*Cartul. de Ramseia* (Rolls Series), i. 232).

[8] Tillmann, *op. cit.*, p. 93, n. 113.

Ferentino appointed the prior of Dunstable to visit all the men's religious houses in the diocese of Lincoln, excepting those of Cîteaux, Prémontré, and the military orders.[1] This in itself is a remarkably early instance of anything approaching a systematic visitation of monasteries in England. There is fuller information about the legate's visitatorial activity at York in mid-August and at Evesham sometime before the council of Reading.

The legate came to Evesham soon after its famous victory, the vindication in the Curia of its exemption from the bishop of Worcester's authority. But no sooner was the battle won than the old enmity of abbot and convent to each other flamed up again. The abbot returned to his tyranny and heeded not the possibility of visitation.[2] When the legate arrived to visit, says Thomas of Marlborough, we imputed many crimes to the abbot and he to us. Then the legate examined individuals, partly in person, partly by his clerks. He inquired into the accusations against the morals of the abbot and, when he left the abbey, commissioned the abbots of Lilleshall and Haughmond to proceed with the inquiry, reserving the correction of spiritual matters to himself. As to the exposure of the abbot's evil life, Marlborough tells us that the abbot met the legate later at the council at Reading, and gained his favour and gave his nephew rents worth ten marks.[3] The main result of the visitation was that a compromise was reached regarding the administration of the house which was agreeable to the convent (fere ad votum nostrum, says Marlborough). This was set down in writing and sent to the legate, who confirmed it.[4] The fact that the abbot threw his promises to the winds as soon as the legate left England did not destroy the whole importance of the latter's visit. The convent now had a written document as a protest against misgovernment, and but for the intervention of the Great Interdict its realization would probably have come earlier than 1213.

St. Mary's Abbey, York, possessed no chronicler of the type of Thomas of Marlborough in the early thirteenth century, and beyond the injunctions given below we know nothing of the visitation of the abbey by John of Ferentino on the Feast of the Assumption (15 August) 1206.[5]

---

[1] *Ann. Mon.* iii. 29.

[2] *Chronicon de Evesham* (Rolls Series), pp. 200–1.

[3] *Ibid.* pp. 202, 246. The details are drawn both from Marlborough's original narrative and from his evidence before Nicholas of Tusculum in 1213.

[4] *Ibid.* pp. 202, 205–21.

[5] Further indication of the legate's presence at York is afforded by a document in the British Museum (MS. Cotton, Vitellius, A. II. fos. 157ᵛ–158). This records the agreement made between Archbishop Geoffrey of York and the dean and chapter of York. The original, which among other matters stated rules for the election of the dean, is said to have been sealed by the legate Cardinal John of S. Maria in via lata, in whose presence the parties promised to observe the agreement.

There seems no means of knowing why this monastery was selected by the legate for inspection, or whether his visit was solicited. At this time the abbot was Robert of Longchamp, brother to King Richard's chancellor, and formerly prior of Ely. He had held the abbacy of York since 1197 and lived in the same office yet another thirty-three years.[1] He was still abbot when the abbey fought for its privileges at visitation against Archbishop Walter Gray,[2] and the abbey chronicler terms him *rector egregius*.[3]

The injunctions do not give the impression of notorious corruption in the monastery. They deal for the most part with the economy of the house and the observance of the rules about food and clothing. The administration had, one may suppose, with time, become perhaps slack, perhaps merely more complicated. So the financial machinery of the abbey is organized, and the abbot is encouraged to make use of the advice of the brethren on convent affairs. This side of the injunctions, which is decidedly pronounced, contrasts with the thirteenth-century customary of the abbey. In the latter the overwhelming authority of the abbot is stressed with few modifications. The passage in the injunctions which bids the abbot take the advice of the seniors, where serious punishment is called for, should be compared with the customary, which says of the abbot : ' ipsius est ponere in gravem culpam et absolvere inde eum qui tali pena meruit excommunicari '.[4]

The injunctions and the customary generally have few points of comparison. The two compilations had different aims. One was to make changes and prohibitions ; the other embalmed customs and rights. Nor is it to be expected that either should give a complete picture of the monastic household. The customary adds to the injunctions details about the monks' clothes (fos. 76ᵛ–77), but says nothing of their cost. From the same source we may learn more about the *hospitarius* (fos. 78–79ᵛ) and find out on what days, with what fare, the hale monks eat at the expense of the infirmarer, as the injunctions imply was sometimes allowable.[5] The *refecturarius* mentioned below does not appear in the customary, but his duties were probably those of the subcellarer who is mentioned, and he occurs in another record of the abbey in this

---

[1] *Vict. County Hist. Yorks*, iii. 108.

[2] *Calendar of Papal Letters* (ed. Bliss), i. 108–9.

[3] MS. Bodley 39, fo. 100. I am indebted to Dr. H. H. E. Craster for the use of his transcript of the chronicle and customary of St. Mary's contained in this volume.

[4] *Ibid.* fo. 68.

[5] ' Occies per annum recreat [infirmarius] totum conventum in circuitu per consuetudinem, excepto festo sancti Iohannis ewangeliste, bis post natale et bis post pasca et bis ad festum sancti Martini in hyeme, semel in festo apostolorum Petri et Pauli, et semel post exaltacionem sancte crucis, et in hiis recreacionibus apponuntur tria fercula plenaria ad magnum prandium et duo ad cenam.' The infirmarer was to provide fowl at the *recreaciones* of Martinmas and Christmas (*ibid.* fo. 82ᵛ).

period.[1] The *prebendarius*, who is coupled with the cellarer in the injunctions, does not occur again in the customary, but is mentioned at intervals from 1258 onwards in the abbey's chronicle.[2] Nor do we find in the customary any account of the abbot's *familia*, of which the visitor speaks. The two chaplain-monks were the usual attendants of a great abbot ; and the legate's ordinance for annual change finds a parallel in the general regulation of the council of Oxford, 1222 (*c.* 33). The notary permitted by the visitor was no doubt a clerk to do secretarial work, not a notary public, first heard of in England much later in the century, and employed in the fourteenth century in English bishops' chanceries.

Among the important administrative regulations of the legate, which mostly may be found in many other ordinances for monasteries in this century, the creation of two treasurers and the careful description of their duties are particularly interesting. Similar officials appear slightly earlier at Christ Church, Canterbury, and become fairly common in English monasteries in the course of the thirteenth century.[3] At York the powers of the treasurers were large, and they were to be the abbot's special advisers. They were to receive the abbot's revenues as well as the convent's, and to pay out only as was necessary to the various offices. These rules struck not only at superfluous expenditure by obedientiaries, but also at the possibility that an obedientiary might retain the yearly surplus of his office. On the other hand, the extreme measure of pooling the revenues of the house was mitigated by the fact that the *bursae* were kept distinct. The demand for quarterly statements of accounts precedes many similar ordinances in English councils, papal legislation, and visitors' decrees.

It is unlikely that the treasurer's was ever a popular office, and we may doubt whether it lasted at York continuously. Against the continuity of the office we should note that in the customary, of later date, the treasurer does not appear among the other obedientiaries, although his office was most important. Moreover, the chronicler, who occasionally mentions monks as having been *bursarii*,[4] records the fact that on 20 November 1301 two treasurers

---

[1] British Museum, Add. MS. 38816, fo. 38ᵛ. Cf. MS. Bodley 39, fos. 116 and 161 (1258 and 1293). The office is found in Lanfranc's constitutions (Wilkins, *Concilia*, i. 337 *seqq.*), and round about the beginning of the thirteenth century at Abingdon (*Chronicon Abingdon*, Rolls Series, ii. 312, 316, 324), Evesham (*Chron. Evesham*, 209), and St. Augustine's, Canterbury (*Customary*, ed. E. Maunde Thompson, ii. 256).

[2] MS. Bodley 39, fos. 116, 161, 164, 166, 192*v*. At Durham a payment is recorded to an officer with this title in 1278, and Canon Fowler translates the word as 'fodderman ' (*Durham Abbey Account Rolls* (Surtees Soc.), ii. 485 and iii. 829).

[3] Snape, *English Monastic Finances*, pp. 39 *seqq.* Only a few years before the visitation of York (for it was since 1202) Archbishop Hubert, visiting Ramsey, 'constituit tres monachos receptores omnium proventuum huius monasterii ' (*Chronicon abb. Ramseien.* (Rolls Series), p. 342).

[4] MS. Bodley 39, fos. 116, 161, 164 (1258, 1293, 1296).

were appointed 'per quosdam'; 'set illa ordinacio parum profuit'.[1] We know that in 1312 there was some such officer in the monastery, for in that year a monk fled from St. Mary's with £60 belonging to the office of the *bursarius*.[2] Five years later the visiting archbishop prescribed the appointment of a bursar to receive all the revenues of the house.[3]

Altogether the visitor's injunctions of 1206 present many features of interest. They are comprehensive and they are early, probably preceding any other known ones prescribed for an English monastery.[4]

This copy of the injunctions (it is obvious from the ending that it is not the original) stands by itself to serve as a flyleaf to a book of much later date, preserved in the Bodleian Library as MS. Digby 186. The injunctions are written, two columns to the page, on the *recto* and *verso*, *a* of a parchment leaf 11¼in. by 8in., in a hand of Henry III's reign. The two preceding fly-leaves are blank, and the following one has a note to the effect that Dom Robert Haworth, formerly abbot of Stanlaw, died on x. kal. Maii. 1304, and gives some family dates of the late sixteenth century. The body of the volume (numbering ninety folios) is written in several hands of the fifteenth and sixteenth centuries. It contains prophetical tracts by John of Bridlington and others ; fos. 45–64 contain a chronicle of England from Brutus to 1307, and at fo. 65 begin the constitutions of the legate Otto (1237) and the commentary of John of Athona upon them. The last section is incomplete. The volume was not originally one whole,[5] but most of the material clearly shows north-country provenance. The book is on paper, the end leaves of some of the gatherings being of parchment.

Bodl. MS. Digby 186, fo. 1.[6]

Iohannes dei gratia Sancte Marie in via lata diaconus cardinalis apostolice sedis legatus omnibus ad quos presens scriptum pervenerit in vero salutari salutem. Ad statum monasterii Sancte Marie Ebor' in melius reformandum presentium auctoritate statuimus ut duo thesaurarii per abbatem de consensu totius capituli vel sanioris partis sine dilatione qualibet eligantur, qui proventus recipiant universos tam ad abbatis cameram quam ad alias

---

[1] *Ibid.* fo. 168ᵛ.   [2] *Ibid.* fo. 185ᵛ.

[3] Register of Archbishop Melton, fo. 133. This visitor allowed the accounts of the abbot's *camera* to be exempt from inspection.

[4] They have points of comparison with three sets of ordinances for foreign monasteries in the registers of Innocent III. The pope confirmed statutes by two different visitors for the abbey of Bourgueil (O.S.B., diocese of Angers) in 1198 and 1207, and gave some statutes of his own making to Monte Cassino in 1215 (*Reg. Innocent III*, Migne, *Pat. Lat.* 214–16, i. 311 ; x. 14, suppl. 211).

[5] In the catalogue of Thomas Allen's books (Bodley, MS. Wood F. 26, no. 33 fo.) the sections which now occupy fos. 16–22 were apparently not in the volume which contained the rest.

[6] Italicized words and letters are omitted in the manuscript.

obedientias pertinentes. Ita tamen quod redditus singularum obedientiarum in singulis bursis seorsum custodiant, et unicuique obedientiario de
bursa sua que ad obedientiam eius necessaria fuerint subministrent. Nec
redditus unius obedientie in alios usus usque ad finem anni qualibet temeri-
tate convertant, sed potius si qua defuerint inspecta necessitate de com-
*m*unibus redditibus de consilio abbatis et fratrum vel sanioris partis eorum
supplere procurent. Similiter etiam si qua de obedientiarum ipsarum
redditibus superfuerint ultra annum, in solucione debitorum convertant
vel in alios usus quos abbas et fratres vel pars sanior viderit expedire.
Volumus autem ut secundum consuetudinem domus antiquam cellerarius
et prebendarius in monasterio statuantur qui, sicut superius est premissum,
de manu thesaurariorum per tallias et scripta recipiant que in usus officiorum suorum fuerint expendenda. Hoc quidem in aliis obedientiariis
observetur, ut videlicet per tallias et scripta recipienda recipiant, et uni-
versi obedientiarii tam de receptis quam *de* expensis reddant quater in anno
coram abbate et senioribus rationem. Ad hoc idem et thesaurarii teneantur. Abbas etiam de ipsorum manibus per capellanos suos expensas
recipiat moderatas, et tam de receptis quam *de* expensis quater in anno
rationem reddere teneatur ; preter hoc quod quotiens pro negotiis domus
egressus fuerit ad remota, in reditu suo et que receperit et que expenderit
cum thesaurariis computabit. Abbas duobus capellanis monachis, uno
advocato, uno notario, et decem servientibus preter pueros ad servicium
eius necessarios, et ad plus equis duodecim, sit contentus ; capellanos de
gremio monasterii sui viros providos et honestos annis singulis assum-
pturus. Ceterum in locis et horis statutis silentium precipimus observari, et
ne quis claustrum preter licentiam exeat districtius inhibemus, nec exeundi
licentia cuiquam nisi assignata causa rationabili tribuatur. Usum etiam
pannorum de Chabilon'[1] nisi fuerint prorsus nigri, et ciphorum argenteorum
monachis inhibemus. Capas etiam et coopertoria et alias vestes nigras
habeant que mediocri pretio comparentur. Nec fimbrias in subselliis nec
pilleos qui hure[2] vocantur habere presumant. Hoc idem precipimus de
abbate. Prohibemus etiam ne de nocte potationi vacare presumant, immo
nunquam et nusquam preter quam in refectorio statutis horis conveniant
ad bibendum.[3] Quod si quisquam forte | sititierit [*sic*] impetrata licentia
cum refecturario ad refectorium solus accedat, ut necessitati subveniat, non
consulat voluptati. Ab hac autem generalitate eos qui in abbatis presentia
fuerint excipimus, et infirmos.[4] Sub interminatione quoque anathematis

fo. 1
recto, *b*

---

[1] This kind of cloth, used for coverlets, took its name from the original place of
manufacture, Châlons-sur-Marne ; but Mr. Salzman shows that Châlons were made
in England at least as early as the middle of the thirteenth century (*English Industries
of the Middle Ages* (2nd ed. 1923), pp. 199–200). The customary of St. Mary's refers to
' chalones ' left by brethren who die in the infirmary, to be given to the hostillar for the
benefit of his guests (MS. Bodley 39, fo. 79).

[2] The earliest example of this use of the word given by the *New English Dictionary*
is much later, *c.* 1290.

[3] The procedure for ' potus post vesperas ' on fast days is minutely described in the
customary of the abbey (MS. Bodley 39, fo. 70ᵛ).

[4] Cf. Council of Oxford, 1222 (c. 48) (Wilkins, *Concilia*, i. 593) : ' Decernimus, ut
nec monachi nec canonici regulares, nisi statutis horis et locis, potationi aut comestioni
vacare praesumant. Si quis vero sitiverit, impetrata licentia, refectorium regulariter
introeat, et sic necessitati suae subveniat, non ut consulat voluptati. Ab hac generalitate
infirmos excipimus, et eos, qui fuerint in obsequio praelatorum.' I have been unable to

prohibemus ne quis sibi quicquam preter abbatis licentiam appropriare vel de hiis que habuerit testari presumat nec quisquam equos vel alia ut vendat carius audeat comparare. Si quid autem apud quemlibet in morte repertum fuerit, quod ei concessum vel permissum non fuerit ab abbate, christiana careat sepultura,[1] sub eadem interminatione precipientes abbati, ut quicquid proprietatis apud aliquem reppererit monachorum accipiat, et de consilio thesaurariorum in communes monasterii usus expendat. Eidem etiam districte precipimus ut claustrum, capitulum et chorum studeat frequentare, nisi ex causa probabili retrahatur ; sitque circa fratres suos super observantia regulari sollicitus et regulariter corrigat quicquid in eis fuerit corrigendum. Ne autem in correctione modum excedat cum aliquid fuerit commissum ab aliquo quod vel eiectionem vel excommunicationem vel penam aliquam graviorem inducat, cum consilio seniorum quod faciendum fuerit exequatur, nec in talibus quicquam grave illis faciat inconsultis. Immo etiam tam interiora quam exteriora negotia domus si ardua fuerint, de conventus vel sanioris partis consilio et assensu procuret. Minora vero cum thesaurariorum consilio procuret. Consensum autem eorum liberum esse precipimus, ne videlicet quicquam ab eis per minas audeat extorquere, vel in eos si consentire noluerint aliquam exerceat ultionem. Nec abbas sine monachorum vel sanioris partis eorum assensu, nec quisquam de monachis aut obedientialibus preter abbatis licentiam, quicquam ab aliquo mutuare presumat, et cum aliquid receperint mutuo thesaurariis assignetur, per eos de mandato abbatis et consilio seniorum in usus necessarios expendendum. Elemosinarius maiorem sollicitudinem et curam adhibeat ut elemosina collecta fideliter et servata pauperibus fideliter erogetur, nec permittat quod quisquam dirripiat que pauperum sunt usibus deputata. Infirmarius quoque sollicite et studiose procuret ut infirmis necessaria congrue ministrentur, nec de redditibus infirmario deputatis ultra quam statutum est hii qui sani fuerint convivia faciant, et que in necessitates infirmorum provida sunt deliberatione concessa ad suas transferant voluptates. Hospitibus etiam iuxta facultatem monasterii congrue precipimus provideri, proviso tamen ne superflua ministrentur divitibus et pauperibus necessaria subtrahantur. Nullus preterea monachorum preter abbatis licentiam depositum recipiat alicuius ne proprietatis culpam sub honesto nomine valeat palliare. Nec abbas sine conventus vel saltem seniorum assensu ultra centum solidos sterlingorum in anno dare, vel terras aut possessiones ad eos spectantes conferre presumat. Ad hec districtius inhibemus ne unquam filiis personarum, ceden | tibus vel decedentibus patribus, paternas ecclesias immediate concedat, promissiones et concessiones quas super hoc fecerunt hactenus tanquam minus canonicas irritas decernentes.[2] Monachi vacent studiosius lectioni ut litteratiores ad manda-

fo. 1
verso,*a*

find the common original of these two regulations. It is conceivable that the man who framed the injunctions also framed acts for a council of Reading, and that those acts were used in the council of 1222.

[1] Cf. 3rd Lateran Council, c. 10 (Mansi, *Ampl. Collectio*, xxii. 224).

[2] Cf. the injunction of Pope Lucius II to the same effect, to the monks of St. Pancras (1144) ; also the pronouncement of Alexander III to the bishop of Worcester. (Wilkins, *Concilia*, i. 423, 477). Innocent III reiterated the rule in the 4th Lateran Council (c. 31) and his successor wrote specially in 1221 to the archbishop of York, regarding conditions in that province. (*Register of Archbishop Gray* (Surtees Soc.), xxvii–xxviii. 140–1).

tum abbatis quotiens opus fuerit exhortationis verbum faciant ad conventum. Si qui autem contra id venire presumpserint, pene subiaceant regulari.

Promulgavit autem memoratus dominus I. apostolice sedis legatus has constitutiones in accessu suo ad monasterium nostrum ad Assumptionem sancte Marie, anno incarnationis Domini millesimo ducentesimo sexto.

ADDITIONAL NOTES

Pp.444-5: The precise date of arrival is unknown, but the reference to his subscription to a privilege of 4 May 1205 (p.445 n.4) cannot be correct.

P.448 para.2: This centralizing measure was not confined to Benedictine abbeys. Cf.R.A.L. Smith,'The "regimen scaccarii" in English monasteries', Trans. Royal Hist. Soc.,4 s.24 (1942) 73-94, reprinted in his Collected papers (1947), and David Postles, 'The bursary of Oseney abbey:a note', Journal of Soc. of Archivists, vol.6 n.1 (1978) 28-30, which points to the foundation of central treasuries in English Augustinian houses in the late 12th and early 13th centuries.

P.449 line 8: Cf. p.448 n.3 and examples of visitation by English prelates cited in C.R. Cheney, Pope Innocent III and England (Stuttgart,1976) 230-1.

VI

Cardinal John of Ferentino, papal legate in England in 1206

DR. HELENE TILLMANN summarized admirably in 1926 what was then known of the legation of John of Ferentino, cardinal deacon of S. Maria in Via Lata, formerly notary and chancellor of the holy Roman Church. Some additional facts were published in this REVIEW in 1931. Not much has come to light since then, but it may be well to collect the additional fragments and detail the known documents which record this legate's activities. The coming of a legate *a latere* (especially when the see of Canterbury was vacant) offered, at least in theory, opportunity for reform and redress of grievances. John came to England less than a year after the death of Archbishop Hubert Walter and was the last ecclesiastic to wield general authority in the province of Canterbury until the belated arrival of Stephen Langton in 1213. The province of York, which the legate also visited, was to be deprived of its head for an even longer period; for Archbishop Geoffrey went overseas in summer 1207, died abroad in December 1212, and was not re-placed by Archbishop Walter Gray until the end of 1215.

The scanty evidence shows that the legate and his deputies held enquiries and heard disputes and complaints in monasteries throughout the length and breadth of England. No trace has been found of the staff which accompanied him from Italy: the mention of a rent given to the legate's nephew does not prove that the nephew came to England.[1] In the only known cases of sub-delegation the legate employed prelates of English Augustinian houses: the abbots of Haughmond and Lilleshall to investigate Evesham, the prior of Dunstable to visit religious houses in the diocese of Lincoln.[2] Most of the evidence naturally comes from monastic sources, and we rely on chronicles alone for the jejune report that Cardinal John held a council at Reading in October, where, according to the *Brut*

[1] *Chron. abb. de Evesham* (Rolls Ser.), p. 202.
[2] *Ibid.* and *Annales monastici* (Rolls Ser.), iii. 29.

y Tywysogion, ' he confirmed the law of the Church throughout the whole kingdom '.[1] No light can be thrown on this event, but it made enough impression on contemporaries for Geoffrey Muscamp, bishop of Coventry and Lichfield, to date one of his acts ' apud Lich ' anno quo celebratum est concilium a Iohanne cardinali apud Redyng '.[2] The celebrated formulary of Marinus of Eboli preserves a letter of Pope Innocent III addressed to the cardinal as papal legate, which orders him to provide for a bishop-elect unable to reside in his see; the text is unfortunately shorn of the names and date which might permit us to fix the circumstances.[3]

Chroniclers who habitually accused all legates of rapacity made no exception of Cardinal John. Lunt found nothing to connect John with the collection of Peter's Pence or the recovery of arrears of the Crusading fortieth,[4] and we have only two records of the procuration-fees he took. The royal custodians of the see of Lincoln spent 54s. this year ' in procuratione legati ', and Ramsey Abbey laid out 40s. ' in hospitio legati '.[5] The legate was not above accepting a rent of ten marks for his nephew from the infamous abbot of Evesham.[6]

The known *acta* of the legate are six in number, to which may be added two documents prepared for his approval but not uttered in his name. None, unfortunately, is dated, none has any list of witnesses, and no seal survives, although the legate's seal is mentioned in nos. 2, 4, and 8 below.

1. *Canterbury, Christ Church.* Letter of the cardinal legate to the prior and convent, copied in Register A (Ch.Ch. D. and C. muniments), whence printed by J. B. Sheppard, *Hist.mss. comm.*, *Report*

---

[1] *Brut y Tywysogion, or the Chronicle of the Princes, Red Book of Hergest version*, ed. Thomas Jones (Cardiff, 1955), p. 187.   [2] Brit. Mus. MS. Harl. 3868, fo. 3ᵛ.

[3] The elect is described as ' T. de . . . '. The only vacant English see, after the filling of Bath and Wells, was Lincoln, after the death of Bishop William, 10 May 1206, but the elect of Lincoln with the initial ' T ' is known. The person in question may have been elected to an Irish see: in Clonfert, Down, and Lismore the first bishops to appear after 1206 were named Thomas. See Fritz Schillmann, *Die Formularssammlung des Marinus von Eboli* (Bibl. d. preuss. hist. Instituts in Rom, t. xvi, 1929), i. 215, no. 1368.

[4] W. E. Lunt, *Fin. relations of the papacy with England to 1327* (Med. Acad. America, 1939), pp. 56, 538, and *cf.* Cheney, ' Master Philip the notary and the fortieth of 1199 ' *ante*, lxiii (1948), 342–50.

[5] *Pipe Roll 9 John* (Pipe Roll Soc., n. s. 22, 1946), pp. 14, 111.

[6] *Chron. abb. de Evesham*, p. 202. Marlborough's account of the legate and Evesham may be compared with the Melrose chronicler's account of the visit of John of Salerno to his abbey in 1202: ' Predictus apostolice sedis legatus apud Melros honorifice susceptus per L noctes et amplius commoratus est, maxime ut controversiam inter monachos de Kelcou et monachos de Melros pacificaret. Qui utrique parti bene pollicitans, nulli satisfaciens, quamplurima dona scilicet auri et argenti necnon et equorum plurimorum ab utraque parte auferens, nulli quicquam commoditatis conferens, litem penitus indeterminatam reliquid.' *Chron. of Melrose*, ed. A.O. and M.O. Anderson (1936), pl. 51. Of John of Salerno Hoveden wrote: ' Non manducavit carnem, vinum et siceram non bibit nec aliquid quo inebriari potuit; sed aurum et argentum sitivit.' *Chronica Rog. de Hoveden* (Rolls Ser.), iv. 175.

VIII, App. i, p. 320*b*. Inc.: 'Volentes indempnitati.' Described in the rubric as 'Cautio I. sancte Marie in Via Lata diaconi cardinalis de consecratione episcopi Bathoniensis', it is a declaration that by legatine authority Jocelin, elect of Bath, has been consecrated in the church of Reading [28 May 1206] and that this shall not prejudice the prior and convent or their church. No witness or date. At Wells are copies of the antecedent documents, including the king's letter of 23 April, recommending the elect to the legate and so, by implication, accepting Cardinal John as legate to England (see *Archaeologia,* lii. 104–7).

2. *Canterbury, St. Augustine's Abbey.* Declaration by the legate that he has inspected original sealed documents relating to the abbey's churches of Milton and Faversham, and has set his seal to collated copies. Original in Canterbury, D. and C. muniments, Chartae antiquae F. 85, printed below, no. 1. For many years before 1206 intermittent dispute had raged between the archdeacon of Canterbury, claiming the usual rights in these churches, and the abbey which claimed immunity for them on the basis of its papal privileges. The dispute was complicated by the king's claim to exercise the patronage of Milton and Faversham, and in 1201 an earlier papal legate, on his way to Scotland, had intervened.[1] By 1206 the king had waived his claim, and his charter of 15 June 1203 was among the titles inspected by John of Ferentino. These titles bore only on the question of patronage, but may have been wanted in the continuing action of the abbey against the archdeacon. The form of the document is of some diplomatic interest. It is written on one side of a long sheet of parchment about 11 by 6 inches, with a narrow fold at the foot which contained a tag for the legate's seal. It has horizontal ruling throughout its length, amounting to fifty-five lines. Two hands have been at work, both of the same style and period, neither of them particularly un-English in appearance.[2] It seems that the first writer began his work on the seventh line, copying the charter of King John, the bull of Celestine III, and the confirmations of Archbishop Hubert and the prior and convent, leaving blank two lines between each document and three and a half lines at the foot above the fold. The second writer then added the legate's *inspexi*, accommodating himself somewhat uneasily to the free space at the top of the sheet. He then filled the three spaces between the following documents with elaborate

---

[1] John of Salerno, who wrote to the pope about the affair, Sept.-Oct. 1201. For the background and details of the dispute see Eric John, 'The litigation of an exempt house, St Augustine's, Canterbury, 1182–1237', *Bull. John Rylands Libr.,* xxxix (1957), 390–415.

[2] There seems to be nothing to support Sheppard's supposition that the second writer was the legate (*Hist. MSS. commission, Report,* v. 442*b*); but the care displayed in the last paragraph suggests drafting by some southern notary rather than a contemporary English clerk. The legate had himself been papal chancellor throughout the year 1205.

pen-flourishes, and explained the purpose of these in the final clause with which he filled the last three lines and a half.

3. *Beaulieu Abbey.* Letter of John, cardinal deacon and legate, to the abbot and convent of Beaulieu (recently founded by King John), recording his arbitration in a tithe-case between them and William of Bodiam. Copied into the duke of Portland's cartulary of Beaulieu (Brit. Mus., Loan 29/330), fo. 26ᵛ, printed below, no. II, by kind permission of his grace the duke of Portland.

4. *Harrold Priory.* Letters patent of the cardinal legate, addressed 'universis Christi fidelibus ad quos presens scriptum pervenerit', making known that the suit over the church of Stevington (co. Bedford) between the nuns of Harrold and Baldwin de Guînes has proceeded before him to the point of the hearing of witnesses and publication of testimony. Because of the withdrawal of Baldwin's proctor, when the legate was on the point of going overseas, he has referred the case to the pope and deposited the attestations under his seal in St. Augustine's, Canterbury, to be shown to the judges whom the pope may appoint. Inc.: 'Ad vestram volumus . . .'. No witness or date. Copied into a psalter, Bristol, Baptist Coll. Ms. Z.c. 23 *ad fin.*, whence printed by C. R. Cheney, in 'Harrold Priory: a twelfth century dispute', *Bedfordshire Hist. Record Soc.* xxxii (1952), 20–1.

5. *Evesham Abbey.* An agreement under seal between the abbot of Evesham and his convent begins with the words: 'Cum I. dei gratia sancte Marie in Via Lata diaconus cardinalis apostolice sedis legatus officio legationis sibi iniuncte in Anglia fungeretur et orta esset controversia inter me abbatem et nos conventum Eovesham super statu domus nostre coram eo, tandem amicabiliter hoc modo sopita est.' It is printed in Dugdale's *Monasticon*[1] from the original, which I have been unable to trace. Thomas of Marlborough says of this agreement: 'misimus eam ad dominum legatum et confirmavit eam.'[2] This suggests a procedure like that which produced no. I below; but in this case the legate adopted a different form, as no. 6 shows.

6. *Evesham Abbey.* A letter of confirmation addressed to the abbot and convent of Evesham. It confirms 'constitutiones quasdam pro statu monasterii et religionis observantia inter vos communi factas assensu et redactas in scripto', and evidently refers to no. 5 above. Inc.: 'Ea que pro statu.' Copied by Thomas of Marlborough into his chronicle, whence printed in *Chron. abb. de Evesham*, p. 221. It is possible that the original was appended to a text of the agreement.

---

[1] *Monasticon Anglicanum*, ed. J. Caley, &c. ii. 23a: 'ex autographo sub sigillis in curia Augmentationum': the document should be in series B of Ancient Deeds in the Public Record Office.   [2] *Chron. abb. de Evesham*, p. 202.

7. *York, St. Mary's Abbey.* Letters patent of the cardinal legate, addressed ' omnibus ad quos presens scriptum pervenerit ', uttering injunctions for the abbey after legatine visitation on 15 August 1206. Inc.: ' Ad statum monasterii.' Copied on a flyleaf of Bodleian ms. Digby 186 fo. 1, whence printed by C. R. Cheney, *ante*, xlvi. 449–52.

8. *York.* An agreement between Archbishop Geoffrey and Simon, the dean, and the chapter of York, which is drawn up in the name of the archbishop, is said to have been reached ' in presentia venerabilis patris nostri domini Iohannis dei gratia sancte Marie in Via Lata diaconi cardinalis sedis apostolice legati ', and it records that ' ad maiorem etiam securitatem presenti scripto dominus legatus ad preces nostras sigillum suum fecit apponi '. There is no witness or date, but presumably the transaction occurred on the legate's visit to York in August (above, no. 7). Copied in a fifteenth-century hand in a register of York, Brit. Mus. MS. Cotton Vitellius A. ii, fos. 157^v–158^r.

Corpus Christi College, Cambridge

I

(Canterbury, D. & C. muniments, Chartae antiquae F. 85. See above, no. 2)

Ego Iohannes dei gratia sancte Marie in Via Lata diaconus cardinalis apostolice sedis legatus autentica domini Celestini, Iohannis regis Anglorum, Huberti archiepiscopi, et conventus Cantuariensis super concessione et confirmatione ecclesiarum de Midelton ' et de Faversham et pertinentium[1] earum inspexi prout videbantur sigillis eorum signata, et ad instantiam abbatis et conventus beati Augustini Cantuariensis autenticorum ipsorum rescriptis meum feci sigillum apponi.

Iohannes[2] dei gratia . . . [printed from the chancery enrolment in *Rotuli chartarum*, ed. T. D. Hardy (Rec. Comm. 1837), p. 105b].

Celestinus episcopus servus . . . [printed from this and other copies in *Papsturkunden in England*, ed. W. Holtzmann (Abh. Gesellschaft der Wiss. zu Göttingen, 1930–1), i. 580–1].

Hubertus dei gratia Cantuariensis archiepiscopus totius Anglie primas et apostolice sedis legatus omnibus sancte matris ecclesie filiis ad quos presens scriptum pervenerit eternam in domino salutem. Ad universitatis vestre notitiam volumus pervenire nos auctenticum scriptum bone memorie Teodbaldi predecessoris nostri sub huius continentie forma inspexisse: T. dei gratia . . . [printed from other copies by A. Saltman, *Theobald archbishop of Canterbury* (1956), p. 282 (no. 56)]. Quia igitur ex iniuncto nobis officio securitati et paci virorum religiosorum volumus ut tenemur providere, quia etiam hiis que a predecessoribus nostris sive ab aliis quibuslibet intuitu devotionis locis religiosis rationabiliter concessa sunt et confirmata nos decet auctoritatis nostre robur inpendere,

---

[1] MS. ' pertinentiis.'   [2] Another hand begins with ' Iohannes '.

prefatas ecclesias et decimas secundum quod in prenotata carta predecessoris nostri T. et etiam in cartis illustrium regum Anglorum
Henrici et filii eius Ricardi quas inspeximus predictis abbati et monachis
sancti Augustini rationabiliter concesse sunt et confirmate nos eisdem ea
qua fungimur auctoritate inperpetuum concedimus et tam presenti
scripto quam sigilli nostri testimonio confirmamus. Hiis testibus,
magistro S. de Siwell ', magistro W. de Sumercote, Simone filio Roberti,
magistro Reinero de Stanford, magistro Gervasio, Roberto de Bristo,
Ricardo de Ringestede, Iohanne de Sancto Ædmundo et aliis multis.[1]

Omnibus sancte matris ecclesie filiis ad quos presens scriptum pervenerit Gaufridus ecclesie Christi Cantuariensis prior eiusdemque loci
conventus perpetuam in domino salutem. Hiis que a prelatis nostris
provide statuuntur, conceduntur, aut confirmantur subditorum est
gratanter prebere consensum, presertim cum viris religiosis, utilitate,
necessitate, vel pietate suadente, aliqua conferuntur. Unde universitatem
vestram scire desideramus quod nos favore religionis quam fovere
tenemur in concessionem a bone memorie Huberto quondam Cantuariensi archiepiscopo dilectis in Christo fratribus abbati et conventui sancti
Augustini Cantuariensis super ecclesiis de Midelton et de Faversam
factam consentientes, ratam et gratam habemus eandem;[2] in qua re
ratihabitionem et assensum nostrum declarantes, huic scripto signum
nostrum duximus apponendum.

Hoc[3] autem adicimus ad cautelam quod cum rescripta conferri cum
autenticis fecissemus nec[4] interlinearis erat in eis nec in ipsis rasuram
invenimus que ipsam redderet de ratione suspectam[5] vel aliquem posset
de iure movere; cartam quoque que inter rescripta ipsa in diversis locis
vacua videbatur ne in ea quicquam posset inscribi notis variis fecimus
annotari.

II

(Brit. Mus., MS. loan 29/330 fo. 26ᵛ. See above, no. 3).

De controversia que fuit inter nos et Willelmum de Bodeham[6]
personam de Inglisham. Confirmatio domini I. apostolice sedis legati
super decimis laborum nostrorum.

[fo. 27ʳ] Iohannes dei gratia sancte Marie in Via Lata diaconus cardinalis
dilectis fratribus abbati et conventui Belli Loci Regis Cisterciensis ordinis
in vero salutari salutem. Cum dominus noster summus pontifex causam
que inter vos et Willelmum de Bodeam personam ecclesie de Inglisham

---

[1] The legatine title assumed by Archbishop Hubert shows that this cannot be
much later than January 1198. The charters of Henry II (1154–58) and Richard I
(1189) are printed in T. of Elmham, *Hist. mon. S. Augustini Cantuar.* (Rolls Series),
pp. 460, 474.

[2] The prior and convent give confirmation *sede vacante*, after the death of Hubert
Walter on 13 July 1205.

[3] The hand which wrote the first four lines resumes with ' Hoc '.

[4] ' int ' added. [5] MS. ' suspecta '.

[6] Master William de Bodeham, a royal clerk, was presented to the church of Ingle-
sham (co. Wilt.) in July 1202 (*Rotuli litt. patentium*, ed. T. D. Hardy (Rec. Comm. 1835),
p. 15). For the appropriation of this church and the nearby church of Coxwell (co.
Berk.) to Beaulieu (1232) see *Charters and docts. of Salisbury*, ed. W. D. Macray (Rolls
Ser.), pp. 255–7.

super decimis laborum vestrorum quos in parochia de Cokeswell'
propriis manibus vel sumptibus colitis vertebatur nobis commisisset fine
debito terminandam, et tam vos quam ipse W. essetis in nostra presentia
constituti, a vobis et eo fuit sub mutua stipulatione x marcarum in nos
pariter compromissum. Nos vero inquisita super hiis tam vestra quam
partis alterius voluntate, de libero vestro et eius assensu arbitrando
statuimus ut vos ecclesie de Inglisham x solidos sterlingorum in festo
sancti Michaelis annis singulis exolvatis et ecclesia ipsa huiusmodi
solutione contenta vos super decimis ipsis non presumat de cetero
molestare, nec vos ei tenemini respondere set sitis a prestatione decimarum
ipsarum inmunes. Si qua vero partium contra hoc venire presumpserit,
parti alteri penam memoratam exolvat et arbitrium nostrum in sua
nichilominus firmitate persistat.

ADDITIONAL NOTES

P.654 line 3: Although John, cardinal deacon of S. Maria in Via
Lata is described by Potthast and Bresslau and almost all later
scholars as 'cancellarius S.R.E.', this description was questioned by von Heckel and seems to be baseless.

P.655 lines 6-10 and note 3: Delete the reference to Marinus of
Eboli. The pope here is probably Innocent IV and the cardinal
Octavian Ubaldini, who became card. dn. of S. Maria in 1244;
he is not named in mss. Vat. Lat. 3925 and 3976.

P.655 No.1 line 2: Reg.A fo.72r (formerly lxxixr).

P.657 No.4 lines 11-12: The psalter was sold at Sotheby's, 13
December 1976, lot 56, to an undisclosed buyer.

P.658 after No.8: 9. A mandate to (Robert) abbot of St Mary's
York and (Alexander) abbot of Meaux, to enforce the sentence
of papal judges delegate for the dean and chapter of York against
Henry de Aquileia about the church of Topcliffe, which the archbishop of York neglects to enforce. R(ichard) de Percy's suit
against the canons is not to be prejudiced. Arrangements for
collecting the fruits of the church are prescribed.
        I. dei gratia S. Marie in Via Lata diaconus car-
dinalis apostolice sedis legatus dilectis fratribus S.Marie Ebor' et
de Melsa Eboracensis diocesis abbatibus in vero salutari salutem.
Exposita nobis dilectorum fratrum decani et capituli Ebor' queri-
monia patefecit quod cum inter eos et Henricum de Aquileia super
ecclesia de Toppeclive questio verteretur, tandem dilectis fratribus
de Kirkeham et de Bridlington' prioribus causa super hoc fuit a
sede apostolica delegata. Qui convocatis partibus et cause meritis

diligenter inquisitis, de prudentum virorum consilio pro canonicis
sententiam promulgarunt, adiudicantes Ebor' ecclesie fabrice
ecclesiam memoratam et venerabili Eboracenci archiepiscopo exe-
cutioni ipsius sententie demandantes. Set ipse illam exequi pro sua
voluntate contempsit. Nos igitur in defectu ipsius exequi volentes,
eandem legationis qua fungimur auctoritate vobis mandamus quatinus predictos decanum et capitulum in possessionem ipsius ecclesie inducatis,omnes illos qui se facto nostro duxerint opponendos
excommunicationis sententia innodantes, et si necesse fuerit subi-
cientes terras eorum sententie interdicti. Per hoc autem nobili viro
R. de Percy in causa que inter predictos canonicos ex una parte ac
ipsum ex altera super eadem ecclesia vertitur nullum volumus preiudicium generari, quoniam res inter alios acta aliis nocere non
potest, nec impediri priorem Sancti Andree quo minus obventiones
eiusdem ecclesie colligat prout ei est a nobis iniunctum et cum
Ivone clerico bladum et ligumina, sicut in aliis litteris legitur, par-
ciatur, que ipsis vendidimus pro satisfactione Romanis mercatoribus exhibenda.

The letter is in BL ms. Cotton Claud.B iii fo.82v(80v) and York,
D. & C. Magnum reg. album ii fo. 95v, included in the report of
the abbots that they have executed the mandate and inducted the
canons in corporal possession. This was probably issued when the
legate visited York in August 1206 and followed a papal mandate to
other delegates to hear the canons' complaint against Richard de
Percy for flouting the sentence in their favour and denying them
possession of the church (5 June 1206:Letters of Pope Innocent III ,
ed. C.R. and M.G. Cheney, no.709 and p.250). Documents of 1218-
22 in these cartularies show that Henry, backed by Richard de Percy,
resisted and that Richard only confirmed the church to the canons
in 1220.

P.658 after no.9: In an inventory of Glastonbury deeds in Cambridge, Trin. Coll. ms.R.5.33, printed by Hearne (J. Glastoniensis
Chronica (Oxford, 1726)ii.383) 'J. legatus Anglie xx dies' appears
in a list of indulgences, after those granted by the legate Nicholas
of Tusculum.

P.659 no.II line 5: add apostolice sedis legatus.

VII

The Earliest English Diocesan Statutes

ALTHOUGH the diocesan laws of the Latin Church in the Middle Ages form a most valuable source for the history of ecclesiastical influence and institutions, they cannot easily be used. Preserved piecemeal, for the greater part in corrupt and unofficial copies, many of the survivors were published by scholars of the seventeenth and eighteenth centuries and have never been re-edited. Their first editors were in no position to produce critical editions or (what was chiefly required) to survey the material as a whole. Giovanni Domenico Mansi, in making his *Amplissima Collectio* (1759 onwards), proceeded—to use Dom Henri Quentin's words—' par superposition '. The task on his hands was too big to permit him to compare and evaluate thoroughly the medieval diocesan statutes which were at that time known. Little was done to improve this situation before the close of the nineteenth century: only Heinrich Finke's early *Konzilienstudien zur Geschichte des 13 Jahrhunderts* (Münster, 1891), indicated the sort of investigation that was needed, which Hefele and Knöpfler, in the second edition of the *Conciliengeschichte*, did not provide. In recent years some advance has been made in sifting the material in various countries.[1] This

---

[1] In *English synodalia of the thirteenth century* (Oxford, 1941) the present writer illustrated the general problem with English examples, and provided a short general bibliography to 1939; see also ' The medieval statutes of the diocese of Carlisle ', *ante*, lxii (1947), 52–7. Since the war the study of French diocesan statutes has much advanced, largely through the initiative of the late André Artonne: see his papers, ' Le livre synodal de Lodève ', *Bibliothèque de l'École des Chartes*, cviii (1949–50), 36–74; ' Les statuts synodaux diocésains français du xiiie siècle au concile de Trente ', *Rev. de l'Hist. de l'Église de France*, xxxvi (1950), 168–81; ' Les synodes diocésains d'Arles de 1410 à 1570 ', *ibid.* xli (1955), 76–84; ' L'influence du Décret de Gratien sur les statuts synodaux ', *Studia Gratiana*, ed. G. Forchielli and A. M. Stickler (Bologna, 1954), ii. 645–56; ' Les statuts synodaux diocésains français ', *Comptes-rendus des Séances de l'Acad. des Inscriptions et Belles-Lettres*, 1955, pp. 55–63. Professor V. L. Kennedy has thrown light on the statutes attributed to Odo de Sully, bishop of Paris, in ' The moment of consecration and the elevation of the Host ' and ' The date of the Parisian decree on the elevation of the Host ', *Mediaeval Studies* (Toronto) vi (1944), 121–50 and viii (1946), 87–96; more thorough and recent work on these statutes, which tends to confirm the attribution of the core of them to Odo, is by the Abbé Louis Guizard, ' Recherches sur le texte des statuts synodaux d'Eudes de Sully, évêque de Paris (1196–1208) ', *Bulletin d'information de l'Institut de Recherche et d'Hist. des Textes*, v (1956), 53–69. See also Dom Jean Leclercq, ' Les decrets de Bernard de Saintes [1141–66] ', *Revue du Moyen Age Latin*, ii (1946), 167–70. P. C. Boeren writes on ' Les plus anciens statuts du diocèse de Cambrai ', *Revue de Droit Canonique*, iii (1953), 1–32, 131–72, 377–415, iv (1954), 131–58. See Louis Guizard, ' L'étude des anciens statuts synodaux des diocèses de France ', *Bibliothèque de la Revue d'Histoire Ecclésiastique*, fasc. 33: Congrès de droit canonique

has shown how often traditional ascriptions of statutes must be modified and how seldom we are presented with a series of synodal statutes which has not undergone some retouching, either by the bishop whose name they bear or by his successors.[1] But even harder problems are raised by statutes which are wholly unascribed in the surviving manuscripts. To determine their origin we can only examine the internal evidence and compare them with other statutes of known provenance. Even if certainty in every case is unattainable, the investigation is worth the effort and may teach us something about other, better authenticated, series of statutes and the method of their compilation. This paper is concerned with three series of statutes: the first was set by Mansi in the *Amplissima* (xxii. 723) under the date 1200 and the title ' Concilium incerti loci '; the second is found in print only in a late and garbled version which David Wilkins published in *Concilia Magnae Britanniae et Hiberniae* (1737), i. 593 and Mansi reprinted (xxii. 1173) as ' Statuta legenda in concilio Oxoniensi edita ', linked to the genuine canons of Oxford, 1222; while the third was given by Wilkins (i. 656, and after him, by Mansi, xxiii. 463), as statutes of an unknown bishop.

I

' Constitutiones incerti loci ' is the title given by Martène and Durand to two series of statutes which they printed in *Thesaurus novus anecdotorum* (Paris, 1717), iv. 147, from a manuscript of the abbey of Corbie (diocese of Amiens). Both were reprinted by Nicolò Coleti in his *Sacrosancta concilia*, xiii (1730), 759 and by Mansi (xxii. 723, 731). The second series (*inc.* ' Baptismus cum reverentia . . . '), save for the last ten chapters (c. 53–62), corresponds to parts of the Parisian statutes attributed to Bishop Odo de Sully (d. 1208).[2] We are concerned only with the first series (*inc.* ' Quia non potest . . . ') printed under this title, ' Constitutiones incerti

médiéval 1958 (Louvain, 1959) pp. 73–87, which refers also to studies outside France. In 1939 appeared Emil Brzoska, *Die Breslauer Diözesansynoden bis zur Reformation* (Bresslau, 1939), on which see the ensuing controversy between Brzoska and Bernhard Panzram in *Ztschr. der Savigny-Stiftung für Rechtsgesch.* (kan. Abt.), lxi (1941), 384–97, lxiv (1944), 336–63. Great advance is marked in Poland by the publication of critical studies and editions by Professor Jakub Sawicki under the title *Concilia Poloniae: Zródła i Studia Krytyczne* (nine volumes, 1945–57, in progress). Dr. Sawicki's important paper on ' Die Entwicklung der Kirchenrechtswissenschaft in Polen 1918–57 ', *Oesterreichisches Archiv für Kirchenrecht*, ix (1958), 243–69 gives a full bibliography of work on Polish synods, pp. 255–60. For Sweden we now have the monograph of Professor Sigurd Kroon, *Det svenska Prästmötet under Medeltiden: dess Uppkomst och Ställning i Samhälle och Kyrka*, Acta historico-ecclesiastica suecana 18 (Stockholm, 1948), with a short résumé in French; for a review by the present writer see *Journal of Eccl. Hist.* i (1950), 120–1.

[1] E.g., for Paris see L. Guizard, *loc. cit.* p. 1 n. 1 above, and for the Norwich statutes see Cheney, *Eng. Synodalia*, pp. 125–36.

[2] The statutes are in Mansi, *Ampl. Coll.*, xxii. 675–86. Chapters 53–62 of the statutes printed at col. 731–5 differ from the corresponding parts of ' Odo ' (*communia precepta*, c. 21–4) but concern the same matters. The series as a whole may be another recension of the Parisian statutes, as Guizard suggests.

loci '. It is our object to show that these statutes, which we will call *CIL*, were compiled in England, and to fit them into the history of the legislation of the English Church. The manuscript from Corbie, which Martène and Durand saw, has not been traced among the numerous remains of that famous library,[1] but another incomplete text in an early thirteenth-century hand has come to light on two folios which form flyleaves to a glossed book of Daniel in Cambridge, Pembroke College MS. 62, which was formerly in the abbey of Bury St. Edmunds.[2]

In a short preamble to the statutes, addressed to the clergy, the legislator declares that his object is to appoint rules of conduct, of dispensing the sacraments, and of behaviour towards the laity. The following sixty-four statutes follow out this scheme fairly systematically. Chapters 1–4 concern cases of irregularity in ordination, chapters 5–16 the ' vita et honestas ' of the clergy with special reference to the sins of *luxuria, superbia,* and *avaritia.* The rest of the statutes is mainly written round the rules for the performance of four sacraments: the eucharist, baptism, penance, and marriage. Scattered among these chapters and following them are some prescriptions which could not fit logically into the scheme: on the maintenance of church fabric, Sunday observance, games in churchyards, and so on. These produce a somewhat disorderly effect on an underlying pattern, as we find in even the most important sets of English diocesan statutes of the thirteenth century.[3] Altogether there is little here to suggest a gradual accumulation of statutes at successive synods, and we may assume for the time being that *CIL* was completed all at one time.

The first step towards determining the circumstances in which *CIL* was issued is to look for parallel passages in other legislation, and they are to be found in plenty; for only half a dozen chapters (7, 38, 40, 41, 57, 61) do not present close verbal parallels with other statutes of known provenance. Parallels with more than one set of statutes may be particularly instructive, and it is those which will be examined here. The present writer pointed out long ago that the canons of Archbishop Hubert Walter in the provincial council of London (or more exactly, Westminster), 19 September 1200, were paralleled in the earliest diocesan statutes of Salisbury (1217 × 1221), Winchester (? 1224), and Chichester (1244 × 1253).[4]

[1] *Cf.* L. Delisle, *Le cabinet des mss. de la Bibliothèque Impériale* [*Nationale*], (Paris, 1868–81), ii. 104–41, 427–8.

[2] The second flyleaf is severely damaged; the text contains the preamble, c. 1–46, and parts of c. 47–55. Since the binding is relatively modern there is no certainty that the flyleaves come from Bury.

[3] *Cf. Eng. Synodalia*, pp. 52–3 (Salisbury) and 90–1 (Worcester).

[4] *Ibid.* pp. 55, 76, 87. The references to the statutes of Salisbury hereafter are to the edition by W. D. Macray in *Charters and docs · · · of Salisbury* (Rolls Series, 1891), pp. 128–63, but in some instances readings from other sources are preferred. The Winchester statutes are quoted from the only known manuscript: Bodleian, Hatton

4   THE EARLIEST ENGLISH

It is therefore of special interest that all these parallels, without exception, are matched in *CIL*.
A few examples will bring out the relationship:

Westminster c. 3	*CIL* c. 36, 35	Salisbury c. 27 [1]
De baptismate vel confirmatione si dubitetur sanctorum canonum statuta sequentes statuimus ut conferatur, quia non dicitur iteratum quod nescitur fuisse collatum. Ideoque baptizentur expositi de quorum baptismo dubitatur, sive inveniantur cum sale sive sine sale.	Similiter de confirmatione si dubitetur conferatur, quia dici non debet iteratum quod nescitur fuisse collatum. Si vero pueros cum sale contingat expositos inveniri baptizentur, si vero sine sale inveniantur expositi et utrum baptizati fuerint dubitetur baptizentur, ita tamen quod ante . . . [as Salisbury].	Si vero pueros contingat cum sale expositos inveniri baptizentur, ita tamen quod ante . . . [as *CIL*]. Similiter de confirmatione quia non debet dici iteratum quod nescitur esse collatum.

Westminster c. 9	*CIL* c. 48	Salisbury c. 45–46
Cum . . . sanctorum patrum statuta declarent decimas de omnibus que per annum renovantur prestandas id inviolabiliter decernimus observandum ita ut occasione mercedis servientium vel messorum decima pars non minuatur. . . . Detentores vero decimarum iuxta Rothomagensis concilii constitutum . . . usque ad satisfactionem congruam anathematis vinculo feriantur.	Decimas autem de omnibus que per annum renovantur dandas decrevimus ita ut occasione mercedis servientium vel messorum ecclesie decima parte non frustrentur. Detentores vero decimarum . . . usque ad satisfactionem congruam anathematis vinculo feriantur. Cum autem hii qui decimas detinuerint . . . [as Salisbury].	Decimas autem de omnibus que per annum renovantur et maxime consuetas decimas dandas decrevimus et districte precipimus ita ut occasione mercedis servientium vel messorum ecclesia decima parte non frustretur. Detentores autem decimarum consuetarum . . . usque ad satisfactionem condignam per censuram ecclesiasticam compellantur. Cum autem hii qui decimas detinuerint . . . [as *CIL*].

Westminster c. 10	*CIL* c. 9	Winchester c. 63
Hiis etiam adnectimus ut clerici non intersint tabernis et publicis potationibus.	Inhibemus etiam ne sacerdotes vel quilibet clerici tabernas frequentent vel publicis potationibus aut spectaculis aut ubi turpia et inhonesta cantantur intersint.	Sacerdotes et clerici publicis non intersint potationibus.

92, fo. 154ʳ. The Chichester statutes are quoted as from Wilkins, i. 688–93. The Westminster canons are in Wilkins, i. 505–8.
    [1] The second sentence is only found in texts AC (cf. *Eng. Synodalia*, pp. 57–8).

Westminster c. 12	CIL c. 58	Salisbury c. 38	Chichester (Wilkins, i. 690a)
Diffamati . . . super crimine de quo vinci non possunt, commoneantur . . . Si vero incorrepti . . . indicatur eis purgatio, et non occasione pecunie captande differatur de die in diem, sed statim primo die si parata fuerit suscipiatur et canonicum numerum non excedat.	Diffamati . . . super crimine aliquo de quo vinci non possunt, moneantur . . . Si vero incorrecti . . . indicatur eis purgatio, que occasione captande pecunie de die in diem nullatenus differatur, sed statim primo die si parata fuerit recipistur et canonicum numerum non excedat. Archidiaconus seu officialis vel decanus contra hoc statutum veniens se noverit ab officio suspendendum nec sine speciali auctoritate domini archiepiscopi vel episcopi relaxandum.	Diffamati . . . super crimine aliquo de quo convinci non possunt, moneantur . . . Si vero incorrigibiles . . . indicatur eis purgatio, que occasione pecunie oblate vel promisse de die in diem nullatenus differatur, sed si parata fuerit statim primo die recipiatur et canonum numerus obser- vetur. Archidiaconus sive officialis eius contra hoc veniens ab officio suo se noverit suspendendum.	. . . diffamati . . . super aliquo crimine de quo convinci non possunt, moneantur . . . Si vero incorrect . . . indicatur eis purgatio, que occasione captande pecunie de die in diem nullatenus differatur, sed statim primo die si parata fuerit recipiatur et canonicus usus observetur. Archidiaconus, officialis, sive decanus contra statutum veniens se noverit ab officio suspendendum.

These examples indicate clearly that *CIL* stands between Westminster, 1200 on the one hand and the Salisbury, Winchester, and Chichester statutes on the other. This could mean either that *CIL* was the common parent of Westminster and the later statutes or that it was a parent of the later statutes, itself derived from Westminster. Two facts point to the latter explanation: the drafting of *CIL* seems to improve on Westminster in neatness at several points, and at one point where Archbishop Hubert's legatine canons of York (1195)[1] provided a basis for his canons of Westminster, Westminster stands between York and *CIL*:

York c. 4	Westminster c. 3	CIL c. 36, 35
Ubi autem puer cuius baptismus ignoratur reperitur expositus, sive cum sale sive sine sale reperiatur, baptizetur, cum non intelligatur iteratum quod nescitur fuisse collatum.	De baptismate vel confirmatione si dubitetur, sanctorum canonum statuta sequentes statuimus ut conferatur, quia non dicitur iteratum quod nescitur fuisse collatum. Ideoque baptizentur expositi de quorum baptismo dubitatur, sive inveniantur cum sale sive sine sale.	Similiter de confirmatione si dubitetur conferatur, quia dici non debet iteratum quod nescitur fuisse collatum. Si vero pueros cum sale contingat expositos inveniri baptizentur, si vero sine sale inveniantur expositi et utrum baptizati fuerint dubitetur, baptizentur . . .

[1] Wilkins, i. 501.

6   THE EARLIEST ENGLISH

Another group of parallels must now be noted. *CIL* c. 5 agrees in substance and for a few words is verbally identical with c. 4 of canons issued by Cardinal Robert de Courson as papal legate, first in a council at Paris in June or July 1213, secondly in a council at Rouen in February 1214.[1] Further on in *CIL* comes a small group of statutes (26–30) which with one exception (27) agree very closely with Courson's canons, c. 9–12. Two examples will illustrate the similarities:

Paris 1213, I. 4	*CIL* c. 5
Inhibemus etiam districtius ne clerici in sacris ordinibus constituti etiamsi beneficiati non fuerint, in propriis domibus vel in alienis publice focarias habeant unde scandalum oriatur. Quod si aliqui contra huius constitutionis tenorem venire presumpserint et ad admonitionem prelati sui focarias non dimiserint et a se prorsus non expulerint, elapsis xl diebus a primo die monitionis noverint se excommunicationis sententie subiacere. Idem etiam de beneficiatis duximus statuendum, adicientes quod post tempus predicte admonitionis, ab officio et beneficio se noverint esse suspensos nec absolvantur vel ad beneficia restituantur nisi gravi ab episcopis suis iniuncta pena.	. . . statuimus ut sacerdotes et clerici beneficiati, vel in sacris ordinibus constituti sive beneficiati sint sive non, . . . continenter ac honeste vivant prout ad sacrum eorum ministerium noscitur pertinere. Nec in domibus propriis vel alienis publice concubinas unde scandalum oriatur tenere presumant set eas a se prorsus expellant et longius faciant amoveri, nisi velint simul officio et beneficiis suis contra hoc agendo privari.

Paris 1213, I. 9	*CIL* c. 26
Ad hec inhibemus districtius ne sacerdotes ignoti de quorum ordinatione non constat ad divinorum celebrationem admittantur, sine litteris testimonialibus vel testimonio bonorum virorum et eos qui contra hec venerint decernimus puniendos arbitrio prelatorum.	Ad hec prohibemus districtius ne sacerdotes ignoti de quorum ordinatione non constat ad divinorum celebrationem deserviendo ecclesias admittantur, nisi de licentia nostra cum per litteras testimoniales vel testimonium bonorum virorum nobis de eorum ordinatione fuerit sufficienter fides facta.

Again we can point to parallels with most of these passages in the Salisbury statutes (c. 6, 7, 70, 19, 18); but the likeness of Salisbury to *CIL* proves nothing about the relations of *CIL* to Courson's canons. A close comparison of *CIL* and Courson at these points gives no clear priority to one or the other. Only one small matter of substance can be adduced as evidence: *CIL* c. 29 (Paris

[1] Mansi, *Ampl. Coll.*, xxii. 820, 900.

I. 11, Rouen 12) forbids priests to demand compulsory payment 'pro annalibus vel tricennalibus vel septennalibus missarum faciendis'; Salisbury c. 18 borrowed this statute from *CIL* or from Courson, but omitted 'vel septennalibus'. I do not know of any other English statutes which mention *septennalia* of masses. May it not be that this was a piece of mechanical copying by the writer of *CIL*, from a legatine canon not intended for England and inappropriate to English custom?

The facts that we have so far considered establish that *CIL* was composed between 1200 and 1221 (the latest possible date for the Salisbury statutes); if it borrowed from Courson's canons it must have been framed after July 1213. The many loans from the Council of Westminster (of which ten chapters reappear in *CIL*) and other parallels with the Council of York, 1195,[1] suggest that *CIL* was English, despite the fact that it is printed from a manuscript in a French library which also contained synodal statutes of Paris and despite the connection with Courson. There is also the evidence of wide diffusion in English dioceses. A detail of substance confirms English composition: c. 64 reads, 'Prohibemus quoque ne denunciatus scotallorum fiat in ecclesiis vel per sacerdotem extra.' So far as is known, the word and custom of 'scotales' were peculiarly English.

An inference about the date of *CIL* may be drawn from its failure to mention the Fourth Lateran Council of 1215. Dangerous as is the argument from silence, it is noticeable that *CIL* has nothing to say about the degrees of consanguinity (whereas the Salisbury statute c. 86 will quote the Fourth Lateran c. 50–51) and requires the laity to be admonished to confess thrice a year without penalizing those who fail to confess annually. The silence of *CIL* is more significant still when compared with derivative passages in Salisbury; thus:

CIL c. 45	Salisbury c. 37
Moneantur laici statim in principio Quadragesime vel pluries in anno cito post lapsum confiteri, et ut ter in anno, scilicet Pascha, Natali, Pentecoste communicent; prius tamen preparari per aliquantulam abstinentiam de consilio sacerdotis faciendam [et] per confessionem.	Confessiones ter in anno audiantur, ter in anno communicare [subditi] moneantur, in Pascha, in Nathali, in Pentecoste; prius tamen preparent se per aliquam abstinentiam de consilio sacerdotis faciendam. Quicunque autem *semel in anno* ad minus *proprio* non confessus fuerit *sacerdoti*, et *ad minus* ad *Pascha eucharistie sacramentum* non perceperit, *nisi de consilio sacerdotis duxerit abstinendum et vivens ab ingressu ecclesie arceatur et mortuus christiana careat sepultura.*

---

[1] *Cf. CIL* c. 33 and York c. 5, *CIL.* c. 54 and York c. 10.

CIL c. 49	Salisbury c. 48, 49
Excommunicatio non passim et absque delectu fiat sed premissa canonica ammonitione. Singulis autem annis in tribus solempnibus festivitatibus. . . .	Sacro approbante concilio *prohibemus ne quis* aliquando *excommunicationis sententiam nisi competenti monitione premissa et presentibus personis ydoneis per quas* sufficienter *si necesse fuerit possit probari monitio,* auctoritate propria *promulgare presumat . . . expedire.* Singulis autem annis in tribus solempnitatibus maioribus. . . .

The italicised words in the Salisbury statutes come from the Fourth Lateran Council c. 21, 47. In the light of these passages where Salisbury seems deliberately to bring *CIL* up to date, we may suppose that the latter belongs to the years between 1200 and 1215.

The point has now been reached when it will be profitable to look at two textual differences between the Corbie text and the Bury text of *CIL*.[1] In the following quotations the italicised words are found only in the Bury text. *CIL* c. 17 is concerned with the care and reverence to be shown towards the consecrated elements in the eucharist, and reads: ' nec ultra septem dies serventur hostie consecrate, *post solutum scilicet interdictum*, set septimana qualibet in die dominica renoventur.' *CIL* c. 19 describes the method of carrying the viaticum to the infirm, and reads: ' lucerna precedente . . . et cruce similiter . . . precedente quoque tintinnabulo *post solutionem interdicti* ad cuius sonitum excitetur devotio audientium.' If (as the evidence already examined suggests) these are statutes issued in England between 1200 and 1215, the interdict in question is probably the general interdict which lay on all England from 24 March 1208 to 2 July 1214. Moreover, since these statutes are instructing parish priests in matters relating to the reserved Host and the viaticum, they would not have been framed at a time when the celebration of mass was wholly forbidden. After the earliest days of the interdict[2] it was not likely that the reserved Host would be found in any English churches until the pope had mitigated the interdict in January 1209 by permitting conventual churches to celebrate mass once a week behind closed doors.[3] But this mitigation did not affect the parish priests until, late in 1212, the pope allowed them to administer the viaticum

---

[1] It is convenient to designate the texts by these names, but we cannot assume that they were written in these places.

[2] In the instructions which probably emanated from one or more of the bishop-executors of the interdict soon after it began, we read: ' Corpus domini sicubi residuum fuerit, reservetur honeste in ecclesia, donec dicatur quid inde fieri debeat, ita quod a nullo sumatur nec a sacerdote nec ab alio ': Avranches, Bibliothèque municipale MS. 149, fo. 109ᵛᵃ (from Mt. S.-Michel), printed Migne, *Patr. Latina*, ccxvii. 192.

[3] Migne, ccxv. 1529.

to the dying and for this purpose to fetch the reserved Host from a conventual church.[1] This may possibly have tempted certain priests to reserve the consecrated Host for rather long periods as the Bury text envisages in c. 17, but no details of the practice of the time seem to have survived. But when the pope permitted the viaticum, he did not lift the embargo on bell-ringing: hence the note in c. 19. The Bury text, then, has limiting dates, July 1212 and July 1214. If one is entitled to read into the statutes a lively hope that the interdict will soon be lifted, then the text must belong to the period after King John had made his peace with the pope on 13 May 1213.

One might argue that the Bury text is a copy of statutes which originated before 1215 but in which this copy incorporated these special provisos because of some later local interdict. I know of no interdict which would meet the case. It would have to be an interdict covering a whole diocese, or at least an archdeaconry, and would have to be only a partial interdict, since the viaticum was permitted. It would also have to be of considerable importance or duration to persuade a copyist that these insertions were worth making. We are driven back to the view that the general interdict on England is the one in question.

It still remains to determine which version of the statutes is the earlier: that containing the references to the interdict or the Corbie text? If the references are insertions made in a pre-existent series of statutes, we must date the original issue between 1200 and 1208, when the interdict began. But before we jump to a conclusion on this point, it will be well to consider by what authority the statutes were framed.

They make no mention of a synod or synodal authority. Nor do they use any term such as *provincia* or *diocesis nostra* which determines the area to which they applied. But two other differences between the Bury and Corbie texts may serve as pointers. First, at most points in the statutes where an ecclesiastical authority is named, Bury reads *archiepiscopus* and Corbie reads *archiepiscopus vel episcopus*; thus c. 16: ' Quilibet autem sacerdos de consensu domini archiepiscopi [*add* vel episcopi C] suum habeat confessorem.' Secondly, in c. 21, to Corbie's prescription ' quod omnes habeant canonem misse secundum consuetudinem ecclesie correctum ' Bury adds, after ' ecclesie ', the word ' Cantur' '.

The possible authorities responsible for *CIL* are three in number: papal legate, archbishop, bishop. Let us examine the possibilities in turn:

(i) If Corbie is the original, its references to archbishop and bishop betoken a legatine authority. We meet with just such provisions in the legatine canons of Hubert at York, 1195, and Otto

---

[1] *Memoriale fr. Walteri de Coventria* (Rolls Series), ii. 205 and *Annales monastici* (Rolls Series), ii. 271.

at London, 1237. Two legates *a latere* visited England between 1200 and 1215: John of Ferentino in 1206, Nicholas of Tusculum in 1213–14.[1] But if the Corbie text is the original, it follows that it must be earlier than 1208, when the interdict began; and the authorship of Nicholas of Tusculum is excluded, attractive as that theory may be. John of Ferentino, on the other hand, came to England within a year after Archbishop Hubert's death and before King John's breach with Rome. Little is known of his activities except in regard to certain monasteries; but several chroniclers report that he held a council at Reading, and from the *Brut y Tywyso-gion* comes the surprising statement that in it ' he confirmed the law of the church throughout the whole kingdom '.[2] Could *CIL* be the unidentified canons of a Council of Reading, held in October 1206? This would agree with its dependence on Archbishop Hubert's canons, the lack of knowledge it displays of the statutes of Odo de Sully, bishop of Paris, and the wide and apparently independent borrowing by later English bishops. These facts are certainly compatible with such an origin, but do not necessarily require this explanation. Several other considerations tell against a legatine authority. First, *CIL* is altogether too modest a set of pastoral precepts to be regarded as a ' confirmation of church law of the whole kingdom '; far less comprehensive than Archbishop Hubert's canons, it hardly touches on any topic which would not interest the parish priest and his assistants. Secondly, certain canons of Robert de Courson of 1213–14 seem to be more probably a source than a derivative of *CIL*; and if this is so, it tells against John of Ferentino as author, though not against Nicholas of Tusculum. Thirdly, both Bury and Corbie versions include, in no less than six scattered chapters, the phrases *sine assensu nostro, auctoritate* or *licentia nostra, sine litteris nostris*, where no legate but a diocesan is plainly intended. This is a strong reason for rejecting that theory that either of the legates, before or during the interdict, was concerned in uttering these statutes.

(ii) Can it be supposed that *CIL* is provincial legislation, issued either by Hubert Walter or Stephen Langton for Canterbury or by Geoffrey Plantagenet for York? This might be, were we to regard

---

[1] For both see H. Tillmann, *Die päpstl. Legaten in England bis zur Beendigung der Legation Gualas* (Bonn, 1926), pp. 92–3, 98–107. For the former see also Cheney, ' The papal legate and English monasteries in 1206 ', *ante*, xlvi (1931), 443–52, and for the latter see also Angelo Mercati, ' La prima relazione del Cardinale Nicolò de Romanis sulla sua legazione in Inghilterra ', *Essays in History pres. to Reginald Lane Poole* (Oxford, 1927), pp. 274–89.

[2] *Brut y Tywysogion or the Chronicle of the Princes, Red Book of Hergest version*, ed. Thomas Jones (Cardiff, 1955), p. 187; the *Peniarth MS. 20 version* (ed. Jones, 1952), p. 83 reads: ' held a stately council wherein to confirm the laws of the church.' The council made sufficient impression to serve as a means of dating an act of the bishop of Coventry: ' Act' apud Lich' anno quo celebratum est concilium a Iohanne cardinali apud Redyng '' Brit. Mus., MS. Harl. 3868, fo. 3ᵛ.

the *archiepiscopus vel episcopus* of the Corbie text as a way of catering
for both the archdiocese and the dioceses of suffragans; but that
would involve giving priority to the Corbie text and assigning
CIL to Archbishop Hubert (who had already issued a more comprehensive code, though less detailed in some particulars) or to
Archbishop Geoffrey, and neither man seems to be a likely author.[1]
It would also involve neglecting the probable connection with
Courson's canons, and interpreting the Bury text as a reissue of
provincial canons for the archdiocese only. That the Bury version
could not be issued to the province is shown by its references to
archiepiscopus where the diocesan authority is intended, and by the
enforcement of the ' custom of the church of Canterbury ' when
other diocesan customs were certainly used within the province.

(iii) The third alternative, that *CIL* was issued in the first instance
for a diocese, raises fewer difficulties. On this showing, the Bury
version is the original and was designed for the archdiocese of
Canterbury: hence the reference to *archiepiscopus* (never to *epis-*
copus), and *consuetudinem ecclesie Cantur* ', and the phrases *sine assensu*
nostro, &c. The statutes, we must assume, were issued during the
interdict. This involves treating the Corbie text as a generalized
version of Canterbury diocesan statutes in which *vel episcopum* has
been added and the *consuetudinem ecclesie Cantur* ' has been dropped
along with the references to the interdict, in order to make a broader
application possible. Whether these changes were made for an
official reissue or unofficially, when and where they were made, is
beyond reasonable conjecture, since we know nothing about the
Corbie text.

The possibility that *CIL* was issued by an archdeacon can be
excluded in view of the use of the personal pronoun at points
where diocesan authority is invoked. The archdeacon is mentioned
only once,[2] and then the use of the singular, *archidiaconus*, is compatible with the theory that *CIL* was designed for the arch-diocese of
Canterbury, which had only one archdeacon at this time.[3] The
absence of more allusions to him and his duties agrees with the
tone of the preamble in suggesting that the statutes were issued
for direct transmission to all parish priests and concerned them
more than diocesan officers. In this respect *CIL* agrees with
Robert Grosseteste's famous statutes for the clergy of the diocese
of Lincoln, which do not mention at all the bishop's subordinates

---

[1] Theoretically, Langton could be the author, 1206–8, transmitting the canons to his
province during the twenty months between his consecration and the interdict, although
he was personally excluded from the country. But this seems so improbable as not to
deserve serious consideration.

[2] c. 59: ' Archidiaconus seu officialis vel decanus contra hoc statutum veniens se
noverit ab officio suspendendum, nec sine speciali auctoritate domini archiepiscopi
vel episcopi relaxandum.'

[3] Cheney, *From Becket to Langton* (Manchester, 1956), p. 6, n. 3.

on whom the application of the rules chiefly depended. In each case the legislator seems to be more concerned with the didactic, pastoral object than with the enforcement of sanctions.[1]

We conclude, tentatively, with the hypothesis that Archbishop Stephen Langton produced these statutes for circulation in his diocese, after his arrival in England on 16 July 1213 and before the lifting of the interdict on 2 July 1214. Seen in this context, *CIL* marks an important stage in the local law-making which was designed to bring order and uniformity to the English Church. The object of the next few pages is to place the statutes in this setting.

Before the end of the twelfth century, the canons of English legatine and provincial councils formed a foundation. Those of Archbishop Richard's Council of Westminster (1175) have a peculiar interest; for as Seckel first observed and Professor C. N. L. Brooke has more amply demonstrated, ' owing to the chance that its canons, incorporated incognito into decretal collections, could appear to be the canons of a general council, the province of Canterbury " legis-lated " for the Church at large '.[2] Before long, we may suppose, English diocesans were uttering precepts in their synods which repeated the canons and bore on similar topics. In the dispute which arose between Archbishop Richard and the exempt abbey of St. Augustine's, Canterbury, in 1182–3, the obligation was laid upon priests of the abbey's churches to attend synods and hear ' prohi-bitiones et precepta sinodalia '; and continental parallels make it improbable that this was an exceptional proceeding.[3] Nor need we rely on conjecture. Roger of Hoveden, writing before 1192, summarizes eight *decreta* which Hugh of Avalon, bishop of Lincoln (1186–1200) issued in his synods.[4] They resemble closely later diocesan legislation. Outside synods, too, a bishop could make laws by issuing mandates to his archdeacons. Bishop Hugh published a general rule relating to Pentecostal processions and payments in a letter to all the archdeacons and officials of the diocese of Lincoln, and Henry Marshal, bishop of Exeter (1194–1206) did the like.[5] Hubert Walter's two councils, 1195 and 1200, pro-vided the provinces of York and Canterbury respectively with

[1] Grosseteste's statutes are printed by Luard, R. *Grosseteste Epistolae* (Rolls Series), pp. 154–66; cf. *Eng. Synodalia*, p. 119.

[2] See Professor Brooke's paper, ' Canons of English Church Councils in the early Decretal Collections ', *Traditio*, xiii (1957), 471–80, at p. 476.

[3] Cheney, *From Becket to Langton*, p. 143. Cf. the practice of the diocese of Poitiers, ' secundum generalem consuetudinem regionis ', described by Pope Innocent III in 1212 (Migne, ccxvi. 543).

[4] *Gesta Regis Henrici II* (Rolls Series), i. 357. For the date and the probability that Roger of Hoveden wrote this chronicle, see Lady Stenton *ante* lxviii (1953), 574–82.

[5] *Registrum antiquissimum of . . . Lincoln*, i, ed. C. W. Foster (Lincoln Record Soc. 27, 1931), 257–58. *Register of John de Grandisson*, ed. F. C. Hingeston-Randolph (Exeter, 1894–99), ii. 785–86.

materials for instructing priests. During the last years of Archbishop Hubert's life, to 1205, there is no clear evidence of statute-making by English bishops,[1] but several of them obtained indults and mandates from Rome to strengthen their hands in tightening clerical discipline.[2] A generation later, Robert Grosseteste was issuing statutes on such authority as this, and the practice may well have started earlier.[3]

After Archbishop Hubert's death we should hardly expect to find much statute-making by English bishops for some years to come. Several bishoprics lay vacant for long periods, the interdict descended on the country in 1208, and few bishops remained at their posts after the king was excommunicated in 1209. It would be rash to suppose that diocesan government went entirely to pieces during the interdict or that absent bishops were completely cut off from their flocks: officials could deputize for them, their mandates could be read in ruri-decanal chapters.[4] The fact remains that there is a gap in the evidence of statute-making until King John made peace with the Church in May 1213. He chose a critical moment to do so.

On April 1213 Pope Innocent III had sent out to the various provinces of the Latin Church a summons to a general council to be held in November 1215.[5] The pope declared the two-fold object of the council in the preamble: ' Of all the desires of our heart we long chiefly for two in this life, namely, that we may work successfully to recover the Holy Land and to reform the Universal Church, both of which call for attention so immediate as to preclude further apathy or delay unless at the risk of great and serious danger.' For the furtherance of reform he ordered archbishops and bishops, during the intervening two and a half years, to enquire carefully about all matters which seemed to call for correction or reform, and to write reports for consideration by the council. This summons was calculated to stir men of good will all over Europe to active measures of reform. In northern France an additional impulse was given by the despatch of Cardinal Robert de Courson as papal legate a latere to preach and organize the projected Crusade.[6] The pope knew his man. The English-born cardinal had long been

---

[1] Some statutes which perhaps come from this time are in Brit. Mus. MS. Royal 7 C. vii, fo. 55ʳ. Cf. From Becket to Langton, pp. 142–3.

[2] Migne, ccxiv. 1034, ccxv. 110, 722–4.   [3] Engl. Synodalia, p. 120.

[4] The forma interdicti (above, p. 8, n. 2) provided: ' Teneantur a decanis capitula et extirpentur crimina tam clericorum quam laicorum in quantum fieri poterit ' (Migne, ccxvii. 191).

[5] Migne, ccxvi. 823–5, and in Selected letters of Pope Innocent III concerning England, ed. C. R. Cheney and W. H. Semple (1953), pp. 144–7.

[6] Migne, ccxvi. 882–3, 827–8 and M. and C. Dickson, ' Le Cardinal Robert de Courson: sa vie ', Archives d'Hist. doctrinale et litteraire du moyen âge, ix (1934), 53–142. For a recent brief summary of Courson's career see A. B. Emden, A biographical register of the Univ. of Oxford to 1500, i. (1957), 498–9.

a teacher of theology in Paris, and was equipped with practical legal knowledge and experience of affairs. A disciple of Peter Cantor, a colleague of Stephen Langton, he seems to have shared their interests to the full in the problems of church government and clerical conduct. The instruction of the parish priest in sacramental doctrine was a matter which had engaged recent bishops of Paris as well as the academic theologians; and the synodal statutes put out in the time of Odo de Sully and his successor were to be a pattern for many other dioceses. It was therefore highly significant that in June or July 1213 the newly-appointed legate published a long series of reforming canons in a council at Paris. They signify not so much novel ideas of Robert de Courson as a programme which had been finding occasional and partial expression during the last few decades in the writings of theologians,[1] the decretals of popes, and the local laws of the churches: a programme which achieved its broadest expression two years later in the Fourth Lateran Council.[2] The legate repeated the canons of Paris in a council at Rouen in February 1214.

The relevance of Courson's legation in France to the problem of the English statutes which we call *CIL* is obvious. Courson, who received his commission on 19 April 1213, arrived in northern France at the very time when Stephen Langton and his fellow-exiles, somewhere in northern France, were awaiting safe-conducts to return to England and were negotiating with King John. We cannot prove that they met, but it would be strange if they did not. They were old colleagues,[3] they had similar ecclesiastical interests,

---

[1] Of Courson, the Dicksons say: ' Tout ce qu'il nous laisse entrevoir dans la *Summa* de la discipline ecclésiastique à cette époque, se retrouve dans les décrets du concile de Paris ' (*loc. cit.* p. 125, cf. 126.). Cantor's importance may be better appreciated now that his *Summa de sacramentis* is being published by J. A. Dugauquier (*Analecta medievalia namurcensia*, Louvain, 1954–   ). For this circle and their interest in legal questions see F. M. Powicke, *Stephen Langton* (Oxford, 1928), especially ch. iii.

[2] In a paper 'Zur Entstehung der europäischen u. der schwedischen Diözesansynode ', *Kyrkohistorisk Årsskrift*, xlviii (1948), 1–31 Sten Gagnér stresses the importance of the legate's council as preparation for the Fourth Lateran, but greatly exaggerates the novelty of its prescriptions. For his theory it is necessary to argue against Odo de Sully's authorship of any of the statutes attributed to him (' Der Sommer des Jahres 1213 bietet sich dar als *terminus a quo* für die Pariser Statuten ', p. 19). For him the legate's demand for annual diocesan synods (' der Synodenforschung unbekannt ', p. 11, actually noted in *Eng. Synodalia*, p. 15, n. 6) 'machen . . . den Ursprung der hochmittelalterlichen Diözesansynode aus ', p. 12. But all this shows a reckless misuse of the evidence for the ' Odo ' statutes and a sad ignorance of earlier decretals and local laws of similar content.

[3] Jacques de Vitry names them together as great preachers and teachers (Dickson, *loc. cit.* p. 67 n. 6), and they had been appointed together to act in a case of arbitration at Paris in 1206, though Langton withdrew (*ibid.* p. 79). In a dubious story about heretics in Paris, Caesarius of Heisterbach says that the matter was reported to the bishop ' et tres magistros legentes de theologia, videlicet decanum Salebergiensem, et magistrum Robertum de Kortui et magistrum Stephanum ' presumably Richard Poore (see below, p. 16), Robert de Courson, and Stephen Langton: *Dialogus miraculorum*, ed. J. Strange (Cologne, 1851), i. 306.

they were both deeply concerned in the political state of England.[1] That Langton should carry into England something of the atmosphere of Courson's legation, that he should take a first step towards reforming the English clergy by issuing statutes for the parish-priests of his diocese, and that a few of Courson's canons should find their way into Langton's statutes—all this is not in the least surprising. It seems strange, rather, that more was not taken over; but this may be because *CIL* is a less ambitious document, with less scope, than Courson's canons,[2] and its author (whoever it was whom the busy archbishop charged with the task of composition) had Archbishop Hubert's canons to work upon. While the conclusion which we reached by considering the internal evidence of *CIL*'s two versions is not proved to the hilt, it is entirely compatible with the circumstances of Langton's arrival in England. The only recorded councils which he assembled during the two years he spent in England after his return in July 1213 were apparently concerned exclusively with matters arising out of the interdict: the indemnification of the clergy and the election of new prelates.[3] But if we are right in regarding *CIL* as his production, he contributed something of importance to the movement for raising clerical standards before the Fourth Lateran Council.

After 1215 English diocesans began to issue long series of statutes for the guidance of their clergy and officials.[4] They necessarily took account of the canons of the Fourth Lateran Council and, after 1222, of those of the Council of Oxford. Sometimes they quoted the very words of these canons; but for the didactic pattern, for the detail, and very often for the wording, they went back to earlier and less exalted models. The draftsmen showed all the ingenuity expected of a medieval notary in adapting old formulas—' sicut nasum cereum '—to new laws or varying local customs. Their

---

[1] *Rotuli litt. clausarum*, ed. T. D. Hardy (Record Comm. 1833–4), i. 165*a* shows that by the month of August 1213 at latest they were in touch on the question of preaching the Crusade in England; and the terms of the king's letter to Courson suggests that they had actually spoken together about the matter (' per quoddam transcriptum quod dominus Cantuariensis archiepiscopus a vobis audierat ').

[2] In the canons of Oxford, 1222, Langton adopted some of Courson's admonitions to bishops: cf. Paris (1213), iv. 6–8, with Oxford c. 1–2.

[3] A council, perhaps not confined to the southern province, at Westminster, 25 Aug. 1213: Waverley annals, *Annales monastici* (Rolls Series), ii. 277 and Roger Wendover, *Flores historiarum* (ed. H. O. Coxe, Eng. Hist. Soc., 1841–4), iii. 263; a meeting with his suffragans, perhaps hardly formal enough to be accounted a provincial council, took place at Dunstable, according to Wendover about 13 Jan. 1214: *Flores*, iii. 278. Langton apparently tried to call together a provincial council at Oxford in May 1215, at the height of the political crisis, but the attempt was abandoned: *Memoriale fratris Walteri de Coventria* (Rolls Series), ii. 220. The Waverley annals (following those of Southwark) speak of Langton's council of Oxford, 1222, as ' concilium suum primum '. *Ann. mon.* ii. 296.

[4] See Marion Gibbs and Jane Lang, *Bishops and Reform, 1215–1272* (Oxford, 1934), pp. 94–179 and *Eng. Synodalia*.

products have both individuality and a family likeness. The chief sources are *CIL* and the statutes attributed to Odo de Sully.

The earliest English post-Lateran statutes may have been those of Richard Poore, bishop of Salisbury (1217 × 21),[1] and their compiler had before him both these series [2] as well as a copy of Courson's canons (either of Paris or of Rouen). A single example will show how Poore used his main sources:

Odo de Sully 3.5	Salisbury c. 24
Ad elevandum parvum de fonte tres ad plus recipiantur; quod enim amplius est a malo est.	Ad levandum puerum de fonte tres ad plus recipiantur: in baptismo maris duo mares et una femina; femina vero a duabus feminis et uno mare suscipiatur. Quod amplius est a malo est. Plures tantum tanquam testes non tanquam patrini si haberi possunt adhibeantur propter varias causas.

CIL c. 33 [3]

In baptismo vero maris duo mares et una femina suscipiant baptizatum. A duabus vero feminis et uno mare femina suscipiatur in baptismo.

Poore had been a pupil of Langton at Paris and was associated with other scholars at home and abroad. One *Summa de penitentia* was dedicated to Poore as dean of Salisbury (1198–1215), and Poore's sub-dean, Thomas of Chobham, was author of another. During the interdict, moreover, Poore was in Paris from 1209 onwards; he was teaching there early in 1213 and may have been teaching while Courson was still in his academic chair.[4] In 1215 Poore attended the Lateran Council. When he became a bishop (at Chichester, 1215 and Salisbury, 1217) it was natural that his pastoral work should bear the marks of these influences. His synodal statutes were a clever mosaic, and as an instrument of diocesan government and clerical instruction they were far more comprehensive and up-to-date than either of the series which had provided much of the material. We need not therefore be surprised that within a few years the Salisbury statutes seem to have been re-published with comparatively little change for the archdiocese of Canterbury.[5] That Langton would recognize the superiority of his friend's statutes to his own series of 1213–14 is understandable; and the speedy displacement of *CIL* by the longer series may account for the weak manuscript tradition.

During the next generation, while Poore's statutes circulated widely in England, other English diocesans not only borrowed them,

---

[1] The short series of William de Blois, bishop of Worcester, 1219 (Wilkins, i. 570–1) may be earlier.

[2] *Cf. Eng. Synodalia*, pp. 51–7. Those passages which I indicated (p. 55) as coming from Archbishop Hubert come in fact (with much besides) from *CIL*.

[3] *CIL*'s source seems to be the Council of York, 1195, c. 4: ' Statuimus ne in baptismate plures quam tres suscipiant puerum de sacro fonte: masculum duo mares et una mulier, feminam due femine et unus mas ' (Wilkins, i. 501*b*).

[4] Migne, ccxv. 1519, ccxvi. 396, 801, L. D'Achery, *Veterum SS. Spicilegium* (1723), ii. 849. *Cf.* above p. 14, n. 3.   [5] *Eng. Synodalia*, pp. 62–5.

but had independent access to the statutes of Odo de Sully which he had found so useful.[1] The same is also true of Poore's other main source: *CIL*. Little as *CIL* is known in its original form, directly or indirectly it filtered through to the statutes of Winchester, Exeter, Chichester, and another diocese, independently of those parts absorbed by Poore.

The statutes of Peter des Roches for Winchester (probably of the year 1224) are singularly compact and business-like, and free from verbal copying of other legislation.[2] They contain only two or three passages demonstrably drawn from *CIL*, but they are passages which do not occur in the statutes of Salisbury:

CIL c. 14	Winchester c. 20
Provideant autem sacerdotes parochias regentes ne vicinis ecclesiis sint dampnosi, recipiendo iniuste parochianos eorum.	Prohibemus insuper ne sacerdotes parochias regentes vicinis ecclesiis sint dampnosi, recipiendo iniuste parochianos eorum ad penitentiam vel ad ecclesiastica sacramenta percipienda.

CIL c. 50	Winchester c. 61 [3]
Inhibeatur etiam omnibus ne pingnus ubi nichil de sorte minuitur retineant postquam de fructibus sortem receperint, deductis expensis.	Inhibeatur omnibus mercatoribus et creditoribus ne pignus aliquod ultra detineant postquam de fructibus sortem receperint, deductis expensis.

Again, the statutes of Exeter (1225 × 37),[4] which are incomplete in the only known text, are mainly derived from the Salisbury statutes; but they too contain a few passages of *CIL* which were not taken over by Poore, *e.g.*:

CIL c. 37	Exeter c. 2
Quia quilibet christianus adultus dominicam orationem scilicet pater noster et simbolum apostolorum scilicet credo in deum scire debet, precipimus quod quilibet sacerdos parochianos suos ut hec addiscant studeat ammonere.	Quia vero quilibet christianus adultus dominicam orationem scilicet pater noster et cimbolum apostolorum scilicet credo in deum patrem scire debet, precipimus quod quilibet sacerdos suos parochianos ut hec addiscant una cum salutatione beate virginis moneat diligenter et inducat. Pueros quoque sepe . . . [as Salisbury c 5].

[1] *Eng. Synodalia*, pp. 82–4 and below, p. 22. An early text of the Odo statutes is preserved in Cambridge, Corpus Christi Coll. MS. 317 fo. 1ʳ; but whether this was written in England or was in English ownership in the thirteenth century is unknown.

[2] *Ibid.* p. 76.

[3] *CIL* c. 50 was also the source of Salisbury c. 47, but this must be separately derived from *CIL*. For a third parallel passage see above, p. 4.

[4] *Eng. Synodalia*, pp. 76–9. Mention of the dean, whose dignity was only created in 1225, provides the *terminus a quo*.

The same is true of Richard de Wich's statutes for the diocese of Chichester (1244 × 53):[1]

CIL c. 25	Chichester (Wilkins, i. 690*b*)
Statuimus etiam ut pensiones ecclesiarum veteres sine assensu nostro non augeantur nec nove imponantur eisdem.	Item statuimus ne pensiones ecclesiarum veteres sine nostro assensu augeantur nec nove eisdem imponantur.

The chief beneficiary of *CIL*, apart from Salisbury, is anonymous and must be considered separately. But it will be best first to look at a famous and widely diffused series of statutes which Mansi printed after Wilkins, without being able to identify it: the so-called *Legenda* of Oxford.

II [2]

The statutes which here call for identification are contained in Bodleian MS. Bodley 843 fos. 122ʳ-125ᵛ; they bear no title and no mark of provenance: the script may be assigned to the first half of the thirteenth century. They may be christened ' Statuta synodalia ' (hereafter *SS*).[3] The first half of *SS* deals in turn with the administration of the seven sacraments; then come fairly clearly marked sections on the archdeacon's authority, the care of churches and church property, tithe, sentences of excommunication, the conduct of the clergy, secular and regular. The last chapter condemns the mistresses of clerks. A very similar text of much of *SS* is in a mid-thirteenth century manuscript, Cambridge, Gonville & Caius Coll. 349 fo. 127ʳ*b*, where it follows without break an abridged version of the canons of Oxford, 1222.

It is the association of late and truncated copies, variously deformed, with the canons of Oxford which has obscured the true nature of *SS*; and the matter has been confused by other selections ascribed to Archbishops Walter Reynolds and Stephen Mepham.[4] These must be cleared out of the way before we consider the whole series of *SS* as it appears in MS. Bodley 843.

Wilkins (i. 593) printed the statutes which he found in the fourteenth century Bodleian MS. Hatton 109 (then Hatton 24) fo. 56ᵛ, and treated them as an appendix to the canons of Oxford: he gave them the title ' Statuta legenda in concilio Oxoniensi edita per dominum Stephanum Langton Cantuariensem archiepiscopum a.d. mccxxii '. Mansi reprinted this text, which we call *Legenda*, to

---

[1] Cf. above, p. 5.

[2] The following account incorporates parts of my former description of the statutes, *ante*, l (1935), 395–8, but differs in some respects from its conclusions, as also from the view expressed in *Eng. Synodalia*, p. 40.

[3] They are shown to be synodal statutes by a time-limit in the penultimate chapter: ' infra spatium sex mensium a tempore huius sancte synodi computandum.'

[4] Cf. below, p. 31.

distinguish it from the related *SS*. Wilkins had tacitly modified the title he found in Hatton 109, which reads: ' Statuta de[*sic*] legenda in synodo edita in consilio Oxon' per dominum Stephanum quondam Cantuariensem archiepiscopum a.d. mccxxii.'[1] This is immediately followed by the *incipit* of the Oxford sentences of excommunication and by the *incipit* of Oxford c. 5 (Wilkins, i. 585, 586). Surely this was but a way of saying that first among statutes to be read in a synod were these parts of the Oxford canons? Then were to be read the statutes which follow, under fourteen rubrics. These, too, were *legenda*, but they did not all emanate from the Council of Oxford.[2] A glance at the choice of canons of Oxford and of *SS* in Caius Coll. 349 supports this conjecture. This selection also begins with the Oxford sentences and continues with c. 5. The intervening chapters of Oxford were not for recital in synod, for they are injunctions addressed by the metropolitan to the bishops. On the same principle, the selection of the canons of Oxford and of *SS* which follows generally omits those concerning the diocesan officials and the regular clergy. In this respect Caius Coll. 349 agrees with the *Legenda* in its omissions from *SS*.[3] We are entitled to infer that these selections were designed for recital in an archdeacon's synod or chapter.

Other groups of manuscripts associate *Legenda* with the Council of Oxford. In a late fourteenth-century collection of canons (Cambridge, Pembroke Coll. MS. 131 fo. 87ʳ) the *Legenda* occur with the title ' Concilium apud Oxon ' secundum celebratum ibidem a.d. mccc vicesimo.' After a preamble which also occurs in Robert Grosseteste's diocesan statutes,[4] this text continues as Caius Coll. 349 with the Oxford sentences and c. 5 and the first chapter of *SS* (' De baptismo '). Unfortunately Pembroke Coll. 131 is defective,

---

[1] The Hatton text concludes (fo. 62ᵛ); ' Expliciunt statuta legenda in synodo ut supra continentur in consilio Oxon'.' Two related texts which follow the canons of Oxford have similar *incipits* to that of Hatton 109 and resemble it in form. They both end: ' Expliciunt constitutiones bone memorie Stephani Langtone archiepiscopi Cantuariensis edite in concilio Oxon' a.d. mccxxii ' (Oxford, Balliol Coll. MS. 158, fo. 138ʳ (late fourteenth century) and Cambridge, Univ. Libr. MS. Ii. 3. 14, fo. 221ᵛ (early fifteenth century)).

[2] Chapter 3 (last sentence), 10 and 14 come from the Council of Oxford c. 11, 28, 8 (ii) and 9 (Wilkins, i. 586–90), while the incorrect rubric of c. 14 (' De vita et honestate clericorum ') suggests that c. 14–16 of the Fourth Lateran were meant to follow, as they do in the two early texts of *SS*.

[3] Since *SS* is not in print, it is worth noting its chief additions to the *Legenda* printed by Wilkins. After c. 6 ' De matrimonio ' is a chapter on the hearing of matrimonial cases; before the last clause of c. 7 ' De ordinibus et ordinandis ' is a chapter on the conduct of monastic ordinands; after c. 8 ' De officio archidiaconorum ' is a chapter urging archdeacons, &c. to exercise justice. At the end come three chapters abridging Fourth Lateran Council c. 14–16, and a long series of precepts ' De statu monachorum et regularium '. The chapter-numbers given here correspond to the series of rubrics in Wilkins's text of *Legenda*. When *SS* comes to be printed a new numeration will be adopted.

[4] R. *Grosseteste Epp.* (Rolls Series), pp. 162–4, beginning: ' Et quia in multis ecclesiis ut credimus non est scriptum Oxoniense concilium. . . . '

but two more manuscripts which have similar titles and the same introductory matter terminate with Fourth Lateran Council c. 14–16 and other material.[1] In four more manuscripts some of the *Legenda* follow the canons of Oxford without a break under the same rubric.[2] Two fifteenth-century texts, which come closer than do most to the text of Bodley 843, follow the canons with a fresh title: in the one case ' Generale consilium Oxoniense ' (Bodleian MS. Selden supra 43, fo. 46^r), in the other ' Constitutiones iste celebrate etiam Oxon' a.d. m—' (Cambridge, Trinity Coll. MS. 1245, fo. 116^v).[3] Another fifteenth-century text (Oxford, Magdalen Coll. MS. 185 fo. 14^r), which agrees closely with the printed text of 1504,[4] precedes the canons of Oxford. It bears the evidently corrupt title: ' Anno regis Henrici viii^o concilium Oxon' celebratum sub Stephano Cantuariensi archiepiscopo et suis suffraganeis anno gratie mccxxx.'[5] A text written about 1400 (Cambridge, Peterhouse MS. 51 (ii) fo. 23^{r}a) includes some extracts from Oxford 1222 and bears the title: ' Incipiunt constitutiones domini Stephani Cant ' archiepiscopi.'[6] These various associations of the *Legenda* with the Council of Oxford may all result from the fact noted in connection with Hatton 109 and its fellows. Parts of the canons of Oxford 1222 were ordered to be recited regularly in synods. To these might be added whole series of statutes which would be suitable to the occasion; they included c. 14–16 of the Fourth Lateran Council, and much other material which was unconnected with the Council of Oxford.

[1] Cambridge, Gonv. & Caius. Coll. 38, fo. 111^r (fourteenth century) and Brit. Mus., Harl. 3705, fo. 70^v (fifteenth century). The title of Harl. 3705 reads: ' Constitutiones Oxon ii^o. Quidam dicunt quod sunt Stephani Langthon edite in manerio suo de Lambeth anno domini m cc—.' Fourth Lateran Council c. 16 also occurs in the midst of *Legenda* in the group of manuscripts represented by Lambeth 171 (see next note).

[2] Lambeth Palace, 171 fo. 16^r (early fourteenth century from Worcester); Bodleian, Rawlinson C. 428, fo. 107^v (copied from the preceding), Bodley 794, fo. 162^r (early fifteenth century); Oxford, Exeter Coll. 31, fo. 222 (late fourteenth century). In these texts the selection of statutes is the following: *Legenda* c. 2 (i), Fourth Lateran c. 16, ' Circa decimas autem . . . ' (*cf.* below, p. 22 n. 1), *Legenda* c. 13 (i), ' Prohibemus etiam sub pena . . . ' (*cf.* below, p. 27 n. 3), *Legenda* c. 1–7 with the additions of *SS* to 6 and 7, *Legenda* 9, 11, 12, 13 (ii). Fragments of a similar selection occur in Brit. Mus. Harl. 335, fo. 43^r.

[3] The following pages of the Trinity Coll. manuscript are headed ' Oxon ii^o ' (cf. *ante*, l. 398, n. 4). The selection in the Bodleian manuscripts is: *Legenda* c. 1–6 (with *SS* addition to 6), *Legenda* c. 7 (ii) (with *SS* addition), ' Item persone et vicarii . . . ' (*cf.* below, p. 22 n. 1), the four last chapters of *SS* ' De statu monachorum ', *Legenda* c. 9, 11, 12, 13.

[4] *Constitutiones legitime seu legatine regionis Anglicane . . . necnon et constitutiones provinciales ab archiepiscopis Cantuariensibus edite* (Paris, 1504), fo. 124^{v}b.

[5] These texts have the following selection: *Legenda* c. 1–7 (omitting parts of 3, 5, and 7 and with *SS* addition to 6), *Legenda* c. 9, 11, 12, 13 (ii) and C. of Oxford c. 50 (ii). The same text is reproduced in the second supplement to W. Lyndwood, *Provinciale* (Oxford, 1679), p. 7.

[6] This selection resembles closely that in Selden supra 43 (above, n. 3) but places the monastic chapters before *Legenda* c. 7.

At first sight, it does not seem impossible that these *Legenda* should have been issued at Oxford in 1222, to provide the bishops with something more directly adapted to the needs of archdeacons and parochial clergy than were the canons of the provincial council. But the theory is unsatisfactory. No early text of the canons is accompanied by the *Legenda*, and nothing in the canons suggests that the circulation of such a document was contemplated. If such a series of statutes had been officially put out by Langton in 1222, it would surely show some trace of *CIL*, which we attribute to Langton and which filled a similar need. It would also have diminished the need for the series, based on the statutes of Salisbury, which we believe to have been issued in the archdiocese between 1222 and 1228.[1] Finally, had the *Legenda* been issued in this important provincial council, we should expect to find a more extensive influence on other synodal statutes of the period.

Having rejected the supposed connection of the *Legenda* with the Council of Oxford, 1222, we can dispose fairly easily of other groups of texts. No less than fifteen fifteenth-century manuscripts agree in their selection from the *Legenda* and agree in the title: ' Constitutiones provinciales domini Stephani [*sic*] Mepham Cantuariensis archiepiscopi edite apud Lambeth.' Lyndwood selected from some such text, but attached the name of Archbishop Walter Reynolds because, ' iuxta quotationem communem ', they were dated 1322. On the basis of Lyndwood's text the Oxford editor of 1679 composed a series which Wilkins reprinted (ii. 512) as the product of a Council of Oxford, 1322. The arguments against all these attributions have been stated before.[2] They conform to the usual pattern of *spurii* included in the legal collections of the fourteenth and fifteenth centuries.

The manuscripts of these statutes which we have so far considered, apart from their various and inadmissible ascriptions, differ among themselves in the material they include. There are some ten distinct combinations among the thirty or more texts. It is barely credible that each of these combinations should represent the work of a separate legislator, and that in every case the provenance should be lost together with nearly all early manuscripts. But although some of the groups of texts were the results of private enterprise in the later Middle Ages, that does not prove that in the beginning there was no genuine series of statutes, compiled by a bishop as legislator and published in a synod. It is hard otherwise to explain how the many *spurii* came to be born. And so we are driven back to consider the claims of *SS*—the text in Bodley 843—to be the genuine origin of the *Legenda* and the rest. *SS* contains almost everything in the later manuscripts which cannot be traced

---

[1] Above, p. 16 and *Eng. Synodalia*, pp. 62–5.   [2] *Ante*, 1 (1935), 414–15.

to some other satisfactory source.[1] It remains to determine the sources of *SS*, its approximate date, and its nature—official or unofficial.

(i) The chief source of the first six chapters is the statutes attributed to Odo de Sully, on the sacraments. The loans are usually word-perfect, often more faithful than the comparable passages in which Richard Poore drew upon the same source. This part of *SS* also draws on the Council of Westminster, 1200, and the Fourth Lateran. The borrowings from Westminster come directly from the canons, and not through the mediation of *CIL*, as do the corresponding parts of Poore's Salisbury statutes. Close parallels between *SS* and the statutes of Salisbury and the canons of Oxford raise the question: which is derived from which? A short sentence in Salisbury c. 22 appears in *SS* in the form of Salisbury's later recensions (' aqua *in qua* domi baptizatus fuerit ') and this may be taken to establish the priority not only of Salisbury, but also of Oxford (for Oxford preceded the later Salisbury recensions). The latter part of *SS* (*i.e. Legenda* c. 7–14 and additional matter) does not rely on Odo de Sully, but continues to draw on the Fourth Lateran and the other sources named above. The final chapter is the statute directed against clerks' mistresses, which Roger Wendover preserves in his *Flores historiarum*, s.a. 1225, as a decree sent out by the archbishop and his suffragan bishops.[2]

(ii) The sources give a clue to the date of the series. Although *SS* incorporates much earlier legislation, it seems to be fairly homogenous. The passages from Salisbury and Oxford do not read like additions to an earlier recension. It is true, however, that the section *De sententiis* (*Legenda* c. 13 with some additions and differences) would have made the most suitable ending to a well-planned series. The chapters which follow may be divided into three parts: (*a*) three chapters *De vita et honestate clericorum*

---

[1] The unidentified passages are three:

(i) The texts attributed to Mepham and Cambridge, Trinity Coll. 1245 (see above, pp. 20–1) have a chapter ' Ne inclusi aliquo modo instituantur sine licentia episcopi ', *inc.* ' Ad hec districtius . . . ', printed in *Constitutiones legitime* (Paris, 1504), fo. 146ᵛ*a*. In the group of manuscripts represented by Lambeth 171 (above, p. 20, n. 2) this is inserted among the canons of the Council of Oxford (*cf. ante*, l. 393). It occurs in Lyndwood's *Provinciale*, lib. 3 tit. 20 c. 2 *ad fin.*, as part of a canon of Archbishop Edmund; it is not found in the ' Edmund ' manuscripts (*cf. ante*, l. 400–2, and *Eng. Synodalia*, pp. 65–7).

(ii) The group represented by Lambeth 171 alone places among the *Legenda* a chapter on tithe which begins ' Circa decimas autem . . . '. This is also found towards the end of some but not all of the manuscripts of ' Edmund ' and is printed in Wilkins, i. 639*b* (c. 40 (i)). In substance, and partly in wording, it is extremely close to *CIL* c. 48.

(iii) The texts in Bodleian, Selden supra 43 and Peterhouse 51 (ii) insert before the monastic chapters: ' Item persone et vicarii infra annum edificent domos in terris ecclesiarum. Capellani non transferantur de loco ad locum nisi de assensu sui archidiaconi nec admittantur in archidiaconatu sine assensu archidiaconi ' (the Peterhouse text, which is extremely corrupt, omits ' nec admittantur . . . archidiaconi').

[2] H. O. Coxe ed. (*Eng. Hist. Soc.*, 1841–4), iv. 104 (Wilkins, i. 607).

are abridged from c. 14–16 of the Fourth Lateran; (*b*) the next twelve chapters concern the regular clergy;[1] (*c*) the last chapter on clerks' mistresses stands inappropriately by itself, whereas it might have been added to the chapters in (*a*) above. It is difficult not to regard both (*a*) and (*c*) as additions made—officially or unofficially— to an original series which included all else. The fact that the twelve chapters on the regular clergy follow *De Sententiis* is hardly an argument for treating them as an addition; for both the Council of Oxford and the Council of London of 1268 offer examples of groups of monastic regulations whose position in a series is shifted by copyists at will. The supposed date of the chapter on clerks' mistresses (1225) suggests that all else was put together between 1222 and 1225. The evidence, admittedly, is not strong, but the handwriting shows that the compilation cannot have been much later.

(iii) The last questions to be asked concern the nature of *SS*: was it officially promulgated or was it a privately compiled *florilegium*? If official, was it intended for a province, or a diocese? Can we locate it in any one diocese? The variety of sources, the care with which they have been blended and modified in *SS*, and those other passages which cannot be traced elsewhere, are features which we see constantly in the genuine diocesan statutes of the period. They do not afford proof that *SS* was genuine legislation, but they suggest that this is the most likely origin. On the assumption that in *SS* we have official statutes, the legislative authority can hardly be in doubt. The diocesan bishop is invoked at all points, and occasionally is referred to in the first person plural. The time-limit in the penultimate chapter implies recital in a diocesan synod.[2] As for identifying the place of origin, the diocese for which the statutes were composed was English (*cf.* c. 7); more we cannot say.

III

'Constitutiones cuiusdam episcopi' (hereafter *CCE*) is the title at the head of some statutes in the British Museum MS. Cotton Vespasian E. iii, fo. 148ʳ (formerly 138), written early in the fourteenth century. The same hand wrote, among other parts of the volume, the preceding item: statutes of Alexander de Stavensby for the diocese of Coventry and Lichfield. The earlier part of the book consists of historical annals and miscellanea relating to the abbey of Burton-on-Trent, and the latter part which contains the statutes may also have been compiled there. Spelman printed

---

[1] The last four chapters occur in Peterhouse 51 (ii), fo. 23ᵛᵇ and in Bodleian, Selden supra 43, fo. 46ʳ. Some parts of the monastic section re-appear in *CCE* (see below, p. 24 n. 2), and parts in a short, unidentified, and mutilated series of monastic ordinances in Cambridge, Corpus Christi Coll. 367 (ii) fo. 52ᵛ (early thirteenth century).

[2] Above, p. 18, n. 3.

the statutes (ii. 230–40) and Wilkins followed him (i. 656–63); they were reprinted from Wilkins by Mansi (xxiii. 463–78).

Like other series of diocesan statutes *CCE* starts with a fairly clear pattern displaying the sacraments in turn, adding at suitable points chapters on the care of churches and conduct of the clergy. But in the last third of the series no very clear order emerges: among other topics are included the behaviour of the regular clergy, tithe, and excommunication. There is no internal evidence to show where *CCE* originated or to prove, what Spelman and his followers state, that it was published in a synod. Spelman dated it ' *circa* 1237 ' but admitted to ignorance of the date. Wilkins set it *s.a.* 1237 but assigned it simply to the reign of King Henry III.

Comparison with other statutes permits some conclusions about the date and the sources. About nine-tenths of the material is paralleled in those statutes of the early thirteenth century with which we have already been directly or indirectly concerned. The problem is to determine the relationship of *CCE* to the others. *CCE* begins, under the rubric ' Ex concilio ', with the creed of the Fourth Lateran Council c. 1, and at various points adds to the sections under the main rubrics a series of *incipits* of other chapters of the general council.[1] This makes it possible to fix the relationship with *CIL*, of which fifty-five out of sixty-four chapters find parallels in *CCE*. For since *CIL* has been shown to date from 1213–14, and since *CCE* must be later than 1215, *CCE* must be derived from *CIL*. After *CIL*, the next most important parallel with *CCE* is the second group of unidentified statutes with which we are concerned: *SS*.[2] Much of *CCE*'s section on the sacraments of baptism and confirmation are found also in *SS*, and since the common sources of all of this are the canons of Westminster, 1200, and the statutes attributed to Odo de Sully, a comparison of discrepant passages is instructive. One small group suffices:

Odo de Sully 4. 1–3	SS c. 2 (part i)	CCE (Wilkins, i. 657a)
Sacerdotes frequenter moneant populum ad confirmationem puerorum. Post baptismum debet suscipi sacramentum confirmationis. Quod si confirmandus adultus fuerit, confiteatur prius, et postea confirmetur. Sepe dica-	Sacerdotes frequenter moneant populum ad confirmationem puerorum. Post baptismum enim suscipi debet sacramentum confirmationis. Quod si confirmandus fuerit adultus, monendus est per sacerdotem loci ut confiteatur prius et	Sacerdotes sepe dicant laicis ne expectent adventum episcopi ad confirmandum, set adducant pueros ad eum ubi eum adesse audierint prope quamcitius poterunt, et ut fascias sive ligaturas competentes, sufficienter scilicet longas et latas,

[1] *Cf.* Wilkins, i. 658–60. The chapters are not numbered in the manuscript.

[2] *CCE* contains parallels with *Legenda* c. 1, 2, parts of 4, most of 5, all of 8, 13 (i), and *SS* additions to c. 6 and most of *SS* monastic chapters.

Odo de Sully 4. 1–3	SS c. 2 (part i)	CCE (Wilkins, i. 657a)
tur laicis ne expectent diu ad confirmandum pueros adventum episcopi, sed ducant eos ad eum ubi adesse audierint prope, et quod possint nomina mutari pueris si velint in confirmatione aut si visum fuerit expedire.	postea confirmetur. Sepe dicatur laicis ne expectent diu ad confirmandum adventum episcopi, set adducant pueros ad eum ubi adesse audierint prope quam citius poterunt, et ut fascias sive ligaturas secum deferant conpetentes, sufficienter longas et latas.	secum deferant. Quod si adultus fuerit confirmandus, monendus est per sacerdotem loci ut confiteatur prius et postea accedat ad confirmationem.

This shows that SS could not possibly be derived from Paris through CCE; for not only are its readings closer to Paris, but it includes a passage omitted by CCE, and preserves the sequence of Paris where CCE transposes sentences. That would not preclude independent borrowing from Paris by the two English statute-makers; but when we find that both SS and CCE intersperse their borrowings from Paris with identical passages drawn from Westminster, 1200 (in the same order in both series), it is clear that CCE is derived from SS. This gives a valuable *terminus a quo*, since SS includes borrowings from the canons of Oxford, 1222.

This has an important bearing on another set of parallels. CCE also seems to be related directly to a series which, as we have seen, drew heavily on CIL: Poore's statutes for Salisbury. At least twelve chapters of Salisbury (including chapters not taken from CIL and not used in SS) are closely paralleled in CCE. In these cases Salisbury must, from a comparison of dates, be the original and CCE the derivative. At points where CIL was Salisbury's source and CCE does not follow CIL exactly, we can see a process of conflation by a draftsman who had both CIL and Salisbury before him;[1] *e.g.*:

CIL c. 60	Salisbury c. 75	CCE (Wilkins, i. 661b)
Moneat quoque quilibet sacerdos inclusum si habeat in parrochia sua ne mulierculam aliquam recipiat in hospitio de nocte.	Moneat quilibet sacerdos viros inclusos si habeat in parochia sua ne mulierculam recipiat de nocte in domo sua, similiter nec mulier masculum nec deposita sine testimonio sacerdotis et virorum fide dignorum.	Moneatque sacerdos quilibet inclusum si habuerit in parochia sua ne mulierculam aliquam recipiat in hospitio de nocte, similiter nec mulier masculum.

---

[1] Probably something like the E text of Salisbury (a fairly late recension, for which see *Eng. Synodalia*, pp. 59–62). Another set of parallels is CIL c. 28, Salisbury c. 19 and CCE in Wilkins, i. 658a.

In borrowing from Salisbury c. 39 on the demeanour of confessors ('In confessione habeat sacerdos . . .', Wilkins, i. 659a), CCE took at second hand one of the Paris statutes (6.3) which CIL had not borrowed, in preference to CIL's brief piece in c. 46: 'In confessionibus vero non nimis perspicaciter scrutentur plebem suam sacerdotes.'

CCE was mainly composed out of the Fourth Lateran canons, CIL, SS, and the Salisbury statutes. A few explanatory clauses here and there and about eight entirely new injunctions towards the end of the series constitute all that seems to be original. The composer does not show himself to be acquainted with any source which can be dated after 1225. One of the last chapters, 'De crucesignatis' (Wilkins, i. 662a), according to the late W. E. Lunt, agrees better with the conditions of the twelve twenties than with those of a later time.[1]

The provenance of CCE is still unknown. It is possible that its vague title covers either an anthology of current statutes formed by some private person, or the draft of an enactment which never saw the light. On the other hand, the series of statutes is fairly consistent and well-organized; the draftsman did not hesitate to modify his sources discreetly and, it would seem, add to them.[2] The fact that borrowings from all the main sources are spread throughout the series suggests that it was composed at one time; there are no obvious afterthoughts or overlaps. The references to episcopal authority are consistent throughout. On balance, then, it is likely to be a genuine piece of legislation by an English—or conceivably Welsh—bishop, published soon after 1222. Its preservation with statutes of Alexander de Stavensby, bishop of Coventry and Lichfield (1224–38) encouraged Miss Jane Lang to think that CCE was produced either by Bishop Alexander or by his predecessor, William of Cornhill (1215–23).[3] But the vagueness of title reduces the likelihood that these are Lichfield statutes if, as seems probable, the scribe was writing within the diocese; and it is common enough to meet with statutes of different dioceses copied alongside of each other.[4] Stavensby's statutes, as Miss Lang observed, are utterly different in style from CCE. What is more, they deal less adequately with some of the same matters; and whereas CCE provides two confessors for priests in each rural deanery ('in quolibet capitulo . . . a nobis constitutis'), Stavensby only demands

---

[1] Financial relations of the Papacy with England to 1327 (Med. Academy of America, 1939), p. 431, n. 2.

[2] There is a clumsiness in the order of sentences under De baptismo between 'Femine etiam commoneantur . . .' and 'Sepe dicatur . . .'. This is explained by the adding of parts of Salisbury c. 28–9 to a passage taken from CIL c. 39.

[3] Bishops and Reform, p. 109, cf. pp. 119-20. Miss Lang also regarded the frequent citation of the Fourth Lateran as a point in favour of her conjecture, since William of Cornhill attended the Council; but the canons of the Fourth Lateran were too well known for this to count as evidence.

[4] Cf. Eng. Synodalia, p. 145.

one in each deanery or at least one in two deaneries.[1] If yet another conjecture be permitted, we would suggest that *CCE* may come from a diocese adjacent to Lichfield and would name Hereford as the most probable of her neighbours. The bishop of Hereford at the time was Hugh Foliot (1219–34). No other diocesan statutes of Hereford are known to exist,[2] while Lichfield's southern neighbour, Worcester, is practically ruled out; for her bishops issued a short series of statutes in 1219 and more comprehensive series in 1229 and 1240, neither of which shows any likeness to *CCE*. A march-land diocese seems possible as the home of *CCE* in view of one of its later chapters: ' Prohibemus . . . ne patroni ecclesiarum laici, sive sint anglici sive alterius nationis, hospitia a clericis beneficiatis extorqueant.' [3] The non-English lay patron can have been nowhere very common in England, but was to be found occasionally in the Welsh march.

IV

Hefele-Knöpfler's *Conciliengeschichte* comments upon *CIL* and the document found with it in the following terms: ' Wenn endlich Mansi (723) und Labbe (759) in den Anfang des 13. Jahrhunderts noch zwei weitere Synoden verlegen, so dürfen wir uns doch ihrer nähern Betrachtung entheben, indem weder Ort noch Zeit derselben näher bekannt, ja wohl ihre Existenz zweifelhaft ist und ihre Canonen nur Zusammenstellungen verschiedener Verordnungen verschiedener Synoden zu sein scheinen.' [4]

Mansi had encountered the same embarrassing feature in the *Legenda* attached to the Council of Oxford: that the same words were to be found in other diocesan statutes far and wide; and his comment was: ' Undenam tanta affinitas, uter ex alio acceperit, dicant docti.' He did, none the less, hazard the guess that there was a body of synodal constitutions which were well-known throughout France and England and which individuals adopted for their own use, re-shaping as it pleased them, this way and that.[5]

---

[1] Wilkins, i. 659*b*, 641–2.

[2] A liturgical book preserves the record of some diocesan statutes of Bishop John Trefnant (1389–1404): ' Sabbato vero solet fieri plenum servitium de S. Maria tantum secundum novellas constitutiones editas in tempore domini Iohannis Tronore episcopi Herfordensis ecclesie, a.d. m ccc nonagesimo quarto in perpetuum per totam diocesim observandas·': *The Hereford breviary*, ed. W. H. Frere and Langton E. G. Brown (H. Bradshaw Soc., 1904–15), i. 354 and iii. xlvi.

[3] Wilkins, i. 661*a*. This is also found in the group of texts of *Legenda* represented by Lambeth 171 (*cf*. above, p. 20, n. 2), which comes from Worcester; but it is unlikely that this version is anything more than an unofficial anthology. Lichfield's Welsh neighbour, St. Asaph, remains another possible place of origin for *CCE*.

[4] *Conciliengeschichte*, 2nd edn., v (1886), 804. The passage is unchanged in Henri Leclercq's French translation, *Histoire des conciles*, V. ii (1913), 1233.

[5] *Ampl. Coll.* xxii. 1181: ' Capi hinc conjectura valet veteres fuisse synodicas constitutiones per totam Galliam et vicinam Angliam celebres, quas varii episcopi in usus suos adoptaverant, in commodum suum hinc inde reformatas.'

Both theories were plausible and each, as our investigation has shown, contains elements of truth. But the tedious pursuit of origins is worth while if it permits us to see more exactly the process that was at work. It is not enough to dismiss a series of statutes as a work of private enterprise, an unofficial compilation, on the ground that all or most of its parts are to be found elsewhere. Nor, in order to account for the frequent reappearance of the same statutes, need we suppose that they originated in legislation for a wider area than a diocese. It appears from our enquiry that in one case we have a genuine series (*SS*) for a particular diocese, which was subsequently mutilated, as it appears in the *Legenda*, taken up by unofficial compilers of law-books who attached various ascriptions to which it was not entitled; but the later mutilations do not affect the authenticity of the original series. Our aim is to determine the precise time and place at which a series was framed; and even if we sometimes fail, we ought not to assume that thirteenth-century bishops found their statutes floating in the air and gave official sanction to what had been unofficial. The three series *CIL*, *SS*, and *CCE* present some particular problems because of their anonymity; but other anonymous statutes can only be identi-fied by internal evidence;[1] and many better authenticated series show just the same characteristics as the three we have been con-sidering. The earliest statutes of Paris were borrowed by bishops of France, England, Sweden, and Germany. Statutes of Nîmes, compiled in 1252, were not only taken over immediately in neigh-bouring dioceses of the Midi (at Béziers, Arles, Lodève, and Uzès) but in 1473 were published almost unaltered in distant Breslau by Bishop Rudolf of Rüdesheim.[2] English statutes did not travel so far, but those of York appear in Chichester and Dublin, those of Salisbury in Durham and Aberdeen.[3] Another statute of Salisbury, on tithe, may lie behind a statute of Archbishop Boniface for the pro-vince of Canterbury,[4] while at the other end of Europe and at a later date statutes framed for the diocese of Poznan in the fourteenth century were incorporated in the provincial statutes of Lwow *c.* 1415–17.[5]

---

[1] Notably those of Winchester and Exeter (*Eng. Synodalia*, pp. 75, 76). It is very common to find statutes of known origin without adequate title: *e.g.* the main text of Poore's and seventeen texts of Grosseteste's statutes.

[2] *Cf.* Artonne, 'Le livre synodal de Lodève' (above, p. 1 n. 1) and Sawicki, 'Die Entwicklung . . .' (above, p. 1 n. 1), pp. 259–60.

[3] For the diffusion of the York statutes see my forthcoming paper on 'A group of related synodal statutes of the thirteenth century', and on the Salisbury statutes *Eng. Synodalia*, pp. 67–73 and Joseph Robertson, *Concilia Scotiae* (Bannatyne Club, Edinburgh, 1866), ii. 30 ff. (Wilkins, i. 614).

[4] Wilkins, i. 698, 719; but it is possible that the connection is the reverse of this.

[5] W. Abraham, *Studia i materiały do historii ustawodawsta synodalnego w Polsce*, nr. 6 (Cracow, 1920), pp. 35–53 which I have not seen; *cf.* Sawicki, *Concilia Poloniae*, vii (Poznan, 1952), 7–38 and 165–6 (French abstract), and the same, 'Najdawniejsze statuty synodalne poznańskie z rękopisu *BOZ* 63', *Studia Zródłoznawcze*, i (Warsaw, 1957), 207 (French abstract).

Returning to the anonymous *CIL*, *SS*, and *CCE*, the enquiry has led to the following probable conclusions: *CIL* was a series of statutes published by Archbishop Stephen Langton for the diocese of Canterbury between July 1213 and July 1214; *SS* was a series of synodal statutes of an unknown diocese issued between 1222 and 1225; *CCE* was compiled not much later than *SS*, also for a diocese which may possibly have been Hereford. To establish the approximate dates and authentic quality of these texts is to enlarge our knowledge of church government in England in the first quarter of the thirteenth century. We see more clearly than ever that the Fourth Lateran was not the *fons et origo* of all later legislation, and in particular we learn that the incoming archbishop of Canterbury applied himself to the questions of clerical instruction and discipline before the disastrous events of 1215 led to his suspension and absence from England. We see, too, that statute-making by English bishops was extensive in the ten or fifteen years after the Fourth Lateran. Thomas de Chobham, subdean of Salisbury, in his *Summa* which was written perhaps during these years, observed that in different regions there were different canons and different rules governing general sentences of excommunication: ' unde oportet quod quilibet sacerdos sciat constitutiones synodales factas in episcopatu suo.'[1] We already knew of six English dioceses with statutes probably framed before *c.* 1230 (Lincoln, Salisbury, Worcester, Canterbury, Winchester, Exeter); to those we can now add *CIL* for Canterbury, and the anonymous *SS* and *CCE*. The very tenuous nature of the evidence by which we know of all these statutes (the named as well as the unnamed) holds out the chance that there was more activity and the prospect that there may be more discoveries.

Corpus Christi College, Cambridge

[1] Quoted by Fr. Leonard Boyle, ' The *Oculus sacerdotis* and some other works of William of Pagula ', *Transactions Royal Hist. Soc.*, 5th ser. v (1955), 93, n. 3. Similarly, a writer at Paris soon after the Fourth Lateran, reckons that parish-priests may be in possession of synodal precepts: ' Si hec et alia sacerdotibus necessaria non promulgantur in synodis vel non continentur in eorum scriptis, consulendi sunt ab eis periti in dubiis casibus et maxime sui prelati et consuetudines episcopatuum attende ' A. Teetaert, ' Le Liber Poenitentialis de Pierre de Poitiers ', *Aus der Geisteswelt des Mittelalters*, Studien u. Texte M. Grabmann · · · gewidmet (*Beitr. zur Gesch. der Philos. u. Theol. des Mittelalters*, Supplementband iii, 1935), i. 323.

ADDITIONAL NOTES

P.1 n.1: English synodalia was re-issued with a new introduction, Oxford,1968. For other general works see Jakub T. Sawicki,Bibliographia synodorum particularium (Monumenta iuris canonici.Series C: Subsidia,vol.2,Città del Vaticano,1967) and Odette Pontal, Les statuts synodaux (Typologie des sources du moyen-âge occidental, fasc.11. Turnhout,1975). For France see further Répertoire des statuts synodaux des diocèses de l'ancienne France,2nd edition,ed. O.Pontal (Paris,C.N.R.S.,1969); Joseph Avril, Les statuts synodaux du diocèse d'Angers (1247-1423): édition critique et commentaire (Paris,1971), and 'Les "Precepta synodalia" de Roger de Cambrai',Bulletin of Medieval Canon Law,n.s.2 (1972) 7-15. For the Parisian statutes of Odo de Sully and their wide diffusion, see O. Pontal, Les statuts synodaux français du XIIIe siècle, précédés de l' historique du synode diocésain depuis ses origines:les statuts de Paris et le synodal de l'Ouest (XIIIe s.) (Collection de documents inédits sur l'histoire de France, Section de philologie et d'histoire jusqu'à 1610. Série in 8°,IX. 1971). For Spain see P. Linehan, 'Councils and synods in XIII cent. Castile and Aragon',Studies in church history,7 (Cambridge,1971)101-11.

P.2 line 20:Langton's statutes (CIL) for the diocese of Canterbury are edited in Councils and synods ii 23-36.

P.18 line 14: The statutes in ms. Bodley 843 (SS) are edited in Councils & synods ii 139-54 as 'Synodal statutes for an English diocese, 1222 x 1225?'.

P.23 line 31:These statutes are edited as 'Constitutiones cuiusdam episcopi,1225 x 1230?' in Councils & synods ii 181-97.

P.27 last para.: Mansi's conjecture is to a great extent justified by the works cited in the edition to P.1 n.1 above.

P.28 n.3:On the relations of the Salisbury and Canterbury statutes on tithe see Councils & synods ii 365,792-4.

VIII

A GROUP OF RELATED SYNODAL STATUTES OF THE THIRTEENTH CENTURY

WHEN in 1944 Father Aubrey Gwynn published 'Provincial and diocesan decrees of the diocese of Dublin during the Anglo-Norman period,'[1] he made one of the most notable documentary contributions of this century to the study of the medieval Irish Church. At last these texts were all edited accurately in a convenient form, two of them for the first time. The laws can throw much light on the peculiar problems of the Church in Ireland from the twelfth to the fourteenth century and on the degree to which prelates of the Irish Church organized their administration on the same lines as that of their colleagues in England. But, in both countries, historians have tended to neglect synodal legislation because the material was scattered and ill-edited. Thanks to Father Gwynn, we are now in a far better position to exploit the Dublin statutes. It is the object of this paper to consider one Dublin series in particular as part of a group of related Anglo-Irish statutes. To discover the origin and relationship of the statutes is necessary to a full appreciation of their historical importance.

We are concerned in the first place with four sets of statutes, from three dioceses. They are :

(1) A long series, printed by Wilkins,[2] s.a. 1217, attributed to Henry de Londres, archbishop of Dublin, but with an editorial note to suggest that they were issued by Archbishop Fulk de Sanford (1256-1271). Re-edited by Father Gwynn (loc. cit., p. 44), they are ascribed by him to Archbishop Luke of Dublin (1230-1255), probably before 1240. The only medieval manuscript known to contain these statutes is the register of the see of Dublin, known as 'Crede Mihi,' dating from late in the thirteenth century,[3] but Wilkins seems to have printed from a seventeenth-century transcript of this manuscript, now British Museum Add. MS. 4785 fo. 30r (formerly fo. 29r)[4]. Their ascription to the year 1217 goes back to Bishop William Nicholson's Irish historical library (Dublin, 1724), and is apparently grounded

1. Archiv. Hib. xi (1944), 31-117.

2. David Wilkins, Concilia Magnae Britanniae et Hiberniae (1737), i. 548.

3. p. 106 of the manuscript. They are printed in J. T. Gilbert's edition of Crede Mihi (Dublin, 1897), p. 119. I am grateful to the Most Rev. Dr. George Simms, archbishop of Dublin, for allowing me to obtain photostat copies, and to the Director of the National Library for supplying them.

4. This bears the date 19 Aug. 1644. It is among Sir James Ware's collections, which passed to Henry Hyde, second earl of Clarendon (Clarendon MS. 28) and

on the report that Archbishop Henry, in a *generale concilium* at Dublin in that year, ' multa utilia de statu Hibernicane ecclesie ordinavit.'[5] Whoever it was who added to Wilkins's text the suggestion that Archbishop Fulk was author may have noticed the resemblance between parts of the Dublin statutes and English statutes of Fulk's day, and may have taken into account the date of the manuscript. Father Gwynn has stated his reasons for ascribing the series to Archbishop Luke : the time of Archbishop Fulk was a time of much disturbance in Dublin, of which the statutes show no trace, Luke was ' the ablest and most conscientious ' of the thirteenth-century archbishops, and one of these statutes re-appears in synodal statutes of Ferns which are dated 9 September 1240.[6]

(2) A long series, printed by Spelman,[7] and by Wilkins (ii. 169), *s.a.* 1289 as statutes of Gilbert of St. Leofard, bishop of Chichester, issued in his synod at Chichester, 6 October 1289. These exist in ' Liber E,' a fourteenth-century register of the see, Chichester, Diocesan Record Office, Ep. vi/1/4 fo. 188r (=Ch).[8] Spelman had access to two manuscripts but these have not been traced.

(3) Two statutes, on grass and trees growing in cemeteries and on the assessment of dilapidations due from the executors of beneficed clergy. These were printed by Spelman (ii. 50) and Wilkins (i. 425), *s.a.* 1153, and attributed by them to Archbishop William of York (St. William) who died in 1154. The editors had taken their text from the Cottonian manuscript Vitellius A. ii fo. 115r (formerly fo. 125r), where it has the title : ' Constitutio synodalis in provincia Ebor'.' The manuscript, probably from York Minster, was written very late in the fourteenth century (=V). The same two statutes are found under the title : ' Constitutiones due synodales ' among records of August 1309 in the register of William Greenfield, archbishop of York, vol. i fo. 144v (=G).[9]

later to James Brydges, first duke of Chandos (d. 1744). Another transcript known to Wilkins is now Trinity Coll. Dublin MS. F.3.16 (842), which came to the College with the mss. of John Stearne, bishop of Clogher (d. 1745). Another transcript, the verification of which I owe to Dr. J. A. Watt, is in Archbishop Marsh's Library, MS. Z.3.1.3 (8) pp. 46-51.

5. Cf. Gwynn, *loc. cit.*, p. 33 n.1. The title ' generale concilium ' affords no proof of the nature of the assembly : cf. *E.H.R.*, l (1935), 197-8.

6. Gwynn, *loc. cit.*, p. 33. The Ferns statutes are printed *ibid.*, p. 55 and in Wilkins, *Concilia*, i. 681.

7. Or more correctly by William Dugdale, who printed the second volume of Henry Spelman, *Concilia . . . Orbis Britannici* (1664), ii. 404.

8. I am greatly obliged to the Archivist, Mr. F. W. Steer, for allowing me to use a microfilm copy of this register.

9. Vol. ii p. 68 of the edition published by the Surtees Society. The former of the two statutes is found by itself in the cartulary of Healaugh Park Priory, B.M., Cott. MS. Vesp. A. iv fo. 165r, *inc.* ' Inter cetera istud statutum fuit editum anno MCCCXI per venerabilem in Christo patrem et dominum Willelmum . . .', printed in *The chartulary of . . . Healaugh* (Yorks. Archaeol. Soc., Record series 92), p. 186.

(4) A long series, printed by Spelman (ii. 438) and Wilkins (ii. 285) as synodal statutes of William Greenfield, archbishop of York, issued at Ripon, 30 September 1306.[10] Spelman printed from the Cottonian manuscript Vitellius D.v fo. 142r (now fo. 1r of the surviving fragments), apparently a register of the church of York, written late in the fourteenth century ; Wilkins followed Spelman. The manuscript is now so badly burnt that only a very few passages, from nine chapters, are legible. (We call Spelman's edition, checked where possible against the manuscript, text D). The statutes, with some variations of order and content to be noted later, are also found in the following texts :

(A) B.M., Cotton MS. Vitell. A. ii fo. 94r (formerly fo. 104r): cf. above, under (3). This has suffered damage by fire and is much rubbed on the first page.

(J) Cambridge, St. John's Coll. MS. 93 fo. 117ra, written in an ugly hand, late in the fourteenth century, following the 'Oculus sacerdotis' of William de Pagula, and followed by the legatine canons of Otto and Ottobono, all in the same hand.

(L) B.M., Lansdowne MS. 397 fo. 252v (formerly fo. 223v), written late in the fourteenth century at Durham, in a miscellaneous register of Durham Cathedral Priory.

Almost all this series is found, ascribed to William Greenfield and rearranged, in the *Provinciale* of York compiled at the order of Archbishop Thomas Wolsey from constitutions of provincial synods held by his predecessors. This was printed by Wilkins (iii. 662) and again, with a translation, by R. M. Woolley (*The York Provinciale*, London, 1931) from the only known manuscript, which once belonged to Bishop Thomas Tanner, now Bodleian MS. Add. C. 64 (=T).

The third item in this list can easily be eliminated from the discussion. These two statutes are in fact the last two of series 4 ; and the archbishop who issued them was William Greenfield, not St. William.[11] This is confirmed by the dating clause which ends series 4 and by Greenfield's reference to both statutes, on different occasions, as his own.[12]

Of the other three series, a connection between 2 and 4 already attracted the notice of Wilkins who, in taking over Spelman's texts, observed that the statutes of York were the same as those of Chichester issued in 1289, but that the archbishop of York added some. Wilkins refrained, therefore, from reprinting all the Chichester statutes, simply indicating how they stood in the York series in relation to the additional matter which he printed. He implied (and probably supposed) that series 4 was derived from series 2. Tout also observed that the bishop of Chichester's statutes

---

10. The dating clause of c. 44 stands in three texts only (DJL).

11. Cf. *E.H.R.*, l (1935), 385.

12. To the first in 1315 (*Reg. W. Greenfield* (Surtees Soc.), iv. 230) and to the second in 1309 (*ibid.*, i. 30).

'became sufficiently well-known to be re-enacted in substance by Archbishop Greenfield in 1306.'[13] One fact which Wilkins did not notice, which was remarked by William Brown when editing the register of Archbishop John Le Romeyn,[14] would seem to fortify the supposition of borrowing by York : William Greenfield, archbishop of York from 1306 to 1315, had been dean of Chichester (?1301-1306)[15] while Gilbert of St. Leofard was bishop (1288-1305).

But the matter is more complicated. In order to determine the date and origin of the different series of statutes we need to compare the Dublin series (1) closely with Chichester (2) and York (4), and to take into account the evidence of other legislation, notably the second and third sets of synodal statutes of Durham, the statutes attributed to Archbishop Godfrey Ludham of York, 1259, the *Provinciale* of York of 1518, and the synodal statutes of Ferns dated 1240.

As so often with the synodal statutes of the Middle Ages, what purports to be the work of one legislator at one time proves to be the work of several hands, spread over an indeterminate period. There is nothing on the face of the Chichester statutes to suggest that they were not composed and issued as a single enactment in 1289. But if we look at the Dublin statutes, we find a reasonable ending at c. 31 (vi) with an order for the regular recital of the statutes in the rural deaneries, after which come several statutes with recognizable parentage in the Council of Lambeth of 1261 and, at c. 42 a second ending, followed by six more statutes. Turning to the York statutes, we see that the clause which precedes the date, at Ripon, 30 September 1306, refers explicitly to the last two statutes only : 'has autem duas constitutiones inter alias synodales a quibuscunque predecessoribus nostris factas incorporari volumus et inter eas in singulis celebrandis synodis solempniter publicari.' Supposing the series of statutes which precedes these two in the existing manuscripts to be the statutes to which they were originally appended, then they were produced by Greenfield's predecessors, and were not new in 1306. The plot thickens when we find that the bulk of Dublin 1-31 is to be found in the same words in York and Chichester.

II

THE first step towards discovering the origin and relationship of the statutes must be the disengaging of the core, common to Chichester, Dublin, and York, from the various additions found in each. A table of chapters will simplify comparison :

13. *D.N.B.*, *s.v.* Gilbert of St. Lifard.

14. *Register of J. Le Romeyn* (Surtees Soc.) i. 360 n.2 : 'his diocesan constitutions (1289) . . . the model of the constitutions enacted in 1306 by Archbishop Greenfield, who had been dean of Chichester under him.'

15. Cf. *Reg. W. Greenfield*, i. p. lviii.

Chichester	Dublin	York
1	1-2i	1
2	2ii	2
3i	2iii	3
3ii	—	—
4-11i	2iv-8	4-11i
—	9[1]	—
11ii-21	10-17	11ii-21[2]
—	—	22[3]
22	—	23
23-24	18	24-25
25-26	—	—
27-28	19-21	26-27i
29	—	—
—	—	27ii
30	22	28i
—	—	28ii[4]
31	23	29
—	24	30
32-36	25-29	31-35
—	30i	36
37	30ii	37
38	—	—
—	—	38-40[5]
39i	31i	41i[6]
39ii	—	41ii
39iii	31ii	41iii
40i	31iii	42i
40ii	31iv	42ii
40iii	—	—
40iv	31v	42iii
40v	31vi	42iv
—	31vii	—
—	32-48	—
—	—	43-44[7]

1. Dublin 9 is printed by Wilkins in the middle of 12.
2. The L text has a longer version of York 13.
3. Only found in L and T texts.
4. Only found in L text.
5. York 39-40 are omitted from L text.
6. York 41-42 are omitted from L text, 42iv from T text.
7. York 43 is missing from T text. 43-44 are the statutes attributed by Spelman and Wilkins to St. William (above, p. 115).

The core, common to the three series of statutes, seems to be Chichester 1-3i, 4-21, 23, 24, 27, 28, 30-37, 39i, 39iii, 40i, 40ii, 40iv, and 40v.[16] It is noteworthy that in all three series these chapters occur in the same sequence. *Chichester* adds to the common core its 3ii, 22 (shared with York), 25, 26, 29, 38, 39ii (shared with York), 40iii. *Dublin* adds to the common core its 9, 24 (shared with York), 30i (shared with York), and all after 31vi. *York* adds to the common core its 22 (after Chichester 21), 23 (shared with Chichester), 27ii (following Chichester 28), 28ii (following Chichester 30), 30 and 36 (shared with Dublin), 38-40 (following Chichester 38), 43-44 (after Chichester 40).[17]

The easy inference from this analysis is that the common core represents an original series of statutes which were adapted and added to by legislators of Chichester, Dublin, and York. So far, we can only say that this core may have been composed originally for one of the dioceses in question, but it could have reached them all from an outside source ; and so far we have no sound chronological data on which to establish their relationship. To advance the enquiry it will be best to look for indications of influence exercised by, or on, other legislation. For this purpose all the statutes, whether or not they belong to the common core, require to be examined.

> 3i, 4, 5, 6, have close affinities to the second series of Durham statutes, 21-22.[18]
>
> 7 is borrowed in Carlisle statutes 82.[19]
>
> 9, 10, agreed with Durham II 25.
>
> 11 (*ad fin.*) agrees with Durham II 2.
>
> 12 is quoted by Archbishop John Thoresby of York (1352-1373) in his canons (Spelman, ii. 602, Wilkins, iii. 69).
>
> 13 agrees with Durham II 29.
>
> 17 is close in substance to Lichfield 4 (Wilkins, i. 641*a*) without being verbally identical. The Lichfield statutes are probably of the period 1224-1237.
>
> 20, 21 are reminiscent of Durham II 34, although the wording is altogether different.
>
> York 22 is only found in the York mss. L and T. In T it is ascribed to Archbishop William Wickwane (1279-85).

16. The numeration of Chichester is adopted here for convenience. We follow the chapter-divisions of Spelman and Wilkins except for joining their c. 3-4. Consequently, Spelman's c.5 becomes our c.4, and so on, to the end. The numeration of Dublin is that of Father Gwynn's edition.

17. York 43-44 are the chapters positively ascribed to Greenfield.

18. These statutes, ascribed by Spelman (ii. 294) and Wilkins (i. 702) to Walter of Kirkham, were issued by Bishop Nicholas, 1241 × 1249. In *English synodalia* (Oxford, 1941), pp. 138-41, I overlooked the evidence of B.M. MS. Stowe 930 fo. 9r.

19. The main body of these statutes is of 1258 × 1259, but this statute is one of a group of later additions, cf. *E.H.R.*, lxii (1947), 55-56.

22 (not in Dublin) is Council of Oxford (1222) c. 35 (Wilkins, i. 590a, end of c. XXVIII).

23 is reminiscent of Durham II 48 *ad fin.*

24 has close affinity with Durham II 46.

25 (not in Dublin or York) is taken directly from the first Chichester statutes of 1244×53, c. 33 (Wilkins, i. 690a).

29 (not in Dublin or York) could be related to Durham II 18, but equally to statutes from elsewhere.

30 is reminiscent of Durham 12, although the wording is quite different.

31 has close affinity with Durham II 13.

Dublin 24 (York 30)[20] requires rectors to be ordained subdeacons. It is difficult to believe that this could have been enacted (though it might survive in reiterated statutes) after the legatine canon of London 1268 c. 29. It agrees in substance with Durham II 15.

32 has affinity with Durham II 16.

33 agrees in substance with Durham II 14.

36 has affinities with Durham II 49.

York 36 (not in Chichester) has affinity with Durham II 50vi (which *might* be later than June 1258).

37 agrees in substance with Durham II 50iv, but the connexion is questionable : each could be an independent revision of the Council of Oxford 3-4.

York 39 (not in Chichester or Dublin) has affinity with Durham III (of the year 1276) 10, and its final sanction may depend on the Council of Lambeth (1261) 22.

York 40 (not in Chichester or Dublin) is a verbatim copy of the Council of London (1268) 12.

York 43 (not in Chichester or Dublin) is borrowed in the Durham statutes of Richard Kellawe (1311×1316) 8, and thence in the additional statutes of Carlisle, 81.

39i has close affinity with Durham II 50i-ii.

39ii (not in Dublin) has close affinity with Durham III (1276) 10.

39iii deserves comparison with both Durham II and Durham III (see below, p. 121).

40ii follows, somewhat distantly, the Council of Oxford (1222) 3 and 5.

40iii occurs as the last of the additional statutes of Bishop Gilbert of Chichester, published in his synod 14 Oct. 1292, (Spelman, ii. 410 and Wilkins, ii. 183), only in the N text.

Dublin 33 has close affinity with Council of Lambeth (1261) 21.

Dublin 34 has close affinity with the same, 20.

20. A reference to the latter part of this statute is made by Archbishop Walter Giffard, 19 Aug. 1276 (*Register of Walter Giffard* (Surtees Soc.), pp. 262-3).

Dublin 35-38 has close affinity with the same, 22-24.
Dublin 39 has close affinity with the same, 27.
Dublin 40 has close affinity with the same, 28.
Dublin 41 has close affinity with Council of Oxford (1222) 27.

The most obvious point emerging from this comparison is the close connexion of the statutes with Durham II (1241×49). If Chichester 39i is compared with Durham and the Council of Oxford, Durham II will appear as intermediary between Oxford and Chichester, and therefore antecedent to Chichester :

Chichester 39i Dublin 31i York 41i	Durham II 50i	Council of Oxford (1222) 1 and 2
Excommunicamus autem (om. autem Du) omnes illos (om. o.i. Ch) qui pacem regis et regni perturbare aut libertates ecclesiasticas et (ecclesie seu iura Ch) precipue huius sacrosancte Cicestrensis ecclesie infringere seu (ac Ch) possessiones ecclesiasticas invadere aut ad bona ecclesiastica manus impias (iniuriosas Du) extendere presumpserint in preiudicium ecclesiastice libertatis.	Sententia excommunicationis innodamus omnes illos qui pacem regni perturbare aut libertates ecclesiasticas infringere seu malitiose ecclesias suo iure privare presumpserint aut invadere aut ad bona ecclesiastica malitiose manus extenderint contra libertates ecclesiasticas.	Excommunicamus omnes illos qui ecclesias malitiose suo iure privare presumunt aut per malitiam libertates earundem infringere vel perturbare contendunt. Item omnes illos excommunicationis sententia innodamus qui pacem et tranquillitatem domini regis iniuriose perturbare presumunt.

Comparison of Chichester 39iii with Durham II 50iii and Durham III 10 shows that Chichester is nearer to Durham III than to Durham II, and therefore probably later than Durham II :[21]

Chichester 39iii Dublin 31iii York 41iii	Durham II 50iii	Durham III 10 (1276)
Omnes etiam (autem DuY) incendiarios, (add et Du) ecclesiarum frac-	Item simili censura percellimus omnes incendiarios, ecclesiarum fract-	Item excommunicamus omnes incendiarios, ecclesiarum fractores,

21. Cf. below, p. 130, n. 46.

tores, veneficos et veneficas, et magicis incantationibus utentes, et hec (hoc *Du*) fieri procurantes ... denuntiamus excommunicationis sententiam incurrere ipso facto.

ores, veneficos et veneficas, ac utentes magicis incantationibus.

veneficos et veneficas, et magicis incantationibus utentes, seu hec fieri procurantes.

The relationship of our statutes to Durham II is not in other instances so clearly the relationship of dependence, but nothing in the other comparable chapters is inconsistent with such dependence.

The conclusion seems irresistible that the compiler of the original series had before him Durham II ; from eighteen of the Durham statutes he selected and re-shaped material. Nor did his borrowing extend only so far as verbal copying ; for when we find a group of our statutes agreeing in purport with Durham II 12, 13, 15, 16, 14, although only 13 and 16 impose their words on our statutes, we can hardly doubt that all five statutes account for similar treatment of the same topics in approximately the same sequence in both series.

These affinities between Durham II and our statutes demand a re-appraisal of what constituted their original core. Comparison of Chichester, Dublin, and York (above, p. 117) led us to limit this core to Chichester 1-3i, 4-21, 23, 24, 27, 28, 30-37, 39i, 39iii, 40i and ii, iv and v. But the borrowings from Durham II seem to include two other chapters : York 30 (Dublin 24, not in Chichester), while verbally different from Durham II 15, agrees in substance and appears between borrowings from Durham II 13 and 16. York 36 (Dublin 30i, not in Chichester) resembles Durham II 50vi, while other parts of Durham II 50 may lie behind the next three chapters common to all three series of our statutes (Chichester 37, 39i, 39iii).[22] We conclude, then, that York 30 and 36 were parts of the original core, and we are now in a position to reconstruct conjecturally the transmission of these statutes and their development.

22. At first sight York 27ii appears to qualify for inclusion (' Nec ultra septem dies conserventur hostie consecrate sed septimana qualibet renoventur '). The last five words of the preceding chapter (=Ch. 28) agree with Durham II 8, and York 27ii is a verbatim extract from the Salisbury-Durham statutes of Richard Poore (Durham I 53) which is specifically referred to in Durham II 9. But the last five words of Durham II 8 come from the Fourth Lateran Council (c. 20) from which our statute (Ch. 28) quotes a slightly longer passage. Moreover, Durham II 9 does not actually quote Durham I 53 (' inspiciant super hoc constitutionem ven. patris Ricardi quondam episcopi Dunelmensis '). Finally, York 27ii is not merely absent from Dublin and Chichester : it is only found in one (L) of the four York texts. We infer that it is, like some other parts of L, a later addition. Having regard to its character and position, it may even be an unofficial addition.

III

At this point it becomes necessary to consider a conflict of evidence. The ' core ' of these statutes, including the first part of the Dublin series, seems to be later than, and dependent on, Durham II, which may be dated 1241 × 1249. But Father Gwynn, in editing the Irish synodal statutes, reprinted from Wilkins (i. 681) a short series for the diocese of Ferns, and noted that the rules for excommunication in the third and following paragraphs are very closely similar to Dublin 31, while an earlier passage appears to depend on Dublin 23.[23] Wilkins's text, said to have been in the possession of Henry, first duke of Chandos, was almost certainly one of the manuscripts of Sir James Ware which passed to the second Earl of Clarendon and thence, via the duke of Chandos, to the British Museum.[24] In these texts the statutes are said to be issued by the bishop of Ferns, in the church of St. Peter of Solsker, Wexford, on the morrow of the nativity of the Blessed Virgin Mary A.D. 1240. If this date is correct, it follows that the Dublin statutes must be earlier than Sept. 1240.

But the Ferns statutes, as they stand, cannot belong to the year 1240. The passage which they have in common with Dublin is precisely that which has been found to derive from Durham II, without possibility of the borrowing being in the reverse direction. Moreover, Ferns inserts two tell-tale phrases in copying the first clause of the excommunications :

Dublin 31i

Excommunicamus omnes illos qui pacem regis et regni perturbare aut libertates ecclesiasticas, et precipue huius sacrosancte ecclesie Dublin' infringere, seu possessiones ecclesiasticas invadere aut ad bona ecclesiastica manus iniuriosas extendere presumpserint, in preiudicium ecclesiastice libertatis.

Ferns 3

Excommunicamus, *et a liminibus sacrosanctae ecclesiae sequestramus* omnes illos qui pacem domini regis et regni perturbare, aut libertates ecclesiasticas, et praecipue sacrosanctae ecclesiae Fernensis infringere, vel suo iure privare, vel possessiones ecclesiasticas invadere, vel ad bona ecclesiastica manus iniuste extendere, *aut aliquid de eisdem bonis auferre, consumere, vel iniuriose* (ms. : incuriose) *contrectare* praesumpserint, in praeiudicium ecclesiasticae libertatis.

23. *Archiv. Hib.*, xi (1944), 33-34, 55-57.

24. Ware had borrowed a text from Daniel Molyneux, Ulster King at Arms (see Gwynn, *loc. cit.*, p. 34). Two copies of the statutes are noted in the catalogue of the earl of Clarendon's manuscripts, nos. 39, 46 (E. Bernard, *Catalogus librorum mss. Angliae et Hiberniae* (1697), II. ii. 7*b*, 9*b*). They are now B.M. Add. MSS. 4788 fo. 139v (formerly fo. 136v) and 4793 fo. 4r (formerly fo. 1r) cf. *Anal. Hib.* ii. 300-302. Comparison of the texts makes it clear that Add. MS. 4788 was Wilkins's exemplar.

124

The first of these phrases ('et a liminibus . . .') is part of the solemn form of excommunication uttered in Westminster Hall in May 1253.[25] The last insertion ('aut aliquid de . . .') corresponds to canon 12 of the legatine Council of London, 1268 : 'quicquam . . . consumere vel auferre aut contrectare presumpserit' ; but the introduction of the adverb 'incuriose' (a mistake for 'iniuriose') suggests that the model was not London, 1268, but the provincial council of Reading, 1279 (Wilkins, ii. 35*b*), where the adverb was added to the legate's 'contrectare.' This is the more probable since a later clause of Ferns, directed against those who do not execute the writ 'de excommunicatis capiendis,' copies the wording of Reading.

Ferns 1 and 4 correspond exactly to statutes from other dioceses. That on tithe (1) is c. 44 of Robert Bingham's statutes, Salisbury II, issued 1238 × 1244, that on excommunication for the withholding of tithe (4) is c. 43 of William Raleigh's statutes for Norwich, issued 1240 × 1243 and c. 60 of the same bishop's Winchester II, issued 1247 × 1249. Whether or not the bishop of Ferns issued statutes in a synod of September 1240 must remain uncertain ; but there is no doubt that the statutes as preserved consist mainly of much later material and cannot therefore help in the dating of the Dublin statutes. There is thus no difficulty in accepting the evidence of Durham II which has already been considered above.

IV

AT some date before 1268, and probably before 1261, but not before the period 1241 × 1249, a series of statutes was somewhere composed for diocesan use,[26] drawing heavily upon those of Nicholas of Farnham, bishop of Durham. It corresponded to the whole of the first part of the surviving Dublin statutes (1–31vi), excluding c. 9.[27] Whether this series was first drafted for Dublin or for York or for some other diocese does not at present admit of absolute proof. The textual variants in our (much later) texts could be explained on either assumption.

On general historical grounds, York seems a natural place for their origin. Archbishop Walter de Gray (1215–1255) was on good terms with his suffragan of Durham and would easily come by the statutes of Bishop Nicholas, while his successor, Sewal de Bovil (1256–1258) was a zealous prelate who, like Nicholas of Farnham, was a personal friend of Robert

---

25. The archbishop of Dublin was present, and Ferns may have borrowed from a recension of the Dublin statutes later than the one represented by this part of the *Crede Mihi* text.

26. With the exception of York 38 (on tuitorial appeals) there is no suggestion that any of these statutes applied to a province ; on the contrary, numerous references imply only diocesan authority.

27. Added marginally in the existing manuscript, by the original hand.

Grosseteste and belonged to the same scholarly circle, concerned about the education of the clergy. Bovil has, moreover, been credited with synodal statutes, though with what justification is doubtful.[28] The archbishops of Dublin, Luke (1230-1255) and Fulk (1256-1271) were active men, but they were far removed from Durham. This consideration should not, indeed, be allowed more than its proper weight ; so many lines of communication are hidden from us. But on general grounds we may think it highly probable that a series of synodal statutes already published in England was taken over and re-issued, with slight modification, by the archbishop of Dublin. We have already seen that the statutes of Ferns were largely composed of borrowings from English legislation. A close examination of other Irish statutes would certainly bring other affiliations to light. To take one series only : the provincial canons of Alexander of Bicknor, archbishop of Dublin 1317-1349,[29] draw largely upon the English legatine and provincial canons of the preceding century without acknowledgment at any point. In the preamble and first ten canons long passages (nearly a half of the whole amount) are lifted verbatim from the preambles to Lambeth 1281 and London 1268 (in the preamble), from c. 12 of Lambeth 1261 (in c. 2), from c. 12 of London 1268 (in c. 3), from c. 13 of Lambeth 1281 (in c. 7), from c. 11 of London 1237 (in c. 8), and from c. 20 of Oxford 1222 (in c. 10).

There is, then, some colour for supposing that the core of statutes which appeared at Dublin in the mid-thirteenth century was drafted in England, probably at York, between 1241 and 1261, when the recent legatine canons of Otto (London, 1237) were much in the minds of English bishops and when the diocesans of Worcester, Lincoln, Norwich, Salisbury, and London, as well as Durham, were issuing important sets of statutes.

IV

A LITTLE more light is thrown on the circumstances in which this core of statutes and the additions were issued at York by comparison with the version of the Wells-Carlisle statutes contained in the British Museum manuscript, Lansdowne 397 fo. 245r (preceding the L text of our so-called ' Greenfield ' series). I have elsewhere tentatively attributed this version to Archbishop Godfrey Ludham of York in 1259.[30] Comparison with

28. J. Bale, *Scriptorum illustrium maioris Brytanniae* . . . *catalogus* (Basel, 1557), p. 312.

29. Printed by Wilkins, *Concilia*, ii. 746 and by Fr. Gwynn, *loc. cit.*, p. 71. Wilkins copied from the Ware transcript of the Red Book of Ossory, now B.M. Add. MS. 4791 fo. 175r (formerly, fo. 183, fo. 180, fo. 45), collated with another transcript, that belonging to Bishop John Stearne. Fr. Gwynn copies from the original Red Book.

30. C. R. Cheney, *English synodalia of the thirteenth century*, pp. 97-109 and *E.H.R.*, lii (1947), 52-57. These statutes have not been printed. To distinguish

the ' Greenfield ' series raises again in an acute form the problem of this attribution. To examine its correctness will involve a somewhat lengthy digression. The ' 1259 ' statutes are a longer series than the forty-seven statutes we have been considering, and they cover some of the same ground far more comprehensively. The series, which originated at Wells between 1252 and 1258, is longer than any earlier series published by an English bishop. It not only has well-arranged and full sections on the administration of sacraments and the conduct of parish priests, but devotes a lot of space to the duties of archdeacons, rural deans, and apparitors, and to the exaction of tithe. The statutes of Wells were carried northwards and published in Carlisle in 1258 or 1259. The ascription of the Lansdowne version to York, 1259, always seemed doubtful, since the statutes must have been published at Carlisle simultaneously or only a few months earlier, and since the only manuscript of the York version was written at Durham a century later. The title, it is true, now reads ' Constitutiones ecclesie Ebor',' but this title is not in the original hand, and a note to the displaced c. 57, which was written by the first scribe, implies that he did not know the statutes to be intended for the diocese of York ; he said : ' Ista constitutio est una de constitutionibus *ante constitutiones Ebor*' [i.e. ' Greenfield '] ad talem signum intus ' (fo. 237v). It is strange, too, that the officials who, in 1306 or later, inserted Archbishop William Greenfield's two statutes in a series of synodal statutes of his predecessors, should have ignored these. Nor is there any trace of them in the *Provinciale* made in 1518 by compilers who had the ' Greenfield ' collection and other documents before them. Since these later compilers had access to statutes which, as we shall see, must belong to the mid-thirteenth century, how came they to miss another important series issued in the same generation ? But the argument from silence is inconclusive.

First, it is unproved that when Greenfield ordered his two statutes to be incorporated among other synodal statutes of some of his predecessors, there existed a single official compilation of York statutes. Perhaps his order stimulated his clerks to compile one ; but this, too, is uncertain. If a compilation did already exist in the archbishop's registry in 1306 it may have been in the form of our texts D and J, where Greenfield's two statutes follow the rest, as 43 and 44. The ' incorporation ' of Greenfield's statutes may, in this event, be represented by our text A, where abridged versions of 43-44 appear before 41-42. But if this was an official compilation, it was not the only collection to be made. For the Durham manuscript, L, has a longer version of 13, adds 22, supplements 27 and 28 (27ii, 28ii), and omits 39-42. The compiler of the *Provinciale* of 1518 may have had a text before him like that of DJ or A ; but if so, he also had access (as we

the York series of ' 1306 ' which we have hitherto been considering from the statutes ascribed to 1259, I shall refer to the series dated 1306 as ' Greenfield ' throughout this section.

have) to a few other statutes dated before 1306.[31] Again, an entry of January 1228 in Walter de Gray's register points to a statute of that archbishop not otherwise known.[32] Thus it is evident that the ' Greenfield ' series did not comprehend *all* the thirteenth-century legislation of the diocese of York. The statutes which we attribute to the year 1259 could have been either overlooked or deliberately set on one side in 1306.

Despite the lack of any manuscript of ' 1259 ' other than the solitary survival from Durham, we have a little positive evidence to counteract the argument from silence. In 1307 the archbishop of York issued a mandate forbidding the prior and convent of Lewes from storing tithes of sheaves, derived from their appropriated churches in the diocese, ' extra solum ecclesiarum contra constitutionem a nostris predecessoribus salubriter editam.'[33] The fact that a little later the archbishop saw fit to issue a general inhibition to the same effect may suggest that the *constitutio* to which he referred was not well known ;[34] but this looks very like a reference to c. 37 of ' 1259 ' : ' Inhibemus ne de bonis ecclesie edificia in solo construant laicali, sed in solo ecclesiarum edificare ut convenit compellantur, ibique fructus ecclesiarum suarum reponant et in solo nullatenus laicali. . .'[35] Nothing on the subject is found in the ' Greenfield ' collection. But if Greenfield had this statute before him in 1307, he presumably had the whole series, for it was as a single series that these statutes came north from Wells. This piece of evidence speaks strongly in favour of the publication of the series at York.

Other possible traces of the ' 1259 ' series have to be taken into account. (i) The statute attributed to Archbishop William Wickwane (1279-1285) in the *Provinciale* of 1518 (III. ix. 5), which is also c. 22 in the L text of ' Greenfield,' exempts wage-earners from paying tithe if their annual earnings do not exceed half a mark. But Archbishop John Le Romeyn, in August 1286, refers to the constitution of his predecessor, William, on this subject and says that it fixed a five-shilling limit.[36] The limit of five shillings is found in c. 74 of the statutes of ' 1259.' Romeyn's mandate seems to prove that there had been a five-shilling limit in York diocese,

---

31. He had York 22 (of ms. L) under an ascription to Archbishop William Wickwane (book III, tit. ix c. 5) and two unascribed statutes, possibly of the thirteenth century (I. iii. 1 and 2).

32. *Reg. Walter Gray* (Surtees Soc.), p. 20 : licence to Richard de Vescy to sell the fruits for the ensuing autumn ' non obstante constitutione nostra, in qua prohibuimus ne aliquis beneficiatus fructus suos ante diem S. Marci Evangeliste vendere possit vel ipsa beneficia impignorare.'

33. *Reg. William Greenfield* (Surtees Soc.), ii. 35.

34. *Ibid.*, ii. 38 : ' Licet a nonnullis nostris predecessoribus atque nobis . . . inhibitum fuerit.'

35. MS. Lansd. 397 fo. 249r as emended by reference to the Carlisle text, Carlisle Episcopal Register II p. 138.

36. *Register of John Le Romeyn* (Surtees Soc.), i. 188.

and to that extent it points to the authenticity of the ' 1259 ' statute ; but how can this be reconciled with the reference to Wickwane ? Two explanations seem possible : *either* Romeyn knew that Wickwane issued a statute on the subject (which is in fact *Provinciale*, III. ix. 5) but mistook ' 1259 ' c. 74 for it ; *or* Wickwane issued (or re-issued) ' 1259 ' c. 74, and a new statute on the same subject (*Provinciale*, III. ix. 5) was issued at some time between Romeyn's mandate of 1286 and the date of writing of L. If it were issued by Archbishop Greenfield or his immediate successors, Melton and Zouch, who were all named William, a later copyist might confuse the Williams and so give rise to the attribution in the *Provinciale*.

(ii) In another place Wickwane apparently modified a statute of ' 1259.' On 7 May 1282 he wrote : ' Licet in statuto nostro synodali statuendo ordinaverimus quod usus Ebor' in singulis parochialibus ecclesiis nostre dyocesis observaretur, ita quod infra annum continuum, a statuto huiusmodi numerandum, per singulos rectores et vicarios de libris usus eiusdem provideretur competenter, communiter tamen reperimus in Notinghamie predicto decreto nostro minime paritum extitisse.'[37] This statute (another example of a statute not included in the later compilations)[38] links up with ' 1259 ' c. 15 : ' Libri secundum usum predictum [*sc.* ' Ebor' vel saltem Sar'] infra biennium provideantur ecclesiis memoratis.'[39] All this justifies the conclusion that the statutes of ' 1259 ' were known, used, and modified at York during the following generation. That they were issued in 1259 and not at some later date rests on the fact that the surviving manuscript retains the time-limit given in the Carlisle statutes ; and this suspicious fact suggests another possibility. Can it be that a copy of the Carlisle statutes was preserved by the archbishop's clerks but never received official publication at York? Though unlikely, this is possible. In any case, there is evidence enough that the ' 1259 ' statutes were known at York. That being so, we have to see whether their existence helps to date the series with which this paper is chiefly concerned.

There is no close verbal similarity between the two sets of statutes. This offers a presumption in favour of pre-1259 issue for the core of the ' Greenfield ' statutes. The ' 1259 ' statutes were imported wholesale from outside, and were not easily susceptible to alteration ; but a draftsman at York in following years could hardly have failed to borrow from them. Some differences of substance point in the same direction. In both series it is laid down that penance shall not be enjoined upon the sick when their confession is heard ; the treatment of this in ' 1259 ' c. 6 is so much more thorough and diffuse than in ' Greenfield ' c. 15 (=Chichester 15) that the latter would hardly have been written if the former were at hand. The

---

37. *Reg. W. Wickwane*, p. 80; cf. p. 295.

38. Perhaps because a time-limit was set in the statute; though in other places (e.g., Salisbury) such statutes were reissued, shorn of their time-limits.

39. For the text of the whole chapter see *English synodalia*, p. 101.

same applies to the statutes appointing confessors in deaneries in '1259' c. 11ii and in ' Greenfield ' c. 7 (=Chichester 7). In one case only does the order seem to be reversed. 'Greenfield ' c. 25 (=Chichester 24) is a verbatim copy of canon 35 of Oxford (1222), which rendered illegal bequests by clerks to their mistresses, though the source of the statute is not stated. ' 1259 ' c. 25 is a modified version of the same canon, referring to it (' prout in concilio Oxon' reperitur esse statutum '). The desire to reproduce exactly the words of the canon of Oxford may well have been prompted by the reference to the canon in the ' 1259 ' statute ; and since the canons of Oxford had, strictly speaking, no authority in the northern province,[40] it was better to be silent about the source. But if in this case a statute of ' Greenfield ' seems to be later than 1259, it is a statute which is not in the ' core ' of the series. That core, if our reading of the evidence is right, certainly preceded the ' 1259 ' statutes.

V

WE have reached the point of dating our 'core' of statutes between 1241 and 1255. And now to what dates can be assigned the various additions to the core made in Chichester, Dublin, and York?

(i) *Chichester*. This is the one series to which a definite date is assigned in the title of one text : 1289.[41] It adds to the original core two of the York additions (Chichester 22, 39ii) in the same positions in the series, and makes fresh insertions at several points without any addition at the end.[42] The first substantial addition found only in Chichester, 25 and 26, comes in part from the statutes of Richard Wich, bishop of Chichester, 1244 × 1253 ; the next two, Chichester 29 and 38, are not datable and have not been found elsewhere. Chichester 40iii requires quarterly pub- lication of the sentences of excommunication, and is a natural appendix to the series of sentences taken over from York. There is nothing to suggest that the statutes were issued piecemeal at Chichester, nothing to prevent our accepting them as a compilation issued as a whole by Gilbert of St. Leofard in his synod of 6 Oct. 1289.

We can well understand why statutes issued at York should re-appear in Chichester in the pontificate of Bishop Gilbert, and why these statutes should not include all those issued at York before 1289. For Master Gilbert, like Master William Greenfield, had been a protégé of Archbishop Walter Giffard. He was appointed to be the archbishop's official in November

40. The ' 1259 ' statutes had, of course, originated in the southern province, at Wells.

41. Reasons have been given above for regarding the date of 1306 in the York series as applicable only to York 43, 44.

42. York 30 and 36 were probably of the original core and were omitted by Chichester (cf. above, pp. 120, 122).

130

1268[43] and was active in his service until 1274 at least ;[44] but he does not appear after this in the registers of the northern province and made his later career in the south.[45] We may safely infer that his synodal statutes stem directly from the York series and that the copy of that series which the bishop possessed was at least ten years old in 1289.

(ii) *Dublin*. The core is represented in this series by 1-31vi, excepting 9. The fact that 9 is added, by the original scribe, to the text in Crede Mihi suggests that he may not have found it in his exemplar of the rest of the series, but there is nothing in its contents to throw light on its date. 31vi pretty clearly closed the series as first issued at Dublin. 31vii is an addition drawn verbatim from the canons of Oxford, which might have been made at any time. Coming to 32-40 we meet with a group of statutes which show much borrowing from the canons of Lambeth (1261) and which must have been composed at one time. Their position in the manuscript makes it most probable that 1-31vi were issued in Dublin 1241 × 1261, and 33-40 soon after 1261. As for the remainder, 41-48, they may have been published at the same time as 33-40 or later, separately or as a group. The final limit is set by the date of the only medieval copy, in Crede Mihi, probably soon after 1275.

(iii) *York*. The additions to the core consist of 22, 27ii, 28ii, (30 and 36, though not in Chichester, were probably part of the core : above, p. 122), 38-40, 41ii, 43-44. Since *York* 23 *and* 41ii are found also in Chichester, we may assume that they were added to the core before Gilbert of St. Leofard left northern parts ; and since 41ii also occurs in the statutes of Durham III, dated 1276, and probably preceded them,[46] we may ascribe these additions to the third quarter of the thirteenth century. *York* 39 probably influenced Durham III, 1 and therefore probably belongs to the same period ; as it seems to echo the Council of Lambeth, it may be dated between 1261 and 1276. *York* 40, being a quotation from the legatine canons of London, 1268, has its *terminus a quo*, and since the legate provided for regular repetition of this canon, it may well have been uttered in synods of 1269. *York* 22, which occurs only in the L text, and under an ascription to William Wickwane in the *Provinciale*, has been discussed already (above, pp. 127-8). Whatever the explanation of the problem it sets, it can hardly

43. *Reg. Walter Giffard*, p. 2.

44. He acted as the archbishop's vicar 3 May 1274 (*Reg. Thomas Corbridge* (Surtees Soc.), i. 47) and was still employed 22 Oct. 1274 (*Reg. Walter Giffard*, p. 295). In Dec. 1274 he was provided and collated to the church of Kirk Ella, Yorks. (*ibid.*, pp. 286-7).

45. Cf. T. F. Tout, *D.N.B. s.v.* Gilbert of St. Lifard. He had certainly left the archbishop's service before the time of Wickwane, cf. *Reg. W. Wickwane*, p. 260.

46. York 41ii, like 41iii (above, p. 12), is related to Durham III, dated 1276. The fact that 41iii belonged to the core of Dublin is a point in favour of dating these chapters before 1276.

be earlier than the pontificate of Wickwane. *York* 38, which denounces tuitorial appeals from the province of York to the court of Canterbury, might be of early date. If it were in a core which had originated in the northern province, it would naturally have been omitted from statutes for Chichester and might have seemed unnecessary in Dublin. But no record of trouble on this topic has been noted before the time of Archbishop Wickwane, when certain men of Beverley appealed for 'tuition' to Canterbury in 1281. The prior and convent of Durham likewise appealed in 1282-1284.[47] Again, in 1289 Archbishop John Le Romeyn threatened Peter de Thuresby and the abbot of Jervaulx with excommunication if they took their lawsuit for tuition to Canterbury.[48] None of these records cites or implies the existence of a synodal ruling on the matter. But the last incident probably occasioned the making of a statute on this subject; for already on 24 November 1291, the archbishop is referring to his synodal statute against appellants to the court of Canterbury, (*Register*, ii. 12). *York* 27*ii*, 28*ii* are additions to the statutes which they follow and provide no internal evidence of their date. As they occur only in the L text, the time (or times) of their issue is altogether doubtful.

VI

THE object of this enquiry has been to determine, so far as possible, the origin and relationship of three sets of diocesan statutes, of Dublin, Chichester, and York, printed by Wilkins under the years 1217, 1289, and 1306 respectively. To sum up quite briefly our findings on them : The Chichester series present the least complicated picture ; they were probably issued at the time stated, in a single series. But this series shows little originality : it depended mainly on the statutes of York. Dublin and York create more problems : they contain a common core which was perhaps composed elsewhere but which very probably originated at York between 1241 and 1255. While this core was in a large measure a new composition, it was influenced at many points by the statutes of Nicholas of Farnham, bishop of Durham (1241 × 1249). We conjecture that this core of statutes was borrowed from York and published in Dublin by Archbishop Luke (d. 1255) or his successor, Fulk de Sanford, before 1261. But this core

47. *Reg. W. Wickwane*, pp. 14, 109, 272 for the first episode ; *Reg. epist. Johannis Peckham* (Rolls Ser.), ii. 494, 645, cf. I. J. Churchill, *Canterbury administration*, i. 461-2, and F. M. Powicke, *The Thirteenth Century*, pp. 493-4, for the second. Since the above was written the tuitorial appeal from Durham to Canterbury has been discussed, with new documents, by R. Brentano, *York Metropolitan Jurisdiction and Papal Judges Delegate*, 1279-1296 (Univ. of California, Publ. in History, vol. 58, Berkeley and Los Angeles, 1959), pp. 39-40, 130, 136, 184-95.

48. *Reg. J. Le Romeyn*, i. 338. For appeals to the court of York for tuition from 1219 onwards, see *Reg. Walter Gray*, p. 135, *Reg. Walter Giffard*, pp. 140-2, *Reg. W. Wickwane*, pp. 169, 297, *Reg. J. de Halton Carlisle* (Canterbury and York Soc.), i. 164-5.

132

accounts only for about two-thirds of the existing Dublin series and a smaller fraction of the statutes of York. In each case the residue was added piecemeal at indeterminate times, which in Dublin may have spread over thirty years, at York over sixty years. Of the York statutes only the last two really belong to the date which the whole series bears : 1306.

If the route by which we have arrived at these conclusions has been long and tortuous, it has at least brought to light some facts of interest about other statutes of York, and about statutes of the English diocese of Durham and the Irish diocese of Ferns. The whole enquiry, too, may serve to bring into sharp relief a few features of this somewhat neglected branch of ecclesiastical law. First, these statutes illustrate very well how the thirteenth-century bishops, legislating for their subjects, seldom troubled to compose a wholly new set of instructions and precepts. They copied, without qualm and without acknowledgment, occasionally re-touching according to taste. Secondly, it was not unusual, once a series of statutes was published, to add to it by a mandate or synodal pronouncement, and the new statute might take the form of insertion or appendix. In neither case would copyists usually trouble to distinguish the various parts, and a composite series of statutes might be entitled equally well with the date of issue of the first or the last of them. Thirdly, our enquiry points to extraordinarily haphazard habits of recording synodal statutes and other diocesan mandates. No single text of the York statutes contains all of those which have survived, and some have not survived at all. It is not surprising, then, to find even in the Middle Ages the same ignorance, neglect, and misunderstanding of the statutes as has been their lot in later times.

ADDITIONAL NOTES

The English statutes discussed here are edited in Councils & synods ii 421-35 (Durham),483-8 (York), and 1082-90 (Chichester).

P.131 ad.fin : On the question of authorship of the Dublin statutes, Fr Gwynn, in a private letter to the writer,23 Nov.1961, suggested that the first 31 chapters were published by Archbishop Luke when he conse- crated St Patrick's cathedral on St Patrick's day, 1254. 'Is it not very probable,' he wrote, 'that a provincial council was held at the time of this solemn consecration of Dublin's new cathedral, built in fine Early English style ? Is this not a very likely background for the promulgation of synodal decrees which are so obviously borrowed from contemporary English synods ?' The Dublin borrowings from York are indeed found only in the first 31 chapters (cf.p.130,above) and the section could be assigned to this occasion. Even so, I would suggest, a newcomer from England in the see, Fulk of Sandford (cons.25 March 1257) was perhaps more likely to promulgate statutes than was Archbishop Luke at the end of his long pontificate (1230-1255). The wording of this section, as well as of the later chapters, indicates statutes issued for a diocese, not a province.

IX

The so-called Statutes of John Pecham and Robert Winchelsey for the Province of Canterbury[1]

Among the legislators of the medieval English Church John Pecham, archbishop of Canterbury, 1279–92, is remembered chiefly on account of canons published in two councils early in his pontificate, at Reading in July-August 1279 and at Lambeth in October 1281. His successor, Robert Winchelsey (1294–1313), less celebrated for his laws, none-the-less is assigned by Lyndwood, the fifteenth-century canonist, nine chapters of the *Provinciale*. The 'Winchelsey' documents and some others described in medieval manuscripts as 'Statuta' or 'Constitutiones' or 'Decreta' of one or other of the two archbishops cannot be immediately or surely connected with any known provincial council. They include texts on questions of almost daily occurrence to medieval archdeacons and parochial clergy: about the calculation of tithe, the duties of stipendiary priests, the obligations of the laity for church repairs. Lyndwood glossed many of them. Modern students of history and canon law commonly cite them. It is, therefore, of some importance to establish the degree of credit which may be allowed to the ascriptions. This study will consider the evidence of the manuscripts and will aim at sorting the genuine statutes from the spurious and the dubious. Some of each kind will be found.[2] The enquiry may not only help to determine the nature of these particular documents, but also may reflect light on other doubtful legislation and illustrate the ways in which laws were framed and customs established in the English Church in the later Middle Ages.

Before considering this material it is well to draw the reader's attention to certain features of English ecclesiastical law-making in the thirteenth century. First, it was not unknown for laws to be projected in one assembly, cast into a mandatory form in another, and only finally re-cast and pub-

---

[1] I am grateful to Sir Maurice Powicke, the Reverend Professor E. C. Ratcliff, and my wife, whose criticisms at various stages in my studying of this material helped to make the argument more cogent and the statement of it clearer.

[2] The problems were briefly faced and some provisional conclusions stated by the present writer in 'Legislation of the Medieval English Church', *Eng. Hist. Rev.*, l (1935), 193–224, 385–417, see pp. 408–13.

lished as canons in a third: this was what happened in councils of 1257, 1258, and 1261.[1] Secondly, conciliar decisions, although put into writing, might never be published in authentic form: this is illustrated by the events of April 1282. At a council of the province of Canterbury which discussed matters of jurisdiction disputed between the archbishop and his suffragans, an ordinance to define and restrict the competence of the Court of Canterbury was drafted as letters patent in the name of the archbishop. But although Pecham's registrar copied the ordinance, a later marginal note in the register reads: 'Ista littera licet fuerit concessa communi consilio archiepiscopi et suorum non tamen fuit sigillata, nec emanavit ad alios sed usque ad duodecimum annum ordinationis archiepiscopi mansit quasi perdita in archivis.'[2] At the same time, other versions of the agreement, written down by various bishops' clerks, gained currency, much to Pecham's annoyance.[3] Thirdly, there were other councils at which decisions of the nature of legislation were taken, which, so far as we know, never became the basis of written enactments. For example, in a council of January 1280 Pecham and his suffragans condemned statutes made in the Benedictine Chapter of the province, but we only hear of this in later correspondence.[4] Then there is a letter (11 November 1290) from Oliver Sutton, bishop of Lincoln, to the vicar of Riseley. The vicar has received a citation from the conservator of privileges of the Hospitallers in England: the bishop tells him not to act upon it, 'cum ad presumptionem quorundam conservatorum finibus sibi concessis nullatenus contentorum reprimendam a venerabili patre domino I. dei gratia Cantuariensi archiepiscopo, totius Anglie primate, suisque suffraganeis iam pridem statutum fuerit condictum seu concorditer ordinatum quod in provincia Cantuar' nullus alius quam episcopi et officiales eorundem citationes conservatorum exequeretur.'[5] The vague expression 'statutum condictum seu concorditer ordinatum' will be noted. No other reference to this decision of the provincial council has been found. Again, when Robert Winchelsey held his first provincial council, 15 July 1295, the Merton chronicler reported: 'constitutiones quasdam a sanctis patribus approbatas sed per mercenariorum incuriam a vi propria vacillantes in medium legitime revocavit; necnon et alias ordinationes prioribus adnectens propter gregis tuitionem decrevit inviolabiliter observari.'[6] But no legislation remains: only a series of draft resolutions and notes of agenda made by the archbishop's

[1] *Eng. Hist. Rev.*, l. 402–6.

[2] Cf. I. J. Churchill, *Canterbury Administration*, London 1933, i. 429–30.

[3] *Reg. Epp. J. Peckham* (Rolls Series), ii. 405–6. Two versions are in Worcester, Record Office, Reg. Godfrey Giffard fol. 133ʳ (with an illuminating letter about the council from the bishop at fol. 134ᵛ). A third version resembling the second is in Bodleian MS. Ashmole 1146 fol. 78ʳ (a Chichester book), and yet another in *Reg. Ric. de Swinfield ep. Herefordensis*, Canterbury & York Soc. 1909, 32.

[4] *Documents . . . of the Eng. Black Monks*, ed. W. A. Pantin (Camden 3rd Series, liv. 1937), iii. 274 and *Reg. Epp. J. Peckham*, i. 150–1, 225, 256.

[5] *Rolls and Register of Bishop Oliver Sutton*, ed. R. M. T. Hill, Lincoln Rec. Soc. 48, 1954, iii. 56.

[6] *Flores Historiarum* (Rolls Series), iii. 279.

chancellor.[1] Finally, a complaint of Pecham's suffragans, quite early in his pontificate, should be remembered: 'Cum metropolitanus in provinciali duntaxat concilio iuxta formam sibi a iure traditam constitutiones edere valeat, petunt ne aliqualiter secus fiat.' The archbishop's reply was 'quod non intendit facere constitutiones contra iuris formam'.[2]

SO-CALLED STATUTES OF JOHN PECHAM

The canons of Reading and Lambeth call for no discussion, since the time of their issue and their authenticity are not in question.[3] But in two places in his great *Concilia Magnae Britanniae et Hiberniae* (four folio volumes, London 1737), David Wilkins printed 'statutes' of John Pecham which do not clearly indicate their origin.[4] These must be scrutinised. Wilkins's first group, printed (ii. 48–9) *sub anno* 1280, covers nine topics, arranged under four rubrics. He found all these texts together in Oxford, Balliol Coll. MS. 158 (then L. 3), a large collection of legatine and provincial canons, written in the late fourteenth century with fifteenth-century additions. Each 'statute' in this group is recorded in other MSS., but they are only assembled thus in the Balliol book and none is found in any book written within a generation of Pecham's lifetime. They are usually ascribed in the MSS. to Pecham without further detail.[5] The first six statutes also form a unity in six other MSS. and it was probably such a text that Lyndwood knew, for he only glosses nos. 1–4 and 6.[6] But, as we shall see, it is inconceivable that the second half of no. 6, which is a mandate for sending proctors to a clerical assembly on 20 October 1283, was issued at the same time as all the other texts which appear under the same rubric. Probably, then, the group was put together from scattered pieces in the fourteenth century; the character and date of one part do not enlighten us about the group as a whole. Each part must be considered on its merits.

1. *On the custody of the Host.* (*'Dignissimum eucharistie sacramentum . . . rigida castigantes'*).

This contains nothing to show whether it was intended for a province or a diocese or whether it was issued in a synod. The reference to archdeacons in the plural tells against its being an enactment for the diocese

---

[1] 'Articuli . . . archiepiscopi in prima sua convocatione per R. de Ros concepta', preserved in the Worcester register of Godfrey Giffard, fol. 392ᵛ. This also has (fol. 260ʳ) agenda for the provincial council of 13 October 1286.

[2] *Reg. Epp. J. Peckham*, i. 332, 334.

[3] The most recent account of the two councils is in Dr. Decima L. Douie's *Archbishop Pecham*, Oxford 1952, ch. iii.

[4] Reprinted in J. D. Mansi, *Ampl. Collectio Concil.*, Venice 1759–98, xxiv. 339–42.

[5] In several MSS. nos. 1–6 are appended to the genuine canons of Reading without any dividing line (M, Oa; for the list of MSS. and *sigla* see below, 33–4). In D the title is: 'Incipiunt constitutiones de Redyngg'. U and Ha are said to be published at London at the New Temple. In some MSS. no. 2 is attached to the canons of Lambeth.

[6] He ascribes all five to Pecham: *Provinciale*, Oxford 1679, 249–50, 36–40, 230–1, 336–7, 313.

of Canterbury: if Pecham issued it, he issued it for the province. Lambeth (1281) c. 1 was devoted to the same topic and Lyndwood, who possessed both, conflated the two without warning in *Provinciale*, iii. 25, 2.[1] The two texts are evidently related, and it is most likely that this statute preceded the Council of Lambeth and was modified therein. The statute disagrees with Lambeth c. 1 in providing for fortnightly, instead of weekly, renewal of the consecrated Host. Lambeth c. 1 provides 'circa deportationem . . . eukaristie ad egrotos, servetur honestas alias et alibi constituta'. This could refer to our statute,[2] and was taken to do so by the annotator of the canons of Lambeth in Cambridge Univ. Library MS. Add. 3575; but prescriptions of this kind were so common in thirteenth-century diocesan statutes that the reference need not be interpreted in this way. Whether the statute was provisionally approved in an earlier provincial council,[3] or was a mandate issued by Pecham in his visitations, or was a draft presented to the Council of Lambeth for discussion, is uncertain; but there is no reason to doubt that it emanated from Pecham, 1279–81.

2. *On the making of chrism ('Cum sacri chrismatis . . . credimus intellectu').*

Not only is this associated with nos. 1 and 3–6 in seven MSS. (DGMUHaUaCb); it occurs in nine other late MSS., sometimes unascribed, but often ascribed to Pecham 'secundum aliquos libros' (FKQSZHb). It is not matched by any other utterance of Pecham. While its date and even its authenticity remain doubtful, there is nothing about it to arouse suspicion.

3. *On commemorating deceased bishops ('Sanctum et salubre . . . studeant nuntiare').*

This recalls Lambeth (1281) c. 27, and probably preceded it. Johnson noted that the two were connected and said: 'perhaps this may be produced as a singular instance of a second law made on the same head, but much less perfect than the first.' But comparison suggests that Lambeth c. 27 was a careful *précis* of this wordy document, omitting only the final clause, which invites exempt clergy to come voluntarily into line with the rest and to notify their intentions 'to us in our next congregation'. It was probably the failure of exempt abbots to attend the Council of Lambeth, 1281,[4] which caused this section to be dropped from the canon. We are still unable to say whether no. 3 was the provision of a council, 1279–81, or a mandate issued by the archbishop.

[1] John Johnson, *A Collection of the Eccles. Laws*, London 1720, remarked upon this. While printing nos. 1–7 after the canons of Reading, he admitted that he found 'no certainty of the time or place'.
[2] Which reads: 'Circumferatur autem cum debita reverentia ad egrotos, sacerdote saltem induto superpellicio et gerente orarium cum lumine previo in lucerna et tintinnabulo sonoro.'
[3] The bishops of the province assembled in council, more or less formally, on five occasions between the councils of Reading and of Lambeth.
[4] Cf. *Reg. Epp. J. Peckham*, i. 237–8, 255; *Reg. J. Pecham* (Canterbury & York Soc. 1908) 150; *Annales Monastici* (Rolls Series), ii. 395–7, iii. 288, iv. 483; *Flores Historiarum* (Rolls Series), iii. 54–5; *Gesta Abbatum S. Albani* (Rolls Series), i. 458–9.

4. *On bishops' indulgences* (*'Item cum salubriter . . . faciant vilipendi'*).

This, like no. 2, is not matched elsewhere. The only reason for assigning it to Pecham is its presence with other apparently genuine texts.

5. *On nuns* (*'Item pro misericordia . . . secularium feminarum'*).

This single sentence is rather an admonition to fellow-bishops ('studeant fratres') than a statute. Of its three parts the first two are covered more fully by nos. 9 and 10 which, as will be seen, provided material for Lambeth (1281) c. 17, 18. We regard this as the draft for a mandate or canon, prepared before May 1281, of which the last part, to restrict residence of boarders in nunneries, was dropped when no. 10 was composed.

6. *On the purgation of criminous clerks* (*'Clerici pro suis . . . studium equitatis'*).

This is not matched elsewhere. It is compatible with the circumstances of 1279–81, for the treatment of criminous clerks came under discussion between king and clergy in November 1280; but in the light of the document which follows no. 6 in all MSS. a later date seems equally plausible. That document, 'De procuratione clericorum', is simply an administrative order that proctors of the inferior clergy shall attend a meeting to be held on 20 October.[1] The meeting is almost certainly that of October 1283, and the mandate was probably uttered in the council at Lambeth, 9 May 1283; its opening words suggest that it was a final injunction, following others delivered orally, in the same way; if so, no. 6 may have been uttered at the same time, but for reasons already stated, the preceding sections in this group cannot all belong to 1283.[2]

7. *On church ornaments* (*'Ad doctrinam presentium . . . vicariis reparari'*).

This is the commonest of statutes attributed to Pecham, and is not easily disengaged from other documents concerned with the obligations of parishioners and incumbents. It might seem to be based on a statute attributed to archbishop Walter Gray of York (d. May 1255); but on close inspection the York statute is found to conflate Pecham's statute and the later versions attributed to Winchelsey and Reynolds; it contains prescriptions far too elaborate for the province of York in the thirteenth century and can only have circulated in that province long after Gray's time.[3] There is, then, no known source for no. 7. Only one comparable statute is found in English synodal statutes of this period: c. 12 of Exeter, 1287 (Wilkins, ii. 139), but this is not verbally connected with no. 7 and

---

[1] For the confusion which has been caused by the lack of a complete date see F. Makower, *Const. Hist. of the Church of England*, London 1895, 361 n. 36.

[2] Text Ha of nos. 1–6 and the summons concludes: 'Edita fuerunt hec statuta London' apud Novum Templum'; this may have arisen from a misunderstanding of the summons.

[3] All MSS. are fifteenth-century or later, all are ascribed to Gray. It figured in the York *Provinciale* of 1518 as Gray's. For printed editions see H. Spelman, *Concilia*, ii, London 1664, 290; Wilkins, *Concilia*, i. 698, iii. 676; Mansi, *Ampl. Collectio*, xxiii. 789, 792; *Chartulary of Cockersand Abbey*, ed. W. Farrer, Chetham Soc. 1898–1909, i. pt. i, 50.

makes much heavier demands upon parishioners. No. 7 is described as Pecham's 'statute' or 'constitution' in ten texts (GHMPGaMaTaYaAbCb), and in Ma is said to be his 'Decretum . . . nuper factum in visitatione sua'.[1] But it nowhere uses the language of command, and has the air of a letter declaratory of custom for the use of archdeacons. Disputes over the obligations of parishioners may have led archdeacons of the fourteenth century to attach the name of Pecham to a document which was not his.[2] On the other hand, the archbishop was an active visitor and his courts would be concerned with disputes over this question. Some sort of directive to archdeacons may well have come from him or his officials.[3] Moreover, the apparent connexion with the Winchelsey-Reynolds statutes suggests, without proving, that no. 7 is a genuine though informal utterance of the archbishop.

8. *On trees in cemeteries ('Ceterum advertentes quod . . . canonica percellemus').*

The opening words show that this did not originally stand alone. It follows naturally upon no. 7, and it is therefore surprising to find that Cb and the closely related G are the only MSS. where nos. 7 and 8 appear together. CbG continue with a passage ('Quocirca devotioni vestre . . . canonica percellemus', not found in MOaKb), which is an order from an archdeacon to his rural deans[4] to publish 'has litteras nostras et contenta in eis'. It remains extremely doubtful whether no. 8 is properly ascribed to Pecham. In favour of its genuineness it may be noted that its wording seems to be known to bishop Peter Quinel at Exeter, 1287, and to archbishop William Greenfield at York, 1306; the preamble also reappears in a revised form in archbishop John Stratford's provincial canon of 1343 (c. 14).[5]

---

[1] Cf. *Reg. Epp. J. Peckham*, iii. p. cxli. In two closely related fifteenth-century MSS. (BbY) the statute is attributed to archbishop *Robert* 'in sua visitatione in diocesi Wigorniensi', and in CaGb to Robert 'suam provinciam visitando'; it is also ascribed to Robert Winchelsey in ZaDb. The appearance of Robert's name is probably the result of confusion with Winchelsey's revised version of the decree. Ea entitles it 'Statuta consilii provincialis Cantuarie'.

[2] Cf. the attribution of 'Casus in quibus simplex sacerdos non potest absolvere' to archbishop Stephen Langton: Wilkins, i. 597, and see *Eng. Hist. Rev.*, l (1935), 400.

[3] See the ruling of William de la Cornere and other clerks of the archbishop concerning the laity's obligations in the chapels of Alvaston and Boulton, near Derby, made at the metropolitan visitation, March 1280 (*Cartulary of Darley Abbey*, ed. R. R. Darlington, Derbys. Archaeol. & Natural Hist. Soc. 1945, i. 239–40, 291–2).

[4] Unless the reference to 'capitulis vestris generalibus' suggests that the writer was a bishop and the recipient an archdeacon; in which case *nostri*, a few lines below, must be emended to *vestri*.

[5] Wilkins, ii. 140, 286, 709. The Exeter statute appears, only slightly modified, in a group ascribed to archbishop Walter in Bodleian MS. Bodley 794 fol. 187ʳ. Here also, following the statute 'de mortuariis' ascribed to Stephen Langton (fol. 187ᵛ) is another statement which is probably a memorandum based on the Exeter statute ('Item quod rector ecclesie habebit omnes arbores . . .'). This occurs in B.M. MS. Harl. 3705 fol. 41ᵛ after no. 8 above, and in All Souls Coll. MS. 42 fol. 254ᵛ and Dublin, Trin. Coll. MS. E.2.22, p. 128; it is re-cast in the form of a statute in Cambridge Univ. Lib. MS. Add. 3575, fol. 289ᵛ.

Wilkins's second group of 'Pecham' statutes, printed (ii. 61) *sub anno* 1281, consists of three parts: two concerning nuns and one about pluralists. Wilkins found them in the Worcester episcopal register (Ob). The only other texts which have been found are UHa (c. 9–11) and MOa (c. 10).

9 and 10. *On nuns* ('*Licet tam venerande . . . sacerdotem absolvi*', '*Ad hec ne . . . tribuerint indiscretam*').

These have the appearance of provincial legislation and the former refers to 'nostra provincia'; but the latter treats 'publicationem huiusmodi edicti' as a time-limit, which does not smack of a conciliar canon. The two statutes are briefly foreshadowed in no. 5 above. These features, and the fact that a text is found in the Worcester register between documents of April and May 1281, become more significant when the text is compared with Lambeth (October 1281) c. 17, 18. Nos. 9 and 10 reappear there, modified in both substance and form, but recognisable. We infer that they fall into the same category as nos. 1 and 3 above and that they were either provisions of a provincial council in 1279–81 or drafts issued by the archbishop in preparation for the Council of Lambeth, October 1281.[1]

11. *On pluralists* ('*Adhec fratres et . . . prebuerunt criminosis*').

This is merely declaratory of the canon of the second General Council of Lyon. It begins by warning bishops who permit pluralism that they are implicated in a sentence of excommunication. This has no place in Lambeth (1281) c. 25, which amplifies Reading (1279) c. 4 against the pluralists themselves. Probably it was an item on the agenda of the Council of Lambeth which found no favour with the assembled prelates.

MS. D of c. 1–6 preserves a text which probably shows how Pecham acted in accordance with his intended canon in his own archdiocese:[2]

De multiplicantibus beneficia ecclesiastica.

Item, omnes qui sibi beneficia ecclesiastica multiplicant contra constitutiones felicis memorie Gregorii pape decimi Lugdun' factas post congregationem domini nostri archiepiscopi et suffraganeorum suorum apud Redingges factam sine dispensatione sedis apostolice excommunicatos esse per totam diocesim Cant' publice et solempniter denuntiari faciatis diebus et locis oportunis, illis dumtaxat exceptis qui dua beneficia huiusmodi postmodum resignarunt vel se super premissis nostre gratie supposuerunt.

The terms of this document make it clear that it was not issued by the archbishop, and point to a mandate by his commissary or by the archdeacon of Canterbury.

---

[1] They are unlikely to have been mandates issued on visitation, since Pecham did not visit the diocese of Worcester until 1282.

[2] The order of nos. 5 and 6 is reversed, and this extraneous piece divides no. 5 from the mandate for proctors. The MS. is a miscellaneous register of Reading Abbey, which does not seem to have had interests in Canterbury diocese.

STATUTES OF JOHN PECHAM AND ROBERT WINCHELSEY

The claim of these eleven texts to be genuine legislation by John Pecham for the province of Canterbury is not very strong. One or two seem to be mere adumbrations of laws (5, 11); some are drafts or mandates, doubtless intended to be superseded by the conciliar canons in which their substance was wholly or partly repeated (1, 3, 9, 10); one may be a genuine but informal directive (7); others (2, 4, 6, 8) have hardly any other recommendation than that in some fourteenth-century MSS. they are ascribed to Pecham. Nevertheless, they have their place in a collection of *Councils*; for during the later Middle Ages these texts were used in just the same way as well-authenticated canons, and Lyndwood incorporated five of them into his *Provinciale*.

SO-CALLED STATUTES OF ROBERT WINCHELSEY

Wilkins printed in his *Concilia* (ii. 278–83) much, though not all, of the material which has to be considered; other printed editions are noted below under the separate entries. It will be necessary to question the authenticity of these documents one by one, but some general features of the evidence call first for comment. In the first place, the twenty texts include different versions of a single statute: six on ornaments, two on stipendiary priests; and the various statutes on tithe overlap in contents. Secondly, the formulae used are not often those which were employed in thirteenth-century provincial legislation: there is never a mention of synodal authority, seldom a sign that the rule concerns the province, and sometimes a complete absence of the usual mandatory verbs, *statuimus*, *precipimus*, and the like. Thirdly, not all MSS. ascribe the statutes to Winchelsey, and the ascription to him often lacks precision about time or place of issue. The most precise time- and place-date given is for a provincial council in 1305 at Merton which almost certainly did not take place.

Some of the statutes were framed, as we shall see, before Winchelsey's day; but that does not necessarily preclude an association with him, for he is reported to have uttered earlier constitutions in his provincial council of 1295 and to have made additions to them.[1] This might explain the reappearance of these statutes under his name. But, when we look at their contents, it is hard to believe that these pieces on tithe and mortuary and church ornaments were what the archbishop conceived to be the most pressing matters when he came to his province: the agenda for the council suggest more serious preoccupations. If these texts are the relics of a larger undertaking in that council, why have they alone survived, and without any reference to the time and place of publication?

Certain of their features might be explained if we could apply to the group as a whole the description found in some MSS. of some texts: 'facta in visitatione metropolitana'.[2] For this might imply a comparatively

---

[1] Above, 15.

[2] In at least ten MSS. of the statute on stipendiaries, in several groups of the statutes on ornaments, and also in a few MSS. of the tithe statute no. 16. In Ka the statute on stipendiaries under this title is followed without break by no. 14.

informal utterance and a variety of versions. Copies might be made by the bishops' clerks from a master-copy in the archbishop's chancery as Winchelsey went his rounds. But if so, it is strange that no copy is in Winchelsey's register or in other surviving episcopal registers. Nor do the formulae of these documents resemble those of Winchelsey's visitation-injunctions: the common forms *iniungendo, iniungimus* never appear. The mention of visitations adds a little to the plausibility of the ascriptions, even when the texts are found elsewhere under other titles. It is just credible that archbishop Robert (and Walter Reynolds after him), in the course of visitation, made an anthology concerning tithe and other topics about laymen's obligations to churches, drawn from synodal statutes of various dioceses; and it is possible that the archbishop passed on this anthology to his subjects by some process of informal publication hidden from us.[1] It is also possible—and indeed likely—that in doing so he would not hesitate to revise the statutes he collected. Or he might issue a brief *résumé* of their substance and add new regulations to them. But to envisage these possibilities is not the same as saying that the archbishop adopted this course or that, if he did, the documents survive. Each text must be judged on its merits.

All these texts concern matters which remained very much matters of local custom. As the archbishop proceeded on visitation, he discovered what were the local regulations in matters of tithe, repair of churches, and so forth, and might be content to call the attention of the clergy in that diocese to the statutes on the subject which they already possessed. Or, he might address special mandates, in the manner of visitation-injunctions reiterating the common law of the Church, to places which seemed specially to need correction. Thus, on 18 May 1301, after visitation, he addressed his mandate to the dean of Bristol, forbidding fixed payments at baptisms, and various other abuses.[2] In 1303 he wrote after visitation to the official of the bishop of London on the matter of tithes wrongfully withheld from London rectors.[3] These were not provincial enactments, but they would bring a body of rules and regulations to the notice of the clergy of a diocese, or archdeaconry, or deanery, by the archbishop's authority, and so the material might be associated with his name. Such a procedure would explain the opening formula of a group of texts on ornaments: 'Inter cetera provisum est et ordinatum.'[4] But the consequent accumulations cannot be regarded as provincial legislation.

---

[1] He seems to announce the intention in writing to the dean of Bristol (18 May 1301) after visitation, when he orders: 'quod mercatores in una parochia commorantes et in alia seldas ubi sua de die exercent mercimonia optinentes quoad decimas et oblationes eo pretextu faciendas et solvendas id communiter observent quod per loci diocesanum super hoc dudum fuerat ordinatum donec cum maiori deliberatione super hoc equitatis tramite pro conservatione iuris cuiusque loci aliter duxerimus ordinandum.' *The Great Red Book of Bristol*, ed. E. W. W. Veale, text, part i (Bristol Record Soc., iv., 1933), 92. Cf. Reg. W. de Geynesburgh, ed. J. W. W. Bund and R. A. Wilson (Worcs. Hist. Soc. 1907–29), 7–8, wrongly dated 1303.

[2] *Great Red Book of Bristol*, i. 91.   [3] B.M. MS. Harl. 335, fol. 15ʳ.

[4] Other miscellaneous documents were included under this head in U and Qa.

STATUTES OF JOHN PECHAM AND ROBERT WINCHELSEY

The confusion is worse confounded by texts which display every sort of corruption. Many of those which ascribe these documents to Winchelsey are in fifteenth-century collections which contain other gross errors of ascription: the pseudo-Langton and pseudo-Edmund statutes, and those of 1175 dated 1065.[1] The men who compiled these collections were seldom interested in the accuracy of an ascription. The fact that a rubricator of an exemplar carried on a running title too far was enough to mislead generations of copyists; and the scribes of a dozen MSS. saw nothing impossible in a title which made Winchelsey archbishop in 1360.[2] The chief reason for supposing that some of these documents were decreed by Winchelsey is the difficulty of explaining on other grounds why they were ever brought together from diverse places of origin and ascribed to him. But the pseudo-Langton statutes present the same difficulty, and the falsity of their ascription admits of no doubt. This *rechauffé* of known synodal statutes with other material of unknown provenance must be seen in its setting; and the setting casts doubts on ascriptions to Winchelsey. Where material which can be traced in earlier statutes reappears in a modified form ascribed to Winchelsey in late MSS., their divergence from the earlier statutes may be the result not of official revision but of local tinkering or scribal error. It is a suspicious circumstance that Winchelsey never seems to be invoked by archbishops or diocesans in the middle part of the fourteenth century when they regulate the behaviour of priests or the liability for tithe and the like.[3] If these texts were recognised as laws with provincial authority the reticence is strange.

1. *On stipendiary priests* ('*Presbiteri stipendiarii necnon* [or *Item statuimus et*] . . . *ecclesiis suis*').

This is the only document with consistent ascription to Winchelsey. Ten MSS. say that it was made in his visitation in 1305 (FKWZAaKaAb BbFbGb) while nearly all the rest agree that the author was Winchelsey and the year 1305.[4] Although some twenty-four MSS. are known, they are mostly in late, lengthy, corrupt collections of provincial canons where they most often stand noticeably apart from other laws ascribed to the same archbishop.[5] With one exception, to be noted, they may all derive from a single late archetype. The only suspicious fact is this absence of any contemporary or sub-contemporary text; in favour of genuineness

---

[1] Cf. *Eng. Hist. Rev.*, l (1935), 398–400 and C. R. Cheney, *Eng. Synodalia of the XIII Century*, Oxford 1941, 65–7.

[2] It is instructive to see the same sort of error produced by the editors of printed editions. Spelman's placing of nos. 1 and 14 under archbishop Simon Mepham is an example; this was probably not authorised by the MS. he copied.

[3] When Roger Martival used no. 1 he did not name Winchelsey or invoke metropolitan authority. When Simon Islip quoted and confirmed no. 4, along with Boniface on tithe and Mepham on oblations, he did not name the authors (his mandate is with Sa).

[4] Fa (now lost), the only unascribed text, was printed by Spelman (ii. 501) *sub anno* 1332; printed by Wilkins (ii. 280–1) *sub anno* 1305.

[5] The exceptions can be seen in the List of MSS. below.

may be alleged the fact that archbishop William Courtenay re-issued the regulation in 1391 under the impression that it was Winchelsey's.[1]

Something like it was in existence early in the century. A mandate dated 24 September 1320 from Roger Martival, bishop of Salisbury, to the archdeacon of Wiltshire, states that the bishop, in visiting his diocese, has discovered the excesses of certain 'presbiteri stipendiarii et alii sacerdotes propriis sumptibus amicorumve suorum suffragiis forsitan sustentati'. The greater part of the mandate is a slightly modified and re-shaped version of our statute, with two omissions.[2] Similar provisions for an oath to be taken by chaplains, without any close verbal parallels, are found in some undated statutes for the archdeaconry of London, probably fourteenth-century.[3] Further evidence comes from the city of London that the subject of stipendiary priests and their oath-taking was a burning question in Winchelsey's day. The 'rectors and curates' lodged a series of complaints to the archbishop and bishops in their provincial council (? in 1309) against friars, hermits, and stipendiary chaplains who invaded their rights.[4] A contract between the rector of St. Martin's in the Vintry and a chaplain (Michaelmas 1304) shows that the practice of taking an oath in such terms as the statute envisages already existed, while another document contains detailed complaint of the rectors to the archdeacon's official against the chaplains and lays down (in different terms from Winchelsey's) the form of oath the chaplains ought to take.[5]

Ten MSS. say that the statute was 'facta in visitatione'; but Courtenay described it as 'in concilio suo provinciali pie statuta'. Despite this assertion, neither version of the original statute mentions conciliar authority, nor has it the normal protocol or ending of a mandate intended for a province. The commoner version implies a command by the use of the subjunctive: 'non recipiant oblationes . . .' in the first sentence, and thereafter uses the future indicative: 'iurabunt . . .' etc. This is not the way in which a provincial canon was usually issued. The exceptional version (that printed by Spelman and Wilkins from Ea) offers a more orthodox form with 'statuimus et ordinamus', etc.; but even here the statute is loosely, not to say carelessly, constructed. Lyndwood's text gives no help, for while it generally follows the commoner version, somebody (probably Lyndwood) seems to have re-touched it, adding an occasional 'decernimus

---

[1] Wilkins, iii. 213 from Lambeth, Reg. W. Courtenay, fol. 76v. Winchelsey's statute was re-published and declared binding throughout the province by archbishop Henry Chichele in a convocation of November 1419 (*Reg. H. Chichele*, Canterbury & York Soc. 1937–47, iii. 59 cf. i. pp. cxlviii–ix). William Lyndwood was prelocutor of the clergy in this convocation.

[2] Salisbury, Diocesan Registry, Reg. Martival, ii. fol. 103v. I owe my knowledge of this document to the kindness of Dr. K. M. Wood-Legh. In two important variants only it agrees with Ea against the commoner version.

[3] B.M. MS. Harl. 335, fol. 12r.

[4] Cambridge Univ. Lib. MS. Gg. 4, 32, fols. 125rb–129rb. Vict. County Hist. *London*, i. 200–1 is at fault in referring to 'capellani *non* stipendiarii' (cf. fol. 129ra).

[5] MS. cit., fol. 118ra, 119va. This is undated, but followed by other complaints dated 15 December 1314 (fols. 120rb–121va); cf. Vict. County Hist. *London*, i. 201, where both are dated 1315.

etiam ut . . .' (237) or 'volumus insuper ac firmiter iniungendo mandamus quatenus . . .' (112), to give the document a more formal air.[1] So far as can be judged from Courtenay's paraphrase, he had the commoner version before him when he renewed the statute in 1391. This was probably the original form. If it was a document put out somewhat informally during visitation, this might explain how the bishop of Salisbury came to turn the statute to his own purposes in 1320 without claiming for it the authority of a provincial council,[2] and the form of Ea perhaps represents a medieval editor's attempt to give the statute a normal appearance, as Lyndwood tried to do. But it must be emphasised once again that the ascription of the statute, in any form, to Robert Winchelsey remains doubtful in view of the lateness of the MSS.

2–7. On church ornaments.

John Pecham, it has been seen, may have been author of a directive on this subject (above, no. 7). Some forty-six MSS. ascribe statutes which are plainly revised versions of Pecham no. 7 to Robert Winchelsey or to his successor Walter Reynolds or to both. The confusion of texts is very great and the classification in six groups which is attempted here is only approximately correct, for we are faced with a corrupt tradition. Complicated and corrupt as it is, there are still some reassuring features. Among the varieties some stand out in MSS. of respectable date and appearance which describe the statute as a decree, either of Robert or of Walter, on his visitation (see nos. 2–3, 7). These make it possible, at least, that the earlier directive is correctly ascribed to Pecham, and that it was officially revised by Winchelsey in the middle years, 1299–1305, when he conducted metropolitan visitations.[3] If his decree arose out of visitation, it may have received an addition in his time, which would account for the appendix in no. 5. It was apparently more thoroughly revised by Walter Reynolds in his visitations, which are recorded between 1314 and 1319.[4] Probably most of the texts have been re-cast or abridged, they have contaminated one another, and the exact wording of the genuine statutes is irrecoverable. But three editions prepared from nos. 2, 4–5, and 6–7 respectively, perhaps get as near as may be to the main stages in the official re-shaping of Pecham's statute.

2. 'Ut autem parochiani certiores . . . compositiones reparari.'

This has never been printed, but is found in six texts (imperfect in various ways) of which two (RrWa) come from early in the fourteenth

[1] Here, as elsewhere, Lyndwood reads 'provincia' where all MSS. read 'archiepisco-patus'.

[2] No metropolitan visitation of Salisbury is recorded by Dr. Churchill between 1285 and 1329. Ea appends to its version of the statute a form of oath, extracted from the statute, and this was printed by Spelman and Wilkins. There seems no reason to suppose that it was officially produced.

[3] Cf. Reg. R. Winchelsey, Canterbury & York Soc. 1952–56, i. xviii ff. He had started to visit his archdiocese in 1296 (ibid., xvi).

[4] Churchill, Canterbury Administration, ii. 36–8, 149.

century. All describe the text as a decree of archbishop Robert in his provincial visitation.[1]

3. '*Inprimis statuit et decrevit . . . incumbit reparare.*'

This is a paraphrase of no. 2. PDbMb have the precise reference: 'iuxta decretum domini Roberti in visitatione sua in episcopatu Vyntonnie post mortem domini Iohannis de Pentys loci diocesani, iure metropolitano interposito, a.d.millesimo ccc quinto.'[2] MO omit the words 'in episcopatu . . . interposito'; Oa is joined to other material under a general heading 'apud Merton a.d. 1305'.[3]

4. '*Ut sciant parochiani . . . incumbit reparare.*'

This is closely similar to no. 2; it uses 'innotescimus' instead of 'notificamus' and lays the obligation to repair books upon the rector or vicar.[4] In G it is unascribed, in Cb ascribed to Robert Winchelsey at Merton, while a later hand in W ascribes it to archbishop Robert on visitation.

5. '*Ut sciant parochiani . . . reparatione indigere.*'

This adds to no. 4 a section ('Item compellendi sunt . . .') which demands specified books and other vestments and the repair of books and vestments.[5] It is printed in *Constitutiones legitime seu legatine Regionis Anglicane* (Paris 1504), fol. 151vb; also, from Fa in Spelman's *Concilia*, ii., London 1664, 433, and from Spelman, collated with F and Ra, by Wilkins (ii. 280 (i)). Twelve MSS. are known; all but E (Winchelsey at St. Paul's) ascribe the statute to Winchelsey at Merton, though four (CKZHb) suggest the alternative name of Langton. Those which bear a date give 1360, except for Hb (1260). In every text except E the statute follows nos. 8–12 (or part) and 17, under the same title. Although all these texts are described as Winchelsey's, G, in giving an interpolated version of no. 2, declares that archbishop Walter was reponsible for adding the objects named in the new section of no. 5.[6] No reliance can be placed on this

---

[1] Wa reads: 'Decretum domini Roberti de Wynchelse de ornamentis ecclesie inveniendis et corrigendis. Hoc est decretum domini Roberti nuper Cantuariensis archiepiscopi in sua visitatione provinciali, inter rectores et parochianos locorum (*add* perpetuis G) temporibus observandum (observandis GWa), inter cetera tenorem continens infrascriptum.'

[2] On 26 December 1304 Winchelsey announced his forthcoming visitation of the diocese of Winchester, and he was in the diocese between 15 January and 20 February 1305 (*Reg. R. Winchelsey*, i. pp. xviii, xli). If the decree was promulgated when he was at Merton (Surrey) on 20 February 1305 this might explain the appearance of this place-name in some texts of these documents; but for official dating the visitation of Winchester diocese fell entirely within the year 1304 (ending 24 March 1305).

[3] Like MOPDb this calls the statute a 'Constitutio generalis'.

[4] Lb is like no. 4 but is very corrupt and omits mention of books.

[5] Oa contains only the new section, in an extremely confused series, under the running title of Winchelsey at Merton.

[6] 'Walterus permissione divina Cantuariensis archiepiscopus addidit huic constitutioni illa quinque (*sic*) superius expressata, viz. legendam, antiphonarium, duo psalteria, gradale, troparium, ordinale, manuale, etc.'

late statement, which may well be a conjecture based upon a comparison of texts of nos. 2 and 7. The obvious corruption of all titles in this group makes it doubtful whether the appendix they preserve comes from Winchelsey or Reynolds.

6. '*Ut parochiani ecclesiarum . . . sumptibus eorundem.*'

This is the version used by Lyndwood, and the ten known MSS. include Ea (ascribed to archbishops Robert and Walter) from which Spelman printed (ii. 434), and Ra (no title) and F (ascribed to archbishop Robert 'et secundum quosdam Simonis Islep'), collated by Wilkins (ii. 280 (ii)) with Spelman's edition. The text incorporates the service-books found in no. 5's appendix as the first item in the list of parishioners' obligations, and makes various other changes. The operative words are now 'volumus decetero et precipimus'. All texts are very late in date and many are closely related in contents. The ascription to archbishops Robert and Walter is common to AKQZEaBbCb, and Simon Islip intrudes as an alternative author in KQZBbCb. Y ascribes to archbishops Robert Winchelsey and William. There is no mention of a visitation, no time- or place-date.

7. '*Inter cetera provisum . . . vicariis reparari.*'

This version may be seen in print in *The Reg. of St. Aug. Canterbury, commonly called the Black Book,* ed. G. J. Turner and H. E. Salter, London, Brit. Acad., 1915–24, i. 356 (from Da). There are eighteen MSS. The group is less homogeneous than no. 6 and several texts are corrupt or incomplete. The authors are again said to be archbishops Robert and Walter, and the occasion is their metropolitan visitations. The preamble is worded differently, the list of objects differs in a few particulars, and the demand for the repair of the nave is omitted. Most texts omit the whole of the last clause ('Cetera autem omnia . . .').[1] Despite many errors and omissions the tradition of this group—it is found in fourteenth-century MSS. from several dioceses—merits consideration. It probably comes nearer to an official version than does the *textus receptus* of no. 6.

8–16. *On tithe.*

Wilkins printed (ii. 278–80) from Fa nos. 8–12 on tithe, followed by nos. 17 and 5. While the tithe statutes must be considered one by one, it is important to remember that when nos. 8–12 are brought together it is usually under Winchelsey's name, and that they are never found together with other tithe statutes attributed to Winchelsey, even when those statutes occur in the same MSS.

8. '*Quoniam propter diversas . . . loci persolverint.*'[2]

This statute is elsewhere attributed to various prelates. It was also

---

[1] It occurs in a form different from that of group 6 in Ka.

[2] This is often followed by a string of references to the *Corpus iuris* and commentators (cf. Wilkins, ii. 278–9).

printed by Wilkins (i. 698–9) as a statute of archbishop Boniface, and there are good reasons for preferring that attribution.[1]

9. *'Quoniam ut audivimus . . . particulariter decimentur.'*

Comparison of this with the Salisbury diocesan statutes of Robert Bingham (1238 × 1244) c. 43 and Giles of Bridport (1257) c. 44[2] shows that no. 9 has only a few words which are not found in one or other of the earlier texts. For 'appulsiones' this version reads 'amotiones', and at the end 'particulariter' is an addition. This links no. 9 with the statutes of Wells (1252 × 1258)[3]; for, although the Wells texts are incomplete, the derivatives of Carlisle and York[4] have this statute (c. 75) and end with the words 'partialiter decimentur'. The connexion is confirmed by nos. 10 and 11. Differences between various MSS. of no. 9 point to two separate and deliberate conflations of the earlier statutes.[5]

10. *'Quid vero pro . . . duximus relinquendum. Item precipimus . . . valeat impedire.'*

Apart from obvious corruptions this proves to be identical with Giles of Bridport's statutes c. 45, which is also found in Carlisle and York c. 76. Some texts, including those printed by Wilkins, transpose the two halves.[6]

11. *'Ad hoc quia audivimus . . . eorum fautores.'*

This is found without significant difference in Carlisle and York c. 77. Where they read 'vicinorum', no. 11 stupidly gives 'vicariorum'. Where Carlisle and York read 'presentis sinodi', this omits 'presentis'. WwYBb present a puzzling variation. After the *explicit* 'eorum fautores' they add the clause 'et sine conscientia . . . habet exposcere', which closes the Carlisle-York statute; they continue with Carlisle-York c. 78 (not about tithe, but about excommunication) before coming to the tithe statute no. 13. As may be seen from the list of MSS., nos. 11–12 are less commonly found in the Winchelsey collection than are nos. 8–10.

12. *'Statuimus etiam quod prediales . . . precipimus observari.'*

This is only attributed to Winchelsey and is always found with nos. 9–11, except for W (mid-fourteenth century) which provides a short anthology entitled: 'Incipiunt constitutiones de Merton de divisione

---

[1] Some were stated in *Eng. Hist. Rev.*, l. 406.

[2] Bingham's statutes are found in B.M. MS. Harl. 52, fol. 119ᵛ, Bridport's are printed in Wilkins, i. 714–20. The numeration of chapters of these and other synodal statutes in the text above is that which will be used in the forthcoming continuation to Haddan and Stubbs, *Councils and Eccles. Documents*.

[3] Cf. Cheney, *Eng. Synodalia*, 97–101.

[4] Cf. Cheney, 'The Medieval Statutes of the Diocese of Carlisle', *Eng. Hist. Rev.*, lxii (1947), 52–7.

[5] Cf. also the use of Bingham, c. 43–4, below 29 n. 4.

[6] Lyndwood gives the text in its original order, immediately following no. 9, in *Provinciale*, iii. 16, 6. Some texts only contain the second part, 'Item precipimus . . .' (e.g. S). Nos. 9–10 are ascribed to the legate Ottobuono in Ta, which in no. 9 reads 'appulciones' and 'particulariter decimentur'.

decimarum.'[1] Here no. 8 (which we attribute to Boniface) comes first.[2] This is followed without break by statutes of John Gervais of Winchester (1262 × 1265),[3] by Bingham's c. 43 (not modified in the fashion of no. 9 above, but abridged), and then by this no. 12 in shortened form. It is followed by Bingham's c. 44,[4] continues with extracts on tithe from the *Decretum*, etc., and drifts into extracts from the canon 'tradita a magistro Simone de Mepham Cantuar' archiepiscopo apud London' que sic incipit: Zelari oportet' [Wilkins, ii. 552]; but at the end of all is written (p. 111): 'Expliciunt constitutiones de Merton.' The collection is of interest in showing how statutes from different dioceses might be brought together under one heading, to the confusion of later generations. Although this manuscript is connected with the diocese of Norwich, it preserves these statutes of the two Wessex dioceses.[5]

If nos. 8–11, with which no. 12 is usually found, had really been issued by Winchelsey, no. 12 would not be a likely addition: its brief opening statements were more thoroughly expounded in the other statutes. But, since nos. 8–11 are not authentic, the case of no. 12 remains open. Serious doubt arises on several grounds: the opening statements are not only very brief but must have been commonplaces by the end of the thirteenth century; neither these nor the last phrase ('quam constitutionem . . . in nostra provincia precipimus observari'), which alone suggests provincial legislation, occur in the one comparatively early text, W. Moreover, the main regulation does not square with nos. 14 and 16. The text does not keep good company in the MSS., and is unlikely to be a genuine statute of Winchelsey.

13. *'Quoniam in signum . . . munusculo circumscripto.'*

This is found in the collection attributed to Winchelsey at Merton a.d. 1360 in Za, where it is preceded by nos. 8, 9, 10 (transposed), 17, Pecham no. 7, and Winchelsey nos. 1, 14, 18. In Y it follows a text of nos. 8 and 17 which ends: 'Expliciunt constitutiones domini Roberti apud Merton archiepiscopi de modo decimandi a.d. m° cc° vicesimo secundo' and a text of nos. 9–11 and Carlisle-York c. 78 entitled: 'Sequntur alie constitutiones apud Merton'; no. 13 is simply entitled: 'Sequitur postea

---

[1] The rubricator also wrote at the head of the page 'Wynchelse Merton', but the first word is partly erased.
[2] For the last words: 'donec . . . persolverint' it reads 'ipso facto'.
[3] Wilkins, ii. 297–8 (c. 62–3).
[4] This follows another series (8, 14, 9, 10ii) in S, ascribed to Winchelsey at Merton. In Ab (fol. 159r 'Inter eccl. rectores') and in R (fol. 55va 'Cum inter rectores') Bingham c. 43–4 are ascribed to Winchelsey. R, which is preceded by nos. 7, 19 and 16, ends: 'Hec est constitutio facta et optime de mundo approbata et per totum mundum adiudicata at per apostolicam sedem confirmata et sic finit hec constitutio'. Bingham c. 43–4 appear among pseudo-Langton material in M fol. 119vb.
[5] Salisbury, D. & C. muniments, Liber evidentiarum C, witnesses to the interchange of statutes between Salisbury and Winchester (cf. *Eng. Synodalia*, 105, 126, 144–5). Statutes of John Gervais of Winchester (c. 62–4, cf. above) appear as 'Constitutio fratris Iohannis Cantuariensis archiepiscopi edita London' a.d. 1280 de decimis et oblationibus' in the fifteenth-century Oxford, Brasenose Coll. MS. 14 fol. 173rb.

una alia constitutio de decimis.'[1] The whole of this statute occurs in Carlisle-York c. 74 and may well have been a statute of Wells. No. 13 takes over from this diocesan source the phrase: 'ecclesiarum nostre diocesis'. There is no reason for accepting no. 13 as a genuine re-issue by Winchelsey.

14. 'Sancta ecclesia constituit . . . decimarum compellatis.'

This was printed without ascription in *Constitutiones* (Paris 1504), fol. 138[ra]. Lyndwood, glossing it (iii. 16, 7, p. 199 cf. app. ii. 36) speaks a little more cautiously than is his wont: 'attribuitur et ascribitur Roberto Winchelsey'. Apart from the appearance of this statute in the unusual series in Za (cf. no. 13) this is not found among other tithe statutes attributed to Winchelsey. It exists in twenty-one MSS., sometimes following no. 1, sometimes following no. 20. It is never ascribed to anybody but Winchelsey, but nine texts (CFKPZFaUaCbMb) are anonymous. In Gb it is called: 'Ordinatio facta a domino Roberto Cant' archiepiscopo in visitatione.' The ascription to Winchelsey is highly dubious, having regard to the terms of the statute, which suggests a mandate from a bishop or an archdeacon to his parish clergy rather than a provincial canon. True, in Lyndwood's text the words 'per nostram provinciam' appear; but these are not found in any manuscript and were probably inserted by Lyndwood himself. The text, as it has reached us, is in an advanced stage of corruption.

15. 'Rectoribus ecclesiarum nobis . . . non presumant.'

An early text, and one other, of no. 2 (GWa) contain, under the same ascription to archbishop Robert on his provincial visitation, a short statute permitting rectors to excommunicate their parishioners for withholding customary tithe and forbidding them to excommunicate by name for any other reason without authorisation. The MSS. are respectable, but this statute is in fact found verbatim among the synodal statutes of Norwich (1240 × 1243).[2] There is no good reason for supposing that Winchelsey made it his own. It is, however, easy to see how the text became associated with him, since, on his metropolitan visitations, he insisted on the rights of rectors in this respect. A mandate to the bishop of London's official[3] shows this, and no 16, if authentic, provides further evidence.

---

[1] The same sequence and ascription of nos. 8, 17, etc. is found in Bb; but here the only heading for no. 9 onwards is a running title: 'Robertus Wynchelsey apud Merton', which has been extended beyond the 'Expliciunt'.

[2] Wilkins, i. 734a (c. 43). It is also in the statutes of London (*Eng. Hist. Rev.*, xxx (1915), 298, c. 74), but the 'Winchelsey' text agrees with Norwich's 'citra conscientiam' against London's 'preter conscientiam'.

[3] B.M. MS. Harl. 335, fol. 15[r], *inc.* 'Quamquam per diversorum . . .'. Winchelsey's visitation of the diocese of London occurred in 1303.

16. *'Quoniam propter diversas . . . post satisfactionem.'*

Four texts (RUQaEb) of the statute on ornaments, no. 7, under the ascription to archbishops Robert and Walter in their visitations, contain a brief injunction on burials (no. 19) and this lengthy statute on tithe. The MSS. are badly corrupted, but at least they stand apart from the usual late and worthless tradition of the earlier texts on tithe, nos. 8–12.[1] In B, a fourteenth-century register of Ely, this statute is ascribed to Robert Winchelsey,[2] in his metropolitan visitation, whereas nos. 7 and 19 are assigned to archbishop Walter in his. The *incipit* and much of the substance of no. 16 agrees with the statute of archbishop Boniface. In its original form this was often attributed in late MSS. to Winchelsey; but here it is considerably modified and amplified. If Winchelsey were responsible for the re-editing, the identical opening sentence might explain the ascription of Boniface's statute to Winchelsey. Most of the statutes on tithe attributed to Winchelsey have been eliminated; this has probably a slightly better claim to be considered his.

17. *On mortuaries ('Quia inter rectores . . . ecclesie reservetur').*

The tithe statutes, nos. 8–12, are commonly followed by this statute on mortuaries and by no. 5 on ornaments. The statute on mortuaries proves to be identical with part of the Salisbury statute of Giles of Bridport (1257) c. 22. The attribution to Winchelsey seems no more probable than its attribution in many other places to Stephen Langton.[3]

18. *On fornicators ('Abiurationes autem fornicariarum . . . precipimus observari').*

Wilkins published this (ii. 283) *sub anno* 1305 from Bb, as a constitution of archbishop Robert. It had already been printed without title in *Constitutiones* (Paris 1504), fol. 150r. The editor of the Oxford *Provinciale* of 1679 described it in his supplement (App. ii. 37) as 'Excerpta quaedam de Matrimonio ex Synodo Wintoniensi celebrata a.d. 1308 Roberto de Winchelsey archiepiscopo Cantuariensi'. He may have added this after a superficial comparison with Spelman's edition (ii. 448) of synodal statutes of Winchester; but the two are not identical. The statute is almost the same as a statute of the diocese of Wells 1252 × 1258 (c. 13).[4] Besides isolated, unascribed texts it is assigned to Winchelsey in FQWZaCb. In M it is noted: 'Hec constitutio dominorum Roberti et Walteri dei

---

[1] Qa is the early fourteenth-century flyleaf of a glossed *Liber Sext* which belonged c. 1370 to the parson of South Walsham St. Lawrence (Norfolk). The mid-fourteenth-century U text is an addition (partly marginal) to the main collection in this volume.

[2] The word 'nuper' may suggest that the exemplar of B was written soon after Winchelsey's death (cf. above, 26 n. 1); but it would be dangerous to rely much on this.

[3] Cf. *Eng. Hist. Rev.*, l (1935), 399, 411. It also occurs in Kb, appended to a conflate version of archbishop Boniface's canons, 1261 (fol. 23r). In Da Ta no. 8 (under the ascription to archbishop Robert at Lambeth) is followed by the whole of c. 22–23 of Bridport, ending with the words 'ecclesiastica coartari'. In YBb no. 8 is followed by the part of Bridport c. 22 contained in no. 17 and all of c. 23: the whole is ascribed to Robert at Merton, 1222! Ww has the Bridport extracts with deleted ascription to Boniface.

[4] This relates its origin to that of nos. 9–11 and 13 above.

gratia archiepiscoporum ecclesie Cantuariensis', and P has a similiar title. None of these MSS. has the authority to justify the Winchelsey ascription; all are of the fifteenth century, and almost all follow this statute with the 'casus in quibus simplex sacerdos non potest absolvere', baselessly attributed to Stephen Langton.[1]

19. *On burials in churches, etc.* (*'Item precipimus quod . . . opera misericordie'*).

Following nine copies of no. 7 on ornaments is a short statute to restrict burials in churches and check the improper use of churches and cemeteries. All MSS. except B (which attributes to archbishop Walter) and P (no title) attribute the two statutes to archbishops Robert and Walter on visitation. Several MSS. are fourteenth century, their version of the statute on ornaments is, as we have seen, plausible, and five of the MSS. contain almost the only statute on tithe (no. 16) which we are disposed to accept as Winchelsey's. As no. 7, if authentic, represents a revision in archbishop Walter Reynolds's time, no. 19 may also belong to Reynolds. The evidence of B is significant here (cf. no. 16).

20. *On the holy-water clerk* (*'A nostris maioribus . . . districtius compellantur'*).

This occurs frequently without ascription in the late collections of provincial canons.[2] It is described as 'per dominum Robertum Wynchelse Cant' archiepiscopum a.d. 1305' in the fifteenth-century portion of W. Lyndwood (iii. 7, 2, p. 142) noted: 'ascribitur in quibusdam libris Bonifacio archiepiscopo et in quibusdam Roberto Winchelsey'. But the two ascriptions can be impartially rejected. This is c. 29 of the synodal statutes of Exeter, put out by bishop Peter Quinel in 1287.[3]

Scrutiny of the tradition of 'Winchelsey' statutes hardly permits one to claim confidently that he was author of any, but a tentative conclusion is possible. Where so much is obscure, the quality of the MSS. is very helpful in balancing probabilities. To discuss this evidence fully would require an analysis of MSS. extending far beyond the limits of an article; but considerations of this sort have always been weighed, even though reference is made to them only in a few places in the foregoing pages. The balance of probabilities favours our treating nos. 1, 2, 5 and (very doubtfully) 16 and 19 as genuine productions of Winchelsey, and no. 7 as the work of his successor, Reynolds. Nos. 3, 4 and 6 appear to be more corrupt versions of 2, 5 and 7. Six tithe statutes (8–11, 13, 15) and three others (17, 18, 20) are found in earlier synodal legislation and have no good claim to be associated with Winchelsey's name. Nos. 12 and 14, not known under any other authentic attribution, are unlikely to be his. So a small harvest of seven somewhat dubious texts is all that can be recovered from the total of twenty.

[1] Cf. *Eng. Hist. Rev.*, l (1935), 400.
[2] It precedes no. 14 (both unascribed) in CFKBbCb. In Ra the running title is 'Wynchelsey'; in Ka the statutes follow no. 1, which is ascribed to Winchelsey.
[3] Wilkins, ii. 147.

STATUTES OF JOHN PECHAM AND ROBERT WINCHELSEY

List of Manuscripts

After each is noted the numbers of the documents ascribed to Pecham (P) or Winchelsey (W) which it contains.

A   Antwerp, Mus. Plantin-Moretus, cat. no. 80 anc. 131. xv c. (fol. 182ᵛ W. 8–10, 17; fol. 202ʳ W. 1).

B   Cambridge, Univ. Lib. Add. 3468. xiv c. From Ely. (fol. 84ᵛ W. 7, 19, 16).

C   Cambridge, Univ. Lib. Add. 3575. xv c. (fol. 288ʳ W. 8–9, 17; fol. 324ʳ W. 6; fo. 330ʳ W. 1; fol. 341ᵛ W. 20, 14).

D   Cambridge, Univ. Lib. Dd. 9, 38. xiv c. From Reading. (fol. 56ᵛ P. 1–6; fol. 58ʳ W. 2).

E   Cambridge, Univ. Lib. Ee. 5, 13. xiv c. (fol 11ʳ W. 5).

F   Cambridge, Univ. Lib. Gg. 6, 21 (olim Eliensis 235). xv c. (fol. 43ᵛ P. 2; fol. 24ᵛ W. 8–12, 17, 5; fol. 67ʳ W. 1; fol. 78ʳ W. 20, 14; fol. 91ᵛ W. 18).

G   Cambridge, Univ. Lib. Ii. 3, 14. xv c. From Oxford, Austin friars. (fol. 209ᵛ P. 1–8, W. 1; fol. 209ʳ W. 4, 2, 15, 5; fol. 212ᵛ W. 8–10).

H   Cambridge, Univ. Lib. Mm. 1, 20. xv c. (ad fin. P. 7).

J   Cambridge, Univ. Lib. Mm. 4, 41. xv c. (fol. 7ʳ W. 7, 19).

K   Cambridge, Corpus Christi Coll. 84. xv c. (fol. 187ʳ P. 2; fol. 29ᵛ W. 6; fol. 30ʳ W. 1; fol. 38ᵛ W. 20, 14; fol. 179ᵛ W. 8–10, 17, 5).

L   Cambridge, Corpus Christi Coll. 189. xiv c. From Canterbury, St. Aug. (fol. 31ᵛ W. 7).

M   Cambridge, Gonv. & Caius Coll. 38. xv c. (fol. 105ᵛ P. 1–6, 10, 8; fol. 118ᵛ W. 3; fol. 120ʳ P. 7, W. 7; fol. 124ʳ W. 18, 1; fol. 126ᵛ W. 14).

N   Cambridge, Gonv. & Caius Coll. 204. xiv c. From Ely, archdeaconry. (p. 150 W. 7).

O   Cambridge, Pembroke Coll. 131. xiv c. (fol. 86ʳ W. 3, 14, 1).

P   Cambridge, Peterhouse 51 (ii). xv c. (fol. 25ᵛ W. 3; fol. 26ᵛ W. 14; fol. 34ʳ P. 2; fol. 37ʳ P. 7, W. 7, 19; fol. 41ʳ W. 18, 1; fol. 43ʳ W. 14).

Q   Cambridge, Peterhouse 84. xv c. (fol. 148ʳ W. 8–10, 17, 5; fol. 154ᵛ P. 2; fol. 163ᵛ W. 6).

R   Cambridge, St. John's Coll. 88. xiv c. (fol 55ʳ W. 7, 19, 16).

Rr   Cambridge, Trinity Coll. 398. xiv c. (fol. iiʳ W. 2).

S   Cambridge, Trinity Coll. 1245. xv c. (fol 136ᵛ P. 2, W. 8, 14, 9, 10, 17, 5, 1).

T   Cambridge, Trinity Hall 18. xv c. (fol. iʳ W. 7, 19).

U   Carlisle, Diocesan Registry, Ep. Reg. II. xiv c. (p. 379 W. 7, 19, 16; p. 424 P. 1–6, 9–11).

W   Dublin, Trinity Coll. E. 2.22 (no. 526). xiv c. (p. 107 W. 8, 12; p. 115 W. 4; p. 130 W. 1) xv c. (p. 162 W. 20, 14, 18, 17).

Ww   Dublin, Trinity Coll. Miscellanea Box VI Under K. xiv c. (W. 9–11, 17).

X   Durham, Univ. Lib. Cosin V. v. 7. xiv c. (fol. 164ʳ W. 2).

Y   Hereford, Cath. Lib. P. 7. vii. xv c. (fol. 123ʳ P. 2; fol. 127ᵛ W. 8, 17, 9–11, 13; fol. 143ʳ P. 7; fol. 149ᵛ W. 6).

Z   Holkham Hall, 226. xv c. (p. 26 W. 8–10, 17, 5; p. 72 W. 6; p. 73 W. 1; p. 103 W. 20, 14; p. 146 P. 2).

Aa   Lincoln, Cath. Chapter Lib. C. 5. 7 (no. 66). xv c. (fol. 62ʳ W. 1).

Ba   London, B.M. Add. 43405. xv c. From Muchelney. (fol. viᵛ W. 1).

Ca   London, B.M. Cotton Cleop. D. iii. xv c. (fol. 190ʳ P. 7).

Da   London, B.M. Cotton Faust. A. i. xiv c. From Canterbury, St. Aug. (fol. 217^r W. 7, 8, 17).
Ea   London, B.M. Cotton Faust. A. viii. xiv c. From Southwark. (fol. 41^v W. 6; fol. 117^v W. 1; fol. 170^r P. 7).
Fa   London, B.M. Cotton Otho A. xvi (lost). ? late xiv c. (fol. 109^v W. 8–12, 17, 5; fol. 138^v W. 1, 14).
Ga   London, B.M. Cotton Vitell. A. ii. xv c. From York minster. (fol. 53^r P. 7).
Ha   London, B.M. Harl. 52. Mid-xiv c. (fol 81^v P. 1–6, 9–11).
Ja   London, B.M. Harl. 237. xv c. From Mountgrace. (fol. 97^v W. 7).
Ka   London, B.M. Harl. 335. xv c. (fol. 15^r W. 7, 19; fol. 66^v W. 8–10, 17, 5; fol. 82^r W. 1, 20, 14).
La   London, B.M. Harl. 2250. xv c. (fol. 94^r W. 1).
Ma   London, B.M. Harl. 2349. xiv c. (fol. 114^r P. 7).
Na   London, B.M. Harl. 3120. xv c. (fol 117^v W. 5, 10).
Oa   London, B.M. Harl. 3705. xv c. (fol. 40^r P. 1–6, 8, 10; fol. 64^r W. 3; fol. 66^v W. 14, 1, 20, 5, 17, 8–10).
Pa   London, B.M. Royal 7 A. ix. xv c. From Southwark. (fol. 60^v W. 14).
Qa   London, B.M. Royal 9 E. ii. xiv c. (fol 1^r W. 7, 16, 19).
Ra   London, Lambeth Palace Lib. 538 (olim 17). xv c. (fol. 97^v W. 8–12, 17, 5; fol. 129^r P. 2; fol. 165^r W. 6; fol. 174^v W. 1; fol. 194^v W. 20, 14).
Sa   London, P.R.O. Exch. K.R. Misc. Bk. 30. xiv c. From Norwich, archdeacon. (fol. 25^v W. 7).
Ta   Oxford, Bodleian, Ashmole 1146. xiv c. From Chichester. (fol. 42^v W. 9, 10; fol. 78^v P. 7; fol. 79^r W. 8, 17).
Ua   Oxford, Bodleian, Bodley 794. Late xiv c. (fol 147^r P. 1–6). xv c. (fol. 187^r W. 7; fol. 189^r W. 14).
Wa   Oxford, Bodleian, Kent roll 6d. Early xiv c. From Tonbridge. (no. rr W. 2, 15).
Xa   Oxford, Bodleian, Rawl. A. 423. xv c. (fol. 15^v W. 2).
Ya   Oxford, Bodleian, Rawl. C. 100. xiv c. (fol. 118^r P. 7; fol. 125^r W. 8, 17).
Za   Oxford, Bodleian, Selden sup. 43. xv c. (fol. 71^r W. 8–10, 17, P. 7, W. 1, 14, 18, 13).
Ab   Oxford, Bodleian, Wood empt. 23. xv c. (fol 153^v P. 7; fol. 174^v W. 1).
Bb   Oxford, All Souls Coll. 42. xv c. (fol 219^r P. 2, W. 8, 17, 9–11, 13; fol. 248^r P. 7; fol. 255^v W. 20, 14, 1; fol. 275^v W. 6; fol. 279^v W. 1).
Cb   Oxford, Balliol Coll. 158. Late xiv c. (fol 165^r W. 4, 1, P. 1–8; fol. 169^r W. 8–12, 17). xv c. (fol. 184^r W. 6; fol. 185^v 20, 14, 18).
Db   Oxford, Balliol Coll. 301. Late xiv c. (fol. 119^v P. 7, W. 3).
Eb   Oxford, Brasenose Coll. 14. xv c. (fol 152^v W. 7, 19, 16; fol. 157^v W. 8–10, 5; fol. 172^v W. 1).
Fb   Oxford, Corpus Christi Coll. 72. xv c. From Bristol, St. Aug. (fol. 55^r W. 1).
Gb   Oxford, Exeter Coll. 31. xiv c. (fol 237^v P. 7, W. 14, 9–12, 7, 1).
Hb   Oxford, Exeter Coll. 41. xv c. (fol. 187^v P. 2, W. 8–10, 17, 5; fol. 202^v W. 6; fol. 204^r W. 1).
Jb   Oxford, Magdalen Coll. 112. xv c. (fol. 224^v W. 1).
Kb   Oxford, Magdalen Coll. 185. xv c. (fol. 11^r P. 8).
Lb   Pasadena, Huntington Lib. HM 932. xv c. (fol. 12^v W. 4).
Mb   Philadelphia, Pa., Free Lib. Carson 4. xv c. (fol. 91^r W. 3; fol. 92^r W. 14).
Nb   Worcester, Cath. Lib. Q. 92. xv c. (flyleaf W. 7).
Ob   Worcester, Record Office, Ep. Reg. G. Giffard. xiii c. (fol. 117^v P. 9–11).

ADDITIONAL NOTES

Pp.16-9: Texts of these statutes are now to be found in C.& S.ii.1118-25.

Pp.23-32:Texts of these statutes are now to be found in C.& S. in the following places:nos 1-7,ii.1382-8;no.8,ii.792-7;nos.9-11,ii.624-5; no.12,ii.1389;no.13,ii.623-4;no.14,ii.1389-91;no.15,ii.352;no.16,ii. 1391-3;no.17,ii.559 no.22(b);no.18,ii.598;no.19,ii.1388;no.20,ii. 1026-7.

P.26: Del. note 2 and read: Between 7 Jan. and 8 Feb. 1305 Winchelsey held visitations 'iure dyocesano' in the diocese of Winchester s.v. (bishop John of Pontoise d. 5 Dec. 1304). He visited Merton priory (Reg. H. Woodlock,i.4,46,98). He held a second visitation in the diocese sede plena by metropolitan authority and is recorded at Merton, 20 and 23 Feb. 1306 (ibid. i.99, Reg.R. Winchelsey,i.494, and P.R.O., CS 85/7/14). If the dating of the decree at Merton may be trusted, it must refer to the second visit. Nothing in the records implies that either visit was the occasion for a provincial council (above,p.21).

P.34: Ad fin. add Pa London,B.M. Cotton Domit.A.iii. xv c. (fo.254v. W.4).

X

Rules for the Observance of Feast-Days in Medieval England

IT IS a commonplace that medieval liturgies of the Latin Church display wide diversity of practice: the ecclesiastical calendar varied from province to province and diocese to diocese, religious orders had their own observances, and a saint's feast might be peculiar to a rural deanery or a single religious house. The study of liturgical calendars has not suffered for lack of students, but another class of calendars also deserves attention. While the pious observance of feasts by the laity did not deeply affect the stately progression of church services as they were regulated in various *Usus* and directed by the precentors of the greater churches, the demands made upon the laity in the matters of attendance at church and abstention from unnecessary work are of great interest. They show the extent to which ecclesiastical authorities thought it possible or desirable to impose the pattern of the liturgical year on the timetable of the layman with his manifold secular occupations. And as with the liturgical calendar proper, so with the calendar of *festa ferianda*[1]—those days when laymen should rest from labour and go to church—custom varied in different times and places.

The object of the present brief study is to comment upon some English lists of *festa ferianda* produced during the thirteenth and fourteenth centuries. It will not try to estimate the extent to which the Church's rules were obeyed or even the way in which they were interpreted. That is a very large topic, already studied partially by several scholars, for which the materials are both abundant and confusing.[2] Reforming bishops,

[1] See Du Cange, *Glossarium*, s.v. 'Feriae sollemnes', 'Feriari', etc. For modern feasts 'sub praecepto' of the Roman Catholic Church see *Codex Iuris Canonici*, c. 1247–9.

[2] The most useful and comprehensive work is Mrs. Edith C. Rodgers, *Discussion of Holidays in the later Middle Ages* (New York, 1940), which makes it unnecessary for me to refer to earlier discussions by B. L. Manning, G. G. Coulton, and others; but Mrs. Rodgers does not deal with the lists which are the subject of this study. For the observance of Sunday in the later middle ages see M. Levy, *Der Sabbath in England* (Leipzig, 1933) and for post-Reformation sabbatarianism W. P. Baker, 'The observance of Sunday' in *Englishmen at Work and Play . . . 1558–1714*, ed. Reginald Lennard (Oxford, 1931), pp. 81–144. I have been unable

sermon-writers, collectors of *exempla*, vernacular moralists, all make plain the common misuse of Sunday and other feasts. The church courts occasionally prosecute shop-keepers and labourers for not observing holidays.[1] But the divergence in practice from the lists which are discussed below are not limited to individual and occasional infractions. Statutes of boroughs and gilds, custumals of manors, account-rolls of many institutions, show that rules were applied which were often at variance with the rules of the ecclesiastical authorities.[2] We ought not to be over-hasty in assuming that the Church's requirements were incompatible with these other regulations. For the canonists and theologians make it quite clear that lists of *festa ferianda* were to be interpreted in no inflexible fashion. Their casuistry was able to distinguish between licit and illicit forms of work, gainful and charitable activities, the duties of hired labourers and servile, as well as between locality and locality, or major and minor feasts. Charity and necessity would be invoked to justify a departure from the rule.[3] Such lists as these, then, were—so to speak—starting-points from which the clergy might proceed to instruct their flock in the right behaviour.

to consult Wilhelm Thomas, *Sonntag im frühen Mittelalter* (Göttingen, 1929. Die Heilige u. die Form: Beihefte zur Monatsschrift für Gottesdienst u. kirchliche Kunst, 6) and Hans Huber, *Geist u. Buchstabe der Sonntagsruhe* (Salzburg, 1958. Studia theologiae moralis et pastoralis edita a professoribus Academiae Alfonsianae in Urbe). J. L. Cate has written valuable papers on 'The English mission of Eustace of Flay, 1200–1', in *Études d'Hist. dédiées à la mémoire de Henri Pirenne* (Bruxelles, 1937), pp. 67–89, and 'The Church and Market Reform in the Reign of Henry III' in *Essays in honor of James Westfall Thompson* (Chicago, 1938), pp. 27–65. For the common law courts and the exchequer see *Handbook of Dates for Students of English History*, ed. C. R. Cheney (1945), pp. 65–6, and J. F. Willard, 'The observance of holidays and vacations by the London Exchequer 1327–36', in *Univ. of Colorado Studies*, xxii (1935), pp. 281–7. For the *dies non legibiles, legibiles festinanter*, and *non disputabiles* of the universities, see Rodgers, pp. 53–62.

[1] See *Depositions . . . from the courts of Durham* [ed. J. Raine] (Surtees Soc., xxi, 1845), pp. 28–30, 32, and B. L. Woodcock, *Medieval Ecclesiastical Courts in the Diocese of Canterbury* (Oxford, 1952), pp. 80–1.

[2] The evidence is often hard to interpret and deserves more attention than it has received. Besides Mrs. Rodgers, see H. S. Bennett, *Life on the English Manor 1150–1400* (Cambridge, 1937), pp. 114–8. Not all the holidays of the customer or hired labourer were major ecclesiastical feasts. Cf. Lyndwood, *Provinciale*, lib. 1, tit. 11, c. 1, *ad verb. Auctoritate ecclesiae* (ed. Oxford, 1679, p. 56b): 'et bene dicit *auct. ecclesiae* quia quaedam sunt solennitates sive feriae quae non indicuntur ab ecclesia, sed aliunde; videlicet a principibus saecularibus quandoque propter victoriam habitam de hostibus vel quia tali die uxorem duxit, vel quia ei filius natus est . . .'.

[3] There was decretal authority: Alexander III (*Extra*, 2.9.3) allowed Norwegian fishermen to catch herring when the shoals came inshore on Sundays or other feasts, excepting major feasts, provided a portion of the catch went to the neighbouring churches and poor; Gregory IX (*Extra*, 2.9.5) allowed legal processes to continue on *festa ferianda* in certain circumstances (cf. *Digest*, 2.12.1). For the discussions of the theologians see Rodgers, pp. 36–45. The English canonist William Lyndwood provides canonistic references in his glosses to *Provinciale*, lib. 2, tit. 3, De Feriis (ed. Oxford, 1679, pp. 99–104).

We must make a further distinction in respect of the documents discussed below. While some of the lists have the character of local legislation, others are doubtful, others again seem to be nothing more than memoranda. The purpose of all such lists is well illustrated by Thomas Chobham, subdean of Salisbury, writer of a widely diffused *Summa de penitentia* in the early part of the thirteenth century.[1] The author, when he comes to speak of the penance to be enjoined on penitents, says:[2]

In primo iniungendum est omnibus penitentibus[3] quod ipsi observent et celebrent dies sollempnes et festivitates institutas per annum in ecclesia. Que autem festivitates debeant[4] celebrari per annum ostendit canon hiis verbis[5]: Pronunciandum est ut sciant tempora feriandi per annum, id est, omnem dominicam a vespera usque ad vesperam, ne iudaismo capiantur. Feriandi vero sunt per annum isti dies: Natalis domini, sancti Stephani, sancti Iohannis euuangeliste, Innocencium, sancti Silvestri, Octave Natalis[6] domini, Teophanie,[7] Purificacio sancte Marie, Annunciacio dominica,[8] sanctum Pascha cum tota ebdomada, Rogationes autem[9] cum tribus [*fo. 58*[v]] diebus, Ascensio domini, sancti dies Pentecostes, sancti Iohannis baptiste, xii apostolorum, et maxime Petri et Pauli qui predicacione sua mundum illuminaverunt, sancti Laurencii, Assumpcio sancte Marie, Nativitas sancte Marie, sancti Michaelis archangeli, cuiuscunque oratorii dedicacio, et omnium sanctorum, et sancti Martini, et sancti Nicholai,[10] et ille festivitates quas singuli episcopi in diocesi sua cum populo collaudaverunt que vicinis tantum circummorantibus indicende sunt, non generaliter omnibus. Relique vero festivitates per annum[11] non sunt cogende ad feriandum, nec prohibende. Indictum vero[12] ieiunium quando fuerit denunciatum ab omnibus observetur. Additur etiam[13] predictis[14] festivitatibus in alio canone[15]: Exaltacio

---

[1] The existing texts show many signs of revision, and in its present form the *Summa* is probably not earlier than the 1220s. An edition of the work by the Rev. F. Broomfield, Ph.D., is in preparation: the first part is an unpublished thesis (Cambridge Ph.D., 1960) deposited in the University Library, Cambridge. Pending its publication see P. M. Quantin, 'A propos des premières "Summae Confessorum"', *Recherches de théologie ancienne et médiévale*, xxvi (1959), 264–306, esp. 284–96.

[2] Printed from Brit. Mus., MS. Royal 8. A. xv, fo. 58[r] (= A), with selected variants of Cambridge, Univ. Lib. MS. Add. 3061, fo. 41rb (= C), both MSS. written mid-13th cent.

[3] *om.* penitentibus C.

[4] debeant C; debent A.

[5] *Decretum Gratiani*, De cons. D. 3, c. 1. The quotation ends at 'ab omnibus observetur'.

[6] *om.* Natalis C.

[7] Ephanie C.

[8] *om.* Annun. dom. C.

[9] *om.* autem C.

[10] *om.* et S. Nicholai C.

[11] per annum *after* cogende C.

[12] *om.* vero C.

[13] autem C.

[14] predictis C; aliis A.

[15] No order respecting the *Exaltatio* of the Cross is found in the *Decretum*, but De cons. D. 3, c. 19, requires the *Inventio* to be solemnized.

sancte Crucis. Per hoc etiam quod dicitur quod festivitates ille sunt celebrande que constitute sunt et[1] consuete et recepte ab episcopis in episcopatu suo comprehenduntur plures festivitates que iam fere ubique[2] consuete sunt et recepte, ut festum sancte Margarete et festum Magdalene, Decollacio sancti Iohannis baptiste, et[3] sancti Dionisii, sancte Cecilie, et[3] sancte Lucie, et[3] sancti Thome Cantuariensis qui tunc non fuit quando predictus canon datus est. Similiter festum sancti Vincencii, et sancti Fabiani et Sebastiani, et sancte Agnetis et sancte Agathe, et[4] sancti Gregorii, et[4] sancti Benedicti, et sancti Georgii. Omnes iste festivitates et plures alie celebrari habent[5] in locis illis in quibus consueverunt celebrari. Grisei tamen monachi quia predicte festivitates non sunt nominatim expresse in canone nolunt eas celebrare, set in illis[6] vadunt ad laborem suum; et inde multum scandalizant laicos simplices. Unde[7] melius esset eis[8] non laborare in illis diebus.[9] Item, per hoc quod dictum est quod dedicacio cuiuslibet oratorii debet celebrari, intelligitur etiam quod festum cuiuslibet sancti in cuius honore fundata est parochialis ecclesia debet celebrari in illa parochia. . . .[fo. 59ʳ] Sunt[10] autem quedam officia que non possunt pretermitti in talibus festivitatibus propter publicam utilitatem, ut veredarii, qui ducunt merces in quadrigis de loco ad locum, nulla die cessant. Similiter coci cotidie preparant cibaria et nullas festivitates celebrant. In multis etiam locis fiunt mercata in diebus dominicis et aliis sollempnitatibus. Omnia ista prohibenda[11] essent si fieri posset; ubi autem fieri non potest, iniungatur transgressoribus quod ipsi agant aliqua alia bona in recompensationem pretermissarum festivitatum. De clericis autem qui corrigunt libros suos et firmant lecciones suas in diebus festivis, non credimus quod peccent nisi sunt tales quod locent operarios suos[12] et accipiant denarios pro libris corrigendis. Sicut enim licet legere et audire euuangelia in ecclesiis, ita licet legere in domibus alios libros, dum modo fiat ad honorem dei et ad utilitatem ecclesie futuram. Sicut enim laicis licet circuire vineas suas et agros suos et arcere nociva animalia et eicere aquam nocivam, quia rivos deducere nulla religio vetuit,[13] et si inveniant[14] sepes vel[15] macerias[16] diruptas licet eas leviter obstruere ad horam ne destruantur

[1] et C; *om.* A.
[2] ubique C; *om.* A.
[3] et C; *om.* A.
[4] et C; *om.* A.
[5] debent C.
[6] *Add* diebus C.
[7] Unde C; ut A.
[8] eis (*after* ut) A; illis C.
[9] Cf. Alexander III's decretal to the bishop of Exeter, protecting the Cistercians' servants and workmen from excommunication by archdeacons and others on this account (*Comp. II*, lib. 2, tit. 5, c. 1, in *Quinque Compilationes Antiquae*, ed. E. Friedberg (Leipzig, 1882), p. 72).
[10] Sicut *cor. to* sunt *in* A.
[11] prohibita C.
[12] locent operarios suos AC; *but MS. Royal 8. F. xiii, fo. 30ʳ reads* locant operas suas.
[13] Cf. Virgil, *Georgics*, 11.268 *sqq.*, quoted by Rodgers, p. 94, who also cites Cato and Columella.
[14] invenerint C.
[15] vel C; et A.
[16] macies C.

segetes et vinee, eodem modo licet clericis in diebus festivis revolvere libros suos et si invenerint mendacia bene licet eis corrigere.

The canon which Thomas Chobham quotes and the additional names which he gives combine to produce the sort of list which circulated in thirteenth-century England, but it does not agree in all particulars with any other which has come to light. This is only to be expected in view of the latitude given by the canon to diocesan regulation,[1] and of Chobham's emphasis on customary additions. In the main series of legatine and provincial canons for England in the thirteenth century there is no list of *festa ferianda*. But some directive was needed if confusion was to be avoided. Chobham implies that parish-priests were expected to instruct the laity in right conduct. His reference to festivals 'constitute et consuete et recepte ab episcopis in episcopatu suo' suggests a measure of diocesan control. Stephen Langton, archbishop of Canterbury, expresses this view in his second synodal statutes for the archdiocese of Canterbury (between 1222 and 1228); a chapter on the celebration of feasts reads:

Quoniam turpis est omnis pars que non congruit suo universo statuimus quod festa consueta uniformiter per diocesim celebrentur nisi alicubi subsit causa specialis a diocesano approbata.[2]

Here Langton probably had in mind liturgical observances as much as the conduct of the laity; but it is to be expected that diocesan statutes will contain lists and that customary practice will give rise to other unofficial lists. They are not liturgical guides.[3] They are made so that parish-priests and other confessors may tell their flock how to behave on feast-days: whether to treat them as holidays, in the modern sense, by abstaining

---

[1] Reiterated by Pope Gregory IX (*Extra*, 2.9.5) when he listed the days when litigation should normally be suspended. Gregory's list resembles that in *Decretum*, De cons. D. 3.1 and adds: 'ceterisque solemnitatibus quas singuli episcopi suis diocesibus cum clero et populo duxerint venerandas'.

[2] C. R. Cheney, *English Synodalia of the Thirteenth Century* (Oxford, 1941), p. 64. For the preamble see Augustine, *Conf.* 3.8.

[3] The difference is evident in those liturgical calendars which bear annotations against certain names or at the foot of each page to indicate the feasts *omnino ferianda* or *tenenda*, or to be kept *preterquam in carucis* or *ab operibus mulierum*. Such calendars are not enumerated below. As examples see *The Hereford Breviary*, ed. W. H. Frere and Langton E. G. Brown, vol. iii (Henry Bradshaw Soc., xlvi, 1915), pp. xxxiv–v, 255–62; *Missale ad usum insignis ecclesiae Eboracensis* [ed. W. G. Henderson], vol. i (Surtees Soc., lix, 1874), pp. xxix–xli; *Liber obituarius aulae reginae in Oxonia*, ed. J. R. Magrath (Oxford Hist. Soc., lvi, 1910), pp. 1–48; Brit. Mus., MS. Egerton 2139, fos. 2–7 (a calendar of Lincoln diocese). Magrath prints (pp. 132–4) from Bodleian, MS. Digby 22, fo. 41ʳ lists (perhaps of SW. French origin) *De festis colendis ab omnibus, infra villam, quoad mulieres. Dies non sessionis* in the Court of Arches are noted in a calendar in Bodleian, MS. Ashmole 1146, fos. 1ʳ–7ʳ (cf. Cheney, *Handbook of Dates*, p. 73). I am obliged to the Rev. F. D. Logan for the information that the calendar was written 1369–70. For notes on *dies non legibiles*, etc., in university calendars see *The Ancient Kalendar of the Univ. of Oxford*, ed. C. Wordsworth (Oxford Hist. Soc., xlv, 1904), pp. 68–103, etc.

from work, or as modified working days.[1] Only in the fourteenth century is there a clear attempt by ecclesiastical authority in England to fix the *festa ferianda* for a whole province.

In that quaint and valuable storehouse of ecclesiological learning, *Statutes of Lincoln Cathedral*, the late Canon Christopher Wordsworth published an erudite note on Holy Days in England.[2] He was printing and illustrating a list of *festa ferianda* for the church of Lincoln which he found in a copy of the year 1523, and along with it he enumerated six other English lists, ranging from '(?) 1222' to '1400'. The dating of several of the lists, including the Lincoln one, caused Wordsworth much trouble, and he did not succeed in resolving his difficulties. As nobody has since returned to the problem or used the material fully, I shall comment on all the lists Wordsworth gave, together with an equal number of lists which he did not mention.

The problem of dating which troubled Wordsworth arises constantly, and it is as well to insist on the fact. The original of any of these lists can only be given a precise date when it is a list closely integrated with a piece of legislation which can itself be dated (cf. nos. 7, 11, 13). The Worcester list (no. 3) provides an example of a list which has been accepted on insufficient evidence as the product of a synod of 1240, because it is found in a manuscript in proximity to statutes of that year; it was probably composed earlier, and re-touched later, than 1240. Again, lists which record the customary practice of certain institutions as employers of labour (cf. nos. 8, 9, 15) may have been copied (as Wordsworth recognized in the case of Lincoln) from much older manuscripts than those which we possess. But whatever the date or authority of the original, the date of the existing texts must always be remembered, for a list of this sort was peculiarly exposed to revision. The list which originated in the Exeter synod of 1287 (no. 7) is a case in point; for we have no contemporary copy of the statutes. If in a case of this sort it is not safe to date a whole list by reference to a single feast which appears in it (for this may be a late insertion), it is equally dangerous to assume that all *festa ferianda* must be dated after their liturgical observance became the subject of a papal or provincial enactment. For many feasts were celebrated in certain regions before the cult was officially made universal,[3] and the demand for more or less

---

[1] What constituted prohibited work was a matter for discussion by the theologians and canonists: see Rodgers, ch. ii. Prohibited activities were *opera servilia.* Cf. Lyndwood, *Provinciale*, lib. 1, tit. 11, c. 1 (p. 56b), ad verb. Caeremoniis (*in fine*) . . . 'ab opere servili, id est a peccato et ab opere impediente vacationem ad deum.'

[2] *Statutes of Lincoln Cathedral*, ed. H. Bradshaw and C. Wordsworth (3 vols., Cambridge, 1892–7), iii. 539–52. For comparable lists in continental ecclesiastical statutes see, e.g. *Sacrorum Conciliorum . . . Amplissima Collectio*, ed. J. D. Mansi (1759–98), xxv. 25, 45 (Coutances), 71 (Bayeux), 455 (Ravenna), 841 (Tarragona).

[3] Lyndwood, glossing Islip's constitution of 1362, s.v. *locorum ordinario*, says: 'ex hoc litera apparet quod episcopus in sua diocesi potest statuere aliquem sanctum solenniter venerari absque auctoritate sedis apostolice. Et hoc intellige verum de sancto per sedem apostolicam prius canonizato' (*Provinciale*, 2.3.3 (p. 103)).

abstention from *opera servilia* was not always determined by the liturgical status of the feast.[1] On the other hand, the existence of a provincial canon of 1329 which orders Good Friday to be observed as a *festum feriandum* enables us to say that any list which does not include Good Friday was probably composed before that year.[2]

1. 'Council of Oxford, 1222' (?)

This list, which purports to be the earliest known, is also the most problematical. The attribution to a celebrated council of the province of Canterbury, held at Osney, outside Oxford, by Stephen Langton, in April 1222, is highly dubious. Some seventy manuscripts exist of the long series of canons published in this council: not one of them contains this. It is first found as c. 8 in Peter Crabbe's edition of the council's canons, and the editor gives only a vague and unsatisfactory account of his manuscript authority.[3] The chapter appears in none of the English editions.[4]

On the face of it, the text is corrupt in its title: 'Haec sunt festa in quibus, prohibitis aliis operibus, conceduntur opera agriculturae et carrucarum'. This cannot apply to the section which immediately follows, on the more solemn feasts, which are to be observed 'sub omni veneratione'. It is applicable rather to the second section, which is introduced with the words: 'Volumus etiam ut alia festa a rectoribus ecclesiarum et capellanis in obsequio divino et laude devotissime celebrentur, minoribus operibus servilibus secundum consuetudinem loci illis diebus interdictis'.

---

[1] When Innocent VI (7 Feb. 1355) ordered the feast of St. Augustine of Canterbury to be kept as a duplex, he ordered cessation from such work as custom forbade on double feasts (*Concilia Magnae Britanniae et Hiberniae*, ed. D. Wilkins (London, 1737), iii. 33 (hereafter referred to as Wilkins, *Concilia*)). But custom prescribed no general rule for double feasts.

[2] Wilkins, *Concilia*, ii. 552, also in Lyndwood, *Provinciale*, 2.3.1. 'Auctoritate etiam presentis concilii districtius inhibemus ne decetero quispiam servilibus ipsa die intendat operibus vel quevis alia exerceat que a pietatis cultu fuerint aliena. Per hoc tamen legem pauperibus non imponimus, nec divitibus prohibemus quin ad agriculturam pauperum promovendam suffragia consueta charitatis intuitu subministrent'.

[3] P. Crabbe, *Secundus tomus conciliorum omnium* (2nd edn., Cologne, 1551), p. 1005, cf. p. 1003. This was reprinted by L. Surius, *Tomus tertius conciliorum omnium* (Cologne, 1567), p. 761, and in the collections of *Concilia* of Nicolini (iv. 237–8), Bini (3rd edn., VII. ii. 828), Hardouin (vii. 117), Mansi (xxii. 1153). It is printed by Wordsworth from Hardouin in *Lincoln Cathedral Statutes*, iii. 539–41. See below, Appendix, no. 1.

[4] The council's canons are printed as a series in *Constitutiones legitime seu legatine regionis anglicane . . .* (Paris, 1504), fos. 121ʳ–124ʳ; *Concilia, decreta, leges in re ecclesiarum orbis britannici . . .* , ed. Henry Spelman (1664), ii. 181–90 (hereafter referred to as Spelman, *Concilia*); *Provinciale* (1679), app. ii, pp. 1–9; Wilkins, *Concilia*, i. 585–93. Although we speak commonly of Spelman's *Concilia*, it must be remembered that the second volume was edited after Spelman's death by Dugdale.

It may be surmised that 'Haec sunt festa . . .' is nothing but a displaced note, which once stood beside the clause: 'Volumus etiam ut . . .'[1] The list of saints cannot in its present form belong to the year 1222, as Wordsworth pointed out,[2] since it includes St. Edmund, confessor, who was canonized in 1247. There is also at least one internal inconsistency which points to revision. The first section contains 'duo festa sanctae Crucis' (i.e. *Inventio* and *Exaltatio*), but the feast of the Invention re-appears in the second section. The inclusion of several feasts which are seldom found in thirteenth-century diocesan lists militates against the ascription of this list to a provincial council of 1222. At the same time, the statement regarding the feast of the Conception B.V.M. 'cuius celebrationi non imponitur necessitas' points to a date before 1329, when Archbishop Simon Mepham's provincial canons were published.[3]

The utter lack of manuscripts and the corruption of the printed text make the ascription of this list to 1222 highly suspect. As it stands, and without further evidence, it cannot be accepted as provincial legislation. Yet the possibility must not be excluded that in another meeting at Oxford the observance of some feast or feasts was orally decreed; and this text, like the next to be considered, may be an imperfect record of the fact. We may even guess a possible occasion. Under the year 1241 the chronicler, Matthew Paris, reports:

convenerunt episcopi Angliae, videlicet archiepiscopus Eboracensis, Lincolniensis, Norwicensis, Carleolensis, cum aliis multis gravibus, religiosis, ac discretis ecclesiasticis personis tractaturi super multiplici desolatione ecclesiae et divinam consolationem postulaturi. Statuerunt igitur quasdam orationes cum jejuniis fieri ab ecclesia generaliter per Angliam. . . .[4]

This must surely be the meeting at Oxford, on 30 November 1241, which was attended by the bishop of Coventry: 'In die sancti Andreae, fuit presens apud Oxoniam in concilio episcoporum, ubi tractum fuit de jejuniis et orationibus pro ecclesia faciendis'.[5] May not the prelates have tried at the same time to improve the observance of *festa ferianda* ? But if the list originated then, its original edition cannot have included the name of St. Edmund, confessor; that at least must be an addition.[6]

---

[1] Cf. the title to the second paragraph of list 6, below, p. 139.

[2] *Lincoln Cathedral Statutes*, iii. 544. The ascription to Oxford, 1222, was accepted by Mrs. Rodgers, p. 102.

[3] Wilkins, *Concilia*, ii. 552, and Lyndwood, *Provinciale*, 2.3.2. This seems to require abstention from work as well as liturgical observance. The feast was treated as a *feriandum* in his list of 1362 (below, no. 12).

[4] *Chronica majora*, ed. H. R. Luard (Rolls Ser., 1872-83), iv. 173.

[5] *Annales monastici*, ed. H. R. Luard (Rolls Ser., 1864-9), iii. 157.

[6] Other possible occasions are a provincial council convened by Stephen Langton in May 1215, described in *Memoriale fr. Walteri de Coventria*, ed. W. Stubbs (Rolls Ser., 1872–3), ii. 220, as abortive, and a provincial council at Oxford in April or May 1250 which was concerned with taxation (*Chronica majora*, v. 100).

2. *Canterbury* (?)

This text, not known to Canon Wordsworth, is contained in Cambridge, Corpus Christi Coll. MS. 337, fo. 37ra. It bears some resemblance to no. 1, but omits entirely Sts. Gregory and Augustine. Besides adding St. Nicholas, it makes the interesting additions of Sts. Dunstan and Alphege, sainted Saxon archbishops of Canterbury, and there are other differences from no. 1. The list is written in a late thirteenth-century hand between a copy of the *Liber scintillarum ven. Bede* (*PL* 88.597) and the tract *Qui bene presunt* of Richard Wetheringsett and the pseudo-Grosseteste *Summa de vitiis*, all written by the same neat hand. M. R. James thought that the book 'came very probably from Christ Church, Canterbury',[1] and this, together with the emphasis laid upon Canterbury saints (although Augustine is missing) points to the list having been designed for observance on the estates of the cathedral priory. It is not cast in the form of a decree uttered in the first person ('Statuimus, etc.'), and there are no grounds for supposing that as a whole it is a piece of legislation rather than a useful memorandum. But the note at the end of the first section: 'Secundum conscilium Oxonie' is of interest, even though it cannot be interpreted certainly. It might refer to all the first section, or to the self-consistent passage ending with the 'dies dedicationis ecclesie',[2] or to the following names of English saints, or only to the last entry: 'dies sancti Aelphegi confessoris [*recte* martiris]'. In any case, it is evidence that already in the thirteenth century a council of Oxford was supposed to have authorized some particular observance.

3. *Diocese of Worcester* (*1218–36*)

This list is found in editions of synodal statutes of Walter de Cantilupe, bishop of Worcester, dated 26 July 1240.[3] While the core of the statutes probably emanated from a diocesan synod of Worcester on that day, the manuscripts incorporate additions and alterations. The re-touching is visible in each of the two versions of a general injunction about *festa ferianda*. This (c. 89 in the forthcoming edition) reads:

[D = Lambeth Palace Libr., MS. 171, fo. 46^v; B = Brit Mus., MS. Cotton Claud. A. viii, fo. 218ra].

Quod autem predecessor noster statuit de festis celebrandis et observandis [*om.* et obs. B, *add* obs. B^2] ne fiant in eis opera servilia, precipimus ab omnibus

---

[1] M. R. James, *Descriptive Catalogue of the MSS. in the Library of Corpus Christi College, Cambridge* (Cambridge, 1912), ii. 168. James's reading of the ex-libris inscription is doubtful.

[2] As Professor Wormald remarks, the list is not in calendarial order, but follows the sequence of a litany in its arrangement.

[3] Spelman, *Concilia*, ii. 240, Wilkins, *Concilia*, i. 663. For the MSS. and the statutes in general see Cheney, *English Synodalia*, pp. 90–109. A new edition will appear in *Councils and Synods, with other documents relating to the English Church*, vol. ii, ed. F. M. Powicke and C. R. Cheney, to be published shortly.

uniformiter observari, nisi forte aliquid specialiter fiat pro veneratione sanctorum in quorum honore vel ecclesie vel altaria consecrantur.

D	B
Dictis autem sollempnitatibus festum beati Nicholai duximus adiungendum. Festa autem Eadmundi confessoris	Dictis autem solepnitatibus [festa *om.* B] beatorum Nicholay et Edmundi archiepiscopi duximus adiungenda. Festa autem

sanctorum Dominici et Francisci in ecclesiis cum novem lectionibus volumus [super hoc *add* B] celebrari. Nolumus tamen per hoc opera laicorum fidelium inpediri.

From the position of St. Edmund in these two versions, it is certain that they represent successive revisions of the 1240 statutes, for St. Edmund was not canonized until 1247, and it is probable that the D version preceded that in B.[1] Text B of the statutes alone contains a list of *festa ferianda*,[2] but this is no integral part of the series. After the ending: 'Expliciunt constituciones domini episcopi Wygornie' comes an Easter Table which occupies the rest of fo. 218^r. Then, on fo. 218^v, come rules for the lectionary throughout the year, on fo. 219^r come arrangements for duplex feasts according to the custom of Salisbury; then, and then only, come the 'Festa ferianda ex toto in episcopatu Wygornie', followed by the 'ferianda in omnibus preterquam in carucis' and the 'ferianda ab operibus mulierum tantum'. These lists, be it noted, do not include the name of St. Edmund; but the name of St. Nicholas is there. At the end is added the sentence relating to Sts. Edmund, Dominic, and Francis which occurs in c. 89, in the form of D, except that St. Edmund is the last to be named. The natural inference is that the lists are those referred to in c. 89 of Cantilupe's statutes: a list issued by Cantilupe's predecessor, Bishop William de Blois (1218–36), with the name of St. Nicholas added by Cantilupe, perhaps as early as 1240.[3] Wulfstan and Oswald are the only Worcester saints to be included.

4. *Diocese of Salisbury (1257)*

This list, not noticed by Canon Wordsworth, is found in synodal statutes of the diocese, printed in Wilkins's *Concilia* (i. 714), and is to be attributed to Bishop Giles of Bridport in the year 1257.[4] Besides two thirteenth-century manuscripts of the whole series of Giles's statutes, this

---

[1] Cheney, *Eng. Synodalia*, p. 95.
[2] Wilkins, *Concilia*, i. 677–8.
[3] The list includes the Translation of St. Thomas the archbishop, which happened in 1220.
[4] Wilkins printed the statutes from Cambridge, St. John's Coll. MS. 62, fo. 107^v (in a collection of didactic and devotional works by several 13th-cent. hands, not originally in one volume). Another late 13th-cent. text of the statutes is in a collection of similar works, Cambridge, Emmanuel Coll. MS. 27, fo. 172^v. An edition showing variants of all manuscripts will appear in the forthcoming *Councils and Synods*, ii.

chapter and the preceding one are copied on the flyleaf of a gradual (Oxford, Bodleian MS. Rawlinson Liturg. d. 3, fo. 111^v) in a thirteenth-century hand. The list also appears at the end of a copy of 'customs in use in the bishopric of Salisbury' printed in Sir Henry Spelman's *Concilia* (ii. 302–4, whence Wilkins, i. 713–4) from Oxford, Corpus Christi Coll. MS. 360, fo. 72^v[1]; here it has the note: 'Constitutio domini episcopi Egidii Sar'.' This text, written *c.* 1300, alone contains the name of St. Catherine after that of St. Mary Magdalene.

On 5 February 1330 Bishop Roger Martival of Salisbury quoted and confirmed the statute of Bishop Giles in a mandate to his archdeacons. They were told to have the order published by rectors, vicars, and parish priests, 'iniungentes eisdem in virtute obediencie quod, recepta harum copia, in aliquibus ecclesiarum et capellarum suarum libris ad memoriam faciant eam scribi'.[2]

The statute differs from most of those printed here, in that it explicitly limits holidays to the feasts which are enumerated (cf. nos. 11 and 13).

5. *Diocese of London (1245–59)*

This list was unknown to Canon Wordsworth. In 1915 the late Canon R. M. Woolley printed synodal statutes for the diocese of London from a late fourteenth-century manuscript in Lincoln Cathedral Libr., B. 6. 7, fo. 6^r (catalogue no. 229).[3] His text concluded with a list of saints' days[4] introduced with the words: 'Ad tollendam diversitatem . . .'. The list itself distinguishes between feasts on which 'omnes operationes prohibeantur' and those on which 'officio sine dampnosa mora celebrato, licet parochianis operaciones necessarias exercere'. Canon Woolley's dating of the statutes '*c.* 1215–22' has to be modified in the light of other texts and after comparison with other legislation of the period. We can now assert confidently that the bulk of the statutes were issued by Fulk Basset, bishop of London, between 1245 and 1259.[5] We can also determine from other manuscripts that Woolley's exemplar was curtailed: in other texts, after the list of saints' days, there follows:

Sane cum omnes electi dei laude digna reverenter sint extollendi, nichil declinavimus illorum honori quem clerus et populus in civitate et extra, tum ex debito tum ex devotione, eis impendere consuevit.[6]

[1] Cf. Cheney, *Eng. Synodalia*, pp. 58, 105.

[2] Salisbury, Diocesan Registry, Reg. R. de Martival, vol. ii, fos. 263^v–264^r. This version makes the same omission as does the St. John's MS.

[3] 'Constitutions of the diocese of London, *c.* 1215–22', *Eng. Hist. Rev.*, xxx (1915), 285–302.

[4] Numbered c. XCIV–CIV; they are c. 90–102 in the forthcoming edition in *Councils and Synods*, ii.

[5] See Cheney, *Eng. Synodalia*, pp. 79–84. The bishop of Lewes's MS. there mentioned is now Brit. Mus., Add. MS. 48344.

[6] This is only found in Brit. Mus., Add. MS. 48344, and Cambridge, Trinity Coll. MS. O.9.28 (no. 1440).

This is followed by a chapter which orders the copying and enforcement of the preceding 'precepta synodalia et prohibitiones' in terms which borrow, like the precedent statutes, from the statutes of Richard Poore, bishop of Salisbury (1217–28). With this, we may suppose, the London statutes, like the Salisbury statutes, were originally brought to a close.

6. *Diocese of Norwich* (?) (*c. 1240*)

In the earliest manuscript of the London statutes (Brit. Mus., Add. MS. 48344), which cannot have been written long after the middle of the thirteenth century, the statutes are followed by a second list of *festa ferianda*. Like no. 5, this was unknown to Canon Wordsworth. It is written in the same hand as that of the statutes. The writer, having set out his list as far as the feast of Sts. Simon and Jude in four columns of eleven lines, to fill the remainder of fo. 8^v, then continued his list in a single narrow column of forty-five lines on the left of fo. 9^r. He reached the bottom with the title: 'Hec sunt festa in quibus post missam excerceantur opera rusticana, set non ante'. The feasts under this head occupy seven lines in a second narrow column. The 'Nota' extends across the rest of the page and likewise occupies seven lines. The remaining space on fo. 9^r is taken up by another hand, not much later in date, in copying two decretals (*Extra*, 4. 20. 7–8). Both the physical arrangement of the list in this manuscript (which appears to be the little commonplace book of some parish-priest), and the form of the final 'Nota', do not suggest a revised synodal pronouncement for the diocese of London. It is arranged in a different fashion from the list in the preceding synodal statutes, and it omits some secondary names in the former list,[1] including all those most closely associated with the city of London. It adds many new names, including a few which point unmistakably to an East Anglian origin: Blaise, Felix, Botulph, Etheldreda.[2] The inclusion of the Translation of St. Benedict suggests that this may have been intended for the parishioners of some church belonging to a Benedictine house. But it was copied by somebody who had just copied synodal statutes of London, and it is hard to believe that there is no connection with the diocese of London. Perhaps it is a list brought from Norwich diocese to one of the Essex parishes (Harlow and Stapleford) of which the Suffolk abbey of Bury St. Edmunds was patron.[3] In any case it belongs to the south-east of England, and is no

---

[1] Alphege, Mellitus, Erkenwald, Dunstan, Ethelbert, Oswald king and martyr, Giles, dedication of St. Paul's, Osith, Ethelburga, Edmund the archbishop.

[2] Professor Wormald remarks the inclusion of Ambrose, who was highly graded at Norwich.

[3] The cathedral priory of Norwich had no churches in the diocese of London. Other Benedictine houses, with churches in London diocese, were the Cluniac priories of Castleacre (Leaden Roding) and Thetford (Finchingfield, White Notley) and the alien priory of Horsham St. Faith (St. Margaret's, Friday Street, London); St. Faith appears in the second section of the list. An alternative explanation is that the owner and copyist of this book held churches in both dioceses of London and Norwich or moved from one to the other.

later than the third quarter of the thirteenth century. The absence of St. Edmund the archbishop, whose feast was widely observed in England, suggests that the writer was copying an earlier list than the one contained in the London statutes, where the feast of St. Edmund figures among the minor festivals of November.[1]

7. Diocese of Exeter (1287)

This list, with its interesting preamble, which recalls Decretum, De cons. D. 3.1, forms c. 23 of the synodal statutes of Bishop Peter Quinel for the diocese of Exeter, 16 April 1287.[2] Here, as in the Salisbury list and the London list, is a clear piece of diocesan legislation. Unfortunately, the surviving twelve texts all belong to the fourteenth century or later and the list has therefore been exposed to the possibility of revision. Differences between the manuscripts suggest that they may have undergone such revision. Thus, St. George is included in four manuscripts only; St. Augustine (Anglorum ap.), absent from one manuscript, is interlined in another, and specifically described as an addition ('et de novo S. Augustini') in a third; St. Margaret appears in one text only; St. Ann, St. Stephen, and St. Edward, king and conf., only in two each. Three manuscripts include Corpus Christi, two of them by way of addition; the Conception of the B.V.M. appears as an addition in one manuscript and is written over an erasure in another, although it appears in the body of all other texts; Commemoratio animarum appears only once, and then as a marginal addition. How far these varieties can be regarded as indications of official revision, how far as the result of scribal enterprise or error, it is impossible to say. Nor is it possible to assign either date or reason to certain erasures in two manuscripts: St. Gregory, the Invention and Exaltation of the Cross, St. John ante portam latinam, the Translation of St. Thomas the martyr, St. Peter ad vincula, St. Laurence, the Decollation of St. John the Baptist, St. Martin and St. Catherine; do they betoken an attempt, in line with many complaints of the later middle ages, to prune a list which had grown excessively long?[3]

8. Barnwell Priory (1295)

This, unlike nos. 4 and 5, is no synodal decree but a list copied by the compiler of a miscellany for the use and information of the Austin canons

---

[1] 'Sancti Eadmundi' does indeed appear in list 6 (November), but the absence of any distinguishing note, such as appears in list 5, shows that Edmund king and martyr must be intended and that there was no possibility of confusion because Edmund the archbishop had not been canonized when the list was made.

[2] The statutes with the following Summula were printed in Spelman, Concilia, ii. 350–403 and Wilkins, Concilia, ii. 129–68, and from these editions passed into the continental collections (Labbe, xi. 1263–1312, Mansi, xxiv. 783–847).

[3] Cf. Rodgers, pp. 81–5, 93–4. The erasure of St. Thomas from the Exeter MSS. may be the work of Henry VIII's reign, when Becket was denounced as a traitor (cf. list 2). The feasts of St. John ante portam latinam, St. Peter ad vincula, St. Martin, and St. Catherine are all absent from Islip's list of 1362 (no. 13).

of Barnwell, outside Cambridge, in the diocese of Ely. It is preceded by a liturgical calendar and followed by a list of episcopal sees in England and Wales. It is possible that the list is based upon a synodal decree for the diocese of Ely, but, if so, the dedication feast of the church of Barnwell and that of St. Giles, the original patron of the priory, have been added. The whole book was edited by J. W. Clark and F. W. Maitland under the title *Liber memorandorum ecclesie de Bernewelle* (Cambridge, 1907). The list occurs on p. 15.

9. *Osney Abbey (c. 1300)*

This resembles no. 7 in being a memorandum copied into an Ordinale, about the year 1300, apparently for the guidance of officers of the Augustinian abbey of Osney (diocese of Lincoln) in dealing with their labourers. It differs from the other lists examined in stating the days when the labourers work, but the long list of vigils implies that the ensuing feast-days were treated as holidays. The distinction between the continuance of work *usque ad vesperas* and *usque ad collationem* is new, and the half-holiday on Saturdays in Lent is noteworthy.[1] The list was published by Dr. H. E. Salter in his edition of the *Cartulary of Oseney Abbey*, i (Oxford Historical Society, lxxxix, 1929), pp. xvi–xvii. It was not known to Canon Wordsworth.

10. *Faringdon (after 1336)*

London, Brit. Mus., MS. Cotton Nero A. xii is a small, neat cartulary and custumal which assembles documents relating to the lands and privileges of the Cistercian abbey of Beaulieu (Hampshire) in its grange of Faringdon (Berkshire, dioc. Salisbury).[2] A list of holidays for the lay-brethren and servants occurs between the charters and the custumal and is written by the same hand as documents dated 1336; it was copied not much later. This was not known to Canon Wordsworth.

The details of the hours for stopping work on vigils may be compared with the particulars recorded at Osney Abbey. In the light of Thomas Chobham's remarks on the Cistercian treatment of holidays quoted above,[3] and the decretal of Alexander III there cited, it is interesting to contrast this list of only twenty-six feasts (apart from Sundays and dedication anniversaries) with the much longer lists of *festa ferianda* from other sources. Archbishop Simon Mepham's recent demand that Good Friday should be kept free of *opera servilia*[4] had not affected the custom at Faringdon.

---

[1] See Rodgers, p. 21, on the objections of some theologians and canonists to this as a piece of judaizing; and cf. B. L. Manning, *The People's Faith in the Time of Wyclif* (Cambridge, 1919), p. 129.

[2] Described briefly by G. R. C. Davis, *Medieval Cartularies of Great Britain* (1958), no. 41. The contents are listed in W. Dugdale, *Monasticon anglicanum* (1817–30), v. 681, note h.

[3] Cf. p. 120.   [4] Cf. p. 123.

FEAST-DAYS IN MEDIEVAL ENGLAND   131

11. *Diocese of Bath and Wells (1342)*

This is the earliest diocesan list of unimpeachable textual accuracy. It was printed by Wilkins from the register of the bishop who published it; but Wilkins only reproduced the text in an abridged and modified form[1]. The feast of Corpus Christi makes perhaps its first appearance in an English list; for it was probably a late interpolation in the Exeter statutes.[2] This was in accord with a mandate by Bishop Ralph's predecessor, John de Drokensford, dated 4 June 1318.[3] There also appear Good Friday[4] and the Conception of the B.V.M., of which the observance throughout the province of Canterbury had been ordered by Archbishop Simon Mepham in 1329.[5]

The mild terms in which the bishop makes his injunction is to be observed ('volumus nostros subditos abstinere et eciam impediri'). Like Bishop Giles of Salisbury (no. 4) this diocesan explicitly limits holidays to the feasts enumerated.

12. *Diocese of Hereford (c. 1348–62)*

A missal which once belonged to Hereford Cathedral Chapter, now Brit. Mus., Add. MS. 39675, contains a list [*fo. 8ᵛ*]: 'Ista festa subscripta omnino ferianda sunt in episcopatu Hereford'.' This is followed by lists of *ferianda* 'preterquam in carucis' and 'ab operibus mulierum'. The lists are printed in *The Hereford Breviary*, ed. W. H. Frere and Langton E. G. Brown, vol. iii (Henry Bradshaw Soc., xlvi, 1915), pp. 251–2.[6] They were not noted by Canon Wordsworth.

Much of the manuscript was written shortly before 1348, for the Translation of St. Thomas Cantilupe of that year is an addition to the calendar. But the *festa ferianda* include the Translation; on the other hand, the feast of Corpus Christi, prescribed for the province of Canterbury in 1362,[7] does not appear. The lists may be dated, then, between 1348 and 1362. But the Conception of the B.V.M. and Good Friday come at the

---

[1] Wilkins, *Concilia*, ii. 711, cf. *Register of Ralph of Shrewsbury*, ed. T. S. Holmes (Somerset Record Soc., ix–x, 1896), ii. 457, 803.

[2] Cf. p. 129.

[3] *Calendar of the Register of John de Drokensford*, ed. E. Hobhouse (Somerset Record Soc., i, 1887), p. 13. This was pursuant to Clement V's decree in the General Council of Vienne, published in *Clementin.*, 3.16.1.

[4] As in lists 1, 2, 6.

[5] Wilkins, *Concilia*, ii. 552; Lyndwood, *Provinciale*, 2.3.1–2.

[6] They were noted by Magrath in *Liber obituarius* (see p. 121, n. 3), p. xxxviii, when the missal belonged to the Rev. E. S. Dewick. The liturgical calendar of a 13th-cent. Hereford breviary bears appropriate marks by a later hand against the feasts which appear in these lists (*Hereford Breviary*, iii, pp. xxxiv–v).

[7] Spelman, *Concilia*, ii. 609–10; Lyndwood, *Provinciale*, 2.3.3 (p. 102), and cf. above, no. 11.

very end of the *omnino ferianda*, after the feast of the dedication; they must
have been added to a previous list composed before the year 1329.

13. *Province of Canterbury (1362)*

This is the first certain piece of legislation for the entire province of
Canterbury to prescribe a long series of *festa ferianda*. The official copy
in the register of Archbishop Simon Islip was edited in Spelman's
Concilia.[1] Unfortunately, an inferior text, dated 1332, was published in
the same volume as the work of Archbishop Simon Mepham, and it was
this text which Wilkins followed.[2]

Unlike most of the earlier lists, the archbishop's does not allow for
variation in the scale of observance. The feasts are fewer than in some
earlier lists, but total abstention from *opera servilia* is demanded for all.
While Islip included in his list the feasts of relatively recent introduction
which the bishop of Bath and Wells had included in 1342 (see no. 11), he
omitted St. Augustine of Canterbury, whose feast had attracted a holiday
in some English dioceses in the thirteenth century; even though a papal
mandate of 7 February 1355 appointed this as a duplex feast throughout
the province of Canterbury.[3] Recently, too, the archbishop had offered
an indulgence to those who observed the feast of Edward, king and
confessor[4]; but Edward is not in Islip's list. The archbishop insisted in
the preamble to the list upon the need to curtail the number of *festa
ferianda*. In keeping with some earlier mandates (cf. nos. 5, 11) he ordered
that none but the prescribed feasts (including those prescribed by individual bishops for their own dioceses) be observed; and he ended with
a complaint and a threat against the fraudulence of hired labourers. It is
highly probable that the archbishop was led to take the unusual course of

---

[1] From Lambeth Palace Libr., Reg. S. Islip, fo. 186^v, formerly fo. 188^v. Texts
with the correct ascription appear in Lyndwood, *Provinciale*, 2.3.3 (p. 101),
Constitutiones legitime (Paris, 1504), fo. 148^r, *Provinciale* (1679), app. ii, p. 57.
Lyndwood reads *servilibus* for *popularium* and omits *Parasceves*.

[2] ii. 500–1, Wilkins, *Concilia*, ii. 560. John Johnson had already remarked
the error in 1720 (*A Collection of all the Eccles. Laws* (1720), vol. ii, *s.a.* 1332).
While the copy in the archbishop's register is addressed to Simon, bishop of
London, and is dated *vii kal. Augusti a.d. 1362, anno consecracionis nostre 13*
(26 July 1362), a 14th-cent. copy at the end of Bartholomaeus, *De Casibus*, in
Lambeth Palace Libr., MS. 205 (fo. 236^v), is shorn of address, preamble, and
ending, and is dated *iv non. Ian. a.d. 1362 anno consecracionis nostre 14* (2 Jan.
1363). It includes (after Inventionis S. Crucis) 'Sancti Augustini Anglorum
apostoli per sedem apostolicam introductam (*sic*)' and (after S. Iacobi) 'Advincula
S. Petri' (followed next by S. Laurencii). In the margin another hand adds
'S. Anne matris Marie' and 'S. Kineburge virginis'. An abstract of Islip's
constitution, perhaps in the form in which it was published by a bishop ('nobis
per suas litteras publicandi districcius iniungendo mandavit') but without title,
address, or date, is copied at the end of a 14th-cent. text of *Oculus sacerdotis* in
Lambeth MS. 216, fo. 111^v: this also includes 'Augustini Anglorum apostoli'
(but inserts it after Corporis Christi). See also *Eng. Hist. Rev.*, l (1935), 212, n. 1.

[3] Wilkins, *Concilia*, iii. 33 (cf. p. 123, n. 1, and n. 2 above).

[4] 22 Feb. 1361: *ibid.*, iii. 47.

legislating on *festa ferianda* for the whole province by the labour unrest of the decades after the Black Death.[1]

14. '*Province of Canterbury (1400)*'

'Hec sunt festa ab omnibus operibus tenenda per constitutionem Ricardi [*sic*] Arundel' Cantuariensis archiepiscopi' is the title of a list written in a fifteenth-century hand in a volume of vernacular works of John Myrc, Brit. Mus., MS. Cotton Claud. A. ii, fo. 152ᵛ. It is printed in Spelman's *Concilia* (ii. 659), with the date 'a.d. 1400 vel circiter'.[2] Wilkins reprinted (iii. 252), tacitly correcting the archbishop's name to Thomas and entered it *s.a.* 1400. Wordsworth noted the list and apparently accepted the ascription.[3] But the authority cannot be regarded as good. No text of the constitution, of which this purports to be an extract or a paraphrase, is known. The canonist Lyndwood, compiling his *Provinciale* under Arundel's successor, did not include this in his title, *De feriis*, or refer to it. The copy as it stands shows signs of revision.

Compared with other lists, this has features both pre-Islip and post-Islip. The significant names of Good Friday and Corpus Christi, which appeared in Islip's list, are missing; all the other names in Islip's list are here, and in addition Augustine of Canterbury, Winifred, Ann, All Souls, Catherine, Chad, and George. Of these the liturgical observance of St. Ann in the province of Canterbury was ordered in 1383, of St. Winifred and St. Chad in 1398, and of St. George in 1416.[4] Local observance did not necessarily wait upon such decrees,[5] but a *festum feriandum* would hardly be imposed upon the entire province before the day was officially appointed in the liturgical calendar. If this were the abstract of a genuine provincial enactment it would be later than 1416; but more probably it is an unofficial fifteenth-century list based upon a pre-1362 list. Its claim to record a provincial constitution of Archbishop Thomas Arundel cannot be upheld.

[1] Cf. Rodgers, p. 102. For a contemporary comment on the constitution see T. Walsingham, *Historia anglicana*, ed. H. T. Riley (2 vols., Rolls Ser., 1863–4), i. 297.

[2] The list is written in a neat book-hand in red and blue, but it does not seem that the colours have liturgical significance. At certain points the word *vigilia* (in blue) occurs. The printed editions omit the *vigiliae* and read at the end *Gregorii* for *Georgii*.

[3] *Lincoln Cathedral Statutes*, iii. 542.

[4] For St. Augustine see above, p. 123, n. 1; for St. Ann see Wilkins, *Concilia*, iii 178–9 (and in *Provinciale* (1679), app. ii, p. 60, and *Wykeham's Register*, ed. T. F. Kirby (2 vols., Hampshire Record Soc., 1896–9), ii. 348); for St. Winifred and St. Chad see Wilkins, iii. 234–6 (and in *Provinciale*, app. ii, p. 62, and *Wykeham's Register*, ii. 481); for St. George see below, p. 134, n. 2.

In list 14 St. Chad appears, with St. George, out of proper order at the end of the list; they must have been additions to the archetype of the Cotton MS. Whether Ann and Winifred (and perhaps others) were also additions inserted in their appropriate places we cannot say.

[5] Thus St. Ann, St. Augustine, and St. George all occur in earlier diocesan lists.

15. *Lincoln* (?*1329–62*)

This list, printed by Canon Wordsworth, was designed simply for the workmen employed by the dean and chapter of Lincoln.[1] It exists in a copy of 1523, but certain features led the editor to date the original much earlier. He pointed to the absence of St. George and the Conception of the B.V.M.; St. George's day was made a *festum feriandum* for the province of Canterbury in 1416,[2] and the Conception was already included in Islip's list in 1362. Unless the Lincoln list disregarded the provincial constitutions, it must have been composed before 1362. The fact that Corpus Christi appears as an addition 'ex nova constitucione papali' does not tell against this, for the feast was celebrated in some English dioceses (cf. no. 11) in deference to the decree in the *Clementines* before Islip treated it as a *festum feriandum* for the province. Moreover, the addition: 'Item dies Pasce modo de novo feriantur', if amended as Wordsworth suggests to 'Item dies Parasceve modo de novo feriatur', would agree with a date soon after Mepham's constitution of 1329.

It is unlikely that the lists enumerated above include all that survive from medieval England, and the naming of these may lead to the discovery of others. To cap them all and override them came the parliamentary statute, 5 & 6 Edward VI, c. 3 (1551–2), on Holy Days and Fast Days.[3] A carefully worded preamble guarded against any superstitious worship of saints, and declared that:

the appointment bothe of the tyme, and allso of the nombre of the daies, is left by thauctoritie of Goddes Worde to the libertie of Christes Churche, to be determyned and assigned ordrelye in every countree by the discretion of the rulers and ministers therof, as they shall judge moste expedyent, to the trewe setting forth of Goddes glorie and the edification of their people.

Ecclesiastical authorities were authorized to punish offenders with ecclesiastical censures and to enjoin penance. The list of feast days set forth in the act resembled that of Archbishop Simon Islip, but reduced the number of days by omitting Good Friday, the feasts of the Conception, Nativity, and Assumption of the Blessed Virgin Mary, the feasts of the Cross, the feasts of Thomas of Canterbury, Mary Magdalen, Laurence, and Nicholas. It was ordained 'that none other daie shalbe kept and commaunded to be kept hollie daie or to abstaine from lawfull bodilie labour'. Even on the approved feasts husbandmen, labourers, fishermen, and others might labour in harvest or when necessity should require.

---

[1] *Lincoln Cathedral Statutes*, iii. 545–7. The source of Canon Wordsworth's text, apparently in a Lincoln Cathedral muniment book, has not been identified.

[2] *Register of H. Chichele*, ed. E. F. Jacob, vol. iii (Canterbury and York Soc., 1945), pp. 8–10; Spelman, *Concilia*, ii. 669; Wilkins, *Concilia*, iii. 376; *Provinciale*, 2.3.4 (p. 103), and app. ii, p. 68.

[3] *Halsbury's Statutes of England* (2nd edn.), vol. 7, Ecclesiastical Law (1949), pp. 1183–5.

APPENDIX

1. 'COUNCIL OF OXFORD, 1222'.(?) P. Crabbe, *Secundus tomus conciliorum omnium* (2nd edn., Cologne, 1551), p. 1005. See above, pp. 123–4.

Haec sunt festa in quibus, prohibitis aliis operibus, conceduntur opera agriculturae et carrucarum.

Statuimus quod festa subscripta sub omni veneratione serventur, videlicet, omnes dies dominici, quinque dies Natalicii, Circumcisio, Epiphania domini, omnia festa beatae Mariae praeter festum Conceptionis cuius celebrationi non imponitur necessitas, Conversio sancti Pauli, Cathedra sancti Petri, festa omnium apostolorum, festum sancti Gregorii, dies Parasceves, feria secunda et tertia et quarta in hebdomada Paschali, dies Asscensionis domini, feria secunda et tertia et quarta in hebdomada Pentecostes, festum sancti Augustini in Maio, duo festa sanctae Crucis, Translatio sancti Thomae martyris, utrunque festum sancti Ioannis baptistae, festum sanctae Margarethae, festum sanctae Mariae Magdalenae, festum sancti Petri ad vincula, festum sancti Laurentii, festum sancti Michaelis, festum Omnium sanctorum, festum sancti Martini, festum sancti Edmundi confessoris et sancti Edmundi regis et martyris, festum sanctae Catharinae, festum sancti Clementis, festum sancti Nicolai, festum dedicationis cuiuslibet*ᵃ* ecclesiae in sua parochia, quodlibet festum illius sancti in cuius honore fundata est ecclesia.

Volumus etiam ut alia festa a rectoribus ecclesiarum et capellanis in obsequio divino et laude devotissime celebrentur, minoribus operibus servilibus secundum consuetudinem loci illis diebus interdictis: festum sanctorum Fabiani et Sebastiani, sanctae Agnetis, sancti Vincentii, sancti Blasii, sanctae Agathae, sancti Felicis, sancti Georgii, sancti Ioannis ante portam latinam, sancti Dunstani, sancti Albani, sanctae Emeldridae, Inventionis sanctae crucis, sancti Stephani, sancti Hieronymi, sanctae Fidis, Dedicatio sancti Michaelis in Monte Tumba, sancti Dionysii, festum Animarum, sanctae Ceciliae, sanctae Luciae, sancti Leonardi.

Haec sunt festa in quibus post missam opera rusticana concedimus, sed antequam, non: Octava beatae Epiphaniae, sanctorum Ioannis et Pauli, Translatio sancti Benedicti, translatio sancti Martini.

Hae sunt vigiliae statutae ad vigilandum: Vigilia Nativitatis domini, Vigilia Paschae, Vigilia Pentecostes, Litania maior, tres dies Rogationum, Vigilia sancti Ioannis baptistae, Vigilia apostolorum Petri et Pauli, Vigilia sancti Laurentii, Vigilia Assumptionis beatae Mariae, Vigilia sancti Bartholomaei, Vigilia sancti Matthaei, Vigilia apostolorum Simonis et Iudae, Vigilia Omnium sanctorum, Vigilia sancti Andreae, Vigilia sancti Thomae apostoli. Ieiunia quatuor temporum in totius anni temporibus: In Martio prima hebdomada ieiunandum est feria quarta et sexta et sabbato, in Iunio in secunda, quod dupliciter observatur a pluribus: in prima hebdomada post Litanias aut in hebdomada Pentecostes, in Septembri tres dies, in proxima septimana integra ante Natalem domini.

ᵃ cuilibet.

2. CANTERBURY (?). Cambridge, Corpus Christi Coll. MS. 337, fo. 37ʳᵃ. See above, p. 125.

Hec festa subscripta ex toto ferianda sunt per annum. Dies Natalis domini cum tota septimana. Dies Pasche cum tribus sequentibus diebus. Dies Pent' cum tribus sequentibus diebus. Dies Epiphanie. Dies Paraceves. Dies Ascensionis. Inventio sancte Crucis. Exaltatio eiusdem. Purificatio beate Marie. Annuntiatio dominica. Assumptio sancte Marie. Nativitas eiusdem. Dies sancti Michaelis. Dies sancti Iohannis. Decollatio eiusdem. Dies apostolorum Petri et Pauli. Dies sancti Andree apostoli. Dies beati Thome apostoli. Dies Conversionis beati Pauli. Dies beati Mathie apostoli. Dies apostolorum Philippi et Iacobi. Dies beati Iacobi [*fo. 37ʳᵇ*] apostoli. Dies sancti Bartholomei. Dies sancti Mathei. Dies apostolorum Symonis et Iude. Dies sancti Luce ewangeliste. Dies sancti Marci ewangeliste. Dies beate Marie Magdalene. Dies sancti Laurentii martiris. Dies sancti Martini confessoris. Dies sancti Nicholai confessoris. Dies Omnium Sanctorum. Dies dedicationis ecclesie. Dies Translationis beati Thome*ᵃ* martiris. Dies sancti Dunstani confessoris. Dies beati Eadmundi confessoris. Dies sancti Eadmundi regis et martiris. Dies sancti Aelphegi confessoris. Secundum conscilium Oxonie.

Hec festa subscripta ferianda sunt in omnibus preterquam in carucis: Cathedra sancti Petri. Dies sancti Barnabe apostoli. Dies sancti Clementis. Dies sancti Vincentii. Dies sancti Oswaldi. Dies sancti Leonardi. Dies beate Katerine.

Hec festa subscripta ferianda sunt ab operibus mulierum: Dies beate Lucie. Dies beate Agnetis virginis. Dies beate Margarete. Dies beate Agathe virginis.*ᵇ*

ᵃ Thome *eras.*
ᵇ This is followed, in the same hand, by verses:

> Christi festa, crucis, Michaelis, festa Marie,
> Festum sanctorum cunctarum lux animarum,
> Sancti festa loci, templi quoque festa sacrati,
> Thomas, Matheus, Mathias, Bartholomeus,
> Iudas atque Symon, os lampadis atque Philippus,
> Barnabas et Paulus, Lucas, socii quoque Marcus,
> Clemens et Stephanus, Laurentius et Nicholaus,
> Matris Marie festa celebrantur honore.

Then the note: Tres sunt dies in quoque anno in quibus si quis sanguinem minuerit aut ipso die aut cito post morietur. Et qui potionem pro infirmitate acceperit, nichil ei proderit. Isti sunt dies: viii kal. Augusti, viii Aprilis kal. et ii kal. Decembris.

———————————

3. DIOCESE OF WORCESTER (1218–36). Brit. Mus., MS. Cotton Claud. A. viii, fo. 219ʳ. See above, pp. 125–6.

[H]ec sunt festa ferianda ex toto in episcopatu Wygornie, scilicet: dies Natalis domini, cum quatuor diebus sequentibus, Circumcisio domini, Ephiphania domini, Depocisio sancti Wolstani, Conversio sancti Pauli, Purificacio beate Marie, Chathedra sancti Petri, sancti Mathie apostoli, Depocisio sancti Osuualdi, Anunciacio dominica, dies Passe, cum duobus diebus, sancti Marci euuangeliste, apostolorum Philippi et Iacobi, Invencio sancte crucis,*ᵃ* Asencio

ᵃ Translatio sancti Wlstani *added in 15th-cent. hand.*

domini, dies Pentecosten, cum duobus diebus, Nativitas sancti Iohannis baptiste, apostolorum Petri et Pauli, Translacio sancti Thome archiepiscopi, sancte Marie Magdalene, sancti Iacobi apostoli, Ad vincula sancti Petri, sancti Laurencii martiris, Asumpcio sancte Marie, sancti Bartholomei apostoli, Nativitas beate Marie, Exaltacio sancte crucis, sancti Mathei apostoli, sancti Michaelis archangeli, sancti Luce euuangeliste, apostolorum Symonis et Iude, festivitas Omnium sanctorum, sancti Martini episcopi, sancti Andree apostoli, sancti Nicholai episcopi, sancti Thome apostoli, omnes dies dominici, festum cuiuslibet ecclesie, dedicacio ecclesie, si fuerit matrix ecclesia per totam parochiam, si capella tantummodo in parochia.[1]

Hec sunt ferianda in omnibus preterquam in carucis: sancti Vincencii martiris, sancti Barnabe apostoli, sancti Leonardi abbatis, sancti Clementis pape et martiris, Translacio sancti Osuualdi episcopi, sancte Katherine virginis et martiris.[b]

Hec sunt ferianda[c] ab operibus mulierum tantum, videlicet: sancte Angnetis virginis et martiris, sancte Margarete virginis et martiris, sancte Lucie virginis, sancte Agathe virginis et martiris. Festa sanctorum Dominici, Francisci, et Edmundi confessoris in eclesiis cum novem leccionibus celebrari volumus; nolumus tamen per hec opera fidelium impediri.

[b] S.Iohannis (?) ante portam latinam preterquam in caruc' *added in later hand* (S.Iohannis (?), *obliterated*) *at foot of page.*
[c] ferienda.

---

4. DIOCESE OF SALISBURY (1257). Cambridge, Emmanuel Coll. MS. 27, fo. 174[rb]. See above, pp. 126–7.

Cum nec[a] unicus dies anni illucescat[b] qui non[c] alicuius vel aliquorum sanctorum venerandis natalitiis decoretur, in quorum laudibus et meritorum preconiis totum tempus a Christi fidelibus quorum suffragiis indigent expendi non indigne meruerunt, hominis tamen conditio, cui dictum est: In sudore vultus tui vesceris pane tuo, nequaquam potest propter occupationes mundanas sanctorum venerationibus iugiter insistere quin necesse habeat corporis necessitatibus providere. Ideoque[d] salva sanctorum reverentia duximus statuendum quod exceptis sollempnitatibus Nativitatis dominice cum iiii[or] diebus sequentibus, Circumcisionis, Epiphanie, Resurrectionis, cum iii diebus, Ascencionis, Pentecosten, cum iii diebus, singulisque sollempnitatibus dominicis, exceptis etiam festivitatibus beate Virginis, apostolorum, et evangelistarum, festivitatibus sancte crucis, sancti Michaelis, sancti Iohannis baptiste, sancti Laurentii, Translationis sancti Thome martiris, sancti Martini, sancti Nicholay, et sancte Marie Magdalene, festis dedicationum[e] in suis parochiis, necnon et sanctorum in quorum honore singule ecclesie construuntur, nullius alterius sancti festivitas ab agricultura et laboribus sine quibus terre coli non possunt parochianis suis indicatur per presbiteros ferianda.[f]

[a] vero.	[b] illuscescat.	[c] nec.
[d] Ideo quia.	[e] fest' dedicationis.	ferienda.

---

[1] Cf. the calendar of the Hereford breviary (no. 12).

5. Diocese of London (1245–59). Brit. Mus., Add. MS. 48344, fo. 8ʳ.[1] See above, pp. 127–8.

Ad tollendam diversitatem que plures duxit in devium et causa fuit scandali, dum quidam rectores ecclesiarum quasdam sanctorum sollempnitates minus celebres officio venerabantur magis sollempni et indicebant observandas, quasdam magis sollempnes minus debito recolebant, precipimus ut mense Ianuario Circumcisionem domini, Epiphaniam, et Conversionem sancti Pauli patroni nostri cum omni honore et debita reverentia servent et iubeant observari. Festa autem sanctorum Fabiani et Sebastiani, Agnetis, Vincentii, debita devotione in ecclesiis venerentur; set officio sine dampnosa mora*[a]* celebrato, licet parochianis operaciones necessarias exercere.

In mense autem Februario Purificacio beate Marie per omnia sollempnis habeatur. In Cathedra sancti Petri et in festo sancti Mathie communes operaciones prohibeantur; operaciones tamen pietatis non inhibemus.

In mense Marcio sola Dominica annunciacio ab omnibus sit sollempnis. In festo beati Gregorii post missarum sollempnia pietatis opera concedantur.

In Aprili festa sanctorum Marci ewangeliste, Erkenwaldi ab omnibus observentur. In festis*[b]* autem sanctorum Ælphegi, Georgii martiris et Melliti post missam operari concedimus.

In mense Mayo festivitates apostolorum Philippi et Iacobi et Invencionis sancte crucis ab omnibus iubemus observari. In festis*[b]* autem sancti Iohannis ante portam latinam, sancti Dunstani, sancti Ethelberti, sint in civitate ista sollempnia propter reverentiam reliquiarum que ibidem continentur.

In mense Iunio festum sancti Barnabe apostoli, Nativitas sancti Iohannis baptiste et festum apostolorum Petri et Pauli, et Commemoratio sancti Pauli sunt sollempniter observanda. Festum autem beati Albani tantum in decanatu Middelsex' propter reverentiam et viciniam iubemus sollempniter celebrari.

In mense Iulio Translatio sancti Thome martiris, festum sancte Marie Magdalene, sancti Iacobi apostoli iubemus [*fo. 8ᵛ*] esse sollempnia. In festo autem sancte Margarete, post missam celebratam, operaciones necessarias fieri concedimus.

In Augusto festum beati Petri advincula, festum sancti Oswaldi maxime in civitate London', festum sancti Laurentii, Assumpcionem beate virginis, festum sancti Bartholomei, festum Decollationis sancti Iohannis baptiste precipimus observari.

In mense Septembri festum sancti Egidii suis peregrinis et in suis ecclesiis sit sollempne. Nativitas beate virginis, festum Exaltacionis sancte crucis, festum sancti Mathei apostoli et ewangeliste, festum sancti Michaelis ab omnibus observentur.

In Octobri Dedicacio ecclesie beati Pauli prima mensis, festum sancti Luce ewangeliste, festum sanctorum Simonis et Iude iubemus ab omnibus observari. Festivitates autem sanctarum Osyde, Ethelburge in suis decanatibus[2] iubemus esse sollempnes.

[1] Other texts are indicated in Cheney, *Eng. Synodalia*, pp. 79–84, and an edition based upon all of them will appear in the forthcoming *Councils and Synods*, vol. ii, where this extract forms chapters 90–102.

[2] The rural deaneries were those of Tendring and Barking, in the archdeaconry of Colchester.

[a] dampno more.
[b] festo.

In Novembri festum Omnium sanctorum summe sit sollempne; dies etiam crastinus, saltem donec sit defunctis per universalis ecclesie suffragia subventum, quies indicatur universis,[c] postmodum libere vacent operacionibus necessariis et pietatis. Festivitates sancti Martini et sancti Eadmundi regis et martiris, sancte Katerine virginis, sancti Andree apostoli, iubemus universis esse sollempnes. Festa autem sancti Eadmundi archiepiscopi Cantuariensis, sancte Cecilie virginis, sancti Clementis post celebracionem divinorum que sollempniter agi debent agrorum culture non negentur.

In Decembri festum sancti Nicholai et sancti Thome apostoli sit cunctis sollempne, et venerabilis Nativitas salvatoris cum festis sollempnibus que sequuntur.

Sollempnitas dominice Resurrectionis et Pentecosten, per quatuor dies, et Ascensionis domini celebrentur.[d] Dedicationes quoque ecclesiarum et earum festivitates in suis locis sollempniter celebrentur. Sane cum omnes electi dei laude digna reverenter sint extollendi, nichil declinavimus illorum honori quem clerus et populus, in civitate et extra, tum ex debito tum ex devocione eis impendere consuevit.

[c] universalis.   [d] celebretur.

---

6. DIOCESE OF NORWICH (?) (*c.* 1240). Brit. Mus., Add. MS. 48344, fo. 8[v]. See above, pp. 128–9.

[H]ec sunt festa in quibus ex toto a servili opere est feriandum:

Nathalis domini, sancti Stephani, sancti Iohannis, sanctorum Innocentium, sancti Thome martiris, Circumcisionis, Epiphanie, Conversionis sancti Pauli. Purificationis beate Marie, Cathedra sancti Petri, sancti Mathie, sancti Gregorii, Annunciacionis dominice, diei Parasceves, Pasce cum die lune et cum die martis nisi aliquis eo die intuitu karitatis alicui egenti carucam accomodaverit, sancti Marci ewangeliste, Philippi et Iacobi, Invencionis sancte Crucis, Ascensionis domini, Pentecostes eodem modo quo Pascha, sancti Augustini Anglorum episcopi, sancti Barnabe, Nathalis sancti Iohannis baptiste, Petri et Pauli, Translationis[a] sancti Thome martiris, sancte Margarete, sancte Marie Magdalene, sancti Iacobi, advincula sancti Petri, sancti Laurentii, Assumpcionis[b] et Nathalis sancte Marie, Bartholomei apostoli, Decollacionis sancti Iohannis, Exaltacionis sancte Crucis, sancti Mathei, sancti Michaelis archangeli, sancti Francisci, sancti Luce, Symonis et Iude, [*fo. 9*[r]] Omnium Sanctorum, sancti Martini, sancti Eadmundi, sancti Clementis, sancti Andree, sancti Nicholai, sancti Thome apostoli, festum sancti loci, dedicationis ecclesie in propria parqchia tantum.

[H]ec sunt festa in quibus, prohibitis aliis operibus, conceduntur tantum opera carucarum:

Fabiani et Sebastiani, Agnetis, Vincentii, Blasii, Agathe, Felicis episcopi Norwicensis, Eadwardi regis, Cuthberti, Benedicti, Ambrosii, Georgii, Iohannis ante Portam Latinam, Botulphi, Albani, Etheldride, Invencionis sancte Crucis,[c] sancti Stephani, Ieronimi, Fidis, Dedicacionis sancti Michaelis, sancti Dionisii,

[a] Translatio.   [b] Assumpcio.
[c] sancte Crucis *om.*

Cecilie, Katerine, Lucie. Comodentur caruce pro deo, alioquin prohibeantur cum aliis operibus: Commemoratio fidelium, festum sancti Leonardi.

Hec sunt festa in quibus post missam excerceantur opera rusticana, set non ante:
Octave Epiphanie, Iohannis et Pauli, Commemoratio sancti Pauli, Translatio sancti Martini, Octave Petri et Pauli apostolorum, Translatio sancti Benedicti, sancti Bricii episcopi.

Nota quod in medio tempore inter festum beati Thome archiepiscopi et Circumcisionis, item inter Circumcisionem et Epiphaniam, item diebus mercurii, iovis, veneris, et die sabbati in septimana Pasche et Pentecosten, si necesse fuerit, exerceantur opera rusticana a tempore misse celebrate usque ad tempus vesperarum, set non ante missam nec post vesperas, nec tempore misse vel tempore vesperarum.

---

7. Diocese of Exeter (1287). Brit. Mus., Harl. MS. 220, fo. 26^r.[1] See above, p. 129.

Circa festa indicenda errare novimus^a quamplurimos sacerdotes dum unus in sua parochia festum aliquod indicit solempniter celebrandum alius idem festum penitus pretermittit, sicque in una parochia homines cessare a laboribus in alia communiter laborare^b sepe contingit; quod absurdum admodum reputantes inhibemus ne sacerdotes alia festa in parochiis suis precipiant solempniter celebrari quam ea que in sacris canonibus sunt expressa vel que cum clero et populo solempniter duximus veneranda. Et ut festorum celebrandorum inter omnes subditos nostros eadem observancia habeatur, festa solempniter celebranda cum clero et populo presenti synodo duximus inserenda. In mense Ianuarii Circumcisionis domini, Epiphanie, Conversionis sancti Pauli^c; in mense Februarii Purificacionis sancte Marie, Cathedra sancti Petri, sancti Mathie apostoli; in mense Marcii sancti Gregorii pape,^{d} Annunciacionis sancte Marie; in mense Aprilis sancti Georgii, sancti Marci evangeliste^e; in mense Maii sanctorum Philippi et Iacobi, Invencionis sancte crucis, sancti Iohannis ante portam latinam,^{f} sancti Augustini Anglorum apostoli^g; in mense Iunii sancti Barnabe apostoli, Nativitatis sancti Iohannis baptiste, apostolorum Petri et Pauli; in mense Iulii Translationis sancti Thome martiris,^{h} sancte Marie Magdalene, sancti Iacobi apostoli; in mense Augusti sancti Petri ad

---

[1] The manuscript is of the late 15th cent. and the additions are in a hand similar to that of the text, probably not much later. This text is chosen as the basis of the forthcoming edition of the statutes in *Councils and Synods*, ii, which will indicate variants of other manuscripts.

^{a} novimus *after* plurimos.

^{b} laborare *after* alia.

^{c} Conv.s.Pauli *erased.*

^{d} s. Gregorii pape *erased.*

^{e} s. Georgii, s. Marci evang. *over erasure.*

^{f} Inv. s. crucis, s. Ioh. ante portam latinam *erased.*

^{g} s.Aug.Angl.apostoli *over erasure.*

^{h} Trans. s.Thome martiris *erased.*

vincula, sancti Laurencii,[i] Assumpcionis sancte Marie, sancti Bartholomei apostoli, Decollacionis sancti Iohannis baptiste[k]; in mense Septembris Nativitatis sancte Marie, Exaltacionis sancte crucis,[l] sancti Mathei apostoli, sancti Michaelis archangeli; in mense Octobris sancti Luce evangeliste, apostolorum Symonis et Iude; in mense Novembris Omnium sanctorum, sancti Martini, sancte Katherine virginis[m], sancti Andree; in mense [*fo. 26ᵛ*] Decembris sancti Nicholai Concepcio sancte Marie[n], sancti Thome apostoli; Natalis domini per octo dies, Pasche per quatuor dies, Ascenssionis domini, Penthecostes per quatuor dies, temporibus suis; festum sancti loci illius cuius est ecclesia, dedicacionis, festum Corporis Christi.[o]

[i] s.Petri ad vinc., s.Laur. *erased.*
[k] Decollacionis s.Ioh.bapt. *erased.*
[l] Exalt.s.crucis *erased.*
[m] s. Martini, s. Kath. virg. *erased.*
[n] s. Nicholai, Concep. s. Marie (*the latter much compressed*) *over erasure.*
[o] dedicacionis, festum Corp. Christi (*compressed*) *over erasure.*

---

8. BARNWELL PRIORY (1295). Brit. Mus., Harl. MS. 3601, fo. 1ʳ. See above, pp. 129–30.

Isti sunt dies in quibus non licet operari.

In die Natalis domini, et iiii° diebus sequentibus, in die Circumcisionis, in die Epiphanie, in die Conversionis beati Pauli, in omnibus festivitatibus beate Virginis, in die Cathedre sancti Petri, in die sancti Mathie, in die Pasche, et tribus diebus sequentibus, in die Dedicacionis ecclesie de Bernewelle,[1] in die sancti Marci ewangeliste, in festo apostolorum Philippi et Iacobi, in utroque festo sancte Crucis, in die sancti Iohannis ante portam latinam, in die Ascensionis, in die Pentecostes, et tribus diebus sequentibus, in die sancti Barnabe apostoli,[a] in die sancte Etheldrede in estate, in Nativitate beati Iohannis baptiste, in festo apostolorum Petri et Pauli, in die Translacionis beati Thome martyris, in die beate Marie Magdalene, in die sancti Iacobi apostoli, in die sancti Petri advincula, in die beati Laurencii, in die beati Bartholomei apostoli, in die Decollacionis sancti Iohannis baptiste, in die beati Egidii, in die beati Mathei, in die beati Michaelis, in die beati Luce evangeliste, in die apostolorum Symonis et Iude, in die Omnium sanctorum, in die sancti Martini,[b] in die sancti Andree, in die sancti Nicholai, in die sancti Thome apostoli.

[a] in die sancti Barnabe apostoli *over erasure.*
[b] In die sancti Martini *lightly deleted by a later hand.*

---

9. OSNEY ABBEY (*c.* 1300). Bodleian, MS. Rawl. C. 939, fo. 117ʳ. See above, p. 130.

Isti sunt dies in quibus operarii Oseneye secundum antiquam consuetudinem solebant operari.

---

[1] The church of Barnwell Priory was dedicated in honour of St. Andrew and St. Giles on 21 April 1191, by William Longchamp, bishop of Ely. The day is noted as *principale festum* in the calendar (*Liber memorandorum*, pp. 6, 222).

Vigilia Epiphanie usque ad vesperas, dies sanctorum Fabiani et Sebastiani, sancte Agnetis, sancti Vincentii, Vigilia Conversionis sancti Pauli usque ad vesperas, dies sancte Agathe, Translatio sancte Frideswythe, in Vigilia Cathedre Petri usque ad vesperas, si extra Quadragesimam evenerit, si autem infra Quadragesimam evenerit, debent operari usque ad collationem, eodem modo in Vigilia sancti Mathie et sancti Gregorii, dies sancti Cuthberti, dies sancti Benedicti, Vigilia sancti Georgii usque ad collationem, Vigilia sancti Marci usque ad vesperas, Vigilia apostolorum Philippi et Iacobi usque ad vesperas, Vigilia Invencionis sancte crucis usque ad vesperas, Vigilia sancti Iohannis ad portam latinam usque ad vesperas, Vigilia sancti Augustini Anglorum episcopi usque ad vesperas, Vigilia sancti Barnabe usque ad vesperas, dies sancti Albani, Commemoratio sancti Pauli, Vigilia Translationis sancti Thome martiris[a] usque ad collationem, dies sancte Margarete virginis, Vigilia sancte Marie Magdalene usque ad vesperas, Vigilia ad Vincula sancti Petri usque ad vesperas, dies sancti Augustini magni doctoris, dies sancti Egidii, vigilia Nativitatis sancte Marie usque ad vesperas, Vigilia Exaltationis sancte Crucis usque ad vesperas, Vigilia sancti Michaelis usque ad vesperas, [fo. 117ᵛ] Vigilia sancti Luce usque ad vesperas, Vigilia sancti Martini usque ad collationem, dies sancti Edmundi regis et martiris, dies sancte Cecilie usque ad collationem, Vigilia sancti Nicholai usque ad collationem, post quintum diem Natalis domini, scilicet vi et vii dies, post tercium diem Pasche et Pentecostes.

Item, sciendum quod in omnibus vigiliis apostolorum in quibus omnes communiter ieiunant et in vigiliis Annuntiacionis et Assumpcionis sancte Marie et in vigilia sancti Iohannis baptiste, sancti Laurentii, et Omnium sanctorum debent operari usque ad nonam tantum. Item, sabbatis in Quadragesima non tenentur operari, nisi de gratia, post prandium.

[a] translationis sancti Thome martiris *erased*.

10. FARINGDON (after 1336). Brit. Mus., MS. Cotton Nero A. xii, fo. 79ʳ. See above, p. 130.

Quibus diebus non laborant conversi et famuli in manerio de Farendon':

In Natali domini et tribus diebus sequentibus, in die Pasche et feria secunda, in die Ascensionis, in Pentecoste et feria secunda, in omnibus solempnitatibus sancte Marie, in festo sanctorum Philippi et Iacobi, in Nativitate beati Iohannis baptiste, apostolorum Petri et Pauli, Iacobi apostoli, Laurentii, Bartholomei, Mathei, Michaelis, Simonis [fo. 79ᵛ] et Iude, Omnium Sanctorum, Martini episcopi, Andree, Thome apostoli.

Quando conversi et famuli dimittunt opus suum:

In vigil' Natalis domini, Pache, Ascencionis, Pentecosten, beati Iohannis baptiste, apostolorum Petri et Pauli, beati Laurentii, Assumpcionis beate Marie, et Omnium Sanctorum, dimittunt operarii opus suum ad nonam, videlicet ad prandium, qui tamen secundum antiquam ordinis consuetudinem usque ad vesperas deberent laborare. In vigiliis vero dictarum sollempnitatum quibus ad nonam dimittunt dicti operarii opera sua ut dictum est, recipiunt plenam mercedem suam, ac si tota die laborascent. In omnibus vero sabbatis et vigiliis omnium aliarum solempnitatum quibus famuli non laborant, [fo. 80ʳ] dimittunt opus suum parum ante solis occasum; in omnibus vero aliis diebus post solis occasum. Diebus vero dedicacionum ecclesiarum in manerio de Farendon' non solent famuli nostri laborare.

---

11. DIOCESE OF BATH AND WELLS (1342). Wells, Diocesan Registry, Reg. R. de Salopia, fo. 273ᵛ. See above, p. 131.

Licet veneranda cunctorum festa sanctorum ad laudem et honorem dei ac devocionem fidelium excitandam solempnizari et in ecclesiis solempniter celebrari cupiamus attentius sicut decet, attentis tamen singulis attendendis circumstanciis, non expedit nec oportet homines ab agricultura seu aliis operibus rusticis revocare vel ab occupacionibus rei familiaris in festis singulis impedire. Considerantes igitur quod in locis diversis nostre diocesis festa sanctorum difformiter inducuntur et in quibus festis nostri subditi ab huiusmodi operibus seu occupacionibus se abstinere debeant a quamplurimis in dubium revocatur, ad huiusmodi dubium removendum et pro nostrorum utilitatibus subditorum in festis infrascriptis et non aliis, exceptis festis dedicacionum ecclesiarum et sanctorum in quorum honorem ecclesie fuerint dedicate ac diebus dominicis, singula festa huiusmodi in mensibus quibus contingunt distincte ponentes, et canones antiquos et sanctorum patrum constituciones in ea parte editas quo ad aliqua recensentes necnon presenti nostra provisione aliqua festa addentes, ab huiusmodi operibus et occupacionibus volumus nostros subditos abstinere et eciam impediri.

In mense siquidem Ianuarii festum Circumcisionis domini, Epiphanie domini, Conversionis sancti Pauli; mense Februarii festum Purificacionis beate Marie, Cathedre sancti Petri, et sancti Mathie apostoli; in mense Marcii festum Annunciacionis dominice; in mense Aprilis festum Parasceve et Resurrectionis domini cum tribus diebus sequentibus, cum in illo vel alio mense contingat, et festum sancti Marci evangeliste; in mense Maii festum apostolorum Philippi et Iacobi, Invencionis sancte Crucis, Iohannis ante portam [fo. 274ʳ] latinam, Asscencionis domini, festum Pentecosten cum duobus diebus sequentibus, et festum de Corpore Christi cum in illo vel alio mense venire contingat; in mense Iunii sancti Barnabe, Nativitatis sancti Iohannis baptiste, et apostolorum Petri et Pauli; mense Iulii festum Translacionis sancti Thome martiris dudum Cantuariensis archiepiscopi, sancte Marie Magdalene, Iacobi apostoli; in mense Augusti festum quod dicitur Advincula sancti Petri, festum sancti Laurencii, Assumpcionis beate Marie, sancti Bartholomei, et Decollacionis sancti Iohannis baptiste; in mense Septembris festum Nativitatis sancte Marie, Exaltacionis sancte Crucis, sancti Mathei, et sancti Michaelis; in mense Octobris festum sancti Luce, et apostolorum Simonis et Iude; in mense Novembris festum Omnium sanctorum, sancti Martini episcopi, et sancti Andree apostoli; in mense Decembris festum sancti Nicholai, Concepcionis beate Marie, sancti Thome apostoli, Natalis domini, sancti Stephani, sancti Iohannis apostoli et evangeliste, sanctorum Innocencium, et sancti Thome martiris dudum Cantuariensis archiepiscopi.

Per hanc autem nostram provisionem statutis canonum seu locorum consuetudinibus circa solempnizacionem seu celebracionem festorum quorumcumque sanctorum in ecclesiis solempniter faciendam non intendimus derogare, nec quo ad actus iudiciales excercendos quicquam circa premissa de iure vel de consuetudine inmutare.

---

12. DIOCESE OF HEREFORD (*c.* 1348–62). Brit. Mus., Add. MS. 39675, fo. 8vb. See above, pp. 131–2.

Ista festa subscripta omnino ferianda sunt in episcopatu Hereford'.

Dies Natalis domini cum iiii^{or} diebus sequentibus, dies Circumcisionis domini, dies Epiphanie domini, dies Conversionis sancti Pauli, dies Purificationis, dies Cathedre sancti Petri, dies sancti Mathie apostoli, [*fo.* 9ra] dies Annuntiationis domini, dies Pasche, cum ii diebus sequentibus, dies sancti Marci, dies apostolorum Philippi et Iacobi, dies Inventionis sancte crucis, dies sancti Iohannis ante portam latinam, dies sancti Ethelberti, dies Ascentionis domini, dies Pentecostes cum ii diebus sequentibus, dies sancti Barnabe, dies Translationis sancti Thome de Cantelupe, dies Nativitatis sancti Iohannis baptiste, dies apostolorum Petri et Pauli, dies Translationis sancti Thome archiepiscopi, dies sancte Marie Magdalene, dies sancti Iacobi, dies sancti Petri advincula, dies sancti Laurentii, dies Assumptionis sancte Marie, dies sancti Bartholomei, dies Decollationis sancti Iohannis baptiste, dies Nativitatis sancte Marie, dies Exaltationis sancte crucis, dies sancti Mathei, dies sancti Michaelis, dies sancti Thome de Cantelupe, dies sancti Luce evangeliste, dies apostolorum Symonis et Iude, dies Omnium sanctorum et Commemoratio animarum, dies sancti Martini, dies sancti Clementis, dies sancti Andree, [*fo.* 9rb] dies sancti Nicholai, dies sancti Thome apostoli, item, omnes dies dominici per annum, dies festi cuiuslibet ecclesie, dies dedicationis ecclesie, si fuerit matrix ecclesia, per totam parochiam, si fuerit capella, in parochia tantum capelle, dies Conceptionis beate Marie, dies Parascheves.

Ista festa ferianda sunt preterquam in carucis.

Dies sancti Vincentii, dies Edmundi confessoris, dies sancti Edmundi regis, dies sancte Katerine, dies sancti Gregorii, dies sancti Augustini Anglorum.

Ista festa ferianda sunt ab operibus mulierum.

Dies sancti Benedicti, dies sancti Leonardi abbatis, dies sancte Agnetis, dies sancte Margarete virginis, dies sancte Agathe, dies sancte Lucie, dies sancte Cecilie.

---

13. PROVINCE OF CANTERBURY (1362). Lambeth Palace Libr., Reg. Simon Islip, fo. 186^v. See above, pp. 132–3.

Simon etc. venerabili fratri nostro domino Simoni dei gratia episcopo Londoniensi salutem et fraternam in domino caritatem. Ex scripturis sacris didicimus^a vicia sepe se ingerere et virtutes esse mentiri dum videlicet sub figmento sanctitatis ad execranda proceditur, et sub specie cultus divini ad abhominabilem deo victimam properatur. Ab exordio nempe condicionis humane die dumtaxat septimo ebdomade statuit omnium conditor ab operibus abstinendum; set succedente tempore gratie militans adiecit ecclesia dies plurimos ab omnibus catholicis feriandum; ex quibus postmodum usus hominum tollerante ecclesia, propter operandi ut creditur necessitatem, nonnullos a feriandi ritu subtraxit et quosdam in diversis catholicorum partibus festivos superaddidit localiter observandos, qui, quamvis a primordiis ob veneracionem

^{a} didiscimus.

sanctorum in festivandi consuetudinem introducti fuerant, inconstancia tamen humana ut plerumque in deteriora labente, quod in electorum dei receptum erat honorem conversum est in blasphemiam et abhominacionem, dum videlicet conventicule, negociaciones, et alia exercicia illicita diebus huiusmodi potissime ingeruntur. Quod vero ad devocionis parabatur compendium in dissolucionis erigitur cumulum, dum in ipsis festivitatibus colitur taberna pocius quam ecclesia, commessaciones habundant et ebrietates uberius quam lacrime et oraciones, lasciviis insistitur et contumeliis magis quam ocio contemplacionis, et quod pretermittendum non est, mercenarii, sine quorum operibus res publica regi non poterit, sub colore licito sic ab operibus mechanicis diebus eciam quos sibi festivos constituunt et sanctorum vigiliis abstinent, licet non minus per ebdomadam capientes propterea de salario; quo utilitas rei publice graviter retardatur, quin pocius impeditur, nec propter dei honorem sicut deceret sabatizant set eciam iuxta premissa deum ipsum et sanctam ecclesiam in diebus huiusmodi per abhominationes suas pessimas scandalizant, tamquam solempnitates ipse ad prophanacionis et perversitatis exercicium gratis fuerunt institute; que quanto magis protenduntur in numero, tanto habundantius cultores abusionum huiusmodi in suis excessibus insolescunt. Ut igitur tam supersticiosis adinvencionibus ac eciam fraudulentis mercenariorum huiusmodi commentis occurratur et eorum attenuetur occasio et memorie sanctorum feriandorum iuxta primam ecclesie institucionem in debita habeantur veneracione, reservata facultate viris ecclesiasticis aliisque maioribus ac sibi ipsis sufficientibus, quorumcumque festorum prout eis placuerit ad dei honorem in ecclesiis suis vel capellis solempniter venerandi, de fratrum nostrorum concilio dies festos presentibus inserere duximus, quibus videlicet ab universis popularium operibus etiam reipublice utilibus per nostram Cantuariensem provinciam fuerit regulariter abstinendum.

In primis, sacrum diem dominicum ab hora diei sabbati vespertina inchoandum, non ante horam ipsam preveniendum ne Iudaice professionis participes videamur, quod in festis que suas habent vigilias observetur. Item, festa Natalis domini, sanctorum Stephani, Iohannis, Innocencium, Thome martiris, Circumcisionis, Epiphanie domini, Purificacionis beate Marie, sancti Mathie apostoli, Annunciacionis sancte Marie, sancti Parasceve, Pasche, cum tribus diebus sequentibus, sancti Marci ewangeliste, apostolorum Philippi et Iacobi, Invencionis sancte crucis, Ascencionis domini, Pentecostes, cum tribus diebus sequentibus, Corporis Christi,[b] Nativitatis sancti Iohannis baptiste, apostolorum Petri et Pauli, Translacionis sancti Thome, sancte Marie Magdalene, sancti Iacobi, Assumpcionis sancte Marie, sancti Bartholomei, sancti Laurencii,[c] Nativitatis sancte Marie, Exaltationis sancte crucis, sancti Mathei apostoli, sancti Michaelis, sancti Luce ewangeliste, apostolorum Simonis et Iude, Omnium sanctorum, sancti Andree apostoli, sancti Nicholai, Concepcionis beate Marie, sancti Thome apostoli, dedicacionum ecclesiarum parochialium, et sanctorum in quorum honore ecclesie parochiales dedicantur, aliaque festa que in singulis dicte provincie diocesibus per locorum ordinarios ex certa sciencia peculiariter indicuntur.

Vobis igitur mandamus quatinus premissa omnia et singula ad singulorum

---

[b] Corporis Christi *interlined and rubricated* (? *same hand*).
[c] Decollacionis sancti Iohannis *follows, expunged and deleted, and not rubricated like the other entries.*

confratrum et suffraganeorum nostrorum noticiam deducentes, eorum cuilibet iniungatis quod moneant et efficaciter inducant clerum et populum sibi subiectum ut festa superius enumerata prout^d suis acciderint temporibus summo opere observent et debito venerentur honore, et ad parochiales eorum ecclesias diebus ipsis reverenter accedant, missarum et aliorum divinorum officiorum complementum exspectent pro ipsorum ceterorumque fidelium vivorum et defunctorum salute deum devote et sinceris mentibus oraturi, sic festorum ipsorum decurrendo solempnia ut ipsi et alii catholici pro quibus oraverint sanctorum quorum festa celebraverint intercessores mereantur habere assiduos apud deum; et quod dicti confratres nostri subditis suis huiusmodi intiment quod reliquis sanctorum festivitatibus inpune poterunt ad opera procedere consueta. Si vero aliqui operarii conducticii occurrerint qui^e festis peculiaribus et non ut prefertur indictis a consuetis operibus cessare presumpserint, ut sic secundum premissa eos defraudent quorum ministerio se astrinxerint, ipsos a supersticionibus huiusmodi canonice compescant et faciant per alios compesci ecclesiasticam per censuram; demandantes insuper predictis confratribus nostris quod eorum singuli nos clare et distincte certificent quid fecerint in premissis citra festum Nativitatis sancte Marie virginis proximo nunc futurum, per suas litteras patentes harum seriem continentes. Vos eciam quatenus vestras civitatem et diocesim concernit premissa omnia et singula studeatis efficaciter adimplere et nos modo consimili reddere certiores. Dat' apud Maghefeld, xvii kal. Augusti anno domini millesimo ccc^{mo} lxii° et nostre consecracionis xiii.

^{d} ut *repeated.*   'qui *over* quod *del.*

---

14. 'PROVINCE OF CANTERBURY (1400)'. Brit. Mus., MS. Cotton Claud. A. ii, fo. 152^v. See above, p. 133.

Hec sunt festa ab omnibus operibus tenenda per constitutionem Ricardi Arundel' Cantuariensis archiepiscopi, videlicet: in mense Ianuarii Circumcisio domini, Epiphania domini, item festum illius sancti in cuius honore ecclesia dedicatur, festum dedicacionis ecclesie; mense Februarii Purificacio^a beate Marie, festum sancti Mathie apostoli—vigilia^b; mense Marcii Annunciacio beate Marie, Pascha cum tribus diebus sequentibus—vigilia; mense Aprili sancti Marci euuangeliste—vigilia in die; mense Maii apostolorum Philippi et Iacobi, Invencionis sancte crucis, sancti Augustini primi Anglorum episcopi,^{c} vigilia—Ascencio domini, dies Pentecosten cum tribus diebus sequentibus— vigilia; mense Iunii sancte Wenefrede, vigilia—Nativitas sancti Iohannis baptiste, vigilia—apostolorum Petri et Pauli; mense Iulii Translacio sancti Thome martiris, sancte Marie Magdalene, sancti Iacobi apostoli—vigilia, sancte Anne matris Marie; mense Augusti vigilia—sancti Laurencii martiris, vigilia— Assumpcio beate Marie, sancti Bartholomei—vigilia; mense Septembris vigilia —Nativitas beate Marie, Exaltacio sancte crucis, vigilia—sancti Mathei apostoli,

^{a} Puricacio.
^{b} *The marking of vigils, some preceding and some following the feasts to which they refer, probably follows an archetype in which they were later additions to the main list.*
^{c} episcopi *omitted.*

sancti Michaelis archangeli; mense Octobris sancti Luce euuangeliste, apostolorum Symonis et Iude—vigilia; mense Novembris vigilia—festum Omnium
sanctorum, Commemoracio animarum, sancte Katerine virginis, vigilia—sancti
Andree apostoli; mense Decembris sancti Nicholai, Concepcio beate Marie,
vigilia—sancti Thome apostoli, vigilia—Nativitas domini, sancti Stephani
martiris, sancti Iohannis apostoli et euuangeliste, sanctorum Innocencium,
sancti Thome martiris, sancti Cedde episcopi, sancti Georgii martiris.

---

15. LINCOLN (? 1329–62). *Statutes of Lincoln Cathedral*, ed. H. Bradshaw
and C. Wordsworth, iii. 545–7. See above p. 134.

Hec sunt festa per annum ferianda et solempniter observanda secundum
consuetudinem ecclesie Linc' ab omni opere faciendo per operarios dicte
ecclesie tam in abstilar', carpentar', plumb' quam locis aliis ad fabricam pertinentibus.

Mense Ianuarii Circumcisio domini, Epiphania domini, Conversio sancti
Pauli; mense Februarii Purificacio beate Marie, Cathedra sancti Petri, sancti
Mathie apostoli; mense Martii Annunciacio beate Marie; mense Aprilis sancti
Marci evangeliste; mense Maii festum Philippi et Iacobi, Invencio sancte
crucis, sancti Iohannis ante portam latinam, et Ascencio domini; mense Iunii
festum sancti Barnabe, Nativitas sancti Iohannis baptiste, apostolorum Petri et
Pauli; mense Iulii festum translacionis sancti Thome martiris, sancte Marie
Magdalene, sancti Iacobi; mense Augusti festum sancti Petri ad vincla, sancti
Laurencii, Assumpcio beate Marie, sancti Bartholomei, Decollacio sancti
Iohannis; mense Septembris festum Nativitatis beate Marie, Exaltacio sancte
crucis, sancti Mathei, sancti Michaelis archangeli; mense Octobris festum sancti
Luce evangeliste, apostolorum Simonis et Iude; mense Novembris festum
Omnium sanctorum, sancti Martini, sancti Hugonis [Deposicio], sancti Clemen-
tis, sancte Katherine, sancti Andree apostoli; mense Decembris festum sancti
Nicholai, sancti Thome apostoli.

Item ex nova constitucione papali festum celebratum de Corpore Christi in
quinta feria post festum sancte Trinitatis est solempniter feriandum. Item in
festo Natalis domini feriantur quinque dies, in festo Pasche quatuor dies, in
festo Pentecostes tres dies. Item dies Parasceve modo de novo feriatur.[a]

Summa feriarum predictarum li; de quibus fiunt duo dies accidentes in die
dominica, scilicet[b] dies Pasche et Pentecostes, unde remanent xlix qui accidere
possunt extra diem dominicam,[c] et l dominice; et lii dies sabbati qui feriantur
per dimidium diem, et xiii vigilie sanctorum, qui faciunt in universum xxxii
dies et dimidium integros.

Summa omnium feriarum per annum, computatis diebus dominicis, sabbati,
et vigiliis, vi^{xx} xiii dies et dimidium, qui faciunt tertiam partem anni et xii[d] dies
et dimidium.

[a] *MS. reads*: dies Pasce modo de novo feriantur, *according to Wordsworth*.
[b] *MS. reads*: similiter. [c] *MS reads*: die dominic.
[d] *MS. reads*: cxii.

X

ADDITIONAL NOTES

P.124 para 2 : For the meeting of 30 Nov.1241 see C.& S.ii.338-40.

Pp.125-9 :   Five of these lists,nos.3-7, are edited in their contexts
in C.& S. :no.3 (ii.318,321-5),no.4 (ii.561),no.5 (ii.653-5),no.6
(655-6),no.7 (ii.1021-2).
The reader is also referred to the index of C. & S.(ii 1421) s.v. Feast-
days, for other legislation on the subject.

XI

The Punishment of Felonous Clerks

IN more than one respect the murder of Thomas Becket disturbed the gradual adjustment of the relations of Church and
State. Earlier custom, in England as elsewhere, provided that
a clerk, convicted and degraded in the court christian, should be
punished in the lay court. The Church had acquiesced in this,
and indeed approved so useful a disciplinary weapon. The canon
law stated the doctrine of clerical immunity, and that sufficed ;
for the practice concerned clerks degraded from their orders.
Never before, it appears, had the Church cared about the fate of
the degraded clerk. Becket led the Papacy to apply its doctrine
of immunity, recognized on all hands, more extensively than it
had been applied before, more extensively than it was applied
elsewhere in the next generation. It was not the assertion of
a new principle so much as the new interpretation of a well-
established one ; but the novelty of it, and its sudden sealing with
Becket's murder, is arresting. Becket's sharp victory over the
custom of the past was not reversed, and in England the punishment of felonous clerks was left entirely to the court christian.

Many years ago F. W. Maitland examined the intentions of
Henry II in respect of criminous clerks, and vindicated the king's
statement of earlier custom.[1] Since then M. Génestal has dealt
very fully with the Becket episode as a part of his broad survey of
the *privilegium fori*,[2] several scholars have investigated Norman
custom,[3] and the later history of the *privilegium* in England has
been studied by Dr. Leona Gabel and Mr. A. L. Poole.[4] Much
has thus been done to clarify the normal procedure against
felonous clerks in the century and a half following Becket's death.
Still it may be permissible to suggest that some distinctions have

---

[1] *Henry II and the Criminous Clerks, ante,* vii. 224–34, reprinted in *Roman Canon
Law,* and *Collected Papers,* ii.

[2] R. Génestal, *Le Privilegium Fori en France, du décret de Gratien à la fin du XIVe
siècle* (Paris, 1921, 1924).

[3] C. H. Haskins, *Norman Institutions ;* S. R. Packard, ' King John and the Norman
Church ', *Harvard Theolog. Rev.* xv, and ' The judicial organization of Normandy
1189–1204 ', *Law Quarterly Rev.* xl.

[4] L. C. Gabel, *Benefit of Clergy in England in the Later Middle Ages* (Smith College
Studies in History, xiv) ; A. L. Poole, ' Outlawry as a punishment of criminous clerks ',
Essays in Honour of James Tait.

216 *THE PUNISHMENT OF FELONOUS CLERKS*

been ignored and some scraps of evidence neglected or misunderstood. This study is concerned with the punishment meted out to felonous clerks, and attempts to distinguish the parts played by secular and ecclesiastical courts.

The evidence under review has been drawn from the reign of Richard I to the reign of Edward II. Naturally it is more abundant in the latter half of the period, but one finds no indication that in the thirteenth century either the lay court or the ecclesiastical suddenly changed its view of clerical privilege. Throughout the period evidence is disappointingly scarce. The canonists are cautious or seemingly contradictory in their statements, the bishops' courts have left no registers, and the terseness of the public records raises far more problems than can be solved. It was, perhaps, as well, having regard to the available material, that legal historians should have monopolized the study of this subject in England.[1] Certain it is that the clerk's privilege has generally been viewed with the unfriendly eye of the common lawyer, a lawyer, be it noted, who cannot claim the benefit of clergy which his predecessors of the middle ages might invoke. The felonous clerk has been labouring under persistent, pronounced unpopularity amongst later writers, fiercer, perhaps, than any anti-clericalism he encountered in an age which knew not the sovereignty of the State. After all, the historian does well to remember that the *privilegium fori* represented in the middle ages not merely the exemption granted by the State to a group of men within it, but rather the jurisdiction of a universal authority which regarded the State, where the correction of the clergy was concerned, as a mere ancillary institution. The superiority of the hierarchy, to be sure, did not gain the recognition that the Church required ; but at least the canonist's view was treated with remarkable respect. Henry II could argue his case with Becket upon the basis of canon law, and it will be several centuries before the lay power will publicly flout a plain statement of the *Decretals.* The medieval lawyer most jealous for the jurisdiction of the Crown would probably attack this matter of felonous clerks by inquiring what the canons demanded. Then he might look for ways of evasion ; but he would avoid formal opposition. An incident in the Newcastle assizes of 7 Edward I is instructive.[2] Robert Sautemareys, a clerk, was convicted by the jury of a murderous assault. ' And the said jurors, being questioned whether Robert Sautemareis were a bigamist or not, say that he married a widow who died eight years ago, before the Council,

---

[1] Stubbs's summary treatment of the subject does not do more for this period than state the English canons in relation to the compromise of Henry II (*Const. Hist.*, §§ 399, 402).

[2] *Northumberland Assize Rolls* (Surtees Soc.), p. 366.

&c. Therefore let him be delivered as such [a convicted clerk] to the bishop. And the bishop is not to take purgation in this case until he have a special mandate from the lord king.' The law which deprived the bigamist of benefit of clergy was a canon of the second Council of Lyons (1274).[1] It answered to the desire of the secular authorities, but it had no retrospective force. Edward I had attributed to it retrospective force in the statute *De bigamis* 4 Edward I,[2] but here was a doubtful case. The king's justices in Northumberland, who would gladly have applied the rule and claimed the clerk, recognized its limitations. We shall be following medieval English practice if we look first for what the canon law permits.

M. Génestal's work makes unnecessary a detailed treatment of the canon law of the subject. From his elaborate discussion emerge several points worthy of emphasis for the present question. The canons and all commentators agree that the felonous clerk, except in certain cases of forfeiture, cannot be judged and condemned by the secular court. The cases of forfeiture vary in different times and places, and until the publication of the *Sext* custom governed them.[3] The bigamous clerk did not lose his privilege finally until 1274 [4] ; for married clerks accused of felony Boniface VIII confined the privilege to those who wore the correct tonsure and dress.[5] Correct tonsure and dress became about the same time the tests of privilege for ' apostate ' clerks, who had taken up worldly occupations. The final case of forfeiture is degradation. The clerk degraded from his orders for some grave offence is reduced to the status of a layman : and although theologians dispute upon the nature of orders and the possibility of re-ordination, the canonists agree that a clerk can, for any offence committed after degradation, be tried and punished as a layman.[6]

The canonical procedure appears to be approximately as follows. Let us suppose that a clerk is accused of murder. When he appears in the secular court he ' pleads his clergy ', and it becomes the duty of the ordinary to claim the case for the court christian. There can only be two or three obstacles to delivery to the ordinary. The clerk may be married, and may still claim his privilege.[7] But if he be bigamous, after 1274 he loses his

---

[1] Cf. Génestal, *op. cit.* i. 62 *seqq.* The canons treated a clerk's marriage to a widow as bigamous.

[2] Pollock and Maitland, *Hist. Eng. Law* (2nd edn.), i. 445.

[3] Génestal, I. vi.   [4] *Ibid.* i. 68.   [5] *Ibid.* i. 100–1.

[6] *Ibid.* i. 3–7, and L. Saltet, *Les Réordinations*, especially pp. 354–60.

The Church's policy about this wavered in the early thirteenth century ; but I have found no case in which the English courts questioned the Church's protection of a *clericus coniugatus*, unless the case of Robert Sautemareys be an example. Cf. Génestal, *op. cit.* i. ch. 4.

benefit ; or he may be incorrectly dressed or tonsured ; or he may have been degraded in the past. In those cases, the canons imply, let him go hang : ' omni privilegio clericali nudatus et coercioni fori secularis addictus '. To every other felonous clerk the Church extends a protection which is formidable. Let the secular court but attempt to judge and punish such an one, and it will feel the force of the Church's spiritual weapons.[1]

In the matter of trial the canon law thus claims practically exclusive cognizance of felonous clerks. Its doctrine of *punishment* opens the way more easily to lay intervention.

The famous decretal *At si clerici* of Alexander III (? c. 1177) suggest two types of action to be taken by the Church against felonous clerks, convicted or confessed. If their crimes warrant it they may be ' suspended from their orders ', or ' perpetually removed from the service of the altar '. But for adulteries and other lesser offences, the bishop may pardon the clerk after penance has been done.[2] Celestine III is rather more explicit in his treatment of grave offences : ' If a clerk in orders be lawfully detected in theft, homicide, perjury, or other crime, and convicted, he is to be deposed by the ecclesiastical judge '.[3] With Innocent III an alternative punishment appears. The pope writes to the bishop of Paris about a clerical forger, and speaks of clerks, ' who, being condemned for this or other grave offence, shall have been degraded '.[4] He proposes that they be handed over to the secular arm for an additional punishment. But regarding the particular forger whose fate was then in question, Innocent uses the words of Ahab, king of Israel : ' Shut him up in prison for ever to do penance, and feed him with bread of sorrow and with water of affliction '. Was this clerk to be degraded before being put back in prison ? We cannot tell. But one would suppose that so great a lawyer as Innocent III meant what he said, and no more. Had the procedure been a matter of course, the pope might indeed take it for granted, but we do not

---

[1] Cf. *Register of Wm. Wickwane* (Surtees Soc.), pp. 37–8, for an action against a royal officer who had hanged a clerk, and Gabel, *op. cit.* pp. 121–2, for the punishment of officers who had outlawed a clerk (from Bishop Grandisson's register), and *infra*, p. 227.

[2] *Decretales*, II. i. 4 : ' Si vero coram episcopo de criminibus in iure confessi sunt, seu legitima probatione convicti, dummodo sint talia crimina, propter quae suspendi debeant vel deponi, non immerito suspendendi sunt a suis ordinibus, vel ab altaris ministerio perpetuo removendi. De adulteriis vero et aliis criminibus, quae sunt minora, potest episcopus cum clericis post peractam poenitentiam dispensare.'

[3] *Ibid.* II. i. 10 : ' Consultationi tuae taliter respondeo quod, si clericus in quocunque ordine constitutus, in furto, vel homicidio, vel periurio, seu alio crimine fuerit deprehensus legitime, atque convictus, ab ecclesiastico iudice deponendus est '.

[4] *Ibid.* v. xl. 27 (*Novimus*) : ' Clericus, qui propter hoc vel aliud flagitium grave, non solum damnabile sed damnosum, fuerit degradatus . . .' It is hardly necessary to call attention to the indifferent use of the words *deponere* and *degradare ;* a distinction only comes to be drawn at a later date (cf. Génestal, ii. 56).

know this. Innocent could be explicit on the same topic on another occasion. When the bishop of London wrote to ask what should be done with clerks guilty of robbery or other great crimes, he replied that, ' having been degraded from their orders, they should be cast into strict monasteries to do penance '.[1] If in the case of the forger the pope had wanted degradation to be part of the punishment, he would surely have said so ? It would seem that Innocent III, like his predecessors, thought that degradation was a suitable punishment for grave offences, but he did not regard it as the only permissible penalty.[2] This was the canonistic opinion of later times. Degradation came to be a penalty confined by canonists to a few offences. Boniface VIII particularly says that imprisonment is a suitable punishment for clerks who have confessed, or are convicted of, crimes : imprisonment *in perpetuum vel ad tempus* ;[3] and the glossator treats this as referring to cases in which the bishop judges that ' such an offence is not worthy of degradation '.[4]

Where the punishment stopped short of degradation, the felonous clerk remained in theory exempt from secular justice. But where the canons speak of degradation they sometimes envisage a further punishment for the degraded clerk. A custom of most respectable antiquity, honoured by the twelfth-century canonists, provided that a degraded clerk should also answer to the lay power for his original offence. This custom Becket opposed. Becket's principle was maintained by the pope at that time, and Henry II is generally supposed to have abandoned any claim to punish felonous clerks after degradation ; the obnoxious clauses of the Constitutions of Clarendon were not applied in England.[5] A little later, *c.* 1177 according to M. Génestal,[6] the decretal *At si clerici* stated explicitly that a degraded clerk ought not to be handed over to the secular court.[7] The Becket episode had reversed the custom and broadened the *privilegium fori*.

[1] *Decretales*, v. xxxvii. 6 : ' Respondemus quod a suis ordinibus degradati, detrudi debeant in arctis monasteriis ad penitentiam peragendam '.

[2] This interpretation of the decretal *Novimus* may explain why later canonists do not appeal to it for a wide interpretation of the occasions of degradation and delivery to the secular court (cf. Génestal, ii. 72–3).

[3] *Sext*, v. ix. 3. The phrase appears (with a reminiscence of the decretal *Novimus* thrown in) in a commission for the delivery of clerks, from Bishop Stapledon of Exeter, 1310 (quoted, Gabel, p. 96, n. 25).

[4] A large part of M. Génestal's second volume (livre i) is devoted to ' les cas de dégradation ', but there is no discussion of alternative penalties.

[5] M. Génestal observes that at Sens Alexander III did not clearly condemn the Clarendon proposal. He only objected to the idea ' quod clerici trahantur ad saecularia iudicia ' (*op. cit.* ii. 23).

[6] *Ibid.* ii. 22, 24, 26–7.

[7] *Decretales*, II. i. 4 : ' Sed non debet quemlibet depositum pro suis excessibus (cum suo sit functus officio, nec duplici debeat ipsum contritione conterere) iudici tradere saeculari '.

Between Alexander III and the publication of the *Decretals* some important modifications were made. Several popes are found recommending precisely the procedure for the condemnation of which Becket had died. They not merely permit the secular court to take and punish a degraded clerk, not merely ' abandon ' him, but actually instruct bishops to ' deliver ' the criminals for a secular penalty. The first is Urban III, to whom the bishop of Paris has written about clerks who forged the king of France's seal. The men are not to suffer loss of life or member, but should be degraded, branded, and forced to abjure their province.[1] Here is the double punishment not only permitted, but demanded and perhaps executed, by the Church.[2] In 1192 Celestine III, having ordered the degradation of felonous clerks, proposes penalties if the degraded clerk prove incorrigible. This word *incorrigibilis* will have a great career among the canonists of the next two centuries, and goes far to explain the apparent incompatibility of the Alexandrine decretal with the later canons. According to Celestine III, the degraded clerk who is incorrigible should first be excommunicated and then anathematized.[3] Finally, the pope sees that the criminal may not be cowed by anathema : and a robber or a murderer might well be less susceptible to spiritual censures than other people are. The Church has done her best with the penalties at her disposal, and ' cum ecclesia non habet ultra quid faciat ', relinquishes the incorrigible to the secular power, ' ita quod ei deputetur exilium vel alia legitima pena inferatur '. The punishment is noteworthy, for the banishing of degraded clerks was known of old and was recommended later. Innocent III followed in Celestine's path. Having taken counsel, he decrees that forgers of papal letters are to be degraded and handed over to the secular authorities for punishment.[4] Elsewhere, in more general terms, he seems to regard delivery to the secular court as a natural consequence of degradation. Delivery to the secular court means that the clerk shall be degraded in the presence of the secular authority, who shall be asked after the ceremony to receive the degraded clerk in his own court :

---

[1] *Decretales*, v. xx. 3 : ' eis nec membrum auferri, nec poenam infligi facias corporalem, per quam periculum mortis possint incurrere, sed eis a suis ordinibus degradatis, in signum maleficii characterem aliquem imprimi facias quo inter alios cognoscantur, et provinciam ipsam eos abiurare compellens, abire permittas '.

[2] M. Génestal probably rightly assumes that the Church inflicted these penalties. But he observes ' marque et *abiuratio terrae* sont en effet des peines essentiellement séculières, dont on ne trouve pas d'autre exemple dans le droit classique ' ; and adds ' le concile de Reims de 1157, c. 1, prescrit cette peine contre l'hérétique, mais sans préciser la juridiction qui doit l'infliger ' (*op. cit.* ii. 32–3, 33, n. 2).

[3] His incorrigibility is presumably failure to perform the penance imposed upon him. Cf. the gloss to *Decretales*, ii. i. 4, *s.v.* Iudici.

[4] *Ibid.* v. xx. 7 : ' Postquam per ecclesiasticum iudicem fuerint degradati, saeculari potestati tradantur, secundum constitutiones legitimas puniendi ' ; although in the particular case he reserves the punishment to the Church (cf. *supra*, p. 218).

but the Church shall intercede for him that he may not suffer sentence of death.[1]

These judgements and rescripts of later popes certainly indicate a departure from the unusually exclusive policy adopted by Becket and Alexander III ; but the divergence is one of policy rather than of principle. It would surely be rash to suppose that the pope of the *Deliberatio super facto imperii*, the pope who gave King John his kingdom, wished to give the State more extensive rights over clergy than Alexander III had allowed. Urban, Celestine, and Innocent, all call upon the State to assist the Church in the suppression of offenders ; they advocate practices which have been declared in the past by royal law [2] and local custom ; [3] but from the canon lawyer's point of view the action of the State is its duty, not its right. It may only act when its aid is invoked. The Church need not appeal to the secular power to coerce her errant members ; but, if need be, she may make the appeal. ' Note that for any crime . . . one *can* be handed over to the secular court ' : so speaks Innocent IV, commenting upon the decretal *Novimus*.[4] *Posse*, not *debere*.

The canonists in practice tend to make delivery to the secular arm a common consequence of degradation by confining the latter penalty to cases of incorrigibility and heresy, where the Church needs lay assistance ; but their view of the matter leaves delivery to the discretion of the Church. From one point of view, the Church limits its own jurisdiction in the period under discussion, refraining from the use of banishment which Becket had used and Urban III ordered, defining cases of forfeiture of privilege. Another aspect shows the gradual elaboration of canonical penalties ; so that a felonous clerk might suffer prolonged and painful punishment and still remain entirely within the jurisdiction of the Church.

The canonists' theory must be compared with the English custom after Henry II. Did the felonous clerk only receive punishment in the court christian, and what penalties did that court inflict ? Was the ex-clerk, degraded in the court christian, liable to a second punishment by the secular authority ? At present, authorities do not agree on the answers to these questions. Maitland says : ' At least in theory there were many punishments at the bishop's disposal. The chief limit to his power was set by the elementary rule that the Church would never pronounce a judgment of blood.' [5] This sums up the canonical position, but avoids the question of usual practice. According to Dr. Gabel,

---

[1] *Decretales*, v. xl. 27 (*Novimus*).

[2] The council of Verneuil (755) agrees very closely with Celestine III's rule (cited, Génestal, ii. 11).

[3] Cf. Norman custom quoted by Poole, *loc. cit.* p. 243.

[4] Quoted, Génestal, ii. 49 n.

[5] Pollock and Maitland, *Hist. Eng. Law*, i. 444.

222 *THE PUNISHMENT OF FELONOUS CLERKS*

' as a rule ', in the later middle ages, ' the clerk convicted of felony was degraded and remanded to the bishop's prison for life '.[1] Mr. Poole has recently advanced ' some evidence to show that during the later years of the twelfth and the first half of the thirteenth centuries felonous clerks were sometimes degraded from their orders and forced to abjure the realm '.[2] Here then are three possibilities to be considered. Was there in use a variety of punishments inflicted by the Church ; or one kind of double penalty inflicted by the Church ; or a kind of double penalty in which the State co-operated with the Church ?

Before the actual records of procedure are examined, it will be as well to consider a few general statements which throw light upon English practice in the period. Henry II had demanded that the clerk who was convicted or who confessed should be degraded,[3] and should be protected by the Church no longer. In other words, the king would respect the Church's claim to judge and punish a felonous clerk, but reserved the right to punish the criminal sentenced in the court christian. Becket made this double punishment the main ground of his objection to the Constitutions of Clarendon ; the king withdrew the obnoxious parts of the Constitutions in 1176 ; and so we might infer, save indications to the contrary, that henceforth in England the felonous clerk was immune from punishment by the secular power.

Bracton certainly supports this notion. According to this great royal judge (who was also archdeacon of Barnstaple),

when a clerk . . . is taken for homicide or other crime and imprisoned, and is demanded for the court christian by the ordinary . . . he shall be immediately delivered without any inquiry being then made. He is not to be set free entirely . . . but kept safely in the bishop's prison (or in the king's prison if the ordinary so wish) until he shall have purged himself of the crime imputed to him, or shall have failed in his purgation, in which circumstance he ought to be degraded. . . . When a clerk thus convicted of a crime shall be degraded, no other punishment follows . . ., except in the case of apostasy.[4]

The most interesting feature of this description is its fidelity to canonistic theory. It gives the State no right to judge or punish a clerk, and if the canons did actually leave room for other penalties than degradation, yet at the time when Bracton wrote, degradation was the usual canonical penalty. Unfortunately, as Dr. Gabel has observed, in one particular Bracton's account is at variance with contemporary practice. The accused clerk was *not* always delivered without inquiry to the ordinary. During

---

[1] Gabel, pp. 110–11. [2] Poole, p. 239, cf. p. 246.

[3] Degradation is not mentioned in the Constitutions of Clarendon, but is assumed in the subsequent controversy.

[4] Bracton, *De Legibus* (Rolls Series), ii. 298–300.

Henry III's reign it was becoming usual for a jury to give its verdict in the secular court, and a clerk convicted by the jury was delivered *pro quali* to the ordinary.[1] Here at least is one discrepancy between the customary procedure and the canons ; and Bracton has ignored the practice of the courts. Mr. Poole thinks that this discredits the rest of Bracton's description, and he is, therefore, prepared to find Bracton wrong when the latter declares degradation to be the only penalty of the felonous clerk. But the two parts of the process are hardly comparable. As Dr. Gabel has suggested, Bracton might regard the process of conviction in the lay court as unessential, a practice growing fairly common in his own day, but contrary to earlier custom, unrecognized by the canons, and having no practical consequence.[2] A secular punishment was a very different matter. Accuracy on this point was supremely important. If there was a custom of delivering degraded clerks to the secular arm or of outlawing them, it was *ex hypothesi* an old custom in Bracton's day, a survival of the period before Becket and Alexander III, vital to the clerk's privilege. If Bracton could ignore this, the archdeacon was prevailing over the royal judge to an unsuspected degree.

Later records give negative evidence which has a cumulative effect. The Statute of Westminster I assumes the practice of indictment in the secular court, but clearly treats the clerk's purgation as the test of his punishment or release.[3] Britton likewise speaks of clerks who are indicted of felony and *mescrus* : they are to be delivered to the ordinary and ' according as the ordinary shall certify us of the acquittance of those clerks, we will cause restitution to be made them of their goods, if they have not fled from our peace '.[4] These two statements simply bear witness to the usual recognition of the *privilegium* in English law ; but one may go farther and say that it would be strange for them to ignore jurisdiction over degraded clerks for the offence punished by degradation, if the secular court claimed the right to ignore the Church's jurisdiction or to add to the Church's penalty.

It remains to be seen to what extent the common practice of the courts corresponded to these statements of the law. Britton has already given a warning that on one point the common law of Edward I's time evades the intention of the canons. The king

---

[1] Cf. Gabel, ch. ii, and Poole, pp. 240 *seqq.* ; cf. *infra*, p. 228, n. 4.

[2] Lyndwood states the ecclesiastical attitude towards conviction of clerks in the secular court, *Provinciale*, v. xiv. 3, *s.v.* Pro convictis, and v. xiv. 2, *s.v.* Eorundem. Cf. Gabel, p. 40.

[3] 3 Edw. I, ch. 2 (*Stat. Realm*, i. 28) : ' Le Rey amoneste les prelaz . . . que ceaus qui sunt enditez de tiel ret, par solempne enqueste des prodes homes fete en la Court le Rey, en nul manere ne les delivrent saunz duwe purgacion ; issi que le Rey neit mester de metre i autre remedie.'

[4] *Britton* (ed. F. M. Nichols), i. 27–8.

224 *THE PUNISHMENT OF FELONOUS CLERKS*

confiscates the chattels of clerks who have fled, even if they eventually surrender and are acquitted.[1] More than this, the secular court will be found constantly to ignore the status of clerical fugitives from justice, and will outlaw them like any lay felon who has fled. There appears to be no canon in the *Corpus Iuris* prohibiting this action, and while the English clergy do sometimes protest against it, the king has a good answer. About the year 1245 the prelates protested that ' if clerks to whom crimes are imputed, being summoned before secular judges, fail to appear, they are banished '. To which the king's reply was as follows : ' When clerks to whom crimes are imputed fail to appear and are not claimed by their prelates, since it is not shown that they are clerks but left unknown . . . they are frequently banished for their manifest contumacy, particularly since, were they clerks, they might safely allege their clerical privilege '.[2] The clergy returned in later years to the same complaint,[3] but the court declaring sentence of outlawry could always argue that the clerk had to prove his status, and so by non-appearance forfeited his privilege. It is hardly necessary to illustrate this practice, which all authorities on the subject have observed,[4] unless it be to emphasize that sentence was passed when the court was obviously in no doubt as to the outlaw's clerical status. At the assizes held at Newcastle 40 Henry III, the jurors presented that ' Alan a clerk of Heyden broke open a chest in the church of Heyden. . . . And Alan at once fled and is suspect. Therefore let him be exacted and outlawed.' [5] The canon of Archbishop Boniface which imposes a penalty on those who outlaw clerks apparently remained a dead letter, like other canons of the series.[6] Cases are as common after 1261 as before.[7]

It sometimes happened that a clerk became an outlaw by making voluntary *abiuratio regni*. A criminal fleeing from justice might take sanctuary in any church and there, making confession, abjure the realm in the presence of the coroner.[8] *Abiuratio* was

---

[1] Cf. *infra*, p. 231.

[2] H. Cole, *Original Documents Illustrative of English History*, p. 356, art. xi.

[3] 1257, 1258, 1261 (Wilkins, *Concilia*, i. 727, 738, 750).

[4] Cf. Pollock and Maitland, i. 447 ; A. L. Poole, p. 243.

[5] *Northumberland Assize Rolls* (Surtees Soc.), p. 86 ; cf. *ibid.* p. 88, and earlier cases in Poole, p. 243. The case of John le Rus, a clerk accused of murder in 1221, is interesting. John fled and ' entered religion ' at Bath. His prior produced him before the royal justices, who delivered him to the Church with the admonition ' that he keep his cloister if he can purge himself ' (*Pleas of the Crown co. Glos.*, pl. 128, cited by Poole, p. 242).

[6] Cf. Lyndwood, *Provinciale*, ii. ii. 1, *s.v.* Contingit (ed. 1679, p. 92*a*).

[7] *Northumberland Assize Rolls*, pp. 345, 362 ; *Oxford City Docts.* (Oxf. Hist. Soc.), pp. 196, 198, 203, 204, 218 (Oxford eyre, 1285, nos. 6, 15, 16, 37, 39, 41, 83) ; *Wm. Salt Soc. Collections*, iv. 212, 213, 214 (Stafford assizes, 56 Henry III) ; *ibid.* vi. i. 262, 272 (Stafford assizes, 21 Edward I).

[8] A. Réville, ' L'*abjuratio regni* ' (*Revue Historique*, 1 (1892)).

a privilege which presented the criminal with an alternative to the penalty of death or mutilation. Since it was regarded by the Church as a merciful institution which saved laymen from the rigours of secular justice, it had no place as a penalty for clerks, who in no circumstances could receive a blood-sentence in the court christian.[1] Yet clerks did, it seems, occasionally flee to sanctuary and there make *abiuratio*. By so doing, they escaped imprisonment and trial by either court. The Church courts could scarcely approve of a practice which set clerks on a level with layfolk ; they claim for their own cognizance clerks who have taken sanctuary. But the lay power seems to have willingly permitted clerks to abjure, and even sometimes forced those to abjure who availed themselves of sanctuary. A clear example of this kind of occurrence is found on the Northumberland assize rolls of 40 Henry III. A Nottinghamshire clerk wounded mortally a Scotsman in Northumberland and ' fled to the church of Corbridge and acknowledged this deed there, and acknowledged that he had been a malefactor in his own country, by the receiving of robbers and other misdeeds ; and he abjured the realm in the presence of the coroner '.[2] In 1286 the Crown is found considering the legality of this practice. The bishop of Lincoln had demanded for the court christian one Richard of Scarborough, a clerk, who wished to abjure. The king ordered the clerk to be handed over to the bishop until the king's council should decide whether abjuration might be made.[3]

A suspect clerk might flee to a church simply to avoid lynching or summary punishment : to give himself time to establish his clergy ;[4] the coroner might force such an one to abjure the realm. This lay at the back of some ecclesiastical complaints, and Edward II granted in 1316 that, according to the laudable custom of the kingdom hitherto in use, a clerk, fleeing for felony to a church to have protection, declaring himself to be a clerk, is not bound to abjure the realm.[5]

---

[1] Cf. A. Réville, ' *L'abjuratio regni* ' (*Revue Historique*, l (1892)), p. 20.

[2] *Northumberland Assize Rolls*, p. 76. Cf. the case of Richard of Fulebroc', clerk, said to have escaped from prison at Ipswich, fled to church, and abjured the realm (1260. *Close Rolls, 1259–1261*, p. 247). Several persons without chattels and in no ward are recorded in the Oxford eyre of 1285 as having abjured : probably some at least were clerks. This record does not usually note the status of clerical prisoners, even when it is incidentally proved (*Oxford City Docts*. pp. 198-219, nos. 17, 22, 23, 30, 88).

[3] *Cal. Close Rolls, 1279–1288*, p. 399 ; cited by Réville (p. 20) from Prynne, *Records*, iii. 358, who prints the letter but misunderstands it.

[4] E.g. Oxford eyre, 1285 : ' Robertus de Pennoby et Johannes de Ardern posuerunt se in ecclesiam S. Aegidii ; et praedictus Robertus cognovit se esse latronem . . . et abiuravit regnum . . . Et Johannes exivit ab ecclesia praedicta, et reddidit se ad pacem domini regis, et . . . liberatus fuit episcopo pro convicto ' (*Oxford City Docts*. p. 219, no. 88). Cf. *infra*, p. 231.

[5] Articuli cleri xv (Wilkins, ii. 461–2) ; cf. *Provinciale*, III. xxviii. 1 (p. 256*a*, and *ibid*. p. 268*b*).

Two cases in Henry III's reign show the lay power attempting to banish delinquent clerks in other circumstances. In February 1226 the king ordered the bishop of Norwich's official to release from the bishop's prison Geoffrey the chaplain, who was imprisoned there at the king's command because he had been in Bedford castle with the king's enemies. The official was to have security from the chaplain that he would leave England immediately.[1] Here the king appears to be enforcing *abiuratio* for treason, without a trial in the court christian. Whether or no this was the intention, the order was rescinded. A month later the king wrote again to the official. Geoffrey is now stated to have been captured in Bedford castle, and imprisoned in the bishop's prison, because he had celebrated divine service while excommunicate in the said castle.[2] The chaplain's treason has been transformed into an ecclesiastical offence, the royal authority for his imprisonment is now ignored. It looks as though Pandulf, as upon an earlier occasion,[3] had asserted the *privilegium fori*, and the king avoided friction by withdrawing the original charge. The second case of abjuration that calls for mention is that of a subdeacon in the diocese of Exeter, 1238.[4] He had been outlawed, in circumstances unknown ; when he returned and was recaptured, his bishop claimed him and admitted him to purgation, in which he was successful. The Crown objected to his going free. An outlaw, it contended, was liable to be hanged, and in this case, in deference to the clerk's status, hanging should be commuted to abjuration. Here the Crown is carrying one stage farther its claim that the clerk who has failed to appear in the secular court to be claimed cannot afterwards plead his clergy. An outlaw could only be given a hearing in any court, if he had been inlawed. There is no question of a double punishment for clerks, and the Crown seeks rather to circumvent than to deny the *privilegium fori*. At a later period the clergy recognize the liability of outlaws to the death-penalty, and on this ground object to the practice of forcing clerks to abjure the realm.[5]

While the lay court regularly asserts its jurisdiction over

---

[1] *Rot. Lit. Claus.* (ed. Hardy), ii. 97a : ' accepta prius ab eo securitate sufficienti quod statim post deliberacionem suam exibit a terra Angl' '. A rather similar order had been issued after the Treaty of Lambeth in 1218 (*ibid.* i. 377a). Dr. Tillmann probably rightly assumes that this was virtually the work of the legate Guala (*Die päpstlichen Legaten*, p. 115).

[2] *Rot. Lit. Claus.* ii. 101a. According to the Dunstable annals, ' capellanus vero castri archiepiscopo liberatus est, per forum ecclesiae iudicandus ' (*Ann. Mon.* iii. 88).

[3] *Ann. Mon.* i. 217. It is not clear that the letter of Pandulf about an imprisoned clerk, in 1219, refers to a criminal, although Prynne reads it so (*Pat. Rolls, 1216–1225*, p. 185 ; Prynne, *Records*, iii. 41).

[4] *Close Rolls, 1237–1242*, p. 122 ; cited, Pollock and Maitland, i. 444, Gabel, pp. 113–14, Poole, p. 245.

[5] Articuli cleri xv.

fugitives, and claims clerks who have forfeited their privilege according to the canons,[1] there can be no doubt that when a man pleaded and proved his clergy and was claimed by the ordinary, the lay court delivered him. Under Henry III the clergy do indeed complain from time to time that clerks are imprisoned by the lay power and withheld when the ordinary claims them.[2] This can only have been an occasional abuse. The king replies to complaints that clerks are arrested by the lay power when there is fear of their flight, and that they are afterwards delivered to their prelates at their request to be judged.[3] The king's letters of 1255 confirm this by ordering a criminous clerk to be handed over to the ordinary ' secundum libertatem predictam [ecclesiasticam] et modum et consuetudinem in regno regis hactenus optentam '.[4] This seems to be the normal procedure in the courts, so far as extant records permit one to observe it. Violence was occasionally done to the privilege of clerks : in 1209 some Oxford scholars were hanged ;[5] in 1299 the bishop of Hereford asked the king to order restoration to sanctuary of a clerk who had fled thither and had been forcibly abstracted and imprisoned in a lay prison.[6] But on the other hand, the lay authorities were sometimes more than necessarily punctilious in their regard for the clerk's privilege. About 1194–5 a chaplain accused of complicity in a murder was said to have been ordained priest by the bishop of Coventry after he had been appealed. It was adjudged that the chaplain should be held until the bishop should deliver him.[7] In 1221 William de Bracy fled to sanctuary, and the abbot of Bordesley came and led him away as a monk.

[1] Stafford Assize Roll, 21 Edward I : ' Richard de Swynescho taken for homicide and robbery was put on his trial and pleaded he was a *clericus :* and it was testified that the said Richard was a bigamist . . . per quod privilegio clericali gaudere non debet. Richard admitted this to be true and put himself on the country ' (*W. Salt Soc. Collections,* vi. i. 284). Cf. *supra,* p. 217.

[2] Cole, *Original Documents,* p. 356 (? *1245*) ; Wilkins, i. 724, 727 *(1257)* ; cf. *infra,* p. 230, n. 1.

[3] ' Responsio. Clerici propter homicidia et alia huiusmodi flagicia in facto deprehensi aut alii appellati seu puplice de huiusmodi notati et accusati, arestantur per potestatem secularem cum de subtractione vel fuga ipsorum timetur, et suis prelatis ad eorum requisicionem iudicandi postea liberantur ' (Cole, p. 356).

[4] *Close Rolls, 1254–1256,* p. 96. An earlier mandate to the sheriff of Devon (1227) should be read in the light of this : the king orders John Attestan', clerk, imprisoned on a charge of murder, to be given reasonable sustenance ' donec secundum consuetudinem regni iudicatum fuerit quid de ipso Iohanne fuerit faciendum ' (*Rot. Lit. Claus.* ii. 188a).

[5] *Ann. Mon.* iv. 54. Cf. the complaints of the clergy, 1237 and 1257, cited by Poole, p. 240, n. 3, and *supra,* p. 218, n. 1.

[6] *Reg. R. de Swinfield* (Canterbury and York Soc.), p. 359.

[7] I.e. until the bishop should send to claim jurisdiction over him and so deliver him from his lay gaolers (*Three Rolls of the King's Court* (Pipe Roll Soc. xiv), p. 2). It is of course possible that the man was in orders when the offence was committed, but if so there would be no reason for mentioning his ordination as priest.

228 *THE PUNISHMENT OF FELONOUS CLERKS*

The justices amerced the abbot for receiving William as a monk, but apparently William did not appear in court and was not punished.[1] In the Somerset eyre 1225 a clerk was not claimed and the court did not proceed to judgement.[2] But clerks could only expect to be delivered from the lay prison if the ordinary came into court to claim them.

A clerk, when claimed, is handed over to the court christian either straightway[3] or after a jury's verdict has been taken,[4] and the records of the secular court take no further notice of his case. The practice is seen particularly clearly in those instances when clerks and laymen are implicated in the same crime. The layman's penalty is stated : the record is silent as to the clerk's fate. In the rolls of the king's court, 1194–5, a woman and a clerk are appealed of a murder and are to come before the justices. The woman is to clear herself by ordeal : *mundet se per ignem,* but no such trial is recorded for her clerical companion.[5] This record is so brief as to leave room for doubt. There is a clearer example from Wells, perhaps belonging to the year 1201. Three brothers were accused of murder. Roger and Henry were outlawed for this. But Hugh came and pleaded his clergy as a subdeacon, ' and let him answer when and where he ought. And the archdeacon claimed [cognizance for] court christian. Let him have it.'[6] So also at Bedford in 1202 four men were accused of a murder. ' Robert and Peter are outlawed by their suit for the said death, and . . . William fled to church and abjured the realm . . . Gilbert confessed . . . And Robert the dean of Bedford craved [cognizance for] court christian, for Gilbert is a clerk, and a subdeacon.'[7] At Northampton in the same

---

[1] *Sel. Pleas Crown* (Selden Soc.), i. 86, no. 135, also in *Rolls of Justices in Eyre* (Selden Soc.), pp. 558–9, no. 1141. Robert of Rushock, suspected of murder, was permitted by King John (for a price) to enter religion as a monk of Worcester, probably (according to Mrs. Stenton) before his conviction (*ibid.* pp. 627–9, no. 1298).

[2] ' Et quia clericus est iudicium ponatur in respectum. Custodiatur. Nullus eum petit ' (*Sel. Pleas Crown,* i. 118, no. 185). Cf. several examples from Edward I's time in Gabel, pp. 42, 44–5, 56–8.

[3] Examples of immediate delivery, apparently without conviction in the secular court, are common in the first half of the thirteenth century : *Somerset Pleas* (Somerset Rec. Soc.), i, nos. 84, 89, 93 (*c. 1201*), no. 1175 (*27 Hen. III*); *Sel. Pleas Crown,* i, no. 54 (*1202*), no. 189 (*1220*); *Rolls of Justices in Eyre,* no. 543 (*1218*); *Bracton's Notebook,* ii, no. 490 (*1231*), iii, no. 1453 (*1220*); *Rot. Lit. Claus.* ii. 203a (*1227*); *Northumb. Assize Rolls,* p. 125 (*40 Hen. III*).

[4] Examples of verdicts from Henry III's reign are given by Gabel, p. 36 (earliest, *34 Hen. III*) and Poole, p. 241 (earliest, *1221*), to which may be added the case of a clerk's delivery to the court christian on the assize rolls *12 Hen. III* : ' It was afterwards testified that he was not guilty ' (*Wm. Salt Soc. Collections,* iv. 70).

[5] *Three Rolls of the King's Court,* p. 83.

[6] *Sel. Pleas Crown,* i, no. 117. True, the record below says ' Hugo et Rogerus qui utlagati sunt fuerunt in thedinga de Chaunedon ', but this is almost certainly a mistake for ' Henricus et Rogerus . . .' (cf. *infra,* p. 235).

[7] *Ibid.* no. 49.

year a charge of violence was brought against a clerk and two
laymen. ' And the dean craved [cognizance for] court christian
for Thomas, and had him, for he is a clerk. And Osbert and
William are outlawed.' [1]

It might be inferred from Henry III's reply to the clergy's
gravamina that clerks were delivered for immediate purgation
as soon as they were captured and imprisoned ; and the records
which have been quoted show the immediate delivery of clerks
by the royal judges. But the two things are not the same.
It seems to have been an established rule that clerks accused of
felony must not be tried or purged until they had pleaded
their clergy before the royal judges who took the pleas of the
Crown. This might, of course, involve imprisonment for years in
a royal or episcopal prison. Consequently, one finds the king
in 1226 granting bail to a clerk accused of murder, until the next
assizes,[2] and commonly ordering his sheriffs and constables to
deliver clerks in their charge to the ordinary : ' to be produced
before the justices when they shall come into those parts, according
to the custom of the realm of England '.[3] The practice explains
and partly justifies the clergy's complaints of delay.

Thus the lay authorities always insisted that the clerk suspected of a felony should establish his clergy by appearing in
the royal court. If he failed to surrender, he was outlawed ;
if he was arrested, he was kept in prison until he could appear
before the royal judges. These customs hamper the *privilegium
fori*, but do not contradict it. The practice of convicting felonous
clerks before their delivery to the court christian suggests a more
direct interference with the claim of the Church to be sole judge.
Although Archbishop Pecham in an undated canon implicitly
accepts the practice,[4] the clergy as a body object to it in 1280.
They complain that ' clerks imprisoned for civil or criminal
offence or delict are not delivered to the ordinary unless judgement has previously been pronounced against them by laymen '.
The king's reply insists that clerks who have been delivered to
their prelate should, before purgation, be presented again in the
lay court, there to be pronounced guilty or innocent, as has hitherto

---

[1] *Earliest Northants. Assize Rolls* (Northants. Rec. Soc.), no. 78.

[2] *Rot. Lit. Claus.* ii. 162a.

[3] *Ibid.* ii. 27a *(1225)*, cf. *ibid.* ii. 26a *(1225)* ; *Close Rolls, 1251–1253*, pp. 155, 277,
286, 312, 317, 345. The practice apparently goes back at least as far as John's reign :
' Mandatum est vicecomiti Linc' quod reddi faciat decano et capitulo Linc' equum
qui fuit W. subdecani Linc' quem ballivi Linc' captum tenent pro morte eiusdem subdecani et Simonem clericum captum pro morte eiusdem per salv' pleg' deliberari
faciat ' *(Rot. Lit. Claus.* i. 54a *(1205))*. Grosseteste and Adam Marsh protest against
it *(Ann. Mon.* i. 424, 425), and in 1257 the clergy states that it sometimes causes a delay
of five or six years (Wilkins, i. 727).

[4] Wilkins, ii. 48–9 *(s.a. 1280)*.

been customary.[1] For what purpose, one may ask, did the lay authorities convict the clerk, if not for the purpose of punishing him later on ? The first conviction of the clerk, in the lay court, gave the lay authorities good justification for retaining temporarily the confiscated chattels of the convict. If the court christian confirmed the sentence of the lay court, the chattels presumably remained in the king's hands.[2] This question of chattels may explain the custom of securing conviction before delivery. It should be noticed that the custom was sometimes of advantage to the accused ; for if a clerk did not plead his clergy and was not claimed by the ordinary, his acquittal in the lay court probably ended the matter.[3] This is suggested by several records. An early case is found on the close rolls of 16 John :

Rex vicecomiti Northampt' salutem. Precipimus tibi quod Robertum Foliot clericum et Hugonem capellanum, qui capti fuerunt et imprisonati eo quod male credebantur et quos nullus appellat ut dicitur, facias deliberari.[4]

Again, at the Warwickshire eyre 1221, Hugh the parson of Pillerton appears in court accused of violence and abduction, and ' defends the whole as a clerk and declines to plead before this court, but without pleading is willing to tell the truth '. He is heard and acquitted, and there is no record of his delivery to the ordinary.[5] Even in cases where the clerk is actually claimed for the bishop and delivered as innocent, one may suppose that there were usually no further proceedings.[6] In one case where a clerk gets a favourable verdict in the lay court, his accuser is told that she may proceed against him in the court christian, if she wish.[7]

[1] ' 15. Item clerici incarcerati ex quacunque causa civili vel criminali vel delicto non liberantur ordinario nisi prius per laicos prolato iudicio contra ipsos.
' Responsio regis. Decrevit dominus rex ut clerici capti pro quocunque reatu per ballivos seculares prelatis eos requirentibus liberentur, representandi tamen ab eis in seculari iudicio cum fuerint requisiti, pronunciandi rei vel innocentes per regis iusticiarios sub testimonio laicorum, ut hactenus fieri consuevit. Quod si prelatus clericum huiusmodi taliter non representaverit, centum libras sterlingorum domino regi solvere compelletur ' (Lambeth MS. 1213, fo. 139ᵛ). The articles, without the dated preamble or responses, are in Cole, pp. 361 *seqq.* ; with the replies they appear in Wilkins, ii. 316, *seqq.* In 1309 the clergy protested against this that ' contra libertatem ecclesiasticam respondetur ' (Wilkins, ii. 318).

[2] The clergy in 1257 argued against the confiscation of chattels of degraded clerks, on the ground that they had not and could not be condemned in a lay court (Wilkins, i. 724) : but the *gravamina* of the following years (1258 and 1261) only object to the penalizing of purged clerks.

[3] Thus Justice Staunton in 1313 : ' You must say that he was delivered after being found guilty by this court, for otherwise he would never have been delivered ' (quoted, Gabel, p. 40).

[4] *Rot. Lit. Claus.* i. 178*b*.

[5] *Sel. Pleas Crown*, i, no. 159 ; cf. *Northumb. Assize Rolls*, p. 350.

[6] Cf. *supra*, p. 228, n. 4 ; *Northumb. Assize Rolls*, p. 365 (7 *Edw. I*) ; *Trans. Bristol and Glos. Archaeol. Soc.* xxii. 161 (*15 Edw. I*) ; *Wm. Salt Soc. Coll.* vi. i. 279, 283.

[7] *Northumb. Assize Rolls*, pp. 91–2 (*40 Henr. III*).

From the canonical point of view, the clerk who had been delivered and had succeeded in his purgation was entitled to restitution of his chattels ; but in practice the chattels were sometimes withheld. That, at least, was the complaint of the clergy in 1257, 1258, and 1261.[1] The complaint may have been justified, but both before and after these years the king is found ordering sheriffs and others to restore confiscated chattels to purged clerks.[2] Apparently, also, clerks who had avoided arrest forfeited their chattels, even though they surrendered and secured acquittal. At Gloucester, 15 Edward I, Robert of Newent, a chaplain, was accused of murder. But the jurors swore that he was not guilty and so he was quit of that. But he had 'in fear fled to the church of the Holy Trinity and kept himself there for two months and afterwards gave himself up to the peace. Therefore let his chattels be confiscated for his flight.'[3] For the restitution of chattels a clerk had to obtain through his bishop[4] letters from the king to the sheriff. In certain of the letters the order for restitution is made *de gracia regis speciali*. This phrase is used by the king in answering the clergy's *gravamina* in 1280 : purged clerks shall have their chattels 'sed non sine sua litera in qua contineatur de restitucione hac vice facienda quia hec restitucio fit de gracia speciali '.[5] The clergy commented unfavourably on this reply in 1309.[6] Thus the Crown, having confiscated a convicted clerk's chattels, still claims them, no matter what his fate in the court christian ; only as a special act of royal clemency will they be returned to a clerk whom the Church acquits. Leaving the *privilegium canonis* intact, the royal courts adopt a threatening attitude towards the *privilegium fori*. While it admits unreservedly the Church's jurisdiction over the persons of clerks, the Crown (at least by the time of Edward I) is vindicating its rights over the property of clerks found guilty in the lay court, just as it had established its jurisdiction in all ordinary civil actions concerning clerks. The principle is stated and not applied. Those responsible for the writ restoring chattels *de gracia regis*

---

[1] Wilkins, i. 727, 738, 750. It had not appeared in Grosseteste's protest against abuses a few years earlier (*Ann. Mon.* i. 424).

[2] *Rot. Lit. Claus.* i. 611a, 636a *(1224)* ; *Close Rolls, 1251–1253*, p. 195 ; *ibid. 1253–1254*, pp. 4, 5 ; *ibid. 1254–1256*, pp. 130, 259 ; *ibid. 1259–1261*, pp. 30, 54. Mr. Poole (p. 242) observes that in one of these cases there was to be further discussion. Against the letter ordering restitution of chattels to Robert of Trevoret is the note ' loquendum est cum consilio regis de hoc brevi ', but we cannot infer that the chattels were withheld (*ibid. 1254–1256*, p. 130).

[3] *Trans. Bristol and Glos. Archaeol. Soc.* xxii. 161. Also the case of Robert Sautemareys, whose purgation was deferred : ' et quia praedictus R. se subtraxerat pro morte praedicta, ideo catalla eius confiscantur pro fuga ' (*Northumb. Assize Rolls* , p. 368). Cf. *Britton*, cited *supra*, p. 223, and Gabel, p. 60.

[4] Cf. *Reg. Wm. Wickwane* (Surtees Soc.), pp. 261, 282.

[5] Lambeth MS. 1213, fo. 140r.   [6] Wilkins, ii. 319.

232 *THE PUNISHMENT OF FELONOUS CLERKS*

speciali presumably are clerics. They go thus far to assert the authority of the State they serve, at the cost of conceding to the Church in practice what stricter ecclesiastics demand as of right.

One fact seems proved by the evidence of the clerical *gravamina*. This withholding of chattels is the only complaint against the Crown in the matter of purged clerks. If, on the ground of the jury's conviction, the Crown had laid hands upon a purged clerk, that would assuredly have been the subject of the chief objection. The clergy have a long list of grievances, protesting indiscriminately against old usages and occasional abuses, but nowhere do they hint that the Crown failed to respect a canonical purgation, except by withholding confiscated chattels.

What was the fate of the *clericus convictus*, delivered to the court christian ? A very large proportion eventually had the opportunity to find compurgators, and the majority succeeded in their purgation.[1] But the purgatorial system was not so called for nothing. The clerk who would at last vindicate his character, with the easy oaths of friends or professional swearers, was first purified by a term of imprisonment. He was usually confined to prison until the royal justices visited his part of the country,[2] and even when he had been delivered to the ordinary for purgation, it was within the power of the bishop to defer the test indefinitely. Pecham ordered that convicted clerks should not be easily set free, or let off with a perfunctory purgation.[3] What may be called the ' purgatory ' of convicted clerks lasted in some cases for many years.[4] Moreover, in Edward I's reign, the Church court was employing the sworn inquisition in certain criminal cases, another indication of its willingness to accept a new procedure in the interest of justice. Accused clerks, whose guilt seemed established by this process, were imprisoned without being given a chance to purge themselves.[5] The procedure was made regular by a mandate of Archbishop Islip to his province in 1351.[6] It is also in the reign of Edward I that one occasionally

---

[1] Cf. Gabel, pp. 113–14.

[2] The clergy protested against this without avail in Henry III's reign (Pollock and Maitland, i. 441).

[3] Wilkins, ii. 48.

[4] See Gabel, pp. 109 *seqq.* The terrors of the medieval prison may explain the frequency with which clerks incur outlawry rather than stand their trial. Besides the many cases of death in prison which might be quoted, the following is a picturesque incident. A clerk was imprisoned at Norwich with a companion, for sheep-stealing. His companion escaped and carried the clerk upon his back to sanctuary, because the latter's feet ' were so putrefied by the duress of the prison that he could not walk ' (*Archaeol. Review*, ii. 210, from Gaol Delivery roll, 14 Edw. I).

[5] Examples in Gabel, pp. 97–8 ; *Reg. J. Romeyn* (Surtees Soc.), ii. 54 ; *Reg. Wm. Greenfield* (Surtees Soc.), ii. 116.

[6] Spelman, *Concilia*, ii. 597 (*Provinciale* (ed. 1679) suppl. ii. 54). There seems to be no reason but prejudice for Maitland to stigmatize this as ' a not very sincere effort ' (*Hist. English Law*, i. 444).

meets with a convict clerk delivered to the ordinary with the
proviso that his purgation be deferred during the royal pleasure ;
in a few cases the bare phrase *absque purgatione* seems to prohibit
purgation altogether.[1] A letter (which incidentally suggests that
the Church court was holding sworn inquisitions) came from
the king to the bishop of Worcester in 1292 : this forbids him
to take the purgation of clerks detained in his prison, whose
crimes are notorious ; but with regard to others he may take
such purgation.[2] This royal action is extremely significant. It
shows at once the growing determination of the lay power to
stop abuses of clerical privilege, and the strict attention to the
clergy's claim to be punished only by their own court. That no
objection was raised by the clergy perhaps indicates the Church's
genuine desire to tighten a lax system.

For clerks who failed in purgation or confessed their guilt,
Maitland says, ' at least in theory there were many punishments
at the bishop's disposal '. It has been seen that the canon
law prescribed sometimes imprisonment, sometimes degradation.
English ecclesiastical records of the period are quite insufficient
to tell us what the most usual punishments were. From the assize
rolls we hear incidentally that about 1202 a clerk was *exordinatus*
for his part in a murder committed in Lincolnshire, and that a
subdeacon was *deordinatus* on a similar charge.[3] A clerk was
degradatus for house-breaking about 27 Henry III.[4] This penalty
of degradation is also mentioned in several ecclesiastical documents
of Henry III's reign. On the other hand, imprisonment is the
penalty proposed by the last canon of the provincial council of
Lambeth 1261. All bishops are to possess strong prisons ; and
clerks habitually and incorrigibly given to crimes for which a
layman suffers the death-penalty shall be perpetually imprisoned.[5]
Two features of this canon have been commonly overlooked.[6]
Perpetual imprisonment is reserved for incorrigibles, and degradation is not mentioned as a part of the penalty. Imprisonment,
in fact, appears here, as later in the gloss to the *Sext*, for an alternative, not a supplement, to degradation. Unfortunately, no
records of the southern province indicate the common practice.
Apparently, the only cases of degradation to be found in bishop's
registers of the period come from the see of York. Here in 1271

---

[1] Pollock and Maitland, i. 444 ; Gabel, pp. 105–9 ; cf. *supra*, p. 217.

[2] *Reg. Godfrey Giffard* (Worcs. Hist. Soc.), p. 410.

[3] *Lincs. Assize Rolls* (Linc. Rec. Soc.), no. 924 (quoted, Poole, p. 244) ; *ibid.* no. 931.

[4] *Somerset Pleas* (Som. Rec. Soc.), i, no. 825.

[5] Wilkins, i. 755. Note that Adam Marsh (a friend of the archbishop) refers to
crimes which bring ' poenam sanguinis in laico, . . . depositionem in clerico ' (*Ann.
Mon.* i. 426). But Adam had died before the Council of Lambeth.

[6] Stubbs, *Const. Hist.* iii.[3] 359 ; Pollock and Maitland, i. 445 ; Gabel, p. 111 ;
Poole, p. 239, n. 4.

Archbishop Giffard degraded a man for stealing church ornaments, and expressly stated that no one ought to punish him further.[1] Forty cases of degradation are described with details in the registers of Romeyn, Corbridge, and Greenfield.[2]

If the felonous clerk were imprisoned by the bishop, the lay court could not touch him. But what if he were degraded ? The canon law admitted that the degraded clerk might in some circumstances be delivered or abandoned to the secular arm : at the beginning of the period delivery was not uncommon, at least on the continent. At first sight, the words of the English episcopate in 1237 seem to agree with this : the bishops as a body protest that clerks are not to be hanged by lay authority ' unless they have been convicted by their own judge and previously degraded '.[3] But this is open to another interpretation : that clerks were only subject to lay jurisdiction if they had for an earlier offence been degraded and forfeited their privilege.[4] Twenty years later, the bishops will press to extremity the argument *non bis in idipsum*, when they protest against the confiscation of a degraded clerk's chattels.[5] In view of this jealous insistence upon privilege, and of Bracton's explicit statement, one ought to demand indisputable record-evidence before admitting that the bishops in 1237 would allow a clerk degraded for a felony to be punished by the lay court for the same offence. If it was usual, it is strange to find no mention in writs ordering the delivery of clerks to the court christian. Presumably a lay officer would have habitually attended at purgations and degradations, but the bishops' registers contain no summons, notification, or other record of his presence. In fact, there seems to be no convincing proof that the lay court in England claimed to impose a second penalty. The cases which might be taken as examples of a double penalty prove upon examination to be explicable in other ways. They may be considered chronologically.

(i) As early as 1180 the Pipe Rolls mention an outlawed clerk ; but, as Mr. Poole observes, he may have been a fugitive.[6]

(ii) *c.* 1194–5, four men were accused of murder and the *curia regis* roll states baldly that they were outlawed ; it continues : ' et Silwester fuit in tithinga Martini de Winterburne et Osb' fuit in eadem tithinga et alii clerici ordinati '.[7] Here the character of

[1] *Reg. Walter Giffard* (Surtees Soc.), p. 242.
[2] *Reg. J. Romeyn*, i. 395–6, ii. 55 ; *Reg. T. Corbridge*, ii. 17, 23 ; *Reg. Wm. Greenfield*, i. 228, 245, 255, 256, 265. All these were clerks in minor orders. When Archbishop Corbridge degraded five clerks in 1303 each ' petit degradari '.
[3] ' nisi coram suo iudice convicti et prius degradati ' (*Ann. Mon.* i. 255).
[4] This may be, as the editor suggests, the reason for the hanging of a clerk reported in the Oxford eyre 1285 (*Oxford City Docts.* p. 223).
[5] *Supra*, p. 230, n. 2 ; quoted, Poole, p. 242.   [6] Cited, Poole, p. 244.
[7] *Three Rolls of the King's Court*, p. 113.

the record definitely suggests that the accused did not appear to stand their trial, and were outlawed as fugitives.

(iii) The same possibility holds in regard to ' Willelmus clericus de Harewedon ', outlawed by the justices in eyre in 1202.[1]

(iv) The case of Ralph, brother of William de Netelham, on the Lincoln Assize Rolls 1202, confronts us for the first time with a degraded clerk. Since this has been adduced as the only example of degradation followed by outlawry,[2] it deserves special attention. William and Ralph were accused of murder, and William cleared himself of the charge. ' Radulfus clericus fuit et convictus in curia cristianitatis exordinatus est.' Later in the roll, among disconnected jottings, comes the entry : ' Radulfus de Netelham utlagatus, fuit in franco plegio Willelmi de Netelham in Suterton.' While one is naturally tempted to assume the identity of the degraded clerk and the outlaw, there appears to be an insuperable objection. The outlaw had been in a tithing ; but, according to various authorities, clerks were not placed in tithings.[3] The evidence of their exemption is not confined to Bracton, whom Morris cites ; it emerges from several court records, including the second case quoted above.[4] Ralph, William of Netelham's brother, must therefore take his place among felonous clerks who were degraded, and of whom nothing more is known.[5]

(v) The case of a subdeacon of Exeter diocese has already come in question.[6] One is not told the reason for his outlawry, but it may well have been because of his non-appearance ; it was only upon his return that he purged himself in the court christian.

(vi) In 27 Henry III a clerk and two others were outlawed in the county court, as accomplices to a murder. Again the record permits the assumption that the men were outlawed as fugitives.[7]

(vii) Lastly, in none of the cases of degradation cited above is a further penalty of any sort mentioned.

To sum up the inferences from these scraps of evidence. It

---

[1] Cited, Poole, p. 240, n. 3.   I have been unable to verify the reference.

[2] *Lincs. Assize Rolls*, nos. 924, 963 ; cited, Poole, p. 244.

[3] Pollock and Maitland, i. 568 ; W. A. Morris, *The Frankpledge System*, pp. 74–5.

[4] Cf. Assize Roll, 5 John : *Willelmus clericus de Adgaresle* fled for a murder ; ' et fuit clericus : in nullo franco plegio manens est, ideo interrogetur ' (*Wm. Salt Soc. Coll.* iii. 96). Cf. Assize Roll, 56 Hen. III : Adam fled for homicide and was outlawed ; ' he has no chattels and is in no tything because he is a clerk ' (*ibid.* iv. 213). A similar case, 21 Edw. I (*ibid.* vi. i. 262) ; another, 14 Edw. I (Norwich : *Archaeol. Review*, ii. 212–13).

[5] An alternative hypothesis is that Ralph the degraded clerk was put in frankpledge and, failing to answer for a subsequent crime, was then outlawed. The form of the second entry definitely suggests that non-appearance (for which the tithing would be amerced) was the cause of the outlawing.

[6] *Supra*, p. 226.   [7] *Somerset Pleas*, i, no. 939.

seems likely that in England during the century and a half which followed the death of Becket, the *privilegium fori* was generally observed in the punishment of felonous clerks. The canonical punishments for the felon are imprisonment and degradation, and the former penalty gradually becomes commoner. Not only do the canonists defend any felonous clerk until he is degraded ; but the English courts admit the ecclesiastical definition of clergy, and do not inflict a second personal punishment upon a degraded clerk. The establishing of the custom of conviction before delivery does not entail a penalty on the clerk who purges himself in the court christian ; it does mean that the convicted clerk who is later found guilty in his own court forfeits his chattels : this is the limit of lay punishment. But the clerk must have proved his clergy. By insistence upon this rule the Crown gains jurisdiction over any clerk who flees from justice or voluntarily abjures the realm.

ADDITIONAL NOTES

This essay is concerned with the practice of English courts, lay and ecclesiastical, about clerks accused of felony, from Henry II to Edward II. The remarks on pp.217-21 on the canon law of the privilegium fori were designed simply by way of introduction. Since the paper was written canonistic doctrines on the subject have been much studied ; and their relevance to Constit. Clarendon c.3 has been discussed in many historical works, those, for instance, of Raymonde Foreville, David Knowles, and Beryl Smalley. Charles Duggan made a notable analysis of twelfth-century canonical opinions in 'The Becket dispute and the criminous clerks',Bull.Inst. Hist. Res. xxxv (1962) 1-28, reprinted in Canon Law in Medieval England; The Becket dispute and decretal collections (London, 1982). For a full and balanced statement see the commentary by C.N.L. Brooke on Const. Clarendon c.3 in Councils & synods,i.857-62. See also Landau,'Ursprung und Entwicklung des Verbotes doppelter Straf-verfolgung wegen desselben Verbrechens in der Geschichte des kanonischen Rechts', Ztsch. der Savigny-Stiftung für Rechtsgesch., Kan. Abt. 56 (1970) 124-56, and B. Schimmelpfennig, 'Die Abset-zung von Klerikern', Mon. Iuris Canonici, series C, vol. 6 (1980) 517-32.
For the practice of English lay courts, the printed judicial records of the 13th-14th centuries are vastly more numerous than those accessible in 1936:a guide to publications before 1971 is in Gross's Bibliography of English history to 1485, ed. E.B. Graves (Oxford 1975). They illustrate more fully many points of procedure and so add precision and a surer chronological framework (e.g., the return of chattels to purged clerks de gratia speciali (cf. pp.231-2) seems from the evidence of the Close Rolls to begin in 1262). More

might now be said about the varying treatment of the clerks charged
with forgery of seals, coins, and documents, about sworn inquests
imposed by bishops, and about instances of long imprisonment
before purgation. Two more cases of degradation in 1244 and 1277
(The London eyre of 1244, ed. H.M. Chew and M. Weinbaum (1970)
no.58 and J.R. Wright, The Church & the English crown 1305-34
(Toronto,1980)p.221 n.167) do not add much to the scarce evidence
noted on pp.233-4. The records show that many accused clerks took
to flight. Particular aspects of the subject are touched on, mainly
elucidating practice and law in a later period, by R.B. Pugh, Imprisonment in medieval England (Cambridge, 1968) and J.G. Bellamy,
The law of treason in England in the later Middle Ages (Cambridge,
1970).Two scholars, in valuable monographs on the Church of the
early 14th century, have exploited both the printed material and
much that is less accessible in P.R.O. files and in Canterbury and
Worcester archives:R.M. Haines, The administration of the diocese of Worcester in the first half of the 14th century (1965) pp.
181-6 and J.R. Wright, The Church and the English crown,pp.217-
22. Dr. Wright judiciously concludes, on the basis of the records
of archbishop Reynolds, that 'the administration of ecclesiastical
discipline depended - probably increasingly - upon the operation of
the secular power'(p.222). J.A. Watt, in 'Edward I and the Irish
Church' ,Medieval studies presented to Aubrey Gwynn (Dublin,1961)
gives (pp.153-6) a well-documented and succinct account of the working of the privilege of the clergy in the common law area of Ireland
concluding that they 'had their privilege in the same way as the
clergy in England'.
The gravamina repeatedly presented to the crown (to a.d.1309 now
printed in Councils & synods,ii) point to occasional blatant disregard
by lay officials;but such cases seldom appear on plea rolls or in
bishops' registers. When Winchelsey ordered action in 1299 against
infringers of the privilege, the bishop of Lincoln reported that no
cases were known in his diocese (Reg. O. Sutton, vi.188). More
often the gravamina turn on curtailments of the privilege imposed
by the lay courts:(1) by denying it in actions (including trespass)
other than prosecutions for felony, and (2) by insisting on the submission of the clerk to plead his clergy, on a jury's verdict before
delivery to the ordinary, on the production of the clerk before the
justices, and so on.The strident complaints on these matters presented by the English Church at the C. of Vienne (printed in Councils &
synods,ii.1353-5) cut no ice. The crown stuck to custom. A decision
of the Rota Romana in the mid-14th century condemning the crown's
customary cognizance of civil actions against clergy was devoid of
practical results and, as Walter Ullmann shows, was no 'more than
a mirror of an ecclesiologically conditioned jurisprudence' (The
papacy & political ideas in the Middle Ages (Variorum reprints,1976,
IX p.461), which may be compared with his remarks in Law and
politics in the Middle Ages (1975)182-4. See also F.W. Maitland,
Roman canon law in the Church of England,pp.59-62, who cites the
decision.

XII

NORWICH CATHEDRAL PRIORY IN THE FOURTEENTH CENTURY.

W HEN Bishop James Goldwell visited his cathedral priory of Norwich in 1492-1493 he demanded the observance of the statutes and injunctions of William Bateman, his predecessor.[1] William Bateman had died in 1355. The renewal in this fashion of a bishop's injunctions after he was dead for 138 years suggests they were of some permanent impor- tance, and that the bishops of Norwich in the intervening period had not been active in legislating for their monastery. Unfor- tunately the surviving episcopal registers of Norwich in the fourteenth century contain no visitation records, which were doubtless preserved in separate books or rolls.[2] How often the cathedral was visited in state by its bishop, " sedens pro tribunali," remains a matter for doubt. Although a later docu- ment speaks of the bishop's septennial visitation, it is unlikely that there was any regularity in practice. Of late have come to

[1] *Visitations of the diocese of Norwich*, ed. A. Jessopp (Camden Soc., 1888), p. 7 : " Statuta et Injunctiones recolendae memoriae domini Willelmi Bateman praedecessoris nostri, alias in visitatione sua facta, praesertim de mulieribus infra cepta monasterii non pernoctandis nec suspecte introducendis, monemus et volumus quod in suo robore permaneant et vigore." For *monemus* (*mnomus* in the MS.), *innovamus* should probably be read.

[2] Professor Hamilton Thompson kindly informs me that Bateman's episcopal register contains no record of this visitation. Jessopp published the later visita- tions (1492-1536) from the paper registers of visitations which Tanner took from Norwich. Fourteenth-century parochial visitations are recorded on three parch- ment rolls in the Bodleian (Norfolk rolls, 16, 17, 18), while another membrane records an inquiry at St. Peter's Priory, Ipswich (1327-1336), (Suffolk rolls, 19, printed in *Engl. Hist. Review*, xlvii. 268-272) ; these likewise must have come from the episcopal archives.

© *The John Rylands Library, Manchester, 1936*

94

light some injunctions delivered to the monastery after Bishop John Salmon's visitation in 1309, but there seems no proper reason for their editor's supposition that this prelate had previously visited the priory twice.[1] Nor does there seem to be proof of any visitation between the times of Salmon and of Bateman.

The latest biographer of William Bateman infers that this bishop was active as a visitor from a consideration of his itinerary. He seems to have begun his primary visitation of the diocese in the summer of 1345, and it may have lasted, with intervals, over four years ; but "no official programme survives."[2] The itinerary suggests that Bateman's visitation of the cathedral priory, resulting in the injunctions which Goldwell saw, took place during his long sojourn at Norwich from November 1346 until late in July 1347.[3] This is confirmed by the evidence of the injunctions themselves. Missing from the episcopal archives, they come to light in two texts which clearly belonged to the cathedral priory.

The John Rylands Library Latin MS. 226 is the original, in the form of a small parchment book, dated at the bishop's palace, Norwich, 5th May, 1347, showing the mark of the bishop's seal applied to the last page.[4] The form of this *libellus* of sixteen pages is interesting, for such documents are scarce. The earlier injunctions of 1309, which have luckily been preserved among the cathedral muniments, were written on one side of a large sheet of parchment, with the bishop's seal appended. Until recently the

---

[1] Injunctions printed by E. H. Carter, *Studies in Norwich Cathedral History* (Norwich, 1935), pp. 19-24, dated " 14 kal. Feb. 1308," i.e. 1308/9 ; on frequency of visitation, see *ibid.*, pp. 7-8, 15, 54. The injunctions of 1309 refer to the archbishop's injunctions, suggesting that Winchelsey had visited the cathedral during his metropolitan circuit of 1304, unless they go back to Pecham's visitation of 1281, when the archbishop apparently visited the cathedral (cf. *Hist. MSS. Commission, Report V*, app. p. 449).

[2] " William Bateman, Bishop of Norwich, 1344-1355," by A. Hamilton Thompson, *Norfolk Archaeology*, XXV. i. (1933), p. 115, cf. p. 110.

[3] According to law Bateman should have commenced his circuit with the visitation of the cathedral (*Sext*, III. xx. 1 §§ 1, 6), but this rule seems seldom to have been observed.

[4] The remains of red wax indicate a pointed oval seal $2\frac{5}{8}'' \times 1\frac{5}{8}''$; this corresponds approximately to the second of Bateman's seals listed in Birch's British Museum Catalogue (no. 2041 : $2\frac{1}{2}'' \times 1\frac{1}{2}''$).

Rylands MS. was bound in one volume with two printed incuna-
bula and a small fourteenth-century manuscript ; the volume belonged in the early sixteenth century to the Sherbrooke family of
Norfolk. On a flyleaf (fo. 1ᵛ of the injunctions) is the inscription :
" Ex codicibus Cuthberti Shirbroke de Rockelande infra decana-
tum de Broke Norwicensis diocesis clerici." Another sixteenth-
century hand has written upon a blank leaf (fo. 10ʳ) : " Robertus
Sherbrook est verus possesser huius libri, testis Thomas Sherbrook Anno Domino."

Bishop Bateman ordered that his injunctions should be
copied, bound, and hung up publicly in the chapter-house for
all to see : ¹ a copy was also to be made within a fortnight for
each of the five cells of Norwich, to be preserved in the same
way. None of these copies is known, but another is found in
the middle of a book from the cathedral priory, MS. 370 in the
library of Corpus Christi College, Cambridge.² To judge by
the hand and other contents of the book in the same hand, this
copy was written not very long after the original. It is a fairly
accurate transcript and is of interest for its omissions, which
correspond with certain passages deleted in the original.

Of the visitor little need be said. Professor Hamilton
Thompson's recent sketch of his episcopate makes it clear that
Bateman lived generally on good terms with his cathedral convent,
of which three priors in succession acted as the bishop's vicar-
general. If, as is probable, Bateman held his visitation in the
early days of 1347, he was making use of a time of enforced

---

¹ Other visitors sometimes ordered their injunctions to be copied, but the
practice was not general. Archbishop Pecham occasionally ordered them to be
copied into the martyrology of the monastery (e.g. *Reg. Epp. J. Peckham* (Rolls
series), iii. 800, 805, 826) ; likewise did Baldock and Segrave, Bishops of London
(*Reg. R. Baldock*, etc. (Canterbury and York soc.), pp. 60, 65, 115, 122, 133, 193).
In the fifteenth century Bishop Gray of Lincoln sometimes ordered his injunctions " to be fastened up in some public and conspicuous place within the
dorter . . . so that every monk have free access to behold and examine the
same." (*Visitations of religious houses . . . Lincoln* (Linc. Record Soc.), i. 106 ;
cf. ii. 216, iii. 319.)

² No. 322 in Thomas James's catalogue. The injunctions have been indexed
by each cataloguer in turn, and were noted by J. Willis Clark in his essay on
William Bateman (*Proc. Cambridge Antiq. Soc.*, IX. iii. 314). Blomefield noted
the MS. but dated the visitation 1345 (*Hist. co. Norfolk* (ed. 1805-1810), iii. 507,
n. 8).

96

seclusion. It was a time at which the famous dispute between the bishop and the abbey of Bury St. Edmunds was at its height. Bateman had attempted to exercise jurisdiction over this great exempt house, and in 1345 Bury appealed for letters of protection out of Chancery. Bateman appears to have relied too much on his favour with the king. He disregarded the royal justices indiscreetly, and suffered the seizure of his temporalities in consequence. He and his household retired to Norwich, to the safety of the cathedral precincts, and remained there from November 1346 to the following July. Professor Hamilton Thompson observes that his friendly relations with the chapter " stood the test of his long residence in the cathedral precincts " during this eight months.[1] One might add that it stood the test of what was undoubtedly a rigorous visitation, in which the bishop found some faults to criticize and some important financial reconstruction necessary.

His injunctions may illustrate the bishop's character, as well as the needs of the monastery for which he was legislating. " His training and tastes were legal," says Professor Hamilton Thompson.[2] No threats or exhortations add savour to these statutes. Bateman eschews the elaborate preamble and the pious reflections which transform the injunctions of Archbishop Pecham and some other visitors into little homilies. After the briefest of prefaces he descends at once to details, arranges his material by paragraphs, and numbers them to make reference easy. The style is not always elegant or terse, but it only becomes cumbersome through care for exact expression : it is the work of a lawyer. If one may not suppose that the bishop himself was responsible for composing the injunctions in this form, at least it reflects some light on the training of his clerks. The topics which are treated suggest that the bishop's main care was for business-like conduct of the priory's money matters. After the first four chapters, which point to a weakening of monastic discipline in the past, the injunctions dwell almost entirely upon the temporal affairs of the monastery. Presents for the monks and an annual subscription to the common funds of the house show that Bateman tempered his authority with a pious solicitude for his church.

[1] *Norfolk Archaeol.*, XXV. i. 125.   [2] *Ibid.*, p. 113.

For the historian of Norwich Cathedral the injunctions provide valuable material, more particularly regarding the economic organization. Other abundant records exist in the form of account rolls. The survey of the obedientiary and manor rolls recently provided by Dr. H. W. Saunders [1] sufficiently indicates how the two sources of information may be made to supplement each other. The existence of accounts and inventories for all departments anterior to 1347 shows that Bateman was no innovator, but legislated against laxity, when he demanded inventories of the obediences (ch. 6) and annual statements from the priors of cells (ch. 7). What may be doubtfully inferred from the injunctions can be proved from the priory records. Bateman's anxiety about the priory's financial state is justified by the monks' own financial statement. The bishop was doubtless shown the *status obedientiariorum* for the years preceding his visitation. These survive. According to Dr. Saunders's analysis,[2] the eighteen departments of the monastery show a total deficit of about £18 in 1345, which had leapt to above £135 in 1346, and rose in the following year to more than £173. Unfortunately the *status* of the next few years are not known, so that it is impossible to gauge the immediate result of Bateman's financial measures. In 1363 the deficit was nearly trebled. At the same time the injunctions should teach us to make deductions from the obedientiaries' accounts very cautiously. The common fund, or *thesaurus*, introduces an imponderable element into the calculations. Incredible though it may seem, Dr. Saunders has apparently not become fully aware of its existence during his study of the Norwich rolls.

Almost as soon as the monastic income began to be dispersed among the several obedientiaries, the visitors of monasteries saw the dangers of the process and attempted to gather together the finances into a centralized system. Treasurers were appointed in one monastery after another to collect the money due to the offices, keep the reserves, and pay to each obedientiary according

[1] H. W. Saunders, *An introduction to the obedientiary and manor rolls of Norwich Cathedral Priory* (Norwich, 1930).

[2] *Op. cit.*, pp. 17, 30, 168. The facsimile of the *status* of another year faces p. 68.

to his needs.[1]   But this institution seems never to have prospered. Instead, a treasury often was set up which had its own sources of revenue, and also levied a tax upon the independent incomes of the obedientiaries.   Thus a common fund was created without much interference with the various offices of a monastery.   Dr. Snape infers that the office of treasurer was instituted for this purpose at Abingdon in the first half of the fourteenth century.[2] At Ely there were both a *thesaurarius* who was an obedientiary and a *custos* of the common treasury.[3]   At Norwich, as these injunctions show, there already existed in 1347 a common fund : " peccunia que pro thesauro extitit hactenus deputata " (ch. 24). Bateman planned to increase it by fines (ch. 17), by sales of woods and other occasional profits (ch. 26), and by annual contributions from each office (ch. 25).   Yet Dr. Saunders declares : " It seems doubtful whether we can claim for Norwich Priory a Treasurer or a Treasury." [4]   The doubt presumably arises over the use of the words " treasure " and " treasury ".   These do not imply a separate obedience.   In this connection they represent respectively a sum of money and the place where it was kept.[5]   It will be noticed that Bateman nowhere refers to treasurers : only to four persons holding each a different key to the treasure (ch. 26).

Some other chapters of the injunctions deserve comment. So little is known of the dean of the manors that chapter 28 is a valuable sign of limits being set to his powers.   What were the rights which he had exceeded, and the revenues which he had appropriated, must be discovered from the rolls of his " perquisites." [6]   Confirmatory evidence occurs in the award by which

[1] See R. H. Snape, *Engl. monastic finances*, pp. 37 seqq.   Cf. the receivers at Waltham in 1191 (*Papsturkunden in England*, ed. W. Holtzmann, i. 584), and other early examples cited in *Eng. Hist. Review*, xlvi. 448.

[2] *Op. cit.*, p. 49.   [3] T. D. Atkinson, *Archit. history of* . . . *Ely*, p. 10.

[4] *Op. cit.*, p. 71, n. 1.   But on the same page Dr. Saunders speaks of the treasurer existing at Norwich as " probably but a temporary convenience." Nor can he be unaware that in 1514 Bishop Nicke ordered the obedientiaries to pay a subsidy into the *thesauraria monasterii* (*Visitations of Norwich*, ed. Jessopp, p. 79).

[5] In the sixteenth century the treasury is the place where muniments of the cells ought to be stored (*Visitations*, pp. 73, 79, 265, 269).

[6] Cf. Saunders, *op. cit.*, p. 44.

Archbishop Arundel in 1411 attempted to settle disputes between the bishop and the prior and chapter.[1]   Here the dean of
the manors, or *custos decanatus*, appears quite clearly as the dean
of the priory's peculiar.   He is no manorial officer, and his title
probably arises from the fact that the priory's jurisdiction coincided with its manors, just as the peculiar deaneries of the see
of Canterbury covered the ancient lands of that church.[2]   To
judge from his accounts of fines for spiritual offences and from
his rights in the probate of wills, the dean of the manors at
Norwich resembled most nearly the archdeacons appointed by
great monasteries;[3] but his title was different.   The closest
analogy is perhaps to be found in Worcester, where the prior
and chapter claim " archidiaconal right in the church of Hallow,
create a dean, appoint an apparitor, summon and celebrate
chapters there, hear cases, correct crimes or claim to, exact fines
from delinquents and turn them to their own use according to
their pleasure."[4]

Not many years before Bateman's visitation of his cathedral,
Pope Benedict XII had issued an important series of constitutions
for the reform of the black monks.   A few years later the English
Benedictine Chapter of 1343 drew largely upon them for its
statutes.   Bateman must have been acquainted with all this
legislation, and perhaps was influenced by it.   Indeed he cites
the constitutions of Benedict XII in ordering officers to present
inventories in duplicate (ch. 6).

Other of his injunctions reflect the papal statutes.   In accordance with Benedict XII's rule he forbids money to be given
to the monks in lieu of clothing ; but he permits a monk to receive
money if his old clothes can be kept respectable until the next
distribution (ch. 12).   This mitigation of the rule is symptomatic
of the change that can be traced at this period in the chamberlain's
rolls of Norwich.   Here, as elsewhere in the later fourteenth

---

[1] Printed in Carter, *Studies*, pp. 52-53, 57.

[2] I. J. Churchill, *Canterbury Administration*, I. 62-63.

[3] Cf., e.g., E. H. Pearce, *Monks of Westminster*, pp. 4-5 ; U. Berlière,
" Les archidiaconés ou exemptions privilégiées de monastères," *Revue Bénédic-
tine*, XL. 116-122.

[4] An undated document, early thirteenth century (*Hist. MSS. Com. Rep.*
XIV. App. viii. 191).

century, the monks came to have their allowance of money to buy clothes.[1] While at first sight the matter may seem too trivial to call for much comment, yet on consideration of other records we see that it has a wide significance. For this same refusal to let monks buy their own clothes is reiterated through centuries, and so widely disregarded that at last the rule becomes obsolete. The persistent demands of reformers and the equally persistent evasions by monks show what an important question was at issue.

St. Benedict had clearly intended clothes to be provided for his monks ; and when monks asked for money instead, it was to satisfy their taste for originality in dress or to provide themselves with pocket-money. The second possibility was the more serious, for it involved a possible breach of the fundamental rule forbidding private property to monks. This offence was made the reason for the prohibition at Westminster in 1268, when the legate Ottobono confirmed injunctions after a visitation by his deputies : the visitors had found that the monks were accustomed to receive money from the chamberlain for clothes and other necessaries, and that they frequently spent it on other things.[2] So, during the thirteenth century, Benedictine Chapters in England thrice repeated the rule.[3] Stephen Langton copied the Chapter in legislating for his province of Canterbury in 1222, and Ottobono made a general decree to the same effect in 1268.[4] In 1315 Cluniac visitors at Lenton Priory found that for some time past the chamberlain had abusively given money for clothing, contrary to the custom at Cluny and other great houses of the Order ; they therefore prohibited such payments and made the

---

[1] Saunders, *op. cit.*, pp. 114 *seqq.* Cf. Chirbury (O.S.A.), 1394 (*Register of J. Trefnant* (Canterbury and York Soc.), p. 23).

[2] " Consuevit monachis eiusdem monasterii pro pelliceis coopertoriis et quibusdam aliis necessariis per camerarios monasterii certa pecunie quantitas annis singulis assignari quam ipsi frequenter in usus alios expendebant " (printed by A. H. Sweet, " A papal visitation of Westminster," *Anglican Theolog. Review*, v. (1922), 33). Apparently the chamberlain's accounts show him buying *pellicia* for the brethren in the fifteenth century (E. H. Pearce, *Monks of Westminster*, p. 15).

[3] *Chapters of the English black monks*, ed. W. A. Pantin (Camden Soc., 1931-1933), i. 11, 39, 80.

[4] *Concilia Magnae Britanniae*, ed. D. Wilkins, i. 592, ii. 16.

rule applicable to the whole province.[1] But when in 1336 Pope Benedict XII proposed that this rule be enforced in Benedictine houses the English black monks evaded the plain meaning of his statute, and departed even further from the spirit of it in their legislation of the following century.[2] The arrangement at St. Albans illuminates their policy. Here, both at the beginning of the fourteenth century and in 1351, abbatial statutes forbade the giving of money in lieu of clothes. But between 1336 and 1349 a special rule was made for the prior : " Because in the Benedictine Constitutions we are warned against monks being given money for food and clothing, and because the prior of this monastery has been wont to receive each year from the chamberlain fifty-two shillings for clothes, which in future cannot be done because of the prohibition of the said statute, the abbot has ordained with legal advice that the prior shall henceforth receive each year from the chamberlain clothes to the value of twenty shillings, and thirty-two shillings of good and lawful money for his groceries and other demands upon him." [3] Thus we see a monk receiving money ostensibly to buy clothes ; but when the prohibition of that practice is enforced, the money is found to be far more than equal to the cost of the clothes ; the monk is allowed to keep the excess, provided it is not expended on the purpose for which the money was given ! [4]

Relaxations of the rule did not stop at this point : by the fifteenth century lawyers were agreed that where an abbot had bound himself to pay money in lieu of clothing, he could not revoke the bond.[5] About the same time that the canonist Lyndwood published his opinion Bishop Gray of Lincoln visited Bardney Abbey and made the following injunction : " Seeing that each monk receives yearly from the common goods of the

---

[1] *Visitations and chapters general of Cluni*, ed. G. F. Duckett, pp. 308-309.

[2] *Chapters of the English black monks*, ii. 11, 131 ; cf. *ibid.*, ii. 113, 116, 118, 123, 181.

[3] *Gesta abbatum mon. S. Albani* (Rolls series), ii. 100, 438, 307.

[4] That the amount was excessive is sometimes shown by the visitor's order for a portion of the clothing-allowance to be stopped, as the punishment of a grave offence ; e.g. 1400 *Reg. of Bp. Stafford, Exeter*, p. 314, cited by G. G. Coulton, *Art and the Reformation*, p. 363.

[5] Lyndwood, *Provinciale*, III. xix. 2 (ed. 1679), p. 205, and the authorities there cited.

monastery only twenty shillings for his habit and bedclothes, and of this they have not had meet satisfaction, we enjoin upon you, abbot, under the penalties written above and beneath, that you cause provision and supply of this their private property (*suo peculio*), inasmuch as it is very moderate, to be made to the monks your brethren without lapse of delay, considering that according to the truth of the Gospel, the labourer in the Lord's vineyard must not be defrauded of his daily penny." [1]

Viewed in conjunction with this common development, the rule that Bishop Bateman made at Norwich seems like an attempt to prevent extreme laxity, with a tacit confession that the old law was out of date. The money which might in some cir-cumstances be paid *pro vestibus* obviously would not be spent on clothes. It went to swell the allowance of pocket-money which at this period every monk of Norwich received. The following chapters of the injunctions show that Bateman recognized the dangers of this system to the principle of poverty, and sought for safeguards.

One of the injunctions concerning clothing was repeated by a visitor at Norwich in 1514. The former injunctions object to the use of worsted cowls and frocks (ch. 11), and the later visitor complains that the monks use frocks of worsted *contra ordinem religionis*. Long before this, it was the subject of a general prohibition among the English black monks. The statutes pro-posed by Henry V to the Provincial Chapter in 1421 included one against the use of fine worsted cloth (*pannus ille nitidus de Worceto*), which was proclaimed to be more military than monastic in style ; the Benedictine Chapter concurred with the king in this condemnation. [2]

On one matter Bateman made an order contrary to the statutes of the Benedictine Chapter. It had for centuries been the practice of monasteries cursed with a rebellious monk to transfer him to another house. The practice was approved by popes and bishops, and the Chapter of 1343 recommended that obstinate and incorrigible monks be transferred to a cell, or to another

---

[1] *Visitations of religious houses . . . Lincoln*, I. 4.
[2] *Visitations of Norwich*, pp. 74, 78 ; *Chapters of the English black monks*, ii. 112, 117, and cf. *ibid.*, 122, 126, 180, 192.

monastery, or be expelled.[1] Bateman, on the contrary, ordered that disobedient monks were not to be sent to cells, but were to be reformed at home (ch. 3). He saw that the monk was exposed to more temptations and fewer beneficial influences in cells where the numbers were too small to permit the regular claustral discipline than in the ordered life of a great establishment of fifty monks. Curiously enough, the bishop's fears were realized nearly two centuries later ; for at the visitation of 1526 the prior of Aldeby stated that the prior of Norwich " is wont to send incorrigible and rebel monks to the cells." The consequences of this appear in the evil report of Brother John Shelton, who had lived more loosely at Yarmouth Priory than at home in Norwich.[2]

The copy of Bateman's injunctions has one significant difference from the original. Before it served as the exemplar of the Corpus MS., the Rylands text was abridged by a series of deletions. The same hand which added titles to the numbered paragraphs, scored through certain passages and wrote " Vacat " in the margin. It is not easy to say why these deletions were made. In chapter 6 the passage omitted first demands that the bishop shall be presented with copies of the inventories of all offices. The rest of the chapter was of temporary interest and would naturally be left out of a copy. Then two whole chapters, 9 and 10, are struck through. These ordered confessors to present to the prior accounts of the oblations they received, which accounts were then to be submitted to the bishop. The third and last passage to be omitted is chapter 25, which arranged for annual contributions to the common treasure from the priors and obedientiaries, as well as from the bishop in his lifetime. All these arrangements have the air of novelty. Bateman does not assert that his predecessors have been shown the accounts, or that confessors used to account for their casual profits. The treasure had existed before, but it may not have

---

[1] *Chapters*, ii. 38, 52. The same Chapter does indeed make the apparently incompatible order that the prelate of a monastery shall not banish monks to cells out of personal spite, but only send blameless monks who will behave themselves (*ibid.*, ii. 51).

[2] *Visitations of Norwich*, pp. 197, 200.

104

been endowed with a fixed income. One is tempted to suppose that these injunctions were particularly distasteful to the prior and chapter, who either appealed against them or tacitly ignored them. Either conjecture seems permissible. Religious houses did occasionally appeal against injunctions,[1] but we have no record of this procedure at Norwich.

The administrative arrangements prescribed by a visiting bishop throw light on the conduct of a monastery, but this sort of action by an external authority might be entirely ineffectual without the agreement of the community. How many bishops visited the same religious house twice? How many took the trouble to enforce their predecessors' rules? While visitors' injunctions indicate what was found at fault, they seldom serve as a safe guide to the remedies that were applied. Better evidence of the ordinary administration of a religious house is provided by the ordinances made by the monks themselves in the conventual chapter. A few fourteenth-century regulations by the chapter of Norwich survive and deserve attention. They are preserved in the form of jottings on end-leaves of a Norwich customary, now in the library of Corpus Christi College, Cambridge (MS. 465). All were not written by the same hand, but the writing is all of the late fourteenth century. They touch on the usual material of customaries—on the duties of various servants in the refectory, on the method of doing penance, on those who come late to meals; but these hardly concern the general organization of the house. Those which are printed below mostly belong to the years 1351, 1370, and 1379;[2] the ordinances relating to the cells may be suitably regarded as a supplement to Bishop Bateman's injunctions. They do not cover the

---

[1] At St. Swithun's, Winchester, in 1327 the bishop withdrew his recent injunctions after an appeal by the prior and convent (*Chartulary of Winchester Cath.*, ed. A. W. Goodman, pp. 113-114). At Merton Priory in 1392 the bishop found that his earlier injunctions were not observed, and the convent at his request lodged a formal protest against them (A. Heales, *Records of Merton Priory*, pp. xci-xciii). About 1360 the prior of Christ Church, Canterbury, asked for the revocation or at least modification of certain of Islip's injunctions, made in his visitation "contra solitum morem et consuetudinem huius ecclesie" (*Hist. MSS. Commission, Report IX.*, app. i., pp. 82-83).

[2] The undated ordinance may belong to the year 1370, for the extract given under that year seems to be an imperfect summary of the other.

same ground, but they at least contribute some fragments to our scrappy knowledge of the monastery's organization.

Injunctions of William Bateman, Bishop of Norwich.[1]

Willelmus permissione divina Norwicensis episcopus dilectis in Christo filiis . . priori et capitulo ecclesie nostre Norwicensis salutem graciam et benediccionem. Ex debito pastoralis officii dictam nostram cathedralem ecclesiam vestrumque singulos tam debito more quam solito visitantes, aliqua circa ecclesie nostre prefate personarumque in ea degencium regimen atque statum remediis comperimus indigere. Cupientes igitur quantum nos, licet indignos ecclesie sue regimini presidentes, inspiraverit trinitas increata medelam singulis debitam adhibere, ordinaciones constitutiones seu iniuncciones infrascriptas faciendas decrevimus, quas vobis sub sigilli nostri munimine transmittentes precipimus et mandamus in virtute sancte obediencie inviolabiliter observari. Et ne prolixitas lecture fastidium generet audienti, ad puncta singula sine quibuscumque preambulis que ornatum dumtaxat detegunt sine fructu sub breviori quo poterimus compendio descendemus.

i.

In primis iniungimus et ordinamus quod . . priores ecclesie nostre prefate qui pro tempore fuerint, qui principalem sub nobis et episcopis qui pro tempore fuerint potestatem et curam tam in

[1] I wish to express my thanks to the Master and Fellows of Corpus Christi College, Cambridge, for permitting my use of MS. 370 for collation here, and of MS. 465, from which extracts are printed below ; also to the Librarian, the Reverend Sir Edwyn C. Hoskyns, Bt., for giving me facilities to consult these manuscripts. The text (R) is that of the original John Rylands Library Latin MS. 226, fos. 2ʳ-9ᵛ. Since this is the original, the readings of C (Corpus Christi MS. 370, fos. 80ᵛ-83ʳ) are only of interest in so far as they follow the corrected version of R : the relevant readings have been noted, therefore, but thirty-seven variants which must be a copyist's errors are not recorded in the footnotes. C has no chapter headings, and owing to the omission of passages deleted in R, the numeration differs. The *gemi-punctus*, originally used to replace a proper name, is inserted without much reason in many places in R ; the scribe of C omits it. Passages deleted in R are printed in parentheses, editorial alterations between square brackets. In the notes R² signifies the reading of a second hand in R. Not all the alterations are by the same hand, but they cannot be safely distinguished.

XII

106

temporalibus quam in spiritualibus optinent super omnes, a quibuscumque ecclesie nostre monachis tam cellarum prioribus et obedienciariis quam ceteris quibuscumque in debita reverencia habeantur ; ita quod procedenti priori qui pro tempore fuerit [fo. 2ᵛ] iuxta eos, presertim in ecclesia claustro capitulo refectorio aulaque communi ¹ singuli sedentes assurgant, stantes reverenciam exhibeant, loquentes vero sibi vel verborum signa facientes capuciis depositis humiliter se inclinent, mandatisque suis iustis et canonicis obediant reverenter.

ii. De esu carnium versus.

Item quod . . prior qui pro tempore fuerit non licenciet monachos ad comedendas carnes in aula nec in cameris ex parte aule, nisi ex causa magna et racionabili quam debita consciencia merito reputaverit iustam fore ; super quo dicti prioris conscienciam oneramus.

iii. De monachis mittendis ad cellas.

Item quod monachi vagi leves et indomiti nullo modo mittantur ad cellas, sed in ecclesia remanentes sub obediencie iugo laudabilius deservire, exemplo copiose multitudinis facilius instruantur et humilius inducantur.

iv. Quomodo monachi se debent habere ad cellas.

Item omnibus et singulis ecclesie nostre . . monachis, in quacumque cella dicte nostre ecclesie commorantibus, in virtute sancte obediencie mandamus firmiter iniungentes quatinus cepta celle non exeant nec extra celle cepta commedant neque bibant sine dicte celle prioris licencia speciali,² quodque a commessacionibus et potacionibus horis indebitis abstinentes, in sacre scrip-[fo. 3ʳ] ture vel canonum studio, si ad hoc apti fuerint, alioquin in oracionibus et devocione se occupent diligenter ; et cum ad spacia recreacionis causa seu alia eos exire contigerit,

¹ At Ely the misericord was sometimes called *aula* (Atkinson, *op. cit.*, p. 135). At Norwich the common hall may have been used for that purpose, and may be the hall which connects the prior's lodging with the claustral buildings. Cf. next chapter.
² Cf. *infra*, chapter ordinance 1370.

de prioris licencia ut prefertur soli non vadant, sed monachus monachum secum habeat ubicumque, vel aliam personam honestam si monachum secum habere non poterit, prout dicte celle prior duxerit ordinandum, cui omnes monachi dum ibi fuerint obediant et intendant et eius iustis mandatis pareant reverenter ; cellarum insuper ecclesie nostre quarumcumque . . prioribus sub virtute obediencie firmiter iniungentes quatinus commonachos suos secum degentes honeste et devote tractent, decenterque in cibo et potu eisdem exhiberi et eorum necessaria vetera dum ibi fuerint competenter faciant reparari,[1] dictosque commonachos ab insolenciis voluptatibus venacionibus dissolucionibus et inhonestatibus quibuscumque cohibeant, eosque horis debitis sacre scripture aut canonum studio aut oracionibus vacare faciant diligenter, eciam cum censuris ecclesiasticis, si hec exigerit rebellio eorumdem ; ad quod faciendum tenore presencium singulis cellarum . . prioribus committimus potestatem.

v. *Quod prior sancti Leonardi reddat compotum.*

Item iniungimus et ordinamus quod prior sancti Leonardi qui pro tempore fuerit singulis annis reddat plenum et spe- [fo. 3ᵛ] cificum compotum de omnibus oblacionibus redditibus et proventibus ad dictum prioratum spectantibus, et de expensis suis et receptis, modo et tempore quibus obedienciarii seu officiarii ecclesie nostre prefate compotum reddere consueverunt ; et quod dictus . . prior nullum opus magnum seu notabiliter sumptuosum incipiat absque . . prioris et seniorum . . capituli consilio et assensu.

vi.[2]

Item ut officiariorum ecclesie nostre prefate cedencium decedencium vel ammotorum gestio cunctis nota alios in officiis substitutos magis reddat solicitos in futurum, statuimus volumus et ordinamus quod omnes et singuli . . priores nostre cathedralis ecclesie et cellarum, ac alii gerentes administraciones huiusmodi bonorum ecclesie preficiendi pro tempore, faciant in eorum novitate duo plena et perfecta eiusdem tenoris inventaria omnium

---

[1] Cf. *infra*, chapter ordinance 1379.
[2] R leaves space for chapter heading.

108

bonorum iuxta formam constitutionis benedictine super hoc edite, (quorum unum . . episcopo qui pro tempore fuerit penes se custodiendum tradere teneantur, altero in archa communi ad futuram memoriam reservato. Et hoc idem per . . priores tam nostre ecclesie quam cellarum et administratores bonorum ecclesie nostre prefate qui nunc sunt post datam dicte con- stitucionis prefectos citra mensem Augusti mandamus decernimus et iniungimus in virtute obediencie plenarie faciendum si in novitate prefectionis eorum id non fecerant ut prefertur).[1]

[fo. 4ʳ] vii. *Quod priores cellarum reddant compotum annuatim.*

Item quod omnes et singuli . . priores cellarum reddant sin- gulis annis infra mensem Iulii compotum generaliter de adminis- tracionibus eorumdem, specificando veram summam omnium receptorum per annum ac valorem consuetum fructuum red- dituum et proventuum dicti prioratus, ac summam expensarum anni illius summasque omnium debitorum et creditorum, verum- que valorem stauri et residui remanentis ; et ista compoti reddicio sub forma prefata fiat annis singulis et temporibus sup- radictis . . priori ecclesie nostre prefate in presencia aliquorum seniorum quos dictus . . prior duxerit eligendos ; et dictum compotum faciant . . priores cellarum prefati personaliter si co- mode poterint, alioquin per epistolas . . priori et capitulo directas, sigillis eorum signatas et clausas, cum cedulis veri compoti sub forma prefata dictis epistolis interclusis.

viii. *De confessoribus.*

Item quod confessores seu penitenciarii per nos deputati et per successores nostros futuris temporibus deputandi [2] mundas manus servent, nullusque confessorum aliquem ad sibi con- fitendum procuret vel alliciat verbo nutu signo opere aut alio quovismodo sed gratis et libere venientes gratis et libere audiat confitentes nullamque peccuniam ab aliquibus eisdem confessis

[1] Com. ; R² deletes, and adds [vac]at in margin.
[2] By the archbishop's award, 1411, penitenciaries were to be appointed by the bishop at the nomination of the prior and seniors. They heard all the monks' confessions ; not merely " reserved " cases, as Mr. Carter supposes (*Studies*, pp. 50-51, 42).

quocumque colore seu modo extorquere vel confessos ad solvendum aliquid eis vel eorum alicui quacumque [fo. 4ᵛ] via allicere presumant, nec aliquid eciam a gratis offerente ante confessionem suam et penitenciam datam ac absolucionem secutam recipiant a confessis, sed omnibus rite libereque peractis gratis oblata gratis accipiant a quocumque.

ix.[1]

(Item quod confessores prefati qui pro tempore fuerint singulis annis infra mensem Iulii . . priori ecclesie nostre in presencia aliquorum seniorum quos dictus . . prior duxerit eligendos reddant generaliter compotum, exprimendo veram et integram summam omnium receptorum et specificando usus in quos expendidit quisquis dictam peccunie summam, aut eius partem si tota expensa non fuerit dicta summa.

x.[2]

Item volumus quod . . priores ecclesie nostre cathedralis qui a dictis cellarum . . prioribus et confessoribus compotum receperint, ut prefertur, formam et modum compotorum omnium et singulorum predictorum infra unius mensis spacium a tempore compotorum receptorum . . episcopo qui pro tempore fuerit si infra diocesim suam fuerit, alioquin a tempore quo primum ad diocesim redierit, significare plene et integraliter teneantur.)[3]

xi. *De vestibus utendis.*

Item quod nullus monachus ecclesie nostre cuiuscumque status dignitatis aut gradus fuerit utatur cuccullis vel froccis de [fo. 5ʳ] Wurstede nec vestibus alterius coloris generis vel figure quam illorum quibus . . conventus uti antiquitus consuevit, sed omnium monachorum quorum est idem cultus eademque regula sit tam in colore quam genere et figura omnium vestium idem usus.

---

[1] R leaves space for chapter heading.
[2] R² (in pencil) *De compoto.*
[3] C om. ; R² deletes, and adds *va[cat]* in margin.

110

xii. *Quod non solvatur pecunia pro vestibus, et cetera.*

Item quod non solvatur alicui monacho peccunia pro vestibus aut aliis necessariis ex debito recipiendis, nisi de . . prioris licencia speciali, et nullo modo detur licencia per . . priorem, nisi ex causa racionabili, et nisi per eum vel alium officiarium suo loco per eum si adesse non poterit deputandum et eciam suppriorem vetera eiusdem generis videantur, et nisi eisdem videatur quod vetera sufficient monacho supradicto, pro honorificencia et statu ecclesie ac persone, usque ad tempus quo iterum nova eiusdem generis necessaria dicto monacho ex debito fuerint ministranda.

xiii. *De pecunia distribuenda monachis annuatim.*

Item quod quilibet monachus ecclesie nostre prefate, exceptis cellarum . . prioribus, pro suis secretis necessitatibus relevandis recipiat singulis annis in festo sancti Iohannis baptiste ii. solidos a priore sancti Leonardi de dicti proventibus [1] . . prioratus,[2] et de proventibus ecclesie de Chalke [3] Roffensis diocesis in festo omnium sanctorum ii. solidos, et de peccuniis que pro OO con-sueverant mi-[fo. 5ᵛ] nistrari in octabis pasche xii. denarios, ac a confessoribus seu penitenciariis eodem festo xii. denarios sterlingorum.

xiiii. *De pecunia solvenda ab officiariis et de legatis.*

Item quod omnia relicta legata et donata ex donacione fidelium . . conventui seu monachis generaliter ecclesie nostre prefate, statim infra trium dierum spacium a tempore quo recepta fuerint, dumtamen sufficere poterint ad distribucionem vi. denariorum singulis monachis faciendam, inter omnes et singulos monachos pro equalibus porcionibus dividantur.[4] Ad hec . . priori sancti Leonardi . . confessoribus ac dictorum proventuum et peccuni-arum receptoribus firmiter iniungimus et mandamus quatinus dictis terminis dictas peccuniarum summas plenarie persolvant singulis monachis ut prefertur, sub pena dupli, quam dupli penam, si terminis simplum solvere distulerint, postmodum eis

[1] R² adds *si sufficerint ;* C reads *proventu si suffecerint.*
[2] Cf. Saunders, *op. cit.,* p. 162, n. 1 and Blomefield, *Hist. Norfolk,* iii. 513.
[3] Cf. Saunders, *op. cit.,* p. 160.   [4] R² adds in margin [P]ena.

quibus dictis terminis simplum solutum non fuerit, infra xx. dierum spacium solvere teneantur.

xv. De pecunia concessa ab episcopo.

Item ut persone nostre dum in hac vita fuerimus et anime nostre cum ab hac luce migraverit in piis monachorum precibus, quod toto desiderio fieri cupimus et oramus, memoria [recencior] [1] habeatur, cuilibet ecclesie nostre monacho ii. solidos sterlingorum, de cistis nostris, in festo natalis beatissimi Thome martiris Cantuar' archiepiscopi ordinamus et volumus annis singulis ministrari quousque altissimo concedente aliquos sufficientes redditus dicte nostre ecclesie perpetuo fecerimus depu-[fo. 6ʳ] tari de quibus pensio prefata [2] monachis omnibus et singulis dicte nostre ecclesie presentibus et futuris perpetuis valeat temporibus ministrari.

xvi. De custodia pecunie claustralium.

Item quod monachi nostre ecclesie, obedienciariis seu . . officiariis exceptis, nullam peccuniam penes se retineant, sed quamcumque peccuniam eisdem pro necessariis deputatam priori suppriori aut aliquibus aliis obedienciariis monachis custodiendam tradant, quam dicte peccunie custodes dictis monachis non retradant nisi ex causis veris utilibus piis aut necessariis allegatis et specificatis expresse, et quas dicti custodes merito reputaverint iustas fore ; super quo dictorum custodum districte conscienciam oneramus.

xvii. Quod pecunia ad necessariorum relevamen et non voluptuose expendatur.

Item ne peccunie ad necessariorum relevamen ordinate in usus voluptuarios convertantur, iniungimus quod nullus monachus, minucionis recreacionis aut alio quovis solacio more solito per presidentis providenciam deputatus, aliqua extranea cibaria aut vinum extra necessitatis casum pro se aut sociis faciat provideri set esculentis et poculentis contententur eisdem per conventus . . officiarios more solito ministrandis. Quod si quis

---

[1] R recenseor ; C recensior.   [2] Cf. Saunders, op. cit., p. 160.

112

peccuniam in vino aut esculentis vel poculentis extraneis in talibus solaciis voluptuose absque necessitatis casu convictus fuerit consumpsisse aut in alios usus convertisse quam illos quos peccunie sue custos approbaverit ut prefertur, preter peni-[fo. 6ᵛ] tenciam in capitulo pro inobediencia sibi merito imponendam, ipsum in subtractione duorum solidorum extunc sibi proxime solvendorum decernimus puniendum, et illos duos solidos quos ex hac causa subtrahendos sibi decernimus, thesauro ecclesie volumus applicari.

xviii. *De elemosinaria.*

Item ut elemosine subsidium cunctis pateat in communi, iniungimus et mandamus quod pueri in elemosinaria per obedienciarios domum tenentes positi ad dictorum obedienciariorum officia revocentur, et in loco illorum et aliorum cedencium vel decedencium in futurum, ad ceterorum per ordinem monachorum instanciam, pauperes eorum consanguinei [1] subrogentur, proviso quod ad illos qui semel suos consanguineos subrogarunt facultas iterum non redeat subrogandi, nisi completo primitus ordine ceterorum ; salva tamen nobis et nostris successoribus potestate ponendi more solito pueros in officio libere supradicto, presertim cum ab . . episcopis predecessoribus nostris dicti officii ac tocius monasterii et ecclesie precipuum processerit fundamentum.

xix. *Item de eodem.*

Ad hec insuper ordinamus quod fragmenta et reliquie cibariorum conventus non familiaribus elemosinarii set pueris predictis pauperibus integraliter ministrentur, et demum ea que eis superfuerint poterunt ex causa dictis familiaribus ministrari. [2]

xx. *De sartore et sutore.*

[fo. 7ʳ] Item quod infra cepta monasterii ordinetur infra unius mensis spacium una habitacio conveniens pro uno communi sartore et alia pro uno communi sutore, et infra idem eciam tempus provideatur de illis duobus ministris communibus ad

---

[1] R² adds *tantum* in margin.
[2] Cf. Ben. Chapters of 1249 and 1278 (*Chapters*, I. 37, 79).

reparanda necessaria vetera monachorum et facienda secrecius ea que eorum ministeriis conveniunt infra cepta, ne reparandorum debilitas extraneis pateat publice in ecclesie vituperium manifestum.

xxi. Quod mulieres non hospitentur infra cepta.

Item quod nulla mulier pernoctet infra cepta monasterii nisi fuerit hospes quam hostelarius in camera debita collocabit; ita quod mulieres laboratrices non admittantur nec ponantur in gardinis nec aliis officinis ad laborandum si masculi ad hoc apti poterunt faciliter inveniri ; alioquin, si mares ad hec officia apti non poterint faciliter inveniri, tunc demum ponantur in gardinis vel locis patentibus et publicis ad facienda ea que eorum officio committuntur ; ita quod non intrent domum aliquam infra cepta monasterii nisi ex magna et ardua causa, videlicet si que visitare voluerit maritum infirmum vel alia simili ; et hoc fiat tantum de licencia monachi obedienciarii dicto officio presidentis, cui dicta domus noscitur attributa.

xxii. Quod arbores non dentur nec vendantur.

Item quod arbores nemorum ecclesie non dentur extraneis nec vendantur [fo. 7ᵛ] absque capituli consilio et assensu, nisi arbores tortuose vel adeo inutiles desiccate quod stantes afferrent incomodum et continue deperirent, et tunc de peccunia ex arborum vendicione recepta fiat mencio specialis in compoto proxime faciendo. Vendicio autem arborum in notabili quantitate non fiat sine episcopi qui pro tempore fuerit consilio et assensu.

xxiii. Quod officiarii non habentes nemora releventur de nemoribus, et cetera.

Item quod obedienciarii nemora habentes suis officiis deputata alios obedienciarios nemora non habentes in suis magnis necessitatibus, consideratis officii indigencia et onere incumbente, ad reparacionem domorum vel molendinorum de arboribus competentibus in moderato tamen numero iuvent et relevent, de consilio tamen et assensu capituli seniorum. Ne tamen nimis frequens subsidium de arboribus ut prefertur dilapidacionem

114

pareat in futurum, volumus quod nec semel nec successive minuantur nemora in notabili quantitate absque . . episcopi qui pro tempore fuerit consilio et assensu.

xxiiii. *Quod pecunia restituatur tessaurarie.*

Item ordinamus quod peccunia que pro thesauro extitit hactenus deputata, in cuiuscumque obedienciarii manibus [fuerit],[1] infra duorum mensium spacium thesaurarie restituatur, sub pena dupli quam non restituentes infra aliorum duorum mensium spacium thesauro applicandam solvere teneantur, nisi ex causa racionabili [fo. 8r] per totum capitulum approbanda se poterint excusare.

xxv.[2]

(Item ut ex multis minutis absque gravi onere singulorum per processum temporis thesauri cumulus augeatur, ordinamus quod . . prior ecclesie nostre cathedralis xx. solidos, celerarius xx. solidos, sacrista xx. solidos, camerarius xx. solidos, elemosinarius x. solidos, cantor x. solidos, infirmarius x. solidos, prior de Norman spitele x. solidos, gardinarius x. solidos, refectuarius x. solidos, quilibet penitenciariorum xx. solidos, si cuilibet ultra xl. solidos quos quilibet ex constitucione bone memorie domini Iohannis de Ely, predecessoris nostri, pro labore ad minus percipere debet in usus suos licitos pro libito convertendos, tantum superfuerit de dicti officii perquisitis, alioquin totum residuum quod ultra xl. solidos superfuerit, alicui eorumdem cui xx. solidi integre non superfuerint ut prefertur ; item prior sancti Leonardi xl. solidos, prior Iernemuthe xx. solidos, prior Lenne xx. solidos, prior de Aldeby xx. solidos, prior de Hoxne x. solidos, de officiorum et prioratuum proventibus, in festis omnium sanctorum et pasche pro equalibus porcionibus annis singulis sub pena dupli infra mensem sequentem proxime persolvenda solvere teneantur. Nos insuper temporibus nostris de gracia volumus ad hunc pium usum de cistis nostris xl. solidos annis singulis eisdem terminis ministrare.)[3]

---

[1] RC *fuerint.*   [2] R leaves space for chapter heading.
[3] C om. ; R[2] deletes, and adds *Va[cat]* in margin.

xxvi. *Quod quarta pars compoti reddatur thesauro et pecunia de ciphis.*

Item quod de residuo quod libere superfuerit post compotum cuiuscumque [fo. 8ᵛ] obedienciarii seu officiarii ecclesie nostre prefate, quarta pars et quecumque peccunia pro ciphis et cocliaribus a conversis seu noviciis more solito recepta seu in futurum recipienda,[1] necnon peccunia que pro vendicione quarumcumque arborum nemorum vel silvarum non ceduarum huius ecclesie nostre recepta fuerit in futurum, thesauro ecclesie integraliter applicetur.

xxvi.[2] *De custodia thesauri.*

Item iniungimus quod thesaurus prefatus continue per dei graciam augmentandus sub tuta custodia iiii. personarum et sub quatuor clavibus diversarum formarum celeriter reponatur ; et quod de thesauro nichil minuatur per x. annorum spacium proximorum ex quacumque causa absque . . episcopi qui pro tempore fuerit et capituli consilio unanimi et assensu, nec postea, nisi ex magna et ardua causa, quam totum capitulum deliberato consilio duxerit approbandam.

xxvii. *Item de eodem.*

Item quod fructus redditus et proventus ecclesie de Chalke, deductis pensionibus priori ecclesie nostre cathedralis celerario ac sacriste alias deputatis et monachorum subsidiis per has nostras iniuncciones superius ordinatis, de cetero communium negociorum ecclesie sumptibus deputentur.

xxviii. *De decanatu maneriorum.*

Item excercicium et regimen officii decanatus maneriorum . . prioris et conventus in dictorum . . prioris et conventus grave dampnum noviter adinventi, cedente [fo. 9ʳ] vel decedente[3] decano qui nunc est, ad morem solitum reducendum decernimus,

---

[1] According to the Benedictine Chapter of 1343 (xiii. 2), the cost of a novice's outfit must not exceed one hundred shillings (*Chapters*, ii. 50).
[2] R *sic :* number repeated.   [3] R *vel decedente ;* C *vero.*

116

dictique officii proventus singulorum annorum in usum et co-
modum ecclesie nostre prefate, pro communium negociorum
ecclesie sumptibus volumus et ordinamus perpetuo deputari.

xxix. De custodia cellarii.

Item iniungimus quod nullus secularis clavem cellarii custodiat in futurum, sed magister cellarii alium socium commonachum
habeat dicto officio deputatum, qui alteram clavem [custodiat],[1]
et liberacioni panis et servisie [2] quandocumque fieri contigerit
absente magistro prefato volumus interesse, ut sic nulla liberacio
fiat de cellario absque alterius eorum presencia personali. Per
hec tamen nolumus dictum magistri socium a conventuali observancia excusari, nisi pro aliqua forsitan hora qua propter
magistri absenciam ipsum in cellario oportuerit occupari.[3]

xxx. De clericis sancte Marie.

Item iniungimus et mandamus quod nulli monachi de cetero
ad missam beate virginis in tabula titulentur [4] nisi poterint et
sciverint saltim in plano cantu sufficienter in cantandi officio
ministrare, salva cuilibet libera more solito facultate alium ad hoc
aptum loco sui si vacare non poterit subrogandi, quibus in virtute
obediencie precipimus quatinus ad locum ministrandi solitum in
misse principio accedentes et usque ad eiusdem misse finem continue remanentes, in cantandi ministerio se occupent diligenter.[5]
Et ut dicte misse intitulati aliique ecclesie nostre monachi
cantare scientes eciam non intitulati ad ministrandum virgini
gloriose in dicte misse officio devocius excitentur, omnibus et
singulis monachis dicte [fo. 9ᵛ] misse interessentibus et cantando
dicte gloriose virgini devote ministrantibus singulis diebus quibus
devote et diligenter cantando ministraverint ut prefertur, xx.
dies de indulgencia concedimus per presentes.

Has nostras iniuncciones mandamus et precipimus futuris
temporibus observari, easque in uno parvo volumine [tran-][6]

---

[1] C custodiat ; R custodire.   [2] Cf. Saunders, op. cit., p. 76.
[3] Cf. injunctions of 1309 : the cellarer or master of the cell may go
early from vespers or high mass (Carter, Studies, p. 20).
[4] C intitulentur.   [5] Cf. injunctions of 1309 (loc. cit., p. 21).
[6] C ; obliterated in R.

scribi ligari ac in capitulo appendi publice ut singulorum monachorum [valeant oculis][1] intueri et in memoria continua retineri.
Earumque copiam singulis cellarum prioribus infra xv. dierum
spacium transmitti volumus et in dictis cellis ad futuram memoriam modo simili custodiri. Dat' in palacio nostro Norwicensi
die quinta mensis maii, anno domini millesimo ccc^{m0} quadragesimo septimo, et consecracionis nostre quarto. In cuius rei testimonium sigillum nostrum presentibus [2] duximus apponendum.[3]

CHAPTER-ORDINANCES OF NORWICH CATHEDRAL PRIORY.

CORPUS CHRISTI COLLEGE, CAMBRIDGE, MS. 465.

[fo. 160^v. *No date.*] Ordinatum est per priorem et seniores
quod quocienscunque claustrales habent licenciam a priore
visitare amicos et parentes quod habeant equos cum decenti
apparatu ab illis qui secundum antiquam consuetudinem solebant
eos invenire.

Item ordinatum est quod omnes existentes in cellis, videlicet
apud Lenne et Iern[muth], quod non exibunt extra dictas cellas
sine licencia petita et capis induti et precipue quando ituri sunt
in villam vel transituri per villam ; nec fratres casualiter de domo
venientes bibant vel manducent in dictis cellis sine speciali
licencia priorum dictarum cellarum petita et optenta. . . .[4]

[fo. 161^r.] Memorandum quod anno domini m^0 ccc^0 li^0
ordinatum erat et decretum quod de cetero prior sancti Leonardi
qui pro tempore fuerit cum omnibus sociis suis ibidem commorantibus in omni principali festo tenentur interesse ad secundas
vesperas, et in recompensacione laboris insoliti concessum est eis
quod quandocunque revocati fuerint cum pannis domi quod non
teneantur esse conventuales usque ad horam primam diei proxime
sequentis nisi quando contig[er]it quod matutine illius noctis
sint in capis et tunc teneantur interesse usque ad cantica iuxta
modum ceterorum fratrum nostrorum de cellis nostris domi
revertentium.

[fo. i^r.] Anno domini m^0 ccc^0 lxx^0 per N[icolaum] priorem

---

[1] C ; obliterated in R.   [2] C om. *presentibus.*
[3] C adds *Hee sunt iniuncciones domini Willelmi de Norwico Norwic' episcopi.*
[4] Cf. *supra*, injunctions ch. 4, and *infra*, ordinance 1370.

ordinatum fuit in capitulo quod omnes existentes in cellis non ibunt in villam nisi cum capis, nec venientes de domo nec comedunt vel bibunt in villa nisi speciali licencia prioris celle petita et optenta, nec exibunt sine licencia prioris celle etc.[1]

[fo. 161^r.] Nota quod anno domini m^0 ccc^0 lxx^0 ix^0 fuerunt diverse dubitaciones per priorem et seniores stabilite et in certum redacte.

Inprimis quod reparaciones fenestrarum super infirmiolo de cetero fiant per cominarium.

Item quod dictus cominarius reparabit ingressum usque infirmariam.

Item quod dominus prior inveniet meremium ad reparandum capellam sancti Edmundi et ad latrinam dependentem super dictam cameram, et sacrista cooperturam plumbi et reparaciones fenestrarum dicte capelle. [fo. 161^v.]

Item quod sacrista qui pro tempore fuerit reparabit fenestras in capitulo.

Item quod nullus de cetero utatur curtis capis sub pena suspensionis caparum.

Item quod infirmarius inveniet lampadem ardentem in introitu infirmarie a festo omnium sanctorum usque ad festum purificacionis sancte Marie et aliis temporibus quociens necesse fuerit.

Item quod hostilarius inveniet unum tortys in infirmaria quando necesse fuerit, et refrectorarius in refectorio eodem modo.

Item quod ministretur cuilibet monacho integre de servicio suo existenti foras per totum diem tam in piscibus quam in carnibus quamvis ex negligencia subcelerarius non premuniatur.

Item quod omnes panes integre in infirmaria remaneant penes servientem infirmarie propter hospites, et infirmos, et comedentes in refectorio et in infirmaria ex gracia sive ex consuetudine cenantes.

Item quod monachi claustrales tam venientes de cellis quam comedentes et cenantes in infirmaria inferiori de cetero habeant focalia de camera domini prioris sufficienter.

Item quod monachi habeant cuvas ac alia aeisimenta in brachiaria ad balniandum ac eciam ad rasturam ; laventur cum eis

---

[1] Cf. preceding note.

placuerit, prout solebant, ita quod non habeant occasionem murmurandi.

Item quod nullus monachus conventualis carnes iantabit alicubi sine licencia speciali petita et optenta et precipue quando comedere in refrectorio per cursum tabularum tenetur [fo. 162ʳ].

Item quod nullus officiarius sine licencia speciali ut predictum est in officio suo presum[ps]erit comedere vel bibere, exceptis illis qui ex antiqua et laudabili consuetudine facere solebant.

Item quod priores cellarum habeant clothsekys ¹ competenter pro pannis sociorum suorum et quod solvant pro reparacionibus sociorum cum eis commorancium sicud tenentur per constituciones domini Willelmi Bateman episcopi.²

Item quod dicti priores providebunt fratribus suis de vectura equorum conpetenter quando mittuntur domi, ac eciam solvant pro expensis sociorum suorum in eundo et redeundo sicud solebant facere.

Item quod infirmarius providebit unum medicum in arte medicine peritum pro conventu sicud solebat facere.³

Item quod celerarius faciet ministrare conpetenter et honeste parentibus et amicis monachorum quando veniunt ad eos secundum statum et gradum eorum et precipue amicis claustralium.

Item quod nullus excusetur a celebracione misse sancte Marie neque de sancto spiritu nisi ipsi qui excusantur a celebracione mangne misse atque missarum episcoporum nuper defunctorum.

Item quod prior sancti Leonardi qui pro tempore fuerit tenetur interesse cum sociis suis ad utrasque vesperas in festo sancte trinitatis ac eciam in omni festo principali in secundis vesperis, sed in nocte trinitatis remanebit apud sanctum Leonardum cum uno monacho et alii duo erunt ad matutinas cum conventu.

Item dictus prior tenetur interesse ad servicium in die cene in vigilia pasche et pentecosten.

Item in vigilia epiphanie dictus prior sancti Leonardi cum

¹ Presumably bags for containing clothes : so O.E.D. ; Ducange interprets as sackcloth. This agrees with the injunctions of 1309 (loc. cit., p. 23).

² Cf. supra, injunctions ch. 4.

³ The medicus appears in infirmarer's rolls of 1394 and after (Victoria co. history of Norfolk, ii. 324).

120

sociis suis tenentur esse in capitulo, et in die epiphanie ad missam et in refrectorio ad prandium si sit dies piscium, sin autem nequaquam.

Item in die purificacionis erunt ad missam sed non in refrectorio ad mensam, si sit dies carnium vel piscium [fo. 162^v].

Item in vigilia Marie Magdalene tenentur interesse in capitulo auscultaturi leccionem obitus fundatoris nostri.

Item in anniversario Herberti et ad commendacionem et oblacionem et in refrectorio ad mensam sed non in vigilia ad dirige.

Item tenentur interesse in capitulo in omnibus vigiliis principalium festorum.

ADDITIONAL NOTES

P.94: BL Stowe charter 336 contains, on both sides of a parchment sheet 570 x 295 mm., ordinances in French vernacular for the Austin canonesses of Flixton uttered by bp William of Norwich, written in a bold black hand, ? s.xiv. If, as a s.xv endorsement asserts, the bp was William Bateman, not William Middleton (d.1286) nor William Ayermine (d.1336), this document may be the outcome of a visitation by Bateman, who often stayed at South Elmham in 1346 and later years (Norfolk Archaeol., xxv.133-7).

P.97 n.1: See also The early communar and pittancer rolls of Norwich ..., ed. E.C.Fernie and A.B.Whittingham (Norfolk Record Soc. Publications, 41.1972).

Pp.98-9: For monastic deans with these functions at Battle and Evesham abbeys see Chron. mon. de Bello, ed. J.S.Brewer (1846) pp. 192-3 and Chron. abbatiae de Evesham, ed. W.D.Macray (Rolls series, 1863) p.210. Cf. A.Hamilton Thompson, 'Diocesan organisation', Proc. Brit. Academy, xxix (1943) pp.152-3 and Cheney, From Becket to Langton, pp.121-2. A 'sigillum officii decanatus maneriorum prioris et conventus ecclesie sancte Trinitatis Norwyci' was attached by Mr Nicholas de Rudham, 30 Oct.1321, to BL Stowe charter 331. The damaged seal remains but the legend is lost. In other places the title of dean was given to a monastic manorial official (see V.H. Galbraith, 'Osbert, dean of Lewes', English Hist. Rev. lxix (1954) pp. 289-302) or to the head of a dependent priory, (see B.R.Kemp, ibid. lxxxxiii (1968) pp.505-15).

P.99 lines 12-7: The Worcester text relating to Hallow is printed and commented on by R.M. Haines, <u>Administration of the diocese of Worcester</u> pp.26-7 and dated after the appropriation of Hallow to the priory in 1268. Haines has much else of great value to say about exempt jurisdictions in Worcester diocese and elsewhere (p.13-30). For English archdeaconries of monasteries see also Jane Sayers, 'Monastic archdeacons' in <u>Church and government in the Middle Ages,</u> ed. C.N.L. Brooke et al. (Cambridge,1976)p.177-203. The sacrist of Ely enjoyed similar rights in parts of the Isle (ibid.p.171).

Pp.117-20: The chapter-ordinances are edited in different sequence, with two short passages here omitted because irrelevant to the injunctions, by J.B.L. Tolhurst, <u>Customary of the Cathedral priory church of Norwich</u> (Henry Bradshaw Soc. vol.82,1948)pp.234-45.
P.117 line 16: Tolhurst (p.242) reads 'exeuntes' in error for 'existentes'.
P.117 line 22: Tolhurst (p.238) reads 'Notandum' in error for 'Memorandum'.

XIII

Letters of William Wickwane, Chancellor of York, *1266–1268*

THE following short collection of letters occupies seven folios of an octavo parchment manuscript now in the Bodleian Library.[1] In fairly recent times it has been tightly bound in calf. There is a note on the front fly-leaf in Thomas Tanner's hand : ' This MS. belongs to Mr. Hill Rector of Stanhow [Stanhoe, Norfolk] Lent me May 1728'. Earlier than this there is no record of ownership, and it is not possible to tell whether the main sections of the manuscript were originally bound together. Documents copied on blank spaces in the middle of the fourteenth century simply show that the book was then in Yorkshire.

---

[1] Since 1855 its shelf-mark has been *Rawlinson* C. 775. (Summary Catalogue 12616.) Before this date, according to a note on the inside of the cover, it had ' neither place nor number '.

The first seven folios contain the Wickwane letters. These compose two gatherings, of which a^3 is missing. This must have been removed before the collection was compiled, since letter XIII continues unbroken from page 4 to page 5.[1] Letter XXII ends at the bottom of page 8 ; page 9 is filled with the second half of another letter written in a different hand. This is a bull of Pope Alexander IV giving dispensations to Sewall de Bovill, March 1255/6.[2] That this leaf was already used when Wickwane's clerk copied his letters is proved by the blots from page 8 appearing at the foot of page 9. The clerk presumably incorporated this leaf in the gathering for the sake of the blank dorse (page 10), where the Wickwane collection continues.

On page 15 a new gathering begins, and with it a new work. This is Glanvill's *De Legibus* written in two late thirteenth-century hands. (The first folio, containing part of the table, is missing.) On page 117 begins an *Ars computandi* and on page 127 a *Forma placitandi*. These are also in late thirteenth-century hands. A commission for a proctor, a charm for tooth-ache, a presentation to a living, and several indentures belonging to the middle of the fourteenth century are copied on pages 12, 14, 115, and 150.

The letters with which we are concerned were written by one person [3] in a small courthand, probably at the time of their composition. They are for the most part clearly written, but have suffered from damp and contain many mistakes of copying. The thirty-two letters can all be connected in some way or other with William Wickwane, chancellor and later archbishop of York. The collection was evidently a humble attempt at a letterbook, of a type prepared by many prelates and monasteries in the later middle ages. The clerk who wrote out these copies of the chancellor's correspondence seldom wrote names in full and most often omitted the date. Fortunately, he did not abbreviate in those places where full names are most useful and interesting ; and he gave enough dates to provide a general guide. Six letters are fully dated : from these and from the evidence of those to which we can supply probable dates we may conjecture that the series is in chronological order, from 2 February 1265/6 to 1268. The undated letters are not incompatible with this view. While we cannot say with certainty who the copyist was, it may well have been Wickwane's clerk, Henry of Sandford. He appears first as a sub-deacon sent to the bishop of Durham for ordination as deacon ;

---

[1] The book is numbered in pages, not folios. The pagination is modern.

[2] Printed *in extenso* in *Les Registres d'Alexandre IV*, no. 1218 (*Cal. of Papal Letters*, vol. i, 1894, p. 328).

[3] With the possible exception of letter XXXI, of which the writing bears close resemblance to the rest, but which was certainly executed with different pen and ink.

two letters relating to this are given (IX and X). It is probably Henry of Sandford again who writes to some friends in the south (he came from the diocese of Lincoln himself), and the author of this letter (no. XIII) is most probably the scribe of the collection. The style of this flowery epistle can be traced also in some of the official correspondence. Finally, letters XXIV and XXV both relate to the ordination of Henry of Sandford as priest, in December 1266. These indications seem sufficient to associate Henry particularly with the compilation of this collection. He occurs many years later as a man whom Wickwane could entrust with a position of responsibility. In 1280 the archbishop appointed him to be curator to the rector of Bainton, who was old and infirm : ' de tua sanctitate et industria confidentes.' [1]

The letters are interesting as they throw light on a little-known period of Wickwane's career, but they do not add much to the archbishop's biography. Letter I (February 1265/6) refers to a recent journey to the Roman Curia on business relating to the church of York. This journey may have been occasioned by the death of Archbishop Ludham and the election of Dean Langton to the see, early in the preceding year. Letter II yields the information, apparently hitherto unknown, that Wickwane held a prebend in the collegiate church of Ripon. What is more important than the biographical material contained in these letters is the general view they afford of the activities of a chancellor of York in the thirteenth century. In a small compass we find Chancellor Wickwane at the daily work of his office. The collection is short enough to be taken in at a glance, but is at the same time sufficiently varied to indicate much of the business which passed through the chancellor's hands.

William Wickwane deals with the churches attached to his office, fulminating against abstracters of tithes (I and III), presenting to a vicarage (XX, XXI), negotiating with the executors of his predecessor in a prebend (XVI, XVII). Letter XXI contains an interesting statement of the rights and duties of the vicar of Newbald. The prebend of Newbald involved Wickwane in considerable trouble, which was only just beginning in the period covered by these letters. Letter XXIII marks the first stage in the dispute, which ended in an adverse judgement for the chancellor. Wickwane entered into possession of this prebend after the death of canon Peter of Ferentino. Ancherus, cardinal-priest of S. Prassede, claimed the prebend by papal provision. The whole matter was threshed out by the legate Ottobono, at first in England and then at Rome, and Pope Gregory X gave judgement for Cardinal Ancherus in October 1272. It was then stated that, whereas Wickwane declared that Archbishop Ludham had con-

[1] *Register of Wm. Wickwane* (Surtees Soc.), p. 105.

ferred the prebend on him on the day of Peter's death, that contention was absurd, since Peter died at Viterbo. Pope Urban IV, on the other hand, had reserved the prebend on the day of Peter's death and next day gave it to Ancherus.[1] A complication is introduced into the story by the fact that during the dispute Ancherus had, by an earlier provision, held the prebend of Warthill and a pension.[2] Immediately after the legate's departure from England in 1268 a composition was entered into by Ancherus and the archbishop and dean and chapter of York, by which the former renounced his former pension and his claim to the Newbald prebend, and received an annual pension of 100 marks. This was finally agreed upon in May 1269.[3] In March 1270/1 the archbishop complained that the chancellor, Wickwane, and Thomas of Ludham, a canon, had not paid the pension to Ancherus.[4] The judgement of 1272, which gave Newbald to the cardinal, released the prebend of Warthill for another foreign nominee.[5]

In his capacity as chancellor, Wickwane had the duty of appointing the *magister scolarum* at York. Two letters referring to this post occur in the correspondence (XI and XII). They afford an early example of a master superseding the chancellor in the actual work of teaching in the cathedral school of St. Peter's, though probably the separation of offices had occurred much earlier.[6] The chancellor's control of education is also illustrated by letter VIII, by which Wickwane permitted John de Blaby to place his two sons at Guisborough Priory with the schoolmaster who taught the poor children maintained there by the convent. The existence of this person at Guisborough does not seem to have been noted hitherto. Chancellor Wickwane's permit should be compared with the injunctions which, as archbishop, he sent to the priory in 1280. The archbishop forbids the teaching of wealthy and important scholars, or even of poor scholars, unless the chancellor approves.[7]

A few of Wickwane's letters concern matters of only temporary

---

[1] *Les Registres de Grégoire X*, no. 81 (*Cal. of Papal Letters*, i. 442–3).

[2] Cf. *Register of W. Giffard* (Surtees Soc.), pp. 110, 170, 126, 138, 116.

[3] *Ibid.* pp. 6–7, 224–5.   [4] *Ibid.* p. 225 ; cf. p. 243.   [5] *Ibid.* pp. 170–1.

[6] The office of schoolmaster distinct from that of chancellor probably arose at York somewhere about the beginning of the thirteenth century. Leach says ' The Canon Law of 1215 [*Extra*, v. v. 4] perhaps stamps the date at which the chancellor finally differentiated himself into the master of a theological school ; the title and duties of the ordinary schoolmaster being confined henceforth to the grammar schoolmaster ' (*Early Yorkshire Schools*, I. xx. Yorks. Archaeol. Soc. Record series, xxvii, 1899). Cf. A. F. Leach, *The Schools of Medieval England*, 1915, pp. 112–13. The statutes of York Cathedral of 1307 refer to the chancellor as ' Cancellarius qui antiquitus magister scolarum dicebatur ' (*Early Yorks. Schools*, p. 13).

[7] *Reg. Wickwane*, printed in *Guisborough Cartulary* (Surtees Soc.), ii. 360 : ' Item scolas onerosas divitum et praepotentium scolarium   et etiam indigentium, prorsus prohibemus ; nisi quatenus Cancellarius noster Ebor. eas ad fructum et utilitatem Monasterii evidentius acceptarit.'

importance. These are recommendations to friends for the chancellor's clerks, and correspondence with the archdeacon of the East Riding about the loan of his house at York. (Letters V, VI, XIV, XV, XIX.)

Some of the letters emanate from the dean and chapter of York : they act on behalf of the chancellor (XXVII, XXX, XXXI), give a receipt for the legacy of a deceased canon (XVIII), and present monks of St. Mary's to the bishop of Durham for ordination, during the vacancy of the see of York (VII). The dean gives a certificate to Mauger of Ripon who has received Orders irregularly from others than his diocesan (XXII).

One letter from the dean and chapter introduces Edmund Mortimer as treasurer of York. On 7 August 1265 Henry III granted the treasurership to Edmund, who at this time cannot have been more than sixteen years old and may indeed have been born as late as 1255. In his letters patent the king stated that after the battle of Lewes he had been forced to issue letters in favour of Amaury de Montfort, whose title to the office he now revoked. Six weeks later the king wrote to enforce his order that Edmund should be given by the dean and chapter a stall in the choir and a place in the chapter.[1] The letter in this collection (XXVI) would certainly be later than this. In 1267 Amaury de Montfort received papal protection against the king's revocation, and next year Roger Mortimer appointed proctors in his son's cause at Rome.[2] The letter from the dean and chapter to the chaplains and tenants of the treasurership was probably written early in 1267.

The last letter of all is an agreement between William le Mo of Barthorpe and his son-in-law. It has no connexion with Wickwane beyond the fact that Barthorpe is in the parish of Acklam (East Riding), and that the church of Acklam (East Riding) was attached to the chancellorship of York.

The letterbook contains nothing startling. It tells us little about Wickwane's life, and where it touches on matters known from other sources it adds nothing of importance. Nevertheless, the collection is sufficiently detailed and sufficiently comprehensive to merit some attention as a picture of administrative machinery at work.[3]

---

[1] *Cal. of Pat. Rolls, 1258–1266*, pp. 436, 451–2 ; *Historians of the Church of York* (Rolls Series), iii. 187.

[2] *Cal. of Papal Letters*, i. 434 ; *Reg. W. Giffard*, p. 82. Cf. C. Bémont, *Simon de Montfort* (transl. E. F. Jacob, 1930), 260. Amaury is described in two Italian documents of April 1271 and April 1272 as treasurer of York (Bémont, *Simon de Montfort*, 1st edition, 1884, pp. 366, 367).

[3] I wish to express my best thanks to Professor A. Hamilton Thompson for his advice and many valuable notes, and to Dr. H. H. E. Craster and Mr. N. Denholm-Young for help with palaeographical difficulties.

MS. Rawlinson C. 775, page 1. [1]

[I]

Suo Th. suus W. salutem et intime dileccionis affectum. Karissime, si p. 1.
prosperamini prosperor, gaudeo si gaudetis. Unde ut vestris successibus
planius me coaptem de vestra continencia et statu regni et domini legati [2]
et de archiepiscopo Ebor' [3] si de eo aliquid audieritis mihi vero satisfacite
per rescriptum. De statu meo vos portitor presencium reddere poterit
cerciores. Scitote quod ubi vos fueritis reputo me presentem, in hiis qui
meum tangunt com*m*odum et honorem. Et quia que de novo emergunt
novo egunt remedio, scitote quod dum eram in curia domini pape pro
negocio ecclesie Ebor' expediendo, spoliaverunt me abbas et conventus de
Melsa, ordinis Cysterciensis,[4] decimis duarum bovetarum terre et dimidie
in parochia de Waugn'[5] et alia gravamina mihi plurima intulerunt. Unde
si placet super hiis impetretis litteram quod moneantur dicti abbas et
conventus quod ablata restituant et de dampnis mihi satisfaciant, alioquin
quod vocentur quod compareant coram domino legato ad diem certum
facturi et recepturi quod postulaverit ordo iuris. Scribatur decano Holderness' quod personaliter faciat monicionem et citacionem. Expediatur
nuncium quam cicius poteritis. Salutetis magistrum Benedictum[6] ex parte
mea. Dicatis si placet procuratori domini Portuensis[7] quod petat litteram
quam misit ei dominus suus a clerico domini archidiaconi Colecestr'[8] quam
recepit sibi vel mercatoribus qui eam sibi traderent tradendam, quia melius
notus talibus *habe*batur.[9] Valete. Datum Ebor', die purificacionis beate
Marie, anno domini m° cc lx quinto [2 February 1265/6].

[II]

Reverendis dominis ac in Christo fratribus capitulo beati Wilfridi Rypon'
W. cancellarius Ebor' salutem et fraterne cari*tatis* amplexum. Mandatum

---

[1] Letters and words in italics are omitted or obliterated in the original. The
headings of several letters, printed between parentheses, are in the margin of the
manuscript.
[2] Ottobono Fieschi, cardinal-deacon of St. Adrian, legate in England from
October 1265 to July 1268, later Pope Adrian V.
[3] There was no archbishop of York at the date of this letter. Ludham had died
on 12 January 1264/5. Dean Langton's election (12 March) was set aside by the pope.
Bonaventura refused the post in November 1265, and Walter Giffard was not provided
to the see until 15 October 1266 (see *Reg. W. Giffard*, p. ii).   [4] MS. *Cystern'*.
[5] The church of Wawne (or Waghen) was appropriated to the chancellorship of
York in 1230. It had previously belonged to the abbey of Aumale, which had conceded
to Meaux Abbey the right of patronage. These rights in it had been transferred to the
archbishop of York in 1227 (*Register of Walter Gray* (Surtees Soc.), pp. 52–3, 158 ;
Chronicon Abbatiae de Melsa (Rolls Series), i. 83). Meaux held considerable property
at Wawne, and the abbey chronicle records disputes with two other chancellors of
York on the matter of tithes claimed by the latter (*Chron. de Melsa*, ii. 76 *sqq.*, 291 *sqq.*).
Wickwane had another dispute with the abbey because it wished to set up water-
mills at Wawne (*ibid.* ii. 82–4).
[6] If, as seems likely, Wickwane's correspondent was in attendance on the legate,
this *magister Benedictus* may be Benedict Gaetani (later Pope Boniface VIII), who is
said to have accompanied Ottobono to England.
[7] John Tolet (O.Cist.), cardinal-bishop of Porto (1262–75).
[8] Either Hugh of St. Edmunds, archdeacon of Colchester in 1260, or Fulk Lovel
who is mentioned as archdeacon eighteen months after the date of this letter. (Le
Neve, *Fasti*, ed. T. D. Hardy, 1854, ii. 338.)
[9] Small hole in manuscript, followed by *batur*.

632　LETTERS OF WILLIAM WICKWANE

vestrum qua decuit reverencia pariter et honore nuper recepi quod hac instanti die Iovis[1] in capitulo nostro Ripon' vobiscum personaliter interessem super arduis ecclesiam nostram ibidem contingentibus tractaturus. Unde quia ex parte mea ad hoc faciendum opportunitas undique non occurrit, dominacioni vestre supplico quatinus, presencia mea non expectata, propositum conceptum exequamini cum effectu, scientes quod quicquid ad dei laudem et ecclesie utilitatem duxeritis faciendum mihi gratum erit pariter et acceptum. Datum Ebor' etc.

[III][2]

p. 2. W. cancellarius Ebor' vicario suo de Waugn' salutem et salutis memoriam. Quia intelleximus quod quidam malivoli, ausu temerario, dei timore postposito, decimas ecclesie de Waugn' debitas a locis in quibus a ministris eiusdem ecclesie percipi consueverant manu sacrilega asportarunt et eisdem reddere noluerunt, vobis mandamus, firmiter iniungentes, quatinus hac[3] instanti die dominica pulsatis campanis et accensis candelis publice excommunicetis in genere, nullam personam nominando, omnes illos qui dictas decimas a locis in quibus solvi consueverant asportarunt et asportatas detinent et eisdem spoliatoribus auxilium et consilium prestiterunt, et quid super hiis feceritis nobis per vestras litteras rescribatis. Valete.

[IV]

Suo A. suus W. salutem cum intime dileccionis affectu. Quia cum loquebar vobis alias eratis occupati mentem meam vobis exponere non potui tunc ad plenum, dileccioni vestre, de qua plenam fiduciam reporto, tenore presencium duxi supplicandum quatinus statum vestrum et domini vestri et familie quem prosperari desidero et quid de statu regni audieritis mihi rescribatis. Salutetis dominum[4] et amicos quos ex parte mea noveritis salutandos.

[V]

Discreto viro et fratri in Christo magistro R.[5] archidiacono Estriding' W. cancellarius Ebor' salutem et fraterne caritatis amplexum. De commoditate in domo vestra Ebor' habita et adhuc si placet habenda vobis regraccior cum affectu, paratus vobis in consimili etiam in maioribus pro viribus complacere, unde si graciam inceptam adhuc absque tedio et dispendio continuare potestis, vicario nostro super hoc velitis rescribere mentem vestram. Valete.

[VI]

(Responsio)
Venerabili viro et confratri suo[6] gracia speciali magistro W. cancellario Ebor' suus R. archidiaconus Estriding' salutem et cum optati successus

---

[1] If the letters are in chronological order (see *supra*, p. 627) this would be Thursday, 4 February, 1265/6.

[2] This very probably follows the action of the abbot and convent of Meaux, as described in letter I.

[3] MS. *hoc*.　　　　　　　　　　　[4] Followed by what appears to be *et* deleted.

[5] Robert of Scarborough. He was archdeacon of the East Riding as early as January 1262/3 (*Reg. W. Giffard*, p. 110). Immediately before this he was chancellor of York, in succession to John Gerveys, who became bishop of Winchester in 1262 (Le Neve, *Fasti*, ed. T. D. Hardy, iii. 163). Robert became dean of York in October 1279 (*Reg. Wm. Wickwane*, p. 1).　　　　　　　　[6] MS. *sui*.

augmento paratam ad beneplacita voluntatem. Quod in domo mea de qua scripsistis commoditatem habetis, gratum mihi est plurimum et acceptum, et utinam in munere residencie vestre personalis in qua si facultates mihi ad presens sufficerent vobis consorcii solacium libenter impenderem, possem vobis in corporali obsequio ad remedium subvenire. Desideranter enim [1] et affectu avido facerem ea omnia pro meo modulo que vobis possent cedere ad honorem. Valete feliciter in domino Iesu Christo.

[VII]

Venerabili in Christo patri et domino reverendo R.,[2] dei gratia Dunholm'   p. 3. episcopo, W.[3] decanus et capitulum Ebor' salutem in domino sempiternam. Presentatos nobis per religiosum virum dominum Symonem[4] abbatem sancte Marie Ebor' monachos eiusdem domus fratrem P. de L.[5] et Michaelem de Burton[6] ad ordinem sacerdotis, fratrem vero B. et fratrem W.[7] ad ordinem diaconi, paternitati vestre auctoritate qua sede Ebor' vacante fungimur mittimus ordinandos. Datum Ebor' .vi. idus Februarii, anno domini m.cc.lx. quinto [8 February 1265/6]. Valeat paternitas vestra diu.

[VIII]

Religioso viro domino . . .[8] priori de Gyseburn' W. cancellarius Ebor' salutem in domino sempiternam. Veniens ad nos Iohannes de Blabi,[9] timens ne filius eius primogenitus, si in loco minus tuto inveniretur, a sua [10] potestate in utriusque dampnum non modicum raperetur et gravamen, humiliter supplicavit quatinus de licencia nostra et favore speciali concederemus eidem filios suos duos posse stare apud Gyseburn' et subesse discipline et regimini illius doctoris qui pueros pauperes quos in domo vestra sustentatis pio[11] caritatis intuitu instruit et informat. Nos vero periculo cuiuslibet precavere volentes eius precibus et aliorum amicorum suorum humiliter annuentes, vobis in favorem et graciam et magistro puerorum vestrorum subsidium et honorem dictos pueros recipiendi, instruendi et informandi in moribus et sciencia usque ad festum quod dicitur Advincula sancti Petri proximo sequens tenore presencium concedimus facultatem. Datum etc.

[IX]

Venerabili in Christo patri ac domino reverendo R., dei gratia Dulmen' episcopo W. cancellarius Ebor' salutem et semperparatum ad obsequia famulatum. Quoniam relacione veridica frequenter audivi quod cultum

---

[1] MS. *sm̄*.   [2] Robert of Stichill, bishop of Durham 1261–74.

[3] William of Rotherfield, also known as William Langton, dean of York until his death in 1279.

[4] Simon of Warwick, abbot of St. Mary's Abbey, York, 1258–96.

[5] Phillipus de Langetofthe (Chronicle of St. Mary's, York, MS. Bodley 39, fo. 121).

[6] Together with Philip of Langtoft he had made profession on the return of Abbot Simon from exile, vii. kal. Jan. 1264. They had both entered the monastery in 1262 ' et ad terminum unius anni deo professi et a conventu in capitulo ut fratres recepti, sed dicto die ab abbate benedicti et plene confirmati ' (Chron. of St. Mary's, fo. 121).

[7] No persons with these initials are recorded in the abbey chronicle as entering the monastery in the four preceding years.

[8] Ralph Ireton, prior of Guisborough, *c.* 1262–80, bishop of Carlisle, 1280–92.

[9] A note on the family of Blaby is given in the *Guisboro' Cartulary* (Surtees Soc.), ii. 19–20.

[10] MS. *sui*.   [11] MS. *pro*.

divinum in ministris idoneis cupitis ampliari et ad hoc opem et operam libenter impenditis ut debetis, dilectum clericum meum H. de Sanford,[1] latorem presencium, subdiaconum, cum litteris dimissoriis sui episcopi et meis sibi pro titulo sufficientibus, paternitati vestre presento, rogans ac supplicans quatinus eundem in diaconum vestra clemencia pietatis intuitu suscipiat ordinandum. Et litteram factum vestrum testificantem eidem si placet concedere dignemini graciose. Valeat paternitas vestra semper in domino. Datum *etc.*

[X]

Venerabili in Christo patri ac domino reverendo R., dei gratia Dulmen' episcopo W. cancellarius Ebor' salutem in domino sempiternam. H. de Sanford Lincoln' dyocesis, subdiaconum, ad ordinem diaconatus promovendum paternitati vestre tenore presencium nostro titulo ac periculo presentamus. Datum Ebor' etc.

[XI]

p. 4. Sibi alteri, id quod sibi epistole vestre tenore inspecto et intellecto mentis exultacio erupit abymo que diu sopita iacuerat et remissa ; nec mirum cum mentes amicorum ea iungantur unione quod quicquid unum amicorum afficit et tangit in alterum transferat vis amoris. Ceterum scitote quod nichil adeo mentis mee proposito residet graciosum quam ea prosequi cum effectu que ad sociorum meorum commodum et honorem debeant redundare. Peticioni vestre pro dilecto mihi magistro J. de Neubald' adquiescerem penitus et faverem, si alterius intercessio pro dicto negocio et pro persona alia michi bene cognita non venisset. Quia igitur regimen scolarum Ebor' quo ad annum futurum magistro W. de Nessam concessi illud honestas transferre in alterum non permittit.

[XII]

Dilecto sibi socio magistro J. de Neubald' W. cancellarius Ebor' salutem cum dileccione sincera. Societatem vestram commodum et honorem desiderans cum affectu peticioni vestre adquiescerem diligenter si mea facultas hoc permitteret et honestas. Quia igitur regimen scolarum Ebor' in alterum transtuli antequam de vestra voluntate mihi aliquid fuerat intimatum, vestra discrescio grave non estimet si quod petitis mea impotencia non adimplet. Valete.

[XIII]

Reverendis dominis et amicis in Christo fidelibus domino R. Pernaut[2] et omnibus confratribus, eorum si placet clericulus in omnibus humilis et devotus H. de S.[3] salutem, reverenciam pariter et honorem. Scitis quod magnum confert absenti solacium inter amicos frequentata visio litterarum. Unde vestre dileccioni constare volo me Ebor' quietis corporalis frui solacio cum domino meo, quem cum iusticie[4] respicio, mentis exultacio propter

---

[1] Cf. *supra*, p. 627.

[2] The identical minims and the abbreviation of *per* make the original form of the name uncertain. Henry of Sandford's correspondents may well have been in the diocese of Lincoln, where Henry first took Orders (cf. letter X).

[3] Probably Henry of Sandford.

[4] *Sic.* The sense seems to demand an infinitive in place of this word to balance *loqui.*

eius benignitatem erupit abymo, quem cum loqui audio sue eloquencie
informacio mea replet[1] viscera huberime habundancia. Karissimi, si
prosperamini prosperor, gaudeo si gaudetis, habentes pro constanti quod
in vestrorum felicitate successuum tanto me maioris affeccionis fervor
accendit quanto vestrum sinceriori semper appeto[2] animo incrementum.
Status igitur vestri certitudinem quem deus conservet incolimem mihi vero
intimetis ut sic vestris successibus planius me coaptem et vicaria pagina
suppleat defectum presencie corporalis, quia vacacionem meam usque ad
tempus quasi abiectam partibus aquilonaribus oportet me parumper pau-
sare. De statu meo vos poterit portitor presencium reddere cerciores. Super
omnibus vero que vestris cedunt honoribus et per | me vestrum poterunt   p. 5.
expediri, de me securissime et confidentissime fiduciam adhibeatis. Com-
mendo me vestris oracionibus de quibus fiduciam concipio et spem firmam
ut me indignum, personam inhabilem et laqueo multorum criminum irre-
titum, dominus per suam graciam in melius reformet et mihi graciam
infundat et ad eius laudem in suo servicio me reddat acceptabilem. Verump-
tamen quia dicitur quod in absencia probatur amicus nec facilius quam per
opera experiri potest amicicia an solida fuerit vel superficialis, quia apparente
presencia mea et precibus meis intervenientibus terram patris mei vestri
agriculture exercicio sepius recreastis et aratri vestri beneficio fecundastis,
me ergo absente maior restat indigencia, tum causa temporalis amissionis
tum causa doloris prehabiti[3] tum causa mee absencie tum causa etatis iam
decrepite. Quicquid ergo pro eo feceritis mihi centies reputo dupplicatum,
quia dicitur quod alterum amicorum gravat et ledit, abire illesum reliquum
non permittit. . Valeat dominacio vestra per tempora longa.

[XIV]
(pro amico)

Salutem et felices ad vota successus. Dileccioni vestre non mea merita sed
portitoris presencium misera scribere me compellit, et vestre mansuetudinis
clemencia audaciam in me excitat in scribendo. Quia igitur nunquam
caritas ab eo inportune petitur cui semper in promptu est habundancius
impendere quam rogetur, pro latore presencium rogo quatinus eius precibus
benignum prebeatis auditum et clemencie vestre dexteram porrigatis eidem
ut benignitatis vestre favore assequatur quod intendit et preces meas sibi
senciat fructuosas.

[XV]

Ad maiorem[4] memoriam suscepti oneris cum honore statum vestrum
prosperari scincero zelantes affectu, de successibus vestris, quos Christus
votiva celebritate fecundet, tanto fervencius desideramus audire iocunda
quanto dulcioris recreacionis solacia nostro desiderio subministrant. Sane
quoniam W. latorem presencium famulum nostrum ad partes vestras
destinamus pro negociis nostris expediendis ibidem, pristine dileccionis
vestre affectum quem non credimus sublimitate mutatum, humiliter re-
quirimus, et rogamus quatinus eidem in hiis que nostrum tangunt commodum et honorem sitis propicii et iuvantes.

---

[1] MS. replent.
[3] MS. prehabite.

[2] MS. appetu.
[4] MS. Et iugem.

[XVI]¹

p. 6. Universis presentes litteras inspecturis Petrus Fauvelis de Florentino procurator venerabilis patris domini Gotifredi, dei gracia sancti Georgii ad
velum aureum dyaconi cardinalis, et dominorum ² Guydonis de Pileo et
Petri Romani, domini pape capellanorum, executorum testamenti quondam
magistri Petri de Ferentino canonici Ebor',³ salutem in domino. Noverit
universitas vestra me recepisse nomine procuratorio et habuisse xxx marcas
sterlingorum de fructibus prebende de Neubald' illius anni quo ipse magister
Petrus decessit, deductis expensis necessariis, a venerabili viro magistro
Willelmo de Wykewan', cancellario Ebor', computatis in hiis duabus marcis
pro cancello et duabus marcis pro pauperibus et quatuor marcis pro
defectibus domorum ipsius prebende, reliquis vero tempore turbaçionis
per barones provincie distractis penitus et dissipatis. De quibus xxxᵃ marcis
protestor et confiteor in procuratorio nomine ipsorum dominorum ab ipso
magistro fore satisfactum, renuncians excepcioni non numerate, non solute
et non tradite mihi pecunie, epistole domini ⁴ Adriani ⁵ et omni iuris auxilio
quod mihi prodesse posset et dicto magistro obesse ; necnon facio prelibato
magistro nomine procuratorio finemque quietacionem et refutacionem atque
pactum pro ipsis fructibus de amplius non petendo. Et ad maiorem
cautelam, ne in posterum aliqua dubitacio valeat exoriri exinde, tenorem
procuratorii predicti presentibus litteris inseri feci qui tenor talis est :

Universis presentes litteras inspecturis Gotifredus miseracione divina
sancti Georgii ad velum aureum dyaconus cardinalis, Gwydo de Pileo et
Petrus dictus Romanus de Ferentino, domini pape capellani, fidei com-
missarii bone memorie magistri Petri de Florentino canonici Ebor', salutem
in domino. Noverit universitas vestra nos instituisse, fecisse ac ordinasse
nostrum verum et legitimum ⁶ procuratorem Petrum dictum Fauvellum
de Florentino ad petendum et recipiendum omnes redditus sive proventus
dicti magistri Petri, scilicet, prebende de Neubald', de Foston',⁷ Ebor'
dyocesis, Malpedream et Petredfeld' ecclesiarum suarum ⁸ Wynton'
dyocesis, componendum, paciscendum, transigendum, compromittendum

p. 7. in arbitrum vel in arbitros iudicio eorum standum | et refutacionem et
quietacionem de dictis redditibus seu proventibus faciendum, finem et
pactum de amplius non petendo et omnia alia et singula faciendum que
verus et legitimus procurator facere potest, ratum et gratum habituri
quicquid idem procurator super premissis et quolibet premissorum duxerit
faciendum. In cuius rei testimonium etc. Anno domini etc.⁹

---

¹ For the following dispute over this prebend cf. Letter XXIII and *supra*, p. 628.
² MS. *domino*.
³ Petrus de Ferentino, or Florentino (cf. commission, below), ' dictus Egiptius ',
was a canon of York at least as early as 1241 (cf. *Cal. of Papal Letters*, i. 203, 301). It
seems probable that he was a canon in 1229 (*Reg. Walter Gray*, p. 29). He apparently
died very early in 1264/5 at Viterbo (*Cal. of Papal Letters*, i. 430, 442, having regard
to the date of Ludham's death : 12 Jan. 1264/5).
⁴ MS. *divi*.
⁵ Ottobono, cardinal-deacon of St. Adrian, papal legate in England, 1265–8.
⁶ MS. *legitamum*.
⁷ This was not a prebendal church. Peter de Florentino was connected with it as
early as 1229 (*Reg. Walter Gray*, p. 29).
⁸ Mapledurham and Petersfield, Hampshire. The former should not be confused
with the place of that name in Oxfordshire (cf. *Vict. Co. Hist.*, *Hants.*, iii. 93).
⁹ The year must be 1265, but a closer dating cannot be given.

Et ego decanus Ebor', perlecto et ascultato coram me procuratorio predicto, ad instanciam et peticionem predictorum cancellarii et Petri procuratoris presentibus sigillum nostrum una cum sigillo ipsius procuratoris fecimus apponi.

[XVII]

Venerabili in Christo patri domino Gotifredo, dei gracia sancti Georgii ad velum aureum dyacono cardinali, Willelmus dictus magister cancellarius Ebor' recommendacionem et cum omni reverencia se ipsum. Noverit dominacio vestra quod per compotum famulorum meorum iuratorum super hoc, inventum est me habuisse xxxª marcas sterlingorum tantum de fructibus prebende de Neubald' eo anno quo magister Petrus de Ferentino predecessor meus decessit, deductis expensis necessariis, reliquis vero tempore turbacionis per barones provincie distractis penitus et dissipatis, de quibus xxxª marcis recepi a Petro Fauvello procuratore vestro ii marcas pro cancello et ii marcas pro pauperibus ipsius prebende atque pro defectibus domorum iiii marcas, residuas solvi feci eidem procuratori in pecunia numerata, prout in litteris patentibus inde confectis plenius continetur. In cuius rei testimonium presenti cedule ad peticionem et instanciam eiusdem procuratoris sigillum meum apponi feci. Actum anno domini etc.[1]

[XVIII]

Venerabili in Christo patri domino Gotifredo dei gracia sancti Georgii ad velum aureum diacono cardinali et aliis executoribus testamenti quondam magistri Petri de Florentino canonici Ebor' Willelmus decanus et capitulum eiusdem loci salutem cum omni reverencia pariter et honore. Noverit dominacio vestra nos recepisse et habuisse a magistro Petro Fauvello procuratore vestro x marcas sterlingorum legatas fabrice ecclesie nostre a dicto magistro Petro concanonico nostro prout in eius testamento plenius continetur. In cuius rei testimonium etc. presenti scripto ad peticionem et instanciam dicti P. procuratoris vestri apponi fecimus signum nostrum.

[XIX]

Salutis sustantivum cum meliore quolibet adiectivo. Pro domino N. de E. clerico nostro dominacionem vestram rogamus quatinus in hiis que penes vos habet agenda precum nostrarum interventu eidem gratam impendere dignemini et favorem. Tantummodo si placet facientes quod preces nostras sibi senciat effectuosas. Valete.

[XX]

(pro sacerdoce ad habendam vicariam)

Dilectis fratribus et concanonicis W. decano et capitulo beati Petri Ebor'   p. 8. W. cancellarius eiusdem ecclesie salutem cum omni reverencia pariter et honore. Ad vicariam prebende mee de Neubald ad meam presentacionem spectantem dominum A. capellanum vobis presencium tenore presento, rogans ac supplicans quatinus eundem ad dictam vicariam admittatis et ipsum instituatis canonice in eadem. Datum etc.

[1] Probably early in 1266.

[XXI]

Universis Christi fidelibus presens scriptum visuris vel audituris W. decanus et capitulum beati Petri Ebor' salutem in domino sempiternam. Noverit universitas vestra nos ad presentacionem dilecti fratris cancellarii et concanonici nostri magistri W. de Wykewan' dominum A. de Rypon' capellanum ad vicariam prebende de Neubald' admississe ipsumque instituisse canonice in eadem. Consistit autem dicta vicaria in toto alteragio ecclesie de Neubald', exceptis decimis lane et agnorum de parochia et decimis de curia dicti canonici provenientibus, ita videlicet quod de curia dicti canonici nichil ad ipsum vicarium nomine decime debeat pertinere. Dictus vero vicarius per se ipsum et ydoneos ministros dicte ecclesie faciet deserviri et omnia onera ecclesie, hoc *est in* luminaribus [1] vestimentis et libris et aliis minutis ornamentis que ad vicarium pertinere debeant, sustinebit. In cuius rei testimonium presens scriptum sigillo capituli nostri duximus roborandum. Datum etc.

[XXII]

Universis presentes [2] litteras inspecturis Willielmus Eboracensis ecclesie decanus humilis salutem in domino. Noveritis quod auctoritate apostolica quam inspicientes Malgero de Rypona presbitero restituimus super vite sue meritis facientes inquiri, cum fame sibi testimonium suffragetur [3] nichilque canonicum obsistere compareret [4] quod ipsum ab officii sacerdotalis execucione deberet totaliter impedire, imposita ei penitencia pro eo quod ab alienis episcopis, preter sui dyocesani licenciam, omnes sacros ordines susceperat, ipsumque ab officio usque ad ascensionem domini suspendentes, secum dispensavimus ut ex tunc de beata virgine et pro defunctis valeat celebrare ; ita tamen quod parochialis ecclesie regimen non subeat quousque litteratura sua competencior eidem imploraverit dispensacionis graciam ampliorem. Quod ne ab aliquibus revocetur in dubium apposuimus presentibus signum nostrum. Datum apud Ebor', die Mercurii in septimana pasche, anno domini m° ccl xvi^to [31 March 1266].

[XXIII] [5]

p. 10. (littere procuratorie)

Venerabili in Christo patri domino Octobono dei gracia sancti Adriani dyacono cardinali, apostolice sedis legato, Willelmus Ebor' ecclesie cancellarius salutem et cum honore debito tanto patri paratam ad beneplacita voluntatem. In causa que inter me et magistrum Adam procuratorem et capellanum venerabilis patris domini Ancheri titulo sancte Praxedis presbyteri cardinalis procuratorio nomine, super prebenda quam in Ebor' ecclesia habeo et possideo, coram vobis vertitur seu verti speratur, Elyam de Fenton', [6] latorem presencium, procuratorem meum facio, ordino et constituo, dans ei potestatem defendendi excipiendi repplicandi reconveniendi transigendi et componendi et in animam meam iurandi de calumpnia et de

---

[1] MS. *hiluminaribus.*   [2] MS. *presentos.*   [3] MS. *suffragietur.*
[4] MS. *compareretur.*   [5] See *supra*, p. 628.
[6] Elyas of Fenton is described at some date unknown as ' capellanus canonicus capelle Eboracensis ' (*Reg. Wm. Wickwane*, p. 333). He appears often in Giffard's register as the archbishop's receiver (*Reg. Walter Giffard*, index, *s.v.* Fenton). In April 1268 it was his duty to pay Cardinal Ancherus's pension of 80 marks (*ibid.* p. 107).

veritate dicenda, et quodlibet iuramentum quod occurrerit exigendum et omnia alia faciendi que verus et legitimus [1] procurator facere potest et debet, necnon et alium procuratorem loco ipsius constituendi vel substituendi quociens viderit expedire. Ratumque et firmum habeo et habebo quicquid per ipsum Elyam vel constitutum vel substitutum ab eo nomine meo actum fuerit in premissis vel in aliquo premissorum. Pro eo eciam et pro constituto vel substituto ab ipso iudicatum solvi promitto sub ypoteca rerum mearum. Idem parti adverse significo. Et quia sigillum meum non est notum sigillum capituli Ebor' ad instanciam meam presentibus est appensum.[2] Datum Ebor'.xiiii. kal. Novembris, anno domini m° cc° lx sexto [19 October 1266].

[XXIV]

Venerabili in Christo patri R. dei gracia Dulmen' episcopo, W. cancellarius Ebor' salutem cum omni reverencia pariter et honore. Pater reverende, legistis et recolistis [3] de oleo in lecythis [4] paupercule, qualiter in vasa non pauca iussione prophetica dispertitum profusioris copie susceperit incrementum, quia celestis benediccionis unda non sistitur quamdiu eius haustui humana devocio preferatur. Vasa igitur sacri liquoris receptiva quia non in contumeliam sed in honorem secundum quod estimo praeparata, paternitati vestre tanquam filius represento magistrum videlicet R. de Napton', virum moribus et sciencia preditum et ornatum, quem ad ordinis suscepcionem non movet ambicio sed fervens devocio caritatis, et H. de Sanford, quem vestra pietas promovit in diaconum, nunc si placet pristina clemencia in presbiterum promovendum. Valeat vestra paternitas semper bene.

[XXV]

Reverendo in Christo patri R. dei gracia Dulmen' episcopo W. cancellarius Ebor' salutem, reverenciam et honorem. Dilectum clericum meum H. de Sanford diaconum tenore presencium paternitati vestre presento meo titulo et periculo in presbiterum ordinandum. Datum Ebor' .xvi. kal. Januarii, anno domini m ccc° [*sic*] lx° sexto [17 December 1266].

[XXVI] [5]

W. decanus et capitulum beati Petri Ebor' universis capellanis, libere   p. 11. tenentibus et aliis thesaurarie ecclesie nostre Ebor' salutem in domino sempiternam. Cum commiserimus custodiam ex certis causis beneficiorum terrarum et reddituum thesaurarie ecclesie nostre Ebor' domino Eadmundo de Mortuomari, ita ut in ministrorum remocione seu subrogacione nostrum sequatur consilium et assensum, faciens de proventibus sue custodie in ministris et ceteris ecclesie pertinentibus congrue deserviri, vobis mandamus quatinus in premissis sibi sitis in hiis que ad vos pertinent intendentes, sequestro preteriti temporis nobis salvo. Datum Ebor'.

---

[1] MS. *legittimus.*

[2] Cf. *supra*, Letter XVI. Wickwane used his own seal for Letter XVII. Durandus leaves it doubtful whether the seal of a cathedral chapter was sufficiently important to authenticate an *alienum negotium* such as this was (*Speculum*, II. ii, § 3. 13. See Boüard, *Manuel de Diplomatique* (Paris, 1929), i. 359–62).

[3] The reference is to the miracle of Elisha, *Vulgate*, 4 Reg. iv (cf. 3 Reg. xvii).

[4] MS. *l'ris.*

[5] See *supra*, p. 630.

XIII

[XXVII]

W. decanus et capitulum beati Petri Ebor' vicario de Burton'[1] salutem. Mandamus vobis quatinus perempter citetis Rogerum de N. quod compareat coram nobis in nostro capitulo Ebor' die Lune proxima post festum sancti Mathie apostoli [21 September], Johanni Pistori, servienti cancellarii nostri Ebor', super quinque mensuris ordei in quibus ei ex causa empcionis tenetur, ut dicit, reponsurus et iuri pariturus. Et ad probacionem citacionis facte nobis presentes litteras remittatis sigillo vestro signatas. Datum Ebor'.

[XXVIII]

(littere deprecatorie domino regi pro indigente)
Vestram clemenciam que super miseriis afflictorum visceribus pietatis semper affluere consuevit excitare nos cogit grandis egestas presencium portitoris, qui per dominum R. Foliot, militem, terris suis et bonis omnibus spoliatur. Piis igitur supplicacionibus regiam maiestatem duximus exorandam quatinus tante malicie more obviet consueto, et dicto spoliato remedio subveniat oportuno. Confidencia siquidem facilius optinendi[2] nobis tribuitur, quod dicta terra de ecclesia nostra tenetur, et precipue de prebenda magistri S. de Rupe chouardi,[3] cuius iura licet absentis pro viribus tueri volumus ut presentis.

[XXIX]

Reverendo domino et patri in Christo W. dei gracia Ebor' archiepiscopo,[4] Anglie primati, suus devotus filius W. cancellarius Ebor' salutem et tam debitum quam devotum ad obsequia famulatum. Reverende paternitatis vestre mandato humiliter recepto et diligenter inspecto, secundum eius tenorem de portitoris presencium moribus, honestate et vita a viris fidedignis, clericis et laicis, religiosis et secularibus, diligencius inquisivi, qui a tempore quo de curia ultimo rediit eundem asserunt laudabiliter conversatum. Et si aliquid in eo processerit quod eius famam et vitam aliquociens obfuscaverit, creditur per confessionem et penitenciam esse purgatum. Quia vero a vobis in hiis et consimilibus iusticia dependet et gracia, ipsum auctoritate vestra quousque graciam vestram optineat ab ordinis sui execucione suspendi. Valete. Datum etc.

[XXX]

p. 12. W. decanus et capitulum beati Petri Ebor' vicario de Acclum[5] salutem in domino. Mandamus vobis quatinus peremptorie citetis Thomam filium Isabelle, parochianum vestrum, quod compareat coram nobis in nostro capitulo Ebor' die Lune [16 January 1267/8] proxima post festum sancti Hillarii, cancellario ecclesie nostre Ebor' et Waltero Clok homini suo super

[1] Professor A. Hamilton Thompson says : ' It is almost certainly one of the two Burtons in the diocese which were in the peculiar jurisdiction of the dean and chapter of York, viz. Burton Leonard near Ripon, or Burton Pidsea in Holderness. There were vicarages in both churches.'
[2] Followed by quod possimus, expunged.
[3] MS. thor' Ward'. No canon named S. de Rochechouart appears in the archiepiscopal registers of the period.
[4] Walter Giffard, promoted 15 October 1266, died 25 April 1279.
[5] Acklam, East Riding, near Malton. The church was appropriated to the chancellorship by Archbishop Gray in 1221/2 (Reg. Walter Gray, pp. 143–4).

eo quod in libertatum nostrarum et ipsius cancellarii preiudicium necnon et ipsius Walteri dampnum non modicum et gravamen fundum ipsius violenter ingressus bona sua asportavit, et alias ei ut dicit molestiam inferre iniuste presumpsit responsurus et iusticie pariturus. Et ad probacionem citacionis facte nobis presentes litteras remittatis sigillo vestro signatas. Datum Ebor' .vii. id. Januarii, anno domini m° cc° lx° septimo [7 January, 1267/8].

[XXXI]

W. decanus etc. vicario de Acclum salutem in domino. Intimatum est quod quidam salutis sue inmemores quandam tenentem nostram, M. de T. nomine, a territorio beati Petri in villa de Barthorp violenter rapuerunt et incarceratam aliquandiu detinere in libertatum nostrarum preiudicium presumpserunt. Cum igitur omnes qui libertates nostras scienter infringunt incurrant excommunicacionis sentenciam ipso facto, vobis mandamus firmiter iniungentes quatinus hac instanti die dominice resurreccionis [1] dictos malefactores denuncietis in genere excommunicacionis sentencie subiacere, inquirentes de eorum nominibus diligenter, de quibus cum vobis constiterit nos de eisdem per vestras litteras cerciorare curetis. Et ad probacionem etc. Datum etc.

[XXXII]

Universis presens scriptum visuris vel audituris W. le Mo de Bartthorpe p. 13 salutem in domino. Noverit universitas vestra quod ego concessi W. Croc genero meo totam terram meam in territorio de Barthorpe cum vii bobus et ii equis et i vacca et cum omnibus superedificatis, cum pratis et pascuis necnon et aliis omnibus eisiamentis et libertatibus predicte terre spectantibus tenendum et habendum sibi omnibus diebus vite mee, reddendo mihi inde xxii marcas pro croppa eiusdem terre, bobus, equis et vacca prenominatis infra 4 annos, quandocunque in vita mea prefatam summam exigere voluero. Ad cuius pecunie solucionem fideliter faciendam infra terminum prenominatum, idem W. gener meus istos fide media obligatos mihi invenit fideiussores, scilicet Ricardum le Waleys et Johannem Bruer. Si autem ante solucionem dicte pecunie mihi faciendam de me abesse contigerit volo quod quantum eiusdem pecunie fuerit insolutum per ordinacionem capellani parochialis ecclesie de Acclum tunc temporis et Walteri de Barthorpe pro anima mea distribuatur infra terminum unius anni. Et sciendum quod prenominatus W. gener meus me in omnibus necessariis tam in victu quam in vestitu honorifice in domo sua sustentabit. Ita quod liceat mihi ele-mosinas pauperibus conferre de omnibus bonis domus dicti W. ut in propria domo mea consuevi ad meam liberam voluntatem. Preterea sciendum quod si sepedictus W. gener meus in aliquibus articulis vel in aliquo prenominatis deficere contingat, liceat mihi cum bonis meis sibi liberatis quandocunque voluero ad propriam domum meam reverti ita scilicet quod predicta terra, animalia et bona prenominata in adeo bono statu mihi solvantur quo prius recepit, secundum visum duorum virorum legalium quos eligere voluero. Cum tamen de pecunia mihi pro predictis bonis soluta sibi satisfecerim, volo etiam quod si instita [2] me incidere contingat in domo predicti W. quod melius animal de domo eiusdem W.,

---

[1] If 1268, Easter day = 8 April.
[2] *Sic.* ? for some word meaning mortal illness.

excepto equo suo, me racione mortuarii ad ecclesiam sequatur. Ut omnia autem ista rata conserventur et inviolata, tam ego quam dictus W. gener meus necnon et fideiussores nominati huic presenti scripto sigilla nostra dignum duximus apponi.

ADDITIONAL NOTES

For William Wickwane as chancellor of the church of York see C.T. Clay, York Minster Fasti, i (Yorks. Archaeol. Soc. Record series vol.123.1958)p.20.

P.636 no.XVI: For Mr. Peter of Ferentino see ibid.ii.58.

P.636 no.XVI line 15, and notes 4 & 5: for domini read divi; del. notes 4 & 5 and read: Gaius Comment.III 121,121a; whence Corpus Iuris Civilis, Inst.III.xx.4, Dig.XLVI.1.26.

P.640 n.3: Clay finds evidence outside the registers of Mr Simon de Rochechouart as canon of York in 1255. He became archbp of Bordeaux in 1275 (ibid.ii.5).

P.641 n.2: For some word...illness. read in fata.

XIV

LAW AND LETTERS IN FOURTEENTH-CENTURY DURHAM : A STUDY OF CORPUS CHRISTI COLLEGE, CAMBRIDGE, MS. 450.[1]

MY general title has grown out of a particular interest. Having been concerned with some parts of a little fourteenth-century manuscript in my college library, I became interested in the setting of these pieces—in the book as a whole, that is—and thence I inevitably advanced to consider the circumstances of composition. This led to Durham, and the conditions in which such a book as this could come into existence there in the first decades of the fourteenth century. Hence the general title. I cannot do justice to so large a theme ; but what I have to say about my chosen manuscript will, I hope, be seen to have some bearing on the matter as a whole. It may also invite you to reflect on even broader questions : how in those days legal and historical texts were copied, official records given publicity, propaganda diffused. It throws a little light, too, on the literary recreations of an ecclesiastical official in the Middle Ages.

The book, Corpus Christi College, Cambridge, MS. 450, is a fat little octavo on parchment of 154 leaves (with an indefinite number of leaves lost at the end). It is in the collection which belonged to Archbishop Matthew Parker (d. 1575) and is paginated and marked at significant passages with the familiar red crayon of Parker or one of his assistants. In appearance it is not very attractive. Nothing proves that it ever belonged to the great monastic library at Durham ; Montague Rhodes James,

[1] A lecture given in the John Rylands Library on Wednesday the 9th of May 1972, here slightly extended by kind permission of the Editor of the BULLETIN. I am obliged to the Master and Fellows of Corpus Christi College, Cambridge, for leave to use their MS. 450, and particularly record my thanks to Dr. R. I. Page, the Librarian, for giving me all possible facilities. I owe much to my graduate class of 1971-2 for their help in studying the contents of the manuscript, and am grateful to my colleague, Mr. T. A. M. Bishop, for advising me about the handwriting.

© *The John Rylands University Library of Manchester 1972*

61

who catalogued the Parker manuscripts in the library of Corpus
Christi College in 1912 opined that its owner had been " a
notarial personage of the diocese of Durham ",[1] and we shall
see that his conjecture was acute, even if it cannot be sub-
stantiated.

The book is a miscellany of treatises, poems, historical documents, legal records—about 120 items in all, most of them
already enumerated by James Nasmith, the scholarly fellow of the
college whose catalogue of its manuscripts was published in
1777. This book was perhaps written between the years 1290
and 1320. From the thirteenth and fourteenth centuries we
have miscellanies in fair profusion in English manuscripts,
each one different from the others. They all deserve study.
Any legal and literary miscellany has various separate claims
upon the historian. If we want to extract from it all the good-
ness we can, it is not enough to pick a few juicy plums out of the
whole pudding (which is what so often happens).[2] It is not
enough to look at the different sections of the book in isolation ;
for a composite volume may represent in its totality the interests
of an individual, even though he did not write it all himself.
Moreover, it may pay to look further afield for other miscellanies
containing some of the same texts. Some years ago Stephan
Kuttner, in discussing a canonistic miscellany (MS. Vat. lat.
2343), pleaded for " an examination of parallel tradition in
other manuscripts " with the object of affording " a glimpse
of patterns of composition which seem to have existed for this
type of books in the thirteenth century of which we know as yet
very little ".[3] Some miscellanies of English law certainly merit
the treatment which Professor Kuttner advocated, notably the

---

[1] M. R. James, *A Descriptive Catalogue of the Manuscripts in the Library of
Corpus Christi College, Cambridge* (Cambridge, 1912), ii. 364. James retained the
numeration of items in the manuscript which Nasmith had provided in his
catalogue ; and these numbers are used in references below.

[2] This has happened with Corpus 450, starting with the extraction of the
proverbs in Anglo-Norman (no. 84) by Le Roux de Lincy, *Le Livre des Proverbes
Français* (2nd edn., 1859), ii. 472-84 : " d'après un MS. de Cambridge du Corpus
Christi Collège. Extraits communiqués par Monsieur Francisque Michel."

[3] " Analecta Iuridica Vaticana (Vat. lat. 2343) ", *Studi e Testi*, 219 [Fest-
schrift Anselm M. Albareda, vol. i] (1962), p. 415.

so-called " London municipal collection ", compiled at least as early as the reign of King John, with which is connected a chain of manuscripts which go down to the collections of Andrew Horn, the London fishmonger, early in the fourteenth century.[1]

The anthology in Corpus 450 is far from being restricted to legal matter. But it has unity in the sense that most of it appears to have been collected and written—neatly though not beautiully—for one person's use : a deliberate compilation, even if it was compiled over a good many years. It is more than mere casual jottings, more than a commonplace book. That it deserves the title of miscellany will, indeed, become apparent as one exposes the contents of the mixed bag. But consider first the three longest and most prominent single items. They hang together : the *Summa artis notarie* of John of Bologna, the *Practica seu usus dictaminis*" edita Bononie ad utilitatem rudium " by Laurence of Aquileia, and a rather amorphous collection, or extracts of a treatise, on grammar. These put our miscellany into a familiar category. In the twelfth and thirteenth centuries grammar, epistolary guides, and treatises on the framing of documents commonly occur between the covers of a single book. It illustrates the alliance of the rhetorical and legal disciplines.[2] Rhetoric had somewhat changed its meaning since classical times, becoming the basic art of literary composition, with an accent on its practical value. This particularly characterized thirteenth-century Italy, where the profession of notaries, which called for learning in the law, included many literary men of distinction. Brunetto Latini is a notable representative, who taught rhetoric and the *ars dictaminis* in Florence, perhaps to Dante Alighieri ; a manuscript of his famous *Livre du Tresor,*

---

[1] See Mary Bateson in *Eng. Hist. Rev.* xvii (1902), 480-511, 707-30, and Felix Liebermann, ibid. xxviii (1913), 732-45. For later bibliography see BULLETIN, I (1968), 286-7, and for the contents of " Liber Horn " in the Corporation of London Records Office, N. R. Ker, *Medieval Manuscripts in British Libraries,* i : *London* (Oxford, 1969), pp. 27-34.

[2] See N. Denholm-Young, " The cursus in England ", *Oxford Essays in Medieval History presented to H. E. Salter* (Oxford, 1934), pp. 68-103 and E. H. Kantorowicz, "Petrus de Vinea in England ", *Selected Studies* (New York, 1965), pp. 213-46 ; cf. R. W. Southern on Peter of Blois in *Medieval Humanism* (Oxford, 1970), pp. 108-28.

63

contains a brief " Sometta in volgare modo ad amaestramento di componere volgarmente lettere ", giving forms of address for official and private correspondence ; and in the *Livre*, written in France during the 1260s, Brunetto speaks of the need for a town governor to have " ses notaires tres bons et sages de loi ki sachent bien parler et bien lire et bien escrire chartres et letres et ki soient bons ditteours ...".[1] The alliance of rhetoric and law encouraged instruction by means of exemplary letters— genuine or fictitious mattered not. The medieval administrator was obsessed with forms. The common use of Latin in official business encouraged the copying of models. In thirteenth-century Rome the compilers of *Summae dictaminis* availed them-selves largely of the resources of the papal archives, from which they borrowed hundreds of exemplary letters which displayed at once the rules of the cursus and the procedure of the curia.[2] Legal textbooks often took the shape of a series of formulas for writs, petitions, and so on, strung on a slender chain of com-mentary. In the secular field England produced as early as the 1180s the so-called Glanvill, *De legibus Anglie*: a legal treatise composed largely of forms of judicial writs; and numerous registers of writs followed during the thirteenth century. Form-ularies of a more eclectic sort continued to be assembled by servants of the Crown. The best-known English example, thanks to Mr. Denholm-Young, is the *Liber epistolaris* of Richard de Bury.[3] Dr. Alfred Brown has recently spoken of two formu-laries compiled by privy seal clerks in the early fifteenth century ; he remarks that for such men " letter-writing itself was a pro-fessional skill. Both Hoccleve and Frye included in their formularies collections of proverbs, phrases, exordies, even forms of wills, as well as old diplomatic letters considered to be good

---

[1] Quoted by Helene Wieruszowski, " Brunetto Latini als Lehrer Dantes ", *Archivio Italiano per la Storia della Pietà*, ii (1957), 171-98, at p. 186. For the *Sometta*, ibid. pp. 193-8. See further, Wieruszowski, " Rhetoric and classics in Italian education of the thirteenth century ", *Studia Gratiana*, xi (= *Collectanea Stephan Kuttner*, i, 1967), 171-207, esp. 189-98.

[2] Cf. C. Lefebvre, in G. Le Bras et al., *Hist. du Droit et des Institutions de l'Eglise en Occident:* tome vii, *L'Age Classique* (1965), p. 340.

[3] *The* Liber epistolaris *of Richard de Bury*, ed. N. Denholm-Young (Rox-burghe Club, 1950).

LAW AND LETTERS IN DURHAM 64

examples of composition, and forms of the letters they wrote day by day."[1]

In the field of ecclesiastical administration it was just the same.[2] Decree 38 of the Fourth Lateran Council (1215), " De scribendis actis ", demanded that " universa iudicii acta " should be committed to authentic writing. This probably explains a new efflorescence of this literature (if it deserves the name of literature) in the Latin Church. At Oxford, before the middle of the thirteenth century, William of Drogheda produced his *Summa aurea*, replete with forms of petitions, citations, and proxies for use in ecclesiastical litigation. In Italy this sort of teaching was standard practice. Here the notarial instrument was the commonest sort of deed ; the art of the notary was taught systematically ; and the textbooks contained an abundance of forms. The contact of this Italian tradition with England is seen in the *Summa artis notarie* found at the front of MS. Corpus 450. John of Bologna wrote it in the 1280s.[3] He had come to England with a new archbishop of Canterbury, John Pecham, in 1279. His book, which he dedicated to the archbishop, is a highly professional work, written by one who had studied in Bologna and practised in the court of Rome. The author says that he wrote it because he found English clerks shockingly ignorant of the right way to draw up deeds and do the paper work involved in appeals to Rome. He would show them how to frame the necessary documents. It was only right that

---

[1] A. L. Brown, " The Privy Seal Clerks in the Early Fifteenth Century ", *The Study of Medieval Records: Essays in honour of Kathleen Major* (Oxford, 1971), pp. 260-81, at p. 264.

[2] For early English ecclesiastical formularies see C. R. Cheney, *English Bishops' Chanceries, 1110-1250* (Manchester, 1950), pp. 123-30 ; Jane E. Sayers, " A Judge Delegate Formulary from Canterbury ", *Bull. Inst. of Historical Research*, xxxv (1962), 198-241 and *Papal Judges Delegate in the Province of Canterbury, 1198-1254* (Oxford, 1971), pp. 46-54 ; F. D. Logan, " An Early Thirteenth-Century Papal Judge-Delegate Formulary of English Origin ", *Studia Gratiana*, xiv (1967) [*Collectanea S. Kuttner*, vol. iv], 73-88.

[3] Edited by L. Rockinger in *Briefsteller und Formelbücher des xi bis xiv Jahrhunderts* (Quellen und Erörterungen zur bayerischen und deutschen Geschichte, ix), pp. 593-712. H. Bresslau, *Handbuch der Urkundenlehre* (2nd edn., Berlin, 1912-31), ii. 258, dated the Summa " about 1281 " : this is certainly too early. For more about John of Bologna see C. R. Cheney, *Notaries Public in England in the Thirteenth and Fourteenth Centuries* (Oxford, 1972), pp. 26-27, etc.

65

in these matters the English Church should copy the usage of the mother of churches.

Whoever owned Corpus 450, he certainly would not have troubled to get (and then to correct with great care) this copy of the *Summa*, if he had not been concerned with the drafting of legal documents for church courts. It would be natural for one with this professional interest to have as well the works on grammar and dictamen which are in Corpus 450. It was natural, too, that he should make copies of some old historic letters which were fine examples of prose style. To these, quite naturally, if he was involved in business-correspondence, he added a dozen or so pages of generalized forms of letters.[1] The fact that they abridge, and omit most of the proper names and dates, shows that they were copied for the sake of their formulas, put together here to instruct in the epistolary art. One gives the standard form of the " bulla que vocatur *post iter arreptum* ", another a royal letter of safe-conduct. Another is the form which a prior and convent used in admitting a person to confraternity. There are letters reporting—favourably—on some monks studying at Oxford. Although reduced to general terms, many of these letters may have been drawn from genuine correspondence. Two of the forms concern Durham, and others may well have originated there. They suggest a professional clerk, with monastic attachments. A document which occurs in a later section of the manuscript, confirms the suggestion. This is the licence granted by Rogerus Mathei de Monte Florum, count palatine of the Empire, to the prior of Durham, to appoint John de B., clerk of the diocese of Durham, to the office of notary public by imperial authority.[2] It is dated 1305.

In " John de B." have we run to earth the " notarial personage of the diocese of Durham " of whom M. R. James spoke (partly, no doubt, on the strength of this document)? If John de B. is not an invented name (perhaps a mere reminiscence of John of Bologna), we have no shortage of possibilities among the clerks

---

[1] Nos. 24-44. Other generalized forms are nos. 46 and 92. No. 24 has the rubric : " Rex archiepiscopo pro clericis suis ne compellantur ad ordines vel residentiam et hec litera in registro cancell'."

[2] No. 63, printed in Cheney, *Notaries Public*, pp. 154-6.

in the service of the bishops of Durham, c. 1300-20 ; but none of these is described as a notary public.[1] In any case, it would not do to jump to the conclusion that the compiler of the book buried his own licence in an abridged form in the midst of dateable documents of a later time. The rubric he gives to this licence : " Forma creandi et investiendi aliquos in officium tabellionatus ", does not suggest a man recording an auto-biographical detail. The inclusion of the licence is none the less a useful pointer. It was unlikely to have come the way of anyone not connected with Durham ; it would interest parti-cularly a clerk who was, or wanted to be, a notary public, or who was concerned on behalf of the prior of Durham in licensing a notary. Pointers of this sort will be observed in the course of analysing other sections of the volume.

Two sections, which comprise together nearly ninety pages of the manuscript, contain no less than thirty-nine papal letters belonging to the years 1295-1318. More than half of them are decretals and constitutions of Boniface VIII and his successors, of universal application and of practical importance to any ecclesiastical lawyer of those days. Of the others ten were of general historical or political interest, while nine bore exclusively or partly on Durham affairs. More will be said about this material later. Similar shading off, from the general and the legal to the local and the rhetorical, is seen in other sections. A text of the decrees of the Fourth Lateran Council occupies a quire and a half in the middle of the book, to be followed immed-iately by two papal privileges of 1265 and 1281 for the Mendicant Orders and a decree of the Second Council of Lyon (1274). Next to this comes King John's announcement of his surrender of his kingdoms of England and Ireland to the pope in 1213 ; a hundred years later this might be described as ancient history

---

[1] John de Buttrewyk, 1300 (*Records of Antony Bek, Bishop and Patriarch, 1280-1311*, ed. Constance M. Fraser (Surtees Soc., vol. 162, 1953), p. 206) ; John de Botheby, 1309-15 (ibid. pp. 136, 154, 160, *Registrum Palatinum Dunel-mense*, ed. T. D. Hardy (Rolls Series, 1873-8), iv. 390) ; John de Byrteley, 1310 (*Reg. Pal. Dunelm.*, iv. 101, 130) ; John de Brunnynghill, 1313 (ibid. ii. 1209, 1210, 1214). Master John de Brunne, 1310, although a notary public, does not meet the case, since he describes himself as a clerk of the diocese of Lincoln.

67

with contemporary interest, when the king's annual tribute to the pope, promised by King John, was being withheld.[1] With this item should be mentioned a group of six letters of Pope Innocent III at the end of an earlier quire and another group of four, with Stephen Langton's first letter as archbishop of Canterbury, in the middle of a later quire. Nearly all of these relate to King John's defiance of the pope over Stephen Langton's election, which brought the interdict on England, but one is the famous letter of Innocent III to the prelates and lay magnates of Germany on the matter of the Empire, May 1199, " Quanta debet esse ".[2] These letters may have been copied here for their historical interest ; but equally they were attractive as examples of the literary style of the Innocentian chancery at its most sonorous and most impressive.

A few other documents come under the head of history, contemporary or earlier. The Sultan Malik al-Ashraf boasts to King Aiton II of Armenia that he has captured Acre in 1291, and the king forwards the letter with an appeal for help to King Edward I of England, a committed crusader.[3] The records of this disaster, still vivid when they were copied into Corpus 450, may have prompted the inclusion of a pair of apocryphal letters allegedly exchanged by the king of the Tartars and Louis IX of France.[4] Then comes a little group of German origin : the declaration of war by Adolf of Nassau on King Philip IV of

[1] W. E. Lunt, *Financial Relations of the Papacy with England to 1327* (Mediaeval Academy of America, 1939), p. 165.

[2] The letters to England are nos. 1, 756, 757, 763, 790, 793, 823, 838, 893 in *Letters of Pope Innocent III concerning England and Wales*, ed. C. R. and M. G. Cheney (Oxford, 1967). The letter on the imperial election (Reg. super neg. imperii, no. 2) is dated in Corpus 450 (no. 19) inexplicably " Lateran, 8 kal. July, 6th year " (i.e. 24 June 1203). Langton's letter (no. 107) is printed by Kathleen Major, *Acta Stephani Langton* (Canterbury and York Soc., 1950), p. 1, n. 1.

[3] The letters are preserved in the *Historia anglicana* of Bartholomew Cotton, ed. H. R. Luard (Rolls Series, 1859), pp. 215-19 and the former in *Registrum Joh. de Pontissara, ep. Wintoniensis*, ed. C. Deedes (Canterbury and York Soc., 1915-24), ii. 481-2, where it is described as the translation of a letter directed " cuidam regi Christiano et postmodum ad Romanam Curiam ". Thomas Hearne printed from the register in his *Adami de Domerham historia* (Oxford, 1727), pp. 727-9.

[4] I have traced no other copies of these exercises in vituperation.

LAW AND LETTERS IN DURHAM   68

France when Adolf allied with Edward I in 1294,[1] the Emperor Frederick II's letter on the death of his captive son, Henry, in 1242,[2] and an exchange between an impostor who claimed to be the resuscitated Frederick and the duke of Brabant and the count of Holland in 1284.[3] Along with Boniface VIII's con-stitution, *Clericis laicos*, and related papal letters concerned with lay taxation of the clergy, the collection includes a copy of the French clergy's riposte to the pope of 1 February 1297 and of the English clergy's refusal to meet Edward I's demand in view of *Clericis laicos*; the copy of the latter is the only early text known of this bold remonstrance.[4]

I end this rough catalogue of the historical miscellanea in Corpus 450 with two documents of a different sort : not papal bulls or state-papers, but anonymous pieces of propaganda. They can be dated precisely to the years 1307 and 1308. The first is a splendidly florid harangue written in the name of " Petrus filius Cassiodori, miles catholicus, pugil Christi devotus " apostrophizing the noble English Church which lies languishing and dejected. He wishes her health, release from the yoke of captivity, and the reward of freedom. Peter attacks the reigning pope, Clement V. Popes, he declares, were not appointed to impose annual taxes and to kill men, but to offer gifts and sacri-fices for sins. Clement appoints to the cure of souls his nephews and relatives and illiterate persons, who are deaf to the bleating of their sheep and fleece them, and reap where others have sowed —and so on. Peter predicts that the Church and its priests

---

[1] Here in the name of " Radulphus ". Printed from the original in *Mon. Germ. Hist.*, *Constitutiones* (Legum sectio iv), iii. 501 no. 524, dated 31 August 1294 ; *Regesta imperii*, VI. ii (1291-8), p. 144 no. 431. Cf. V. Samanek, *Studien zur Geschichte König Adolfs* (Sitzungsberichte Akad. Wiss. Wien, Phil.-hist. Kl. 207, ii (1930)), 140 et sqq. and F. Trautz, *Die Könige von England und das Reich*, 1270-1377 (Heidelberg, 1961), pp. 136-7.

[2] In the letters of Peter de Vinea, liber 4 ep. 1, ed. J. L. A. Huillard-Bréholles, *Hist. diplomatica Friderici secundi* (Paris, 1852-61), vi. 29-30.

[3] The letter of the pseudo-Frederick was printed from this manuscript in *Mon. Germ. Hist.*, *Scriptores*, xxiv (1879), 462, n. 1. The reply was apparently printed from another manuscript by Lorsbach, *Florentii litterae* (Herborn, 1802).

[4] Printed hence in *Councils and Synods of the English Church*, ii, ed. F. M. Powicke and C. R. Cheney (Oxford, 1964), p. 1157. Bartholomew Cotton had a text of the letter, but did not copy it.

69

will be ruined unless Edward I, *rex christianissimus,* and the magnates (*potentes regni*) are persuaded to resist the conspiracies and arrogance and pride of this man, Clement, whose exactions from England further the greedy designs of France. According to a chronicler who reproduces this letter, it appeared early in 1307 while Edward I was holding his parliament at Carlisle. The king was listening to a formal protest against the pope's extortions when, lo, this letter as it were floated down from Heaven into the council and was read out in the hearing of king, cardinal nuncio, and all the prelates and others present. The harangue was intended, it seems, to get the clerical and lay notables to join forces in a demonstration against the pope.[1]

The second piece of propaganda is of a different kind. Otherwise unknown, it remains unlikely that the compiler of Corpus 450 composed it. He entitles it : " Lamentacio quedam pro Templariis." In five small pages the author (who was probably a French secular clerk) writes a reasoned defence of the Order of the Temple against monstrous charges brought by the French king's lawyers in 1307-8 ; but he writes in white heat, with savage partisanship. It is not anti-papal in tone : a writer early in 1308 could still hope that Pope Clement would intervene to save the Templars ; but its appeal is to the doctors and scholars of Paris, not to the pope. So far as I know, this is the only surviving text, and it is the sort of utterance which it would have been unsafe to publicize a few years later, when the Pope dissolved the Order.[2]

So far I have concentrated on those parts of Corpus 450 which, if not homogeneous, at least hang together, suggesting legal, rhetorical and historical interests in the compiler, interests of a fairly austere sort. But the *Summa* of John of Bologna is in fact followed by a quire with matter of very different sorts. It opens with the *Apocalypsis Golie episcopi* and

---

[1] Printed by Bale and Fox in the sixteenth, and by Goldast and Prynne in the seventeenth, century. The latest edition is of the text in *The Chronicle of Walter of Guisborough,* ed. H. Rothwell (Camden 3rd series, vol. lxxxix, 1957), pp. 371-4. Messrs. Richardson and Sayles doubt whether the letter was publicly read in the council (*Eng. Hist. Rev.* liii (1938), 431).

[2] Printed from this text in *Medieval Miscellany presented to E. Vinaver* (Manchester, 1965), pp. 65-79.

others of the " goliardic " satiric poems composed late in the twelfth century and directed against the court of Rome and curial officials and women. The Rhenish " Archpoet " is represented by his famous *Confessio Golie*, " Estuans intrinsecus ", and there are other poems from the *Carmina Burana*. This verse is followed by extracts from the pseudo-Aristotelian *Secreta Secretorum* and the Latin translation of the life and sentences of Secundus philosophus. As appendages to the grammatical section there are a few extracts from the early fathers, and Anselm and Bernard, and Petrus Alfonsi, the twelfth-century Spanish converted Jew. Scattered about the book are other short pieces of Goliardic and other Latin verse and extracts from the Alexander legends. All this was very old stuff in 1300 : no modern literature among it. Just one section of the book contains Anglo-Norman vernacular writings. They start with the manual of the French language by Walter de Bibbes-worth, written for the instruction of English youth[1] ; jingles, pious poems, and proverbs of the thirteenth century follow. But this vernacular part of the book occupies only twenty-five pages out of 308. Apart from these literary pieces, which leaven the legal, formal, and historical bulk of the book, there are only a few scraps of in-filling, where the original copyist had left part of a page or leaf blank. The scraps include at least two brief items (three lines " de baculo pastoris " and six lines on the honour and burdens of prelacy) which suggest that the writer had aspirations to high office ; but it would be unwise to form an opinion on such trifles. As a whole, the book is orderly and is not cluttered, like so many medieval miscellanies, with recipes for making ink and cures for gout.

This summary of the contents of the manuscript has already thrown up various pointers towards Durham. To locate the compilation as a whole at Durham is not to say that it was all written there ; and it may be argued that the compiler had acquired his *Summa* of John of Bologna and his decrees of the

---

[1] Usually dated, by its editor, Annie Owen (Paris, 1929) and others, *c.* 1280-90. Re-dated by A. C. Baugh " in the decade 1240-50, and almost certainly not later than 1250 " (" The Date of Walter of Bibbesworth's Traité ", *Festschrift für Walther Fischer* (Heidelberg, 1959), pp. 21-33, at p. 33. I am obliged for this reference to Mrs. C. R. Sneddon.

71

Fourth Lateran Council (written in hands which do not reappear elsewhere in the book) before he built up the volume as it stands. But the closer we look at the documents scattered all through the book, and compare them with the contents of manuscripts which are known to come from Durham, the more evident the Durham connection becomes. For his copy of the *Practica* of Laurence of Aquileia the writer chose a quire to match in size the John of Bologna ; and since the quire was completed in the same hand with a letter about the reinstatement of the prior of Durham in 1301, we may conclude that the whole quire was written by a monk or clerk of Durham (though not necessarily at Durham). One detail is revealing. In copying the last group of papal documents the scribe has inadvertently dated the constitution of Pope John XXII on the church of Toulouse (1317) at *Dunolm'* instead of *Avenon'* : a tell-tale mistake.

Even so, big question-marks still stand over the compiler and his work. What were the man's contacts in Durham : was he a monk of the great cathedral priory or a clerk employed by the monks, or was he an official of the bishop, or simply a cleric beneficed in the diocese? How did he come by all that he copied, including the stuff devoid of any obvious Durham flavour? What can we learn from it all about his interests? What does it tell us about law and letters in the remotest north of England in the early part of the fourteenth century?

Durham may have been remote from the main centres of population and learning, but the church of St. Cuthbert was represented by bishops of outstanding magnificence and a venerable Benedictine community. They were nobly housed and dominated the north-east both spiritually and temporally. They were co-heirs of the independence and culture of Anglo-Saxon Northumbria.[3] At certain times the cathedral monastery

---

[3] For the degree of temporal independence enjoyed by the bishops, see C. M. Fraser, *A History of Antony Bek* (Oxford, 1957) and " Prerogative and the Bishops of Durham, 1267-1376 ", *Eng. Hist. Rev.* lxxiv (1959), 467-76, and Jean Scammell, " The Origins and Limitations of the Liberty of Durham ", ibid. lxxxi (1966), 449-73. For the ecclesiastical situation see F. Barlow, *Durham Jurisdictional Peculiars* (Oxford, 1950) and R. Brentano, *York Metropolitan Jurisdiction and Papal Judges Delegates 1279-96* (Univ. of California Publ. in History, vol. 58, 1959).

produced notable historians and poets, and there are signs that around the year 1200 canonistic studies were cultivated at Durham.[1] By the late Middle Ages the monastery possessed a large, fine library which we know through its medieval catalogues and surviving books.[2] The opportunities were there, then, for the theologian, the historian, the poet, and the lawyer. But in most long-lived institutions the history of learning proceeds by fits and starts. A general view of the Durham community over more than five hundred years conceals the troughs and depressions. There were periods of quiescence. When in 1311 the bishop commended one of the monks for his scholarly eminence, he observed : " a saeculo enim non est auditum quod aliquis in ecclesia Dunolmensi adeo profecerat in scriptura quod sacrae theologiae meruit esse doctor."[3] During the first twenty years of the fourteenth century the library was perhaps relatively neglected ; as the century advanced the signs of more acquisitions and more use of the library appear. With Uthred of Boldon in the second half of the century, and John Wessyngton in the beginning of the fifteenth century, Durham scholarship revived. Probably the regular drafting of monks to the university of Oxford and their coming and going had something to do with it.[4] But for the years just after 1300 we have the words of the contemporary monk, Robert Graystanes, that the prolonged violent battle between Bishop Antony Bek and his monks not only cost the monastery enormous sums

[1] For the historians see H. S. Offler, *Med. Historians of Durham* (Inaugural Lecture, Durham, 1958). Of the poets Lawrence of Durham is the most noted. For canonistic texts closely associated with Durham see S. Kuttner, *Repertorium der Kanonistik, 1140-1234*, i (Studi e Testi, 71, 1937), 472, W. Holtzmann in *Revue d'Hist. Ecclés.* l (1955), 405-6, and C. R. Cheney in *Studia Gratiana*, xi (1967) [Collectanea S. Kuttner, vol. i], 37-68.

[2] *Med. Libraries of Great Britain : a List of Surviving Books*, ed. N. R. Ker (2nd edn., Royal Hist. Soc., 1964), pp. 60-76, and works there cited.

[3] *Reg. Palat. Dunelm.* i. 45-6.

[4] See R. A. B. Mynors, *Durham Cathedral Manuscripts* (Oxford, 1939), p. 4 ; W. A. Pantin, in *Oxford Formularies* (Oxford Hist. Soc., N.S. iv, 1942), pp. 219-45, " Two Treatises of Uthred of Boldon on the Monastic Life ", *Studies in Med. Hist. presented to F. M. Powicke* (Oxford, 1948), pp. 363-85, " Some Medieval English Treatises on the Origins of Monasticism ", *Med. Studies presented to Rose Graham* (1950), pp. 189-215 ; M. D. Knowles, " The Censured Opinions of Uthred of Boldon ", *Proc. Brit. Academy*, xxxvii (1951), 305-42.

73

of money and the lives of a prior and four monks ; it was generally demoralizing. "Once the dispute started", he says,
"the superiors were more occupied with litigation than with
observance of the cloistered life. There were unauthorized
confabulations, inordinate journeyings, a general dissoluteness.
... The superiors were either too preoccupied to correct the
sinners or else shut their eyes to offences for fear of rebellion."[1]
After Bishop Antony Bek's death in 1311 came the peaceable
Richard Kellawe, formerly a monk of the house ; but his days
were disturbed by the depredations of the Scots, and the passage
of the royal armies to and from Scotland brought disorders and
disasters to Durham.[2] Bishop Richard Kellawe's death in
October 1316 was the signal for a long and costly wrangle over
the choice of a new bishop. The monks elected brother Henry
de Stanford, but in the end he had to give way to the queen's
candidate, Lewis de Beaumont, consecrated in 1318. This
bishop (who lived till 1333) was on bad terms with the monks,
and involved them in expensive lawsuits. In short, the atmosphere was not conducive to the contemplative life or theological
study.

Such erudition as there was in the monastery was probably
adapted to law and administration. And in these spheres the
bishops' service offered similar encouragement to men of literary
taste and legal acumen. The records show Bek and Kellawe
providing their clerks with benefices and giving dispensations
from residence for study-leave. These bishops were surrounded
by university graduates, several of them specifically said to be
doctors of law. Kellawe's letters of dispensation and his indulgences are framed in very flowery terms.[3] Kellawe's clerk
can quote Ovid as well as the Bible.[4] When in 1319 Bishop
Lewis de Beaumont published statutes for his consistory court,
he required the commissary general to have an examiner " who
would be wise in the interpretation of laws and of the significance of witnesses' words, and who would know how to
translate carefully their statements out of the mother tongue

---

[1] *Historiae Dunelmensis Scriptores Tres*, ed. James Raine (Surtees Soc., vol. 9,
1839), p. 90.   [2] Ibid. p. 96.
[3] E.g. *Reg. Palat. Dunelm*. i. 102, 442, ii. 778.   [4] Ibid. i. 602.

into Latin ".[1] The business of both the bishops and the cathedral priory meant that they built up their own stores of muniments and with them, we must suppose, office-books : formularies, texts of canon law, notes on the history and liberties of their church, tax-assessments, and so on. These resources would be available on the spot to the studious monk or clerk.

Despite the endemic disputes between Bishops Bek and Beaumont and their chapters, it would be unwise to think that the resources of both the bishopric and the monastery were not to a large extent equally available to the lawyers and administrators and monks in this agitated, vigorous, small society. We know that Antony Bek borrowed law-books from the cathedral library, for it was a matter of complaint when he did not return them.[2] Richard Kellawe employed the monk-theologian, Master Geoffrey Haxeby, as his commissary general, and Geoffrey represented both the bishop and his community at the provincial council of York, held in 1311 to investigate the case of the Templars.[3] Kellawe, we are told, appointed other Durham monks to his episcopal household.[4] On the other hand we find the secular clerk who serves both bishop and monks at different times. Master Richard de Eryum (Eryholme-on-Tees, Yorks. NR) had been educated by the monks, pensioned by them, and beneficed in a prebend of their collegiate church of Howden. But in 1311 and 1312 Richard was Bishop Richard Kellawe's official, and in 1313 he had the bishop's dispensation from residence in the rectory of St. Nicholas, Durham, in order to take his degree in civil law. In 1316 he was back in the bishop's service, but also acted as proctor for the monks. By 1320 he was commissary of Bishop Lewis de Beaumont and, according to Graystanes, gave the bishop guidance and advice to the detriment of the monks. A few years later, having exchanged his prebend of Howden for a prebend of York, he entered the king's service, after the fashion of so many canons of York, and went overseas on diplomatic missions.[5]

[1] H. Spelman, Concilia (1639-64), ii. 481.   See Fraser, Hist. of Antony Bek, pp. 103-4, for lawyers in Bek's employment.   [2] Reg. Palat. Dunelm. iv, p. x.
[3] Councils and Synods, ii. 1328-9.   [4] Hist. Dunelm. SS., p. 94.
[5] See esp. Hist. Dunelm. SS., pp. 103-4 ; Reg. Palat. Dunelm., i. 9, 87, 100,

75

I have laboured these features of Durham in the early part of the fourteenth century—the tradition of learning, the library, the flurry of business and litigation which involved all the *literati* in and around the cathedral city—because I believe that Corpus 450 reflects the time and the place. This belief finds support in the reappearance of the same and similar material in other manuscripts coming from this time and milieu. I wish to refer briefly to four.

First, not far away from Corpus 450, on the next shelf of Corpus Christi College library, is another early fourteenth-century book very like it in size and format : MS. 445. It contains a well-known Italian manual, the *Summa dictaminis* of Richard de Pofi, which abounds in sample forms of papal letters. This is preceded by two folios with three forms of letters which concern Durham ; two of the three are in the episcopal register of Richard Kellawe. A fourth letter which follows is Pope Clement V's release of King Edward I from his oath to observe the charters (1 January 1306).[1] The handwriting of Corpus 445 and parts of Corpus 450 is so similar as to suggest the same man at work on both.[2]

(2) The *Summa* of Richard de Pofi reappears in British Museum ms. Lansdowne 397. This book can be identified in a catalogue of 1421 at Durham, where it was then kept among the cartularies and reference-books in the monastic chancery.[3]

474, 475-6, ii. 753, 784, 808, 1207 ; *Reg. T. Corbridge* (Surtees Soc., vols. 138, 141, 1925-8), i. 147 ; *Reg. W. Greenfield* (Surtees Soc., vols. 145, 149, 151-3, 1931-40), iii. 55, v. 289 ; *Ruchard d'Aungerville, of Bury* (Surtees Soc., vol. 119, 1910), pp. 181-3 ; *Historians of the Church of York* (Rolls Series, 1879-94), iii. 237-40 ; John Le Neve, *Fasti Ecclesiae Anglicanae 1300-1541 : Northern Province*, ed. B. Jones (1963), p. 84; *Calendar of Patent Rolls 1324-1327* (1904), p. 1.

[1] Cf. *Reg. Palat. Dunelm.* ii. 1125-7, i. 69. The release of Edward I from his oath is addressed to the bishop of Coventry and Lichfield, whereas the original (P.R.O., SC 7/10/36) from which Rymer printed (*Foedera*, I. ii. 979) is addressed to the bishop of Worcester.

[2] The hand of MS. 445 seems to be that of the section of MS. 450 mainly devoted to generalized forms, pp. 127-40.

[3] *Catalogi veteres librorum eccl. cath. Dunelm.* (Surtees Soc., vol. 7, 1838), p. 124, letter P. Duffus Hardy (*Reg. Palat. Dunelm.* iv. 483-531) discussed the book and printed extracts. He supposed (pp. 485-6) that Prior Wessyngton bought the book ; but an earlier connection with Durham seems probable. Cf. Pantin, *Hist. Essays in honour of James Tait* (Manchester, 1933), pp. 210-11.

Much of the book was written long after Corpus 450, and only reached its final form under Prior John Wessyngton, after 1414. Its earliest sections may not have originated in the Durham chancery. But the smaller items are significant. For several in-fillings at the end of John of Bologna's *Summa* in Corpus 450 turn up again in Lansdowne 397 in just the same form ; and the Lansdowne miscellanea, like Corpus 450, includes King John's surrender of his kingdoms and the letter of Pope Gregory X to the Emperor Michael Palaeologus applauding his return to unity with the Latin Church.[1]

A third manuscript from Durham (Bodleian MS. Laud misc. 402) yields the *Practica dictaminis* of Laurence of Aquileia, of which a copy is in Corpus 450. In the Laudian manuscript it is accompanied by six documents of the year 1313 which are all to be found in one group in Richard Kellawe's episcopal register.[2]

With a fourth manuscript we come to a book which displays the predominant features of Corpus 450, that is, legal and rhetorical formularies and papal constitutions. This is Durham Cathedral library MS. C.IV. 24, which was given by William of Gisburne, a monk senior enough to be Bishop Richard Kellawe's commissary in 1311 and distinguished enough to be in the running for the priorate in 1322, a man described by Robert Graystanes as a man of great piety and learning. His gift to the cathedral library is a larger and more imposing volume than Corpus 450, but it has points in common with the whole group of manuscripts under consideration. C.IV. 24 has a great wealth of formulary material. Like Corpus 445 and Lansdowne

---

[1] These letters occur in Lansdowne 397 at fos. 132^v and 132^r respectively, in Corpus 450 at pp. 234 and 278. Cf. Lansdowne 397 fo. 97^v with Corpus 450 p. 52 for identical *trivia*. Lansdowne 397 fo. 8^v has a " Taxacio bonorum episcoporum episcopatuum Anglie " almost identical with the list in Corpus 450 p. 107 (no. 21), in a similar hand, and certainly from a common source.

[2] Laud misc. 402 fos. 28^v-31^r (all in one hand of early fourteenth century) and *Reg. Palat. Dunelm.* i. 444-8, 444, 448-9, 449, 449-50. The last of these letters is followed in Laud misc. 402 fo. 30^v in the same hand by a letter of Roger de Seton, canon of York, about the church of Coniscliffe, dated at Durham, September 1275. At fo. 15^v is a letter of Archbishop William Greenfield to the dean of Pontefract about the church of Womersley, 6 November 1315, found in *Reg. W. Greenfield*, ii. 225-7.

77

397 it has the *Summa* of Richard de Poſi, and also parts of well-known thirteenth-century collections of letters. It has six out of the ten letters of Innocent III preserved in Corpus 450. Like Corpus 450, again, it contains some recent papal constitutions and documents of recent continental history.[1]

If we cannot establish direct links between these various manuscripts, it is none the less pretty clear that they drew on the same local sources and reflect, in a measure, the same interests in their compilers. But comparison of Corpus 450 with other Durham miscellanies still leaves room for speculation and enquiry about the origin of some of its contents. The older literary pieces were probably all to be found in the cathedral library, where the medieval catalogues record copies of Petrus Alfonsi, the Apocalypse of Golias, and Secundus philosophus.[2] The Emperor Frederick's letter on the death of his son was to be found among the letters of Petrus de Vinea. As regards the contemporary miscellanea, the letter of Peter, son of Cassiodorus, is, I have remarked, in a chronicle, and that part of the chronicle was written at Durham, according to its latest editor.[3] For that matter, it turns up in miscellanies from Christ Church, Canterbury, and from Whalley Abbey in Lancashire. We need not wonder how such a piece passed from hand to hand, seeing that it was produced in a parliament attended by clerics from all over the country. The lament on the Templars, unknown elsewhere, might have been picked up by a Durham student at Paris in 1308,[4] and a clerk of Durham might take special interest in the Lament ; for although the Order of the Temple had no preceptory in the diocese, Bishop Antony Bek, as patriarch of Jerusalem, was the senior commissioner appointed by Clement V, with the archbishops of Canterbury and York and others, to enquire into the charges against the Templars in Great Britain.

---

[1] See the description in Thomas Rud, *Codicum MSS eccl. cath. Dunelm. catalogus classicus* (Durham, 1825), and Karl Hampe in *Neues Archiv*, xxiv (1899), 522-4. For William of Gisburne see *Reg. Palat. Dunelm.* i. 10-2, cf. 77, 110-1, 207 etc. and *Hist. Dunelm. SS.* p. 102.   [2] *Catalogi veteres*, pp. 25, 33, 56.

[3] *Chronicle of Walter of Guisborough*, p. xxxi.

[4] The (spurious) complaint of Pope Boniface VIII against Nogaret, addressed to the university of Paris, was copied at Carlisle into the bishop's register (*Reg. J. Halton* (Canterbury and York Soc., 1913), ii. 50-52).

The bishop's muniments were certain to include the bulls of
Clement V about the Templars which were copied into Corpus
450 : the bull of 12 August 1308, " Regnans in celis ", which
ordered an enquiry, to be followed by a general council ; and the
bull of 6 May 1312, " Considerantes dudum ", which suppressed
the Order. And Bek's earlier activities as a diplomatic agent of
Edward I may account for three of the German documents in
this miscellany ; for the bishop was among the king's envoys to
Adolf of Nassau in 1294 and was in Brabant when Adolf declared
war on Philip of France. We might also attribute to Bek's
position as patriarch of Jerusalem after 1306 the copies of letters
about the Orient, were there not a more direct source at hand :
the Franciscan Hugh, bishop of Byblos, in the county of
Tripoli. For Friar Richard of Durham, who composed the so-
called Lanercost Chronicle (to 1297), reports edifying conversa-
tions with Bishop Hugh, who gave him information and stories
about Tripoli, while he was staying as an exile in the northern
Franciscan custody of Newcastle during the 1290s. Later on,
Bishop Hugh accompanied Antony Bek on his visitation of
Durham in 1300; and in 1305 Bek tried and failed to secure
for him the revenues of the priorate of Coldingham, a cell of
Durham in Lothian.[1]

Granted that many features of Corpus 450 seem to locate its
owner in the Durham circle of clerks and lawyers about the
years 1300 to 1320, what can be learnt from a section of the
contents which I have reserved for discussion to the last : the
contemporary papal letters and constitutions? I have already
mentioned them, but they deserve separate attention. They
range from the first year of Boniface VIII to the second year of
John XXII—from 1295 to 1318—and they occupy most of two
separate sections of the book which add up to almost one third
of the volume as it now stands.[2] As already noticed, they are not
all of one sort. Nine of the thirty-nine concern Durham :
the visitation of the convent, the restoration of the prior, the

---

[1] A. G. Little, *Franciscan Papers, Lists and Documents* (Manchester, 1943),
pp. 35, 46 ; Fraser, *Hist. of Antony Bek,* pp. 60, 132, 148, 164, 194. Bishop
Hugh eventually obtained the episcopal see of Pola, ibid. pp. 165-6.

[2] Pp. 141-90 and 266-308. A few other documents are interspersed.

bishop's appointment as patriarch, the reservation of the bishopric, provisions for clerks to be beneficed in the diocese. These present no problem ; they will have formed a necessary part of the local muniments—either the bishops' or the monks'—and so were ready to hand.[1] But how did the other papal pronouncements reach Durham? Half a dozen in Corpus 450 had a general political interest rather than a Durham interest or legal importance[2] : such letters as that of Boniface VIII exhorting Edward I to make peace with the king of France, and that of John XXII denouncing Edward II's enemies. Since some of these are found in the episcopal registers of York and Carlisle and fall within the pontificates of Bek and Beaumont, whose registers are lost, it is not unreasonable to suppose that they may originally have reached the bishops of Durham by the same channels. English episcopal muniments stored many such documents of public interest and many were copied, though unsystematically, into bishops' registers. Bishop Oliver Sutton of Lincoln kept copies of certain apostolic letters and constitutions of the lord Boniface in a *pokettum* in his house at Theydon Mount in Essex in 1297, and he had Boniface VIII's announcement of (his election to the papacy copied into his register.[3]

How such letters reached the provinces of the Church is an extremely interesting question.[4] They might get as far as the

---

[1] Nos. 51 (1301), 61 (1302), 90 (1306), 99 (1313), 100 (1316), 108-9 (1317), 113-113A (1318), and related documents of papal officials : 23 (1301), 52 (1301). The missing part of no. 113A, including the date, 6 June 1318, can be supplied from the papal register, Reg. Vat. 68, fo. 299^r (*Registres de Jean XXII, Lettres Communes*, ii. no. 7421, *Calendar of Papal Letters*, ii. 177).

[2] Nos. 35, 45, 49, 91, 93, 101.

[3] *Rolls and Register of Bishop Oliver Sutton*, ed. R. M. T. Hill (Lincoln Record Soc., 1948-69), vi. 15, v. 76-79, cf. iii, p. lxxviii.

[4] On 17 November 1260 Alexander IV wrote to princes and prelates throughout Europe to resist the Tartar invasions (Potthast, *Reg. Pontificum*, no. 17964, etc.). The letter to the Lord Edward survives in original (P.R.O., SC 7/3/24, whence *Foedera*, I. i. 403) ; the letter to the archbishop of Canterbury was copied in the annals of Burton Abbey (*Annales monastici* (Rolls Series, 1864-9), i. 495-9) and elsewhere (Brit. Mus., MS. Harl. 64, fo. 182^r) ; that addressed to the archbishop of York was sent with a covering letter from him to the bishop of Durham, and preserved at Durham (MS. C.IV. 24, fo. 70^r). The whole procedure for

metropolitan, at least, by the hand of an official papal messenger. That procedure probably applied to the announcements of papal elections, demands for taxes, summonses to councils ; others were obtained by the king's agents in his interest, were brought by his messengers from the Curia, and circulated by royal authority to the prelates.   Beyond this, we can only speculate on how a private collector might satisfy his curiosity about current affairs.   Northern chroniclers came by several of the bulls we find in Corpus 450, maybe from episcopal sources.

But the main interest of the compiler of Corpus 450 was, as we have seen, legal.   Twenty-five of the thirty-nine modern papal letters and constitutions are legal in character.   The compiler did not excerpt them from official law-books, apart from two copied from the *Liber Sextus* (published in 1298).[1] For the rest, they appear in small groups in Corpus 450, mostly with their original dates and roughly in chronological order. Their texts have not undergone the revision they show in the official law-books.   We must remember that this was a great era in the uttering of papal constitutions.   And the onus seems generally to have been laid on the governed to find out the law by which they were governed.   There was no *Acta Apostolicae Sedis* published twice a month.   For papal pronouncements the lawyers in the provinces depended largely on friends and agents in the Curia to keep them up to date.   Such men were com-missioned to get copies for English prelates of relevant-seeming documents in Rome or Avignon.   About 1314 the prior and convent of Worcester wrote to their *specialis clericus* in the Curia, saying : " Please send us news of the Curia, with any new con-stitutions, if there are any."[2]   In 1319 an English notary public at Avignon got leave to make a certified copy from the papal register of a recent constitution of John XXII, which was later

publishing " Regnans in celis ", 12 August 1308, delivered by two papal *cursores* to the archbishop of Canterbury, is seen in *Reg. Simonis de Gandavo* (Canterbury and York Soc., 1934), i. 325-34.

[1] Nos. 53, 54 : " De veneratione sanctorum " (*Sext*, 3, 22, 1) and " De regulis iuris " (*Sext*, 5, 12, 5).

[2] *Liber ecclesiae Wigorniensis*, ed. J. Harvey Bloom (Worcs. Hist. Soc., 1912), p. 7.

81

copied into the register of the bishop of Rochester[1] ; since the bishop was in the Curia at the time, he probably commissioned the copy. When on 23 July 1302 Boniface VIII gave his judgment, " Debentes superioribus ", in the Durham dispute over visitation, the bull was given into the hands of the litigants ; and thence, we may suppose, it found its way to Corpus 450.[2] But since the decision was of vital interest to other monastic cathedral chapters of England, the monks of Worcester and Canterbury soon procured copies. They may have got their texts from Durham, or their agents in Rome may have copied from the papal register. This was not all. " Debentes superioribus " also turns up with other " constitutions " of Boniface VIII in some continental collections which gathered together decretals under the title *Extravagantes*, because they lay outside the big official law-books of Gregory IX, Boniface VIII, and Clement V. Evidence from all over Europe points to a casual but fairly prompt diffusion by private enterprise of short collections and single constitutions. It is noteworthy that in the cathedral library at Durham there is a volume, perhaps given about the year 1300, with a large collection of " extravagant " decretals. Among them are eight of Boniface VIII which occur in Corpus 450, mostly in the same order.[3] If the writer of Corpus 450 was in the service of so important a prelate as Antony Bek, bishop and patriarch, or had access to the episcopal archives of Durham, he was well placed to come by this material. He may even have been himself at some stage a proctor of the bishop or the prior of Durham in the Curia, in a specially favoured position. We do not know.

[1] *Reg. Hamo de Hethe* (Canterbury and York Soc., 1948), i. 345-8. For notarial exemplifications from the papal registers of Innocent III (1213 and 1215) authorized by the auditor of causes in 1283, see E. Martin-Chabot, *Mélanges d'Archéologie et d'Histoire* (Ecole française de Rome), lxx (1958), 431-4.

[2] No. 61. An original is noted in the fifteenth-century " Magnum repertorium " of Durham muniments, as no. 8 of the Bonifacian bulls. It was copied into cartularies : Fraser, *Hist. of Antony Bek*, pp. 86-87. Cf. *Registres de Boniface VIII*, no. 4730 and *Extravagantes communes*, 1, 7, 1.

[3] Durham Cath. Libr. MS. C. II. 2 fos. 9ᵛ-10ʳ, 261ʳ. The manuscript was given by brother Gilbert de Shyrburn, who was a senior monk by 1300. For other canonistic contents of the MS. see Walter Ullmann, *Cambridge Hist. Journal*, ix (1949), 261, n. 16.

What can be said by way of conclusion about the manuscript and its compiler? Taking the broadest possible limits, the miscellany began to take shape not earlier than 1290 and was being continued at least as late as 1318 (for we must remember that it stops in the middle of a mandate of John XXII dated 6 June 1318). It shows what was available to a compiler who, at any rate during the later years, was associated with Durham. To see the matter in perspective it may be a good thing to look beyond the parallels we have so far remarked in manuscripts from Durham, and recall that these kinds of documents, and in some cases the very same documents, turn up in miscellanies in other times and places in England. For the literary tastes and the opportunities to come by historical and legal texts, displayed in Corpus 450, were by no means peculiar to Durham, or for that matter to England. Other manuscripts of John of Bologna's *Summa* and the *Practica* of Laurence of Aquileia and Mr. Denholm-Young's lists of other dictaminal works in manuscripts of the thirteenth and fourteenth centuries in England[1] show that there was an English demand for manuals of this sort.

Two examples, neither of them drawn from Durham, will illustrate the frequent combination of such manuals with legal and historical material. MS. Peniarth 390C in the National Library of Wales was written in the main during the 1260s, the " Liber epistolaris " of Richard de Bury (later bishop of Durham), in the collection of Lord Harlech, was written about 1324-6. Both contain treatises on dictamen and collections of epistolary forms. Not only has the Peniarth manuscript a manual, " Quot sint genera dictaminum " and the " parva compilacio magistri Bernardi [de Meung]" [2]; it includes a text

---

[1] " The cursus in England."

[2] For manuscripts of Bernard de Meung with bigger collections of forms see M. Manitius, *Gesch. der lateinischen Literatur des Mittelalters* iii (1931), 307 and F. J. Schmale in *Mitteilungen des Inst. für österreich. Geschichtsforschung*, lxvi (1958), 23 ; and Denholm-Young, " The cursus ", p. 92 for five manuscripts in England. The Peniarth text appears to be hitherto unnoticed ; the " parva compilacio " (p. 91) is here followed by " Littere de maiori compilacione magistri Bernardi " (p. 115). I am obliged to Mr. B. G. Owen and Mr. Daniel Huws, of the National Library of Wales, for information about Peniarth 390C.

83

of Glanvill, *De Legibus Anglie.*[1] It also contains groups of documents not wholly reduced to anonymous forms, connected with Henry of Lexington, bishop of Lincoln, the diocese of York, and Burton Abbey in the mid-thirteenth century. Richard de Bury's bulky book draws on a much wider range of documents. It, too, has business letters from several English bishops' offices (Lincoln, Lichfield, and Durham). It includes the letter of Peter the son of Cassiodorus and several of the letters of Popes Boniface VIII and Benedict XI found in Corpus 450. Each manuscript contains one of the letters of Innocent III which are found in Corpus 450, with other related letters absent from the Durham collection. A large proportion of the " Liber epistolaris" is taken up with the official diplomatic correspondence—the more florid products of the papal and royal offices of state—likely to appeal and to be of practical use to a royal clerk with literary pretensions and with ambitions in the field of diplomacy.

With regard to papal letters and state-papers in these miscellanies, it is worth underlining the fact that although this was an age when official channels of publication were inadequate, access to public records was not jealously guarded. Both administrators and chroniclers found their way to the sources. What has been said about the distribution of papal bulls applies to other sorts of documents. The letter of the French clergy to the pope regarding " Clericis laicos ", 1 February 1297, (Corpus 450 no. 34), was copied into at least three English bishops' registers, at Canterbury, Carlisle, and Hereford. Contemporary chroniclers often laid hands on authentic copies or drafts of state-papers, though the ways by which they got them are usually hidden from us. The chroniclers of St. Albans, from the early thirteenth century onwards, are celebrated

---

[1] The combination of a Glanvill text with ecclesiastical forms of letters occurs in a much humbler miscellany of the same period, Bodleian MS. Rawl. C. 775. It contains, with Glanvill, an *ars computandi* and a *forma placitandi*, and thirty-two letters, partly abridged. Most of the letters are on official business of William Wickwane as chancellor of York, 1266-8, but five of them concern his clerk, Henry of Sandford, who may well have composed and copied them all. Empty spaces in the book were later filled with a form of proxy, a charm for toothache, a letter of presentation, and several fourteenth-century Yorkshire indentures. See *Eng. Hist. Rev.* xlvii (1932), 626-42.

LAW AND LETTERS IN DURHAM

for their zeal, if not their accuracy, in copying documents. They had been preceded by Roger de Hoveden. Some of the documents found in Corpus 450, from Innocent III onwards, had been copied by Hoveden, Wendover, and Rishanger. The Norwich chronicler, Bartholomew Cotton, writing in the 1290s, had ten of the texts included in Corpus 450. The casualness of official transmission was an encouragement to both the chronicler and the miscellany-maker to take copies of important documents that came their way.

With some possible sources of Corpus 450 in mind, can we approach closer to its owner than M. R. James did when he described him as "a notarial personage of the diocese of Durham"? I imagine a clerk with a reasonable training in letters and a professional interest in the law. He makes this miscellany for his own use. He begins, perhaps, in early days when he is studying in the schools by buying or copying a few short treatises, and adds literary and theological quotations, proverbs, ribald Latin poetry, and some vernacular verse of a staider sort. As time goes on, and he is employed at Durham, he has access to ecclesiastical archives. He copies, or an underling copies at his order, public documents and formulas which may " come in useful some day ". The nature of the material relating to Durham suggests that he may have served both bishop and cathedral priory. The general historical material points to a lively mind, an interest in the problems which arose for a clergy under two rules of law, a lack of sympathy with Boniface VIII over clerical taxes and with Clement V in his handling of the scandal of the Templars. Master Richard de Eryum, who incepted in civil law about 1314, might just conceivably be the man. Certainly he had served both the bishop and the convent of Durham for a decade before he became a canon of York and went into royal employment. But any attempt to put a name to the compiler seems to be idle speculation. Were I simply looking for a name I should have to admit total defeat.

What I have been looking for is the sort of man who might have compiled Corpus 450 and the circumstances in which such a miscellany as this could take shape. In this quest I hope that your time and mine has not been entirely wasted. Miscellanies

85

of this kind, which survive from many centres, in many parts of Europe, deserve careful study, even when they are hard to analyse simply and are not superficially exciting. They can throw light on the training and tastes of a particular class of men. In the nature of their education, and to some extent in their outlook and occupations, it is often difficult to distinguish servants of the Crown in the early fourteenth century from the servants of nobles and bishops and great monasteries. They showed versatility in changing masters. The men who served civil and ecclesiastical governments in the West were trained in law and letters ; and the same men participated in the counsels of bishops and monasteries as in the counsels of kings and princes and municipalities. They were both salaried and beneficed. Of late, the part played by such men in the composing of differences between Church and State and in the development of what is usually called the "lay spirit" in government has become better recognized. The background and rewards of these men and their multifarious activities are adumbrated in recent works.[1] A. B. Emden's compact accounts of Englishmen who passed through Oxford and Cambridge illuminate the careers of the professional lawyers and administrators. Corpus 450 and other miscellanies like it may tell us more about this class.

[1] E.g. F. J. Pegues, *The Lawyers of the Last Capetians* (Princeton, 1962) ; J. R. Strayer, *Les Gens de Justice en Languedoc sous Philippe le Bel* (Toulouse, 1970) ; W. R. Jones, "Patronage and Administration : the King's Free Chapels in Medieval England", *Journal of British Studies*, ix (1969), 1-23 ; J. H. Denton, *English Royal Free Chapels 1100-1300* (Manchester, 1970) ; A. L. Brown, "The Privy Seal Clerks in the Early Fifteenth Century".

ADDITIONAL NOTES

Pp.62-3: The mss. are very numerous, and the modern literature copious and increasing, on the medieval art of letter-writing and on anthologies of letters, genuine and fictitious. See Giles Constable, Letters and letter-collections (Typologie des sources du moyen-âge occidental, fasc.17. Turnhout,1976); Rudolf Schieffer and H.M. Schaller, 'Briefe und Briefsammlungen als Editionsaufgabe', in Mittelalterliche Textüberlieferungen und ihre kritische Aufarbeitung (Beiträge der MGH Historikertag, Mannheim, 1976. MGH,1976) pp. 60-70; John Taylor,'Letters and letter-collections in England 1300-1420', Nottingham Medieval Studies xxiv (1980) 57-70. In Scriptorium xxv (1971) 19-24 and pl. 7-8 M.-C. Garand describes 'un bréviaire portatif de droit' (Vatican ms. Borgia lat. 355). It is a pocket-book of unusual format, apparently prepared (1283-4) by or for an Italian notary, Bartholomew de Jordano of Ferentino, containing several short treatises of canon and civil law. Syon abbey library had a volume (T. 50) which combined a formulary of letters on diverse subjects with a treatise of Giles (? of Bellamera) 'Super formam electionis', constitutions and decretals of Innocent III, tituli and extracts from Extra, notabilia on the Digest, and 'alia notabilia iuris ecclesiastici et regni' (Catalogue, ed. M.Bateson, p.193).

P.77 line 21: The copies of the letter of Peter son of Cassiodorus from Canterbury and Whalley are in BL ms. Add.6159 fos.99v,108rv and BL ms. Add.10374 fo.15r. It is also to be found in Cambridge, C.C.C. ms. 358 fo.36v and in the Liber epistolaris of Richard de Bury.

P.81 line 22: The first five of the Bonifacian constitutions in Corpus 450 (Pott.24061-3,24060,24064) are also found in Durham C.II.2 fos.9v-10r and, in slightly different order, in archbishop John Romeyn's register (fos.153r-154v) at York (I am obliged to Dr David Smith for xerox copies) and in Bartolomew Cotton's Historia anglicana (RS) 265-80. For the interest of these texts (especially Pott.24063) for legal doctrine see P. Landau,'Zum Ursprung des "Ius ad rem" in der Kanonistik', Proceedings 3rd International Congress of Med. Canon Law, Mon. Iuris Canonici, Series C vol.4 (Città del Vaticano, 1971) 83-4.

P.83 line 1: William Wickwane's collection is here,no.XIII. A short series apparently assembled (1318-39) in the office of Anthony Bek(II), chancellor,later dean,of Lincoln, and then bishop of Norwich, is in BL ms.Harl.3720.

P.84 line 28: Mr. Richard de Eryum appears in 1304 and 1310 as a poor clerk seeking a benefice from Malton priory (Reg. T. Corbridge, i.147, 279-80, Reg. W.Greenfield,iii.55). He often appears in Durham and York registers in 1311 and after. Mr. A.J. Piper kindly calls to my notice Durham,Misc.ch.4937, of 9 Feb.1303, in which Richard de Eryum, clerk,pledges himself under his seal to serve the prior and convent of Durham 'circa causas et negocia eorum ecclesie sue ubilicet expedienda...'.

XV

NOTARIES PUBLIC IN ITALY
AND ENGLAND IN THE LATE MIDDLE AGES *

I

It must not be supposed from my title that I have
come to talk about the institution of notaries public in
Italy. In such a company as this, that would be impertinent
on my part, and temerarious. My aim is simply, as a student
of history, to see in what respects the notary public, when
he appeared in England, copied the Italian notary, and
to see what mark he left on English society and government,
even though his profession made much less impression than
did the notarial profession in its homeland. The social
and constitutional features of Italy and England in the
thirteenth century were — of course — widely different.
It is therefore a matter of some interest to discover at
what points and in what branches of human activity the
notary public assumed in England some of the tasks which
his brother performed in Italy.

In Italy, at the beginning of the thirteenth century,
the institution of notaries public is already fully formed;
both civil and ecclesiastical government have traditions of
written record having probatory force which came from
the highly sophisticated classical Roman world. The Empire
possessed public registries to furnish official copies of legal
transactions in private law. The Romans also submitted
certain private transactions to the judgement of a court

* A paper read in the Facoltà di Giurisprudenza in the Università degli
Studi di Siena on 26 September 1979.
    To reduce the footnotes, I have not cited authorities for particular state-
ments, if they can be easily traced in the index to my *Notaries public in
England in the XIII and XIV centuries* (Oxford, Clarendon Press, 1972)
(= *NPE*).

and the court recorded the judgement in authentic writing. The conveyance of property was confirmed by the *in iure cessio*. In the Mediterranean world of the early Middle Ages we find the *instrumentum publicum* produced and authenticated by a *notarius*, or *iudex*, who is treated as a *publica persona*. In Italy, by the twelfth century, notaries appear who claim authority from the pope or the emperor to draw up public instruments, certified by their subscription and special mark ; and these instruments are treated as valid *ubique terrarum* - not only in Rome or in papal territory or the empire [1]. In Italy (and in some other parts) by this time the civic or the episcopal notary keeps a cartulary or register of the deeds he drafts, and such registers (at least by the thirteenth century) are deposited in public custody. In England there is nothing like this.

In Anglo-Saxon England men could convey land without writing, and when in the twelfth century a written charter became a usual method of record, it was not always surrounded by the trappings of the law. The scribe of a later cartulary of the abbey of Bury St Edmunds noted that the names of some ot the abbey's early benefactors were unknown: « Cognoscat tamen lector quia ex magna parte hec cognitio periit, quoniam olim multa sancto Edmundo sine cartis data sunt » [2]. Alternatively, in the Anglo-Saxon period and after, the record of a title might be inscribed in a precious liturgical book. « It fortified the title, not so much by a mode of authentication which could possibly satisfy any rational system of jurisprudence or objective test of credibility as by its sacral, magical quality ». Another register of Bury tells how Abbot Ording vindicated the franchise of the abbey in the joint county court of Norfolk and Suffolk, about 1150: « et sciendum quod ista cronica prescripta clare patet in psalterio capelle domini abbatis usualiter iacente coram eo » [3]. But by this

---

[1] G. DURANDI, *Speculum iuris*, Lib. II partic. II De instr. editione § 8.23 (ed. Basileae 1574, p. 659b) and *NPE* pp. 4-5.

[2] F. HERVEY (ed.) *Pinchbeck register* (1925), II, p. 282.

[3] *Ibid.*, II, p. 299 (the sacrist's register), cf. *NPE* p. 7.

time a record of legal importance was commonly committed to a sealed writing; and in thirteenth-century England the term *instrumentum publicum* generally means a document which has been sealed by competent authority [4]. The seal is now used universally for authenticating conveyances and other contracts, testamentary wills, the judicial sentences of the courts, and all manner of documents needed for transacting diplomatic and commercial affairs. Ecclesiastical corporations and officials have their seals of office; municipal corporations, gilds, and individuals have begun to possess them.

In the year 1237 the papal legate in England, Otto cardinal deacon of S. Nicola in Carcere, held a council at London and published canons. Among other matters he addressed himself to improving the procedure of ecclesiastical courts and to detection of forgeries. In these canons we read, in so many words, that « publici notarii non existunt » in England, and again: « tabellionum usus in regno Anglie non habetur » [5]. Otto did not try to force a new *publica persona*, the notary public, on a country where the institution was unknown. Instead, he demanded more careful control of the *sigillum autenticum* which every holder of ecclesiastical office ought to possess. The notary public was still a long way away.

II

He first appears in England, to my knowledge, as draftsman of a public instrument twenty years after the legate Otto's council. On 18 December 1257 a notary

---

[4] E.g. in 1225 the bishop and chapter of Salisbury seal a cathedral statute and call it « instrumentum publicum ». *Register of St Osmund* (Chron. and memorials of Gt Britain and Ireland no. 78, 2 vols. London 1883-4), II, p. 42. In 1258 Christ Church, Canterbury, seal a conventual « instrumentum publicum ». *NPE* p. 4 n. 3.

[5] Cf. C.R. CHENEY and F.M. POWICKE (edd.) *Councils & synods with other documents relating to the English Church, vol. II: 1205-1313* (Oxford 1964), II, pp. 257-8, cc. 27-28.

public named John drew up a contract between Earl Richard de Clare and a proctor of the Marquess William de Montferrat, for the marriage of the marquess to one of the earl's daughters ; the contract was made in the queen of England's chamber in Westminster Palace, in the presence of King Henry III and his Provençal queen, Eleanor. If both parties to the contract had been English, it would probably have been drawn up as a bipartite chirograph, with the seals of the two parties attached.

Between 1257 and 1280 we find about a dozen alien notaries public and two or three English employed in England to draw up and authenticate public instruments. Not surprisingly, the instruments mostly concern foreigners. One records the will of the Provençal bishop of Hereford. Another is a contract between one of the queen's uncles (Peter of Savoy) and the count of Geneva. Others concern claims by Italians to English benefices arising from papal provision, and a debt incurred by the bishop of Winchester to Florentine bankers. Several of these occurred in the course of the legation of Cardinal Ottobuono (later Pope Adrian V) in England, 1265-68. Another, made at the Domus Templi, London, in 1279, records receipt by merchants of the Lucchese firm of Riccardi of 2000 marks from the collectors of a papal tenth for the Holy Land[6].

About this time a notary public from Siena worked in England for various employers and samples of his work remain in English ecclesiastical archives. He prepared documents of 21 March 1278 and 15 July 1280 at London as *Ildebrandinus Bonadote de Senis, sancte Romane ecclesie auctoritate notarius publicus*, and may be the « Ildebrandus publicus notarius » who was paid between 1277 and 1282 by the executors of Walter of Merton, bishop of Rochester, « for writing and innovating appeals »[7].By 1282 he had

---

[6] For notaries active in these years see *NPE* pp. 15-25. For a facsimile of the receipt given at the Temple in 1279 see B. KATTERBACH and C. SYLVA-TAROUCA (edd.) *Epistolae et instrumenta saec. xiii* (Exempla scripturarum, 2. Vatican, 1930), no. 33. It incorporates vernacular Italian receipts.

[7] J.R.L. HIGHFIELD (ed.), *Early rolls of Merton College* (Oxford Hist. Soc. n.s. 18, 1964), pp. 142-5.

added to his title *et imperiali auctoritate iudex ordinarius ac notarius*. His instruments included exemplifications of proxies and mandates in lawsuits, and of appeals to the Roman Curia - by the bishop of Durham against the archbishop of York, by the bishop of Worcester against the archbishop of Canterbury. Professor Brentano also found in Florentine archives an instrument prepared by Ildebrandino at London on 4 May 1284 of a transaction concerning Florentine merchants and Yorkshire wool [8]. We do not know what sort of business first brought Ildebrandino to England, but these records show that he found employment in several quarters for six years, from 1278 to 1284.

III

The years during which Ildebrandino da Siena was active in England were critical for the notariate there. In January 1279 Pope Nicholas III made provision of an English Franciscan resident in the Curia, John Pecham, to the archbishopric of Canterbury. When Pecham entered the see he brought a faculty from the pope to appoint within a year three suitable men to the office of notary public. We can, I think, identify in his service during the next few years the three Englishmen whom he appointed: John Alani of Beccles (who had been the bishop of Hereford's proctor in the Curia, 1276-79), John de Sancto Martino of Lewes, and William de Holyam. Equally important is the fact that the archbishop brought with him from the Curia an Italian notary public: *Iohannes quondam Iacobi de Bononia apostolica et imperiali auctoritate notarius publicus*. Giovanni da Bologna remained in the archbishop's service for several years, but may have preferred the Italian climate to the English; for he is found doing English business in the Curia from 1282 onwards, and is not heard

---

[8] R. BRENTANO, *York metropolitan jurisdiction...* (Univ. of California publications in history 58. Berkeley, 1959), pp. 192-3.

of in England again. He did, however, dedicate to the archbishop his « Summa de his que in foro ecclesiastico occurrunt notariis conscribenda », dated by Rockinger 1289.

The preface to the *Summa* is illuminating. This experienced Italian notary came to the Ultima Thule of Canterbury in the spirit of a missionary, bringing the notarial gospel of Bologna and the Curia to barbarian English clerks. He deplores the total lack of training in the *ars notarie* of the archbishop's clerks. He will show them how to draft the documents required in ecclesiastical business. « Since the most holy Roman church is mother and mistress of all, it is right and proper that all should, so far as possible, imitate her in all their records of legal processes (*in omnibus suis processibus*) ». He gives a large selection of formulas and formal letters in the *Summa*, drawing on his English practice and introducing names of English litigants, proctors, and notaries. Giovanni da Bologna, like other writers of *Artes*, teaches the whole matter of writing business-letters, and does not confine himself to public instruments. So he may have contributed to the general development of letterwriting in England. Be that as it may, his service with John Pecham coincided with the employment of more and more notaries public by English bishops, and his *Summa* circulated in England. Conditions in the Western Church as a whole were favourable: the growth of papal taxation, provisions to benefices, a tendency of the Curia to draw litigation to Rome instead of delegating to the provinces. In just the same period — from the 1270s onwards — notaries public appear in northern France, the Netherlands, Germany, Poland, and other regions where, not long before, the *usus tabellionum* was said to be unknown, even when local notariates existed [9]. All the northern countries received some of their earliest experience of notaries public from the operation of papal taxes.

[9] *NPE* p. 23 n. 3, p. 33 n. 1.

IV

A few words should be said about the documents which the English notary issues. You can tell at once that he is a disciple of the Italian by observing the diplomatic features of his instruments, the civilian terminology, even the way he gives his name. Some few notaries even adopt a distinctly un-English style of handwriting. Very briefly I indicate a few of the diplomatic features, and first of all the personal name of the writer. In the century when notaries first appear in England, the Englishman generally described himself by a cognomen (often topographical), such as Henry of Colchester, and the like. The father's christian name was, as a rule, omitted. If it was used, it was in the form « Henricus filius Ricardi de Colecestria ». But from the first arrival of the English notary public, his subscription to an instrument of his follows the Italian usage. Iohannes quondam Iacobi de Bononia is matched by Andreas quondam Guilielmi de Tange, Iohannes Alani de Beccles, Ricardus natus Philippi Lovecock de Twyverton. The « Guilielmi » of Andrew Tange even copies Italian orthography: in England it would normally be « Willelmi », and Andrew Tange himself uses the common « Willelmus » when he refers in his instruments to others of that name. Another feature of the notary's description of himself is not derived from Italy. The English notary is usually a clerk and is most often described as « clericus... diocesis ». But the meaning of this and the intention in stating it are obscure [10].

The whole pattern of the notarial instrument departs from the epistolary form adopted in nearly all other English legal instruments. Instead, it begins commonly with an invocation, *In dei nomine amen*, and continues in the form

---

[10] *NPE* pp. 87-89. The practice is found in other northern countries (*ibid.*, p. 29 n. 1).

of a declaration by the notary, recording the act in question. The dating often copies Italian precision in stating the hour of the day and the street or even the house or the room where the transaction occurred. Moreover, the Italian method of indicating the day of the month is sometimes used: for example, *die lune quintodecimo die exeunte mense Octobris*. The indiction and the pontifical year of the reigning pope are added to the year of the nativity. Showing more scrupulosity than most English scribes, the notary public is at pains to record in his eschatocol all the points in the preceding text at which collation has led to scribal correction [11].

These features show obvious imitation of a civilian tradition.

V

During the fifty years or so after the coming of Giovanni da Bologna, English ecclesiastical records become far more copious than before. They permit the assertion that an English bishop of the mid-fourteenth century habitually kept one or two notaries public more or less permanently employed. If the notary was a clerk he was recompensed with benefices, if he was a layman, with a stipend and clothing. The bishop's *scriba* or *registrarius* was normally a notary. Pope Boniface VIII had given a push in this direction when in 1302 he gave sentence in a case in which the monks of Durham cathedral tried to exclude the bishop's clerks from accompanying him into their chapter-house on his canonical visitation. Boniface

---

[11] *Ibid.*, pp. 126-9, 138 n. 2, 163, 171. Corrections on the notarial rolls which record Edward I's adjudication on the Scottish succession are discussed in the volumes (highly important for notarial practice in England) by E.L.G. STONES and GRANT SIMPSON (edd.) *Edward I and the throne of Scotland 1290 - 1296: an edition of the record sources for the Great Cause* (2 vols. Oxford 1978), I, 77-8, II. 273, 375. For John de Cadomo's corrections on royal privy seal warrants see P. CHAPLAIS, *Mr John de Branketre and the office of notary in Chancery, 1355-1375* in *Journal of Soc. of Archivists* 4. 3 (1971), p. 171.

pronounced that the bishop might take with him a clerical notary to record the proceedings. The very next year the bishop of Worcester invoked and applied the Durham judgment when he visited Worcester cathedral. Eventually, it was included in *Extravagantes communes*, 1. 7. 1.: « Debent superioribus » [12].

Certain aspects of this notarial invasion of England raise interesting questions. In the first place, I observe that all the notaries who practise in England are styled notaries public by apostolic or imperial authority. They may also mention the authority of the prefect of Rome, but nobody less august, less remote, than these authorities. Sometimes they have received their title from the pope directly (and they may even cite the folio of the chancery register in which their faculty is recorded), [13], or they have received it from a prelate authorized by the pope (but they never mention him). If they claim imperial authority, it is derived through one of the mysterious delegates of the emperor, such as Rogerus de Monte Florum and Bassianus de Alliate, though he is never mentioned. What I find baffling are three questions: 1) why the one authorization is obtained rather than the other; 2) why the two are sometimes obtained by one man; and 3) why, when we see the emperor's substitutes at work, they are found in the neighbourhood of the papal Curia at Avignon? Can any explanation be had from the custom of the Italian notariate? The early Italian visitors to England include both imperial and papal notaries, and Ildebrandino da Siena uses both titles in his later documents, though not in the earliest. The authorization by the prefect of Rome of notaries who practise ouside the city also seems to deserve further enquiry.

---

[12] *NPE* pp. 36-37. For its diffusion see C.R. Cheney, *Law and letters in fourteenth-century Durham: a study of Corpus Christi College, Cambridge MS. 450* in *Bull. of John Rylands Univ. Libr. of Manchester* 55 (1972-3), pp. 60-85, at p. 81.
[13] *NPE* pp. 73-74.

VI

But how could a notary public follow his profession in England? Most often the notary in England acted specifically in his capacity of *public persona* to write documents for use in ecclesiastical courts. There, indeed, and only there could he expect his « public » quality to be recognized. In other fields there were strict limits set to the utility of a deed *sub manu publica*, for the English common law would not countenance it. It smelt of Roman civil law, and this had no standing in England.

When the notary public first set foot in England, the English common law had already evolved its methods of conveyancing, with charters bearing seals, witnessed and warranted. The civil courts of the land had their own formularies, registers of writs. Already in the twelfth century the royal exchequer and chancery were prepared to strengthen private contracts by giving (or rather, selling) official enrolment of private charters. To record a settlement before judges there was the *finalis concordia*, an indented chirograph; and after 15 July 1195 this document, drawn up by the king's court after genuine litigation or a fictitious lawsuit, took the secure form of a tripartite indenture, of which one part, the « foot », remained in official custody. The earliest *pes finis* exists, with the endorsement: « Hec est primum cyrographum quod factum fuit in curia domini regis in forma trium cyrographorum secundum quod [constitutum est per?] dominum Cantuariensem et alios barones domini regis ad hoc ut per illam formam possit fieri recordum traditum thesaurario ad ponendum in thesauro anno regni regis Ricardi VI° die dominica proxima ante festum beate Margarete coram baronibus inscriptis » [14].

---

[14] *Feet of fines Henry II and Richard I* (Pipe Roll Soc. 17, 1894), p. 21 « dominum Cantuariensem ». Hubert Walter, arch-bishop of Canterbury and at that time also justiciar of England.

Before the end of the thirteenth century the gracious jurisdiction of the Crown extended over another type of private contracts — mercantile debts. At the same time the municipal courts were registering transactions in land and relevant title-deeds [15]. In short, English record-keeping was now too highly developed to require, or permit, the intrusion into the system of the public instruments and *protocolla* of the notaries. This explains why so many notarial instruments carry an authentic seal as well as validation by a notary public. It is to be observed that Giovanni da Bologna only provides formulas for production in ecclesiastical courts.

VII

The idea has grown up among English legal historians that the English government of the fourteenth century disliked this alien institution. One piece of evidence seemed to support this. King Edward II, in a writ of 26 April 1320, forbade the employment in England of notaries *imperiali auctoritate* [16]. This was avowedly a demonstration that « rex Anglie habet imperium in regno suo ». Edward II was acting in line with the king of France, Philip le Bel. But Edward did not go so far as the French king and establish a royal notariate in England, nor did he proscribe apostolic notaries. Indeed, Edward II and Edward III both supplicated the popes, from time to time, to get faculties for notaries public.

In certain types of action the royal chancery itself used the notary as a *publica persona* to produce public instruments. When it issued a document which touched the disputed border-land of civil and ecclesiastical matters, the official responsible for deciding on the form of the document knew that sooner or later it might figure in

---

[15] G.H. MARTIN, *The registration of deeds of title in the medieval borough* in *The study of medieval records: essays in honour of Kathleen Major* (Oxford 1971), pp. 151-73.

[16] T. RYMER (ed.) *Foedera* (London 1816-30), II. i, p. 423.

litigation in the Roman Curia, where authentication by a notary would carry weight. There was also another consideration: the notarial form was a convenient means of multiplying copies for internal departmental use. For instance, the public instrument by which in 1320 the new bishop of Winchester renounced and disclaimed certain words in his papal bull of provision was prepared in three notarialized copies to be deposited respectively in the chancery, the wardrobe, and the treasury of the exchequer. Above all, the king's government made use of notaries public in its diplomacy.

Between 1291 and 1296 King Edward I was much concerned in the succession to the throne of Scotland. He claimed to be overlord and judge, and in order to establish his right and justify his action in the eyes of foreign powers he caused public instruments to be prepared with a long narrative of the stages in the succession dispute and with authentic copies of the documents in the case. Notarial exemplifications were made, then and later, which gave an account of « the Great Cause », somewhat biased in favour of the king's authority, written in several copies on parchment rolls, containing 19 to 42 membranes each, and measuring about 12 to 25 metres long [17].

Again, in all the negotiatione between England and France during the Hundred Years War notaries public were used. Whenever truces or treaties are in question, some of the documents of the debate are drafted or transcribed by permanent officials of the king's wardrobe or chancery who have studied law in a university and who are notaries by apostolic (or by apostolic and imperial) authority. The chief among them are civil servants of great reputation and wealth. Several become bishops. John Thoresby, notary by apostolic authority in the royal chancery in 1336, at a salary of forty marks, becomes archbishop of York from 1352 to 1373. After Thoresby's promotion, Dr Pierre

---

[17] STONES and SIMPSON (above, n. 11). Vol. I gives a meticulous account of the genesis of the rolls and estimates the credibility of the notarial records.

Chaplais finds John of Braintree, a chancery clerk « of the first bench » or « the second bench », in the post of « notary in chancery » for twenty years, charged with drafting treaties, specializing on diplomatic affairs. These were his chief duties, and he sometimes added to his title of notary public by apostolic and imperial authority that of *regis scriba*. If the words « notary in chancery » do not certainly indicate that in his day there was a distinct office and a title, office and title had emerged by the end of the century [18].

VIII

The most distinguished notaries were mainly employed in business of Church and State, and it is the public records which preserve most of their writings. But they did not necessarily spend all their time in working for a bishop or an officer of the Crown. For the civil service of medieval England was an ill-defined body of men who, in varying degrees, undertook work for private clients. Other notaries public depended on the fees paid for scribal work by private persons. This work included public instruments on various occasions when laymen and clerics were involved in legal transactions outside the scope of the Common Law - matters relating to marriage and legitimacy and testamentary dispositions and the resignation of church benefices, which were the concern of church courts. Notarial authentication was particularly useful in commercial dealings which involved aliens. An English private seal was not « bene cognitum » in Italy, and an Italian merchant's seal was not acceptable in England; so, on each side, it was commonly fortified by the sign of a notary. The Hundred Years War occasioned a special class of business for English notaries in the drafting and certifying of letters for prisoners of war about their ransom and release [19].

---

[18] See CHAPLAIS, above n. 11, and for the title *regis scriba*, ibid., p. 189.
[19] *Ibid.*, pp. 170, 179-81.

In the private branch of notarial activity there was a sharp contrast with the state of things in southern Europe. Once the English notary public had taken the oath required on admission to the papal or imperial notariate, he did not submit to any other body of rules or enter a civic gild. He was not roped into an organized corporation, like the London Company of Scriveners (or professional scribes). In London and some other English towns the gild of scriveners recorded its members' names at admission and entered in the register of the gild the autograph sign or paraph of every member. Not so the notary public, who was not matriculated and not controlled. It followed from this that the English notary was not called upon, like the southern notaries, to keep registers of his acts for which the local authorities would make provision to ensure their permanent survival [20]. Because of insufficient local control, fraudulent and ignorant practitioners brought the notarial profession into disrepute at the end of the fourteenth century, when Pope Boniface IX ordered the archbishops of Canterbury and York to conduct an enquiry into the credentials of all English notaries. No evidence survives of any enquiry outside the diocese of London, where 13 out of 61 notaries summoned to exhibit their licence and establish their *bona fides* failed to appear [21].

IX

Neither in England as a whole nor in London or any other town did notaries public form themselves into a corporation with the power which a professional body can wield. But for a proper estimate of their influence one must

[20] Cf. G. CATONI & S. FINESCHI, *L'archivio notarile di Siena (1221-1862): Inventario* (Pubblicazioni degli Archivi di Stato. LXXXVII, Roma, 1975), pp. 13-14. For a protocol book from the archiepiscopal archives of Pisa see Gero Dolezalek (ed.) *Das Imbreviaturbuch des erzbischöflicher Gerichtsnotar Hubaldus aus Pisa Mai-Aug. 1230* (Forschungen zur neueren Privatrechtsgeschichte. Max Planck Institut für Europäische Rechtsgeschichte. 13, 1969).
[21] *NPE* pp. 92-94.

look beyond their ranks to see the permeation of notarial
style and practice among all persons concerned with legal,
political, and commercial business. By the fourteenth century, in the academic centre of the university of Oxford,
clerks were receiving practical instruction in the drafting
of business-letters and the art of conveyancing. Formularies
and copies of continental *artes dictaminis* abounded. Their
teaching was applied in offices of both Church and State.
Senior civil servants compiled, or caused to be compiled,
anthologies of dictaminal treatises, standard formularies
suitable to their business, and genuine old well-turned
letters to serve as models for new ones. Richard de Bury,
keeper of the king's privy seal and chancellor, who became
bishop of Durham (1333-45) was responsible for such a
compilation. He was not a notary public, but a talented
diplomat with literary tastes, of whom Petrarca speaks
respectfully. About 1420 one Thomas Hoccleve, a clerk
of the privy seal who was also a poet, assembled a bulky
classified collection of royal letters of all kinds, and Édouard
Perroy, studying diplomacy in the reign of Richard II,
described others of the same sort [22].

In ecclesiastical administration, the English bishop's
secretariat evolved a strictly official register for certain
classes of episcopal business, and this served, to some extent,
as formulary. But the lawyers and scribes who served
bishops and archdeacons, and who were often notaries public,
kept and handed on their own homemade formularies and
cartularies. These untidy books were unofficial and were
often neglected and lost when their owners died; but during
the past fifty years enough of the survivals have been
identified to show the part they played, and notarial doctrine
played, in the government of the English Church. I have
discussed elsewhere a few of these witnesses to the practice

---

[22] E. PERROY (ed.), *The diplomatic correspondence of Richard II* (Camden
3rd series 48. Royal Hist. Soc. 1933), pp. XV XXVII; supplemented by A.L. BROWN
in *The study of medieval records* (above, n. 15), pp. 260-81.

of ecclesiastical chanceries [23]. Lately an even rarer survival has come to light. Cambridge University Library MS. Add. 7318 is a paper book of about 80 pages, about 285x110 mm. in a rough parchment wrapper. It records sketchily about 800 small transactions of burgesses of the monastic borough of Bury St Edmunds, c. 1460-1464, prepared by some professional scrivener. It is a series of memoranda designed to assist the writer in engrossing contracts, receipts, loans, indentures of apprenticeship, and wills [24]. Here is an anonymous English equivalent of the Italian book of *protocolla* in a non-notarial setting.

[23] *NPE* pp. 46-51, *English bishops' chanceries 1100-1250* (Manchester, 1950), pp. 119-30, and *Law and letters* (above, n. 12). See also the formulary of an ecclesiastical lawyer of the late XIV century: D.M. OwEN (ed.) *John Lydford's book* (Devon & Cornwall Record Soc. n.s. 20 and Hist. MSS. Commission JP 22, 1975).

[24] A.E.B. OwEN, *A scrivener's note-book from Bury St Edmunds* in *Archives*, XIV. 61 (1979), pp. 16-22.

INDEX

Abbreviations used are bp for bishop,C. for Council,card.
for cardinal,ch. for church,dn for deacon,pr. for priest.
Not all the entries for particular councils and prelates
which appear in study I are separately indexed. Names
of religious Orders appear as Aug(ustinian),Ben(edictine),
Cart(husian),Cist(ercian),Clun(iac). Places are located
by county in England and Wales,by department in France.
An asterisk indicates an additional note.

-of bpric: I 215 n.2;
VIII 114
-of borough: XV 183
-notarial: XV 174,186-8
Rhetoric: IV 579; XIII 634-5;
XIV 62-4,73,82-3
Ripon(N Yorks),collegiate ch.
of: XIII 628,631-2
Ripon,A. and Malger de:
XIII 638
Rochechouart,Mr Simon de:
XIII*640
Rota Romana: XI*
Rouen(Seine-mar.),prov.
councils of: I 200,202-3,
205,212,395,397

Sabbatarianism: X 117 n.2,
130 n.1
Saint Albans(Herts),Ben.
abbey: V 445; XII 101
-chroniclers of: I 400,
403 nn.3-5,IV 577-8;
XIV 84
Saints,cult of: X 122
Salerno,John of,card.and
legate: VI 655 n.6,656
Salisbury,bps of
Herbert Poore: IV 578-81
Richard Poore,statutes of:
I 204,387,401; VII
passim
Robert Bingham,statutes of:
I 399-400; VIII 124;
IX 28-9
Giles of Bridport,statutes
of: I 399; IX 28,31;
X 126-7
Roger Martival: IX 24-5;
X 127
-dean Richard Poore: V 445;
VII 16
-subdean Thomas Chobham:
VII 16,29; X 119-21
-diocese,feast-days in:
X 126-7,137
Sancto Martino of Lewes,
John de: XV 177
Sandford,Sanford,Henry of:
XIII 627-8,634-5
School,monastic: XIII 629,
633
Schoolmaster of York: XIII
629,634
Scotales: I 398-9
Scotland,'The Great Cause':
XV 180 n.11,184
-provincial councils in:

I 199 n.3
Scriveners'Company of London:
XV 186
Seal,authentic: XIII 639 n.2;
XV 175-6,182-3
-not widely known: XIII 639;
XV 195
Secreta secretorum: XIV 70
Secundus,philosopher: XIV 70,77
Seton,Roger de: XIV 76
Sherwode,William: I 216 n.3
Siena,Ildebrandino Bonadote da:
XV 176-7,181
'Summa summarum': I 214
Sunday observance: X 117 n.2,
118
Synod,episcopal,annual:
I 200; inquisitors in:
I 204-5; preliminary to
council: I 206
Synodal statutes: VII passim;
interchange and diffusion
of: VII 27-9; IX 29 n.5
Synodus,episcopalis s.,
generalis s.: I 196-7

Tange,Andrew: XV 179
Tartar invasions: XIV 67,
79 n.4
Taxation,papal: V 444; VI
655; XV 178
-royal: IV 577-84
Templars,trial of: XIV 74,
77-8,84; 'Lamentacio' for:
XIV 69,77
Testes synodales: I 205 n.3
Thoresby,John: XV 184; and
see York,archbps
Topcliffe(N Yorks),ch.of: VI*
Treasure,thesaurus,and
treasurer,monastic: V*448-9;
XII 97-8,103,114-5;
thesauraria = muniment-room:
XII 98,and = treasurership:
see York

Urban III,pope: XI 220-1
Urban IV,pope: XIII 629

Vienne,C.of(1311-2): XI*
Visitation,of monasteries:
XII passim; XV 180-1;
legatine: V passim; 654-5;
metrop.: I 412-3; XII 94
n.1,98-100
frequency of: XII 93
injunctions after: 206,
V 447-52,XII 93-120;

INDEX OF MANUSCRIPTS

The list does not index all subsidiary manuscripts
cited in nos.I and IX which were later used and
indexed in Councils & synods, II pp.1395-1402. For
the older reference 'B.M.', BL (British Library)
is now used. An asterisk indicates an additional note.

Aberystwyth
National Library of Wales
  Peniarth 390C: XIV 82-3

Avranches
Bibliothèque Municipale
  149: VII 8 n.2

Bristol
Baptist College
  Z.c.23: VI 657

Cambridge
Corpus Christi College
  317: VII 17 n.1
  337: X 125,136
  358: XIV*
  367: VII 23 n.1
  370: XII 95
  445: XIV 75
  450: XIV passim
  465: XII 104-5,117-20
Emmanuel College
  27: X 126 n.4,137
Gonville & Caius College
  44: I 215 n.3,219 n.2,
    394-5
  235: I 215 n.9
  349: I 395-7; VII 18-9
Pembroke College
  62: VII 3-18
  131: VII 19
St John's College
  62: X 126 n.4
  93: VIII 116
Trinity College
  0.9.28 (1440): X 127 n.6
University Library
  Add.3061: X 119-21
  Add.3575: I 212 n.1; IX 17
  Add.7318: XV 188

Canterbury
Chapter Library
  Chartae misc. F.85: VI
    656,658-9
  -L.138a: I 215 n.4
  -0.138: I 215 n.4

Ch.Ch. letters 2 no.225:
  III 578 n.4

Chichester
West Sussex Record Office
  Liber E: I 115

Dublin
Archbishop Marsh's Library
  Z 3.1.3 (8): VIII 114 n.4
Archbishop's Registry
  'Crede mihi': VIII 114
Trinity College
  F.3.16: VIII 114 n.4

Durham
Cathedral Library
  C.II.2: XIV 81
  C.IV.24: III 582-4; XIV 76-7
Cathedral muniments
  Misc. ch. 4937: XIV*

Hereford
Cathedral Library
  P.7.vii: I 212 n.1

Holkham House
  226: I 212 n.1

Lewes
Bishop of: now London, BL,
  Add.48344

Lincoln
Cathedral Library
  B.6.7: X 127

London
British Library
  Add.4783: VIII 114
  Add.4788,4793: VIII 123-4
  Add.4791: 125 n.29
  Add.6159: XIV*
  Add.10374: XIV
  Add.29436: II 488 n.4
  Add.38816: V 448 n.1
  Add.39675: X 144
  Add.48344: I 215 n.9; X 127